Greenhill Books

ONCE THERE
WERE TITANS

NAPOLEON'S GENERALS AND THEIR

BATTLES, 1800–1815

ONCE THERE WERE TITANS

NAPOLEON'S GENERALS AND THEIR BATTLES, 1800–1815

by Kevin F. Kiley

Greenhill Books, London
MBI Publishing, St Paul

Greenhill Books

Once There Were Titans
Napoleon's Generals and Their Battles, 1800–1815

First published in 2007 by Greenhill Books, Lionel Leventhal Limited,
Park House, 1 Russell Gardens, London NW11 9NN
www.greenhillbooks.com
and
MBI Publishing Co., Galtier Plaza, Suite 200, 380 Jackson Street, St Paul,
MN 55101-3885, USA

British Library Cataloguing-in Publication Data
Kiley, Kevin F. Once there were titans : Napoleon's generals and their battles, 1800–1815
1. Generals – France – Biography 2. Napoleonic Wars, 1800–1815 – Campaigns 3.
France – History, Military – 1789–1815 I. Title
940.2'7'092244

ISBN-13: 978-185367-710-6

Library of Congress Cataloging-in Publication Data available

For more information on our books, please visit
www.greenhillbooks.com, email sales@greenhillbooks.com
or telephone us within the UK on 020 8458 6314.
You can also write to us at the above London address.

Edited and typeset by Palindrome
Maps drawn by John Richards

Printed and bound in Great Britain by Creative Print and Design (Wales), Ebbw Vale

To Matthew McCoy Helms (1990–2004)

A Titan in his own right, and one to ride the river with. You left us too soon, young one, before you reached your full potential. You are greatly missed, but we'll meet again on green fields of friendly strife where we'll again be undefeated.

Requiescat in Pace

'The Last Round for the Keeper'

And, as always, to my lovely wife Daisy, who, with the late Ann Elting, shares the title of 'the last widow of the Napoleonic Wars'. And to my beloved son Michael, who is the blood of my heart. May he be the first of the family in several generations who will not have to march towards the muttering guns. Without them, this book could never have been written.

Virtute et Valore

CONTENTS

MAPS

TABLE OF BASIC MILITARY MAP SYMBOLS

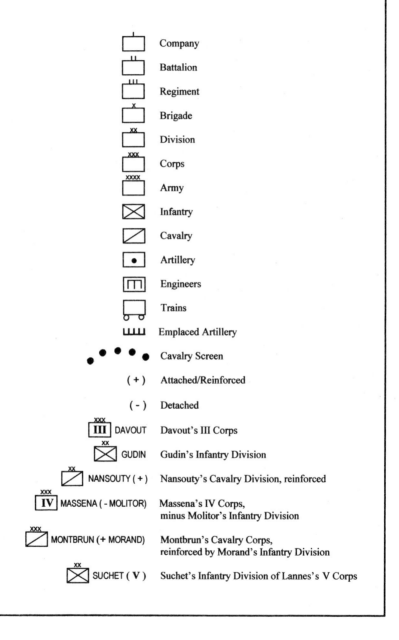

Company

Battalion

Regiment

Brigade

Division

Corps

Army

Infantry

Cavalry

Artillery

Engineers

Trains

Emplaced Artillery

Cavalry Screen

(+)   Attached/Reinforced

(-)   Detached

DAVOUT   Davout's III Corps

GUDIN   Gudin's Infantry Division

NANSOUTY (+)   Nansouty's Cavalry Division, reinforced

MASSENA (- MOLITOR)   Massena's IV Corps,
minus Molitor's Infantry Division

MONTBRUN (+ MORAND)   Montbrun's Cavalry Corps,
reinforced by Morand's Infantry Division

SUCHET (V)   Suchet's Infantry Division of Lannes's V Corps

ILLUSTRATIONS

ACKNOWLEDGEMENTS

This volume was, to use a time-worn phrase, 'a long time coming.' Its genesis and inspiration was John Elting's organisational history of the Grande Armée, *Swords Around a Throne: Napoleon's Grande Armée*. After reading that magnum opus of the instrument of war created by Napoleon, I had the great fortune to meet and spend many hours with Colonel Elting in his home in Cornwall-on-Hudson, New York, about four miles above the United States Military Academy at West Point. That visit in 1989 opened up an entire new world for me, and gave me the gift of a long and lasting friendship with a man whom I consider one of the best historians of the Napoleonic period and who is still the authority on the Grande Armée. He was friend, mentor, teacher, surrogate father and confidant, and we shared great times with our myriad common interests. He was a man for the ages.

Books are not written by authors alone. Family and friends contribute both materially and morally to their creation, even if they are unaware of it. First and foremost, my gratitude is due to two men without whose faith in my writing, and great patience with my failings, this project would never have seen the light of day. Lionel Leventhal, my publisher and friend, and his son, Michael Leventhal, an editor with the patience of Job, have been steadfast in their support, friendship, and loyalty. Thank you, gentlemen.

Kate Baker, also of Greenhill books, saw this book into print. She gave timely advice, ever-needed support, and is a gracious lady without whom this book would have remained in editorial confusion.

Jonathan North was both supportive and helpful, as usual. Without Jonathan's support over the years, I would not be writing for publication. He graciously gave permission to use material from some of his many publications.

Robert Burnham, of the Napoleon Series, has been more than helpful over the years, and his website is the premier Napoleonic site on the internet. His support and friendship are gratefully acknowledged, as are the myriad members of the site and all that they contribute to Napoleonic scholarship and debate, especially Tony Broughton, Robert Ouvrard, Dominique Contant, Yves Martin, Tom Holmberg, Alexander Mikaberidze, Caroline Miley, Kate Luchini, Howie Muir, David McCracken, Fausto Berutti, Susan Howard, Chris Gibbs, Ned Zuparko, Steven Smith, Jerry McKenzie, Robert Mosher, Robert Goetz, Daryl Hosking, and last, but certainly not least, Allan Mountford, who, among others who have contributed to the overall knowledge of the Napoleonic period through debate, research, and sharing material that might otherwise remain silent. Many of these fine ladies and gentlemen are Napoleonic scholars in their own right, and together they form an unofficial 'brains trust' for the period.

Keith Rocco, military artist and historian, was gracious in allowing the use and publication of his superb artwork for this volume. Meissonier and Detaille live again in Keith's fine artwork, and he is the only American military artist that I know of who paints in the Napoleonic period. His painting of the charge of the Polish Light Horse at Somosierra in 1808 perfectly captures the spirit of the Grande Armée, the *Feu Sacré*.

Thanks also go to Peter Harrington for his expert assistance on this volume as well as on my last effort, *Artillery of the Napoleonic Wars*.

There are three men without whom I would not be writing and could not have done as much as I have done with this book. Digby Smith has been a good friend for years and it was his idea that I first suggest to Greenhill that I do a book. His support has been unwavering, and his knowledge and expertise of the period has been invaluable.

Evan Pawley was instrumental in providing much of the material on the Consular Guard in the Marengo chapter. His research skills are unmatched and he has unearthed material that has been invaluable.

Donald Brown has been a constant inspiration for me for quite some time. He is a gentleman and a scholar, an expert analyst and consummate historian for whom I have nothing but respect and admiration. His sense of humour and style and just plain common sense continue to prove that common sense is not a common virtue. He has been a stalwart supporter of my work, an inspiration to always attempt to excel, and a good friend.

All three of you have been of invaluable assistance and this volume would still be a pile of notes without your assistance and support.

John Walsh has helped immeasurably with material for this volume. His outstanding article on the stand of the 84th Ligne at Graz in 1809 is a model of research and presentation.

Don Graves, authority on the Niagara frontier of that forgotten war, the War of 1812, has been both an inspiration and a great help. He has been instrumental in the completion of the two books that I have attempted, and is a good friend, a fellow artilleryman and comrade-in-arms 'and a good man to have around.' He reviewed the manuscript and gave many helpful suggestions regarding the British army.

Karen and Dave Helms, while not contributing materially to this volume, have contributed immensely both morally and spiritually. They lost their eldest son, Matt, tragically and much too early, during the writing of this volume. Parents should never have to bury their children. Matt and his parents and siblings have been constantly in my thoughts during this time. I was privileged to be Matt's coach and friend, and no one could have better friends and neighbours than the Helms. Karen is a colleague as well as friend, being a teacher as I am. Dave is a Master Gunnery Sergeant in the United States Marine Corps and has recently returned from his second combat tour in Iraq. He personifies the motto of the Marine Corps, *Semper Fidelis*, and I only wish I could have been with him on this last tour. Both of them are a constant source of support and inspiration.

After wearing my country's uniform for almost three decades I began another career as a teacher. I have taught seventh and eighth grade for the past ten years, and it has been a wonderful time. Young people today are magnificent, and if any worry that the following generations are not up to the task of taking up the torch, there are two places to go and be reassured. The first are the battlefields of Afghanistan and Iraq, where the traditions of the Armed Forces of the United States are being valorously upheld. The Emperor would be proud of these men and women who selflessly serve and are all volunteers. They possess the *Feu Sacré* which the Emperor believed was the essential quality of a soldier. The second are the classrooms around the country where these youngsters are being educated. I am very proud to be a teacher of young people, and they never cease to amaze and fascinate me. As the eminent American historian, Henry Adams, once said, 'A teacher affects eternity, he can never tell where his influence stops.' My students have taught me more than I could ever hope to teach them. To my students, the athletes I coach, and my colleagues at Hunters Creek Middle School, this book is also dedicated. There will be an essay to follow.

As a retired Marine I do miss my old profession greatly, but there is a time for everything. Fortunately, I am honoured and privileged to work with other retired Marines who also teach. Three of them in particular I am privileged to work with 'on the fields of friendly strife' as football coaches. We have been together a long time, and they are a constant inspiration to me and the young men we coach. Tom King, Mark Pegram, and Joe Posney have helped me with this volume more than they will ever know. They are leaders and teachers of the first rank, and they lead by the force of personal example. It is a humbling experience to be numbered among them, much as d'Artagnan was fortunate to be counted alongside Porthos, Athos and Aramis. Up-downs on the whistle, gentlemen.

My family has had to put up with my moods, temper, and frustration, as well as the trials, and tribulations of writing this volume, and for their patience and continued love and good will I am eternally grateful. My wife Daisy is 'the stuff that dreams are made of' and my son Michael is an unending source of joy and satisfaction. They are always there when needed, and Michael has given his own unique additions to the text with his busy hands. This book is really for them.

And finally to my good friend, mentor and teacher, Colonel John Elting, whose knowledge and guidance are sorely missed, as are our long talks in his study. His presence has been with me for the entire writing of this volume and I do hope he would approve. The last thing he wrote to me before he died, fittingly at his desk in that great study, was '*Vive l'Empereur!*'

Note

Biographical data on the general officers in the text has been taken from *Dictionnaire Biographique de Généraux et Amireaux Français de la Révolution et de l'Empire (1792–1814)* by Georges Six, the biographical sketches in *A Military History and Atlas of the Napleonic War* by Vincent J. Esposito and John R. Elting and David Chandler's *Napoleon's Marshals*.

The vignettes at the beginning of the chapters are based on actual events that occurred during the Consulate and Empire. Where appropriate, the source has been footnoted for ready access for the reader. Any errors in the text or recounting the events are solely the author's.

INTRODUCTION

Their service was hard. Their names are remembered. JOHN ELTING

And all those men . . . what were their names? JULES MICHELET

12:00 15 July 1804 Les Invalides, Paris France
The clattering cavalcade came to a slow, gentle halt in front of the ancient cathedral on the Isle de Paris in the middle of the River Seine. The scarred veterans, the Chasseurs à Cheval of Napoleon's Guard, both led and followed the green Berline carriage. The Chasseurs were preceded by the Grenadiers à Cheval of the Guard, big men on big black horses, who were veterans of Marengo and other fights, referred to as 'the gods' for their manner and bearing. The horses of the procession were curried and combed to perfection, and occasionally their shoes caused sparks on the cobblestone pavement.

Out of the Berline stepped Napoleon Bonaparte, late First Consul of the French Republic and soon-to-be crowned Emperor of the French. The honour guard of Grenadiers à Pied and Chasseurs à Pied of the Guard snapped to attention and with a precision generally unknown in the armies of the Revolution, presented arms to their commander-in-chief. At the uplifted mace of their drum major, the band of the Grenadiers à Pied played 'Let Us Watch o'er the Empire' and to the rumble of drums and the crash of cymbals the ceremony to honour the most worthy of France began.

But this day was not about Napoleon or his soon-to-be imperial majesty. Today, the deserving soldiers and civilians of the French Empire were to be recognised and awarded the new award authorised by Napoleon and his Council of State, the Legion of Honour. This award was open to all, both military and civilian. The only criterion was distinguished service to France. It was the first such award in French history.

As Napoleon entered the domed church at the Invalides, followed by grim generals who had led the armies of the Republic through nine years of war, he made his way quickly to the dais from which he would bestow the award to the deserving. On either side of Napoleon's chair were his stepson Eugène and Murat, both respected veterans who themselves would wear the cross. These two would in turn announce the next award recipient and hand to Napoleon the Cross of the Legion of Honour that the First Consul would pin on their uniform or appropriate civilian attire.

Those who had won weapons of honour during the long wars of the Revolution were automatically granted the new honour, and officers and men were there to be decorated with the new cross. Wounded and lame veterans were also present and those who had given limbs for France were being helped forward by soldiers in dress uniforms who had been detailed for this honourable duty.

From his place in line, quite near the front of those to be honoured, Grenadier Jean-Roche Coignet, who had been put down for a weapon of honour on the battlefield of Montebello by General Berthier himself, watched the assembly of veterans and worthy civilians who were awaiting their cross. Some of the severely wounded veterans could not mount the steps either to the Church or to the First Consul's dais without assistance and some were in obvious pain still from their old wounds. As their names were called and they moved forward to speak to and be spoken to by Napoleon, some of the worst-maimed veterans would sometimes break down, overcome by being awarded their 'bit of metal and ribbon' by their head of state. Napoleon knew many of these men by name and rank and those he remembered had their ears pinched and some were even offered snuff from the First Consul's own snuff box after being decorated.

Finally, Coignet's name was called and he stepped forward, being instantly recognised by the First Consul, resplendent in his full dress uniform of a Grenadier à Pied of the newly christened Imperial Guard . . .[1]

Sweeping across Europe like a juggernaut, the Titans of the French Republic and Empire had led swarming masses of volunteers, conscripts and sullen regulars that swept the armies of the kings before them, gobbling them up if they stood to fight and pursuing them if they ran. Kings and princes who had for years sowed the seeds of reactionary and repressive rule now reaped the fruits of change that came as violent shocks like huge tidal waves on the rocky shores of entrenched conservatism.

Undisciplined, mutinous regulars, led by former sergeants and still wet-behind-the-ears subalterns and inexperienced volunteers dragged along by unwashed, fanatic *sans-culotte* generals were followed by the grimmer Represent-atives on Mission and the spectre of the guillotine; all willing, but inexperienced, conscripts led by officers who were now professionals in all but name, all tributaries forming a gigantic torrent to rid Europe of its kings. All Europe defeated for a moment, they again went forward to spread *liberté, egalité* and *fraternité* among all of Europe's peoples. Ragged conscripts and the remnants of the regulars and volunteers swarmed forward under their now experienced generals, who operated under the threat of a 'Republican shave'.[2] Somehow they trium-phed against all odds through disaster, victory and the incompetence and neglect of a succession of revolutionary governments.

The kings, thoroughly alarmed, vowed not to let the fledgling Republic survive. Giants rose among the experienced French survivors to lead them again into the fire behind tattered battle flags with honours such as *'le Terrible'* and *'Incomparable'*[3] emblazoned on their tricolours. Louis Desaix, Antoine Richepanse, Louis Davout and Charles Decaen emerged from the masses in the armies on the eastern marches, where most of them served Moreau who later turned traitor. Lazare Hoche, Amedée La Harpe, Barthélemy Joubert, Jean Kléber and Kléber's friend, the gallant young François Marceau, thumped their raw troops into shape and led them against the enemies of the Republic. All five of these promising officers were dead on the field of honour, or by disease and assassin-ation,[4] before the end of the Revolutionary Wars and the emergence of Napoleon as First Consul. Yet, they had led their divisions and armies to a string of victories over the professional armies of the Kings.

In the secondary theatre of Italy, a young, nondescript Corsican general named Bonaparte was taking apart Austrian and Sardinian armies with terrify-ing regularity. Knocking Sardinia out of the war and setting up client states in northern Italy, this grim general and his even grimmer subordinates led their starving, half-mutinous demi-brigades to a further string of unexpected and decisive victories and humbled the pope. Experienced generals – the talented and respected Berthier, the 'Big Prussian' Augereau,[5] and the wily Masséna – willingly served their general in chief and they dictated peace at the very gates of Vienna.

Out of misty legend to the terrifying rumble of the Grande Armée's drums come vague and dusty images of the generals who led it. Old before their time, these officers damned and led the eager volunteers of 1792, the sullen conscripts of 1800, the determined veterans of 1805 and 1806, the ragged, frozen scarecrows their Emperor called his 'men of bronze' through snow, ice and masses of revenge-minded Muscovites in 1812 and the scared, much too young conscripts – the famous 'Marie-Louises'[6] – and the older National Guard 'fathers of families', through the heartbreak, bitterness, mud and despair of 1813 and 1814, finally to the last desperate days of 1815. Professionals because they learned their trade if they survived, these sometimes half-educated, iron-hard men led one of the greatest armies in history the length and breadth of Europe and finally to the Valhalla of enduring legend to stand beside Arthur, Roland and the Cid and their immortal legions.

Who were these men who led the first mass armies in history to defeat the professional armies of Europe? They came from varied backgrounds and maintained different beliefs, but they all rallied to the tricolour when *La Patrie* was in danger. They were honed by war and hardship and many knew no other life. They marched behind the rumble of the Grande Armée's drums and their terrible Emperor on his grey horse, to the muttering of the guns on the horizon and repeatedly and unhesitatingly leading their men into the fire. Their survivors became Marshals or commanders in the formidable Imperial Guard, packing their kit year after year to make war on the enemies of what became the French Empire. But who, really, were they, and what has been their contribution to the art of war?

The armies of the kings of Europe who opposed and fought the Revolution set the seed of continued conflict and had to gather the sometimes bitter harvest. What arose from that maelstrom has not been seen since. Some of these commanders were former enlisted men from the old Royal Army, such as André Masséna and François Lefebvre. Masséna was noted as being able to manoeuvre his regiment better than any of its officers.[7] Lefebvre was an excellent tactician and an outstanding combat leader. When occupying a German town Lefebvre announced to the populace that they had come to bring them *liberté, fraternité* and *egalité*. However, if anything took place without his permission, they would be shot!

Others were former nobles and had been commissioned before the Revolution. Louis Nicholas Davout,[8] Emmanuel Grouchy, Etienne Nansouty, Louis Narbonne (properly Narbonne-Lara) and Louis Desaix were in this category. Davout, originally a cavalryman, who would become Napoleon's most reliable subordinate and be known as the 'Iron Marshal,' was a protégé of Desaix. Grouchy, an excellent cavalryman, would eventually be blamed for Waterloo, but was much abler than either he or subsequent generations realised. An excellent cavalry commander, he was tough, intelligent and a proven combat leader. Nansouty, formerly of the Maison du Roi, would become a noted heavy cavalryman and would command the Guard Cavalry in the dark days of the later Empire. Desaix, whom Napoleon considered the best balanced of his generals, gained a solid reputation in Germany, conquered Upper Egypt,[9] and saved the day at Marengo, there being shot dead leading the 9e Légère to the attack.

Napoleon mourned his loss. Narbonne, former royalist, would make the Russian campaign at the age of fifty-seven only to die in Germany the next year from a fall from his horse.

Others joined up when the tocsin sounded in '92, Jean Lannes being a perfect example. Joining a volunteer unit he was quickly elected lieutenant and earned his subsequent promotions on the battlefield. Blunt and loyal in his relationship with Napoleon, he was also a close friend. Despising politicians, he once bluntly told French Foreign Minister Charles Talleyrand, a proven scoundrel who betrayed both Napoleon and France, to his face that he was nothing but a silk stocking full of fresh manure.[10]

It is a plain, hard fact that Napoleon would not have achieved what he did without the generals and marshals who served him and France, no matter his genius and great innate ability. Some, it is quite true, were 'human projectiles who required the Emperor's aim and impulse'. Others were definite millstones around the Imperial neck. However, as a group they were arguably the greatest collection of military talent to ever serve one man. Few commanders in military history were better served by their subordinates. Baron Ernst Odeleben, another Saxon officer attached to Napoleon's staff remarked that Napoleon had the knack of training commanders. Carl von Clausewitz, no lover of the French or Napoleon, stated,

> You have to have seen the steadfastness of one of the forces trained and led by Bonaparte . . . seen them under fierce and unrelenting fire – to get some sense of what can be accomplished by troops steeled by long experience in danger, in whom a proud record of victories has instilled the noble principle of placing the highest demands on themselves. As an idea alone it is unbelievable.[11]

Odeleben remarked of the new Grande Armée of 1813, built around the survivors of 1812, that

> the good military bearing, which predominated in this raw army, sprung, as it were, from the earth and assembled by the wave of a wand, was truly admirable . . . the military spirit, the activity in marches, and the bravery of the young troops so rapidly formed and opposed to experienced soldiers excited no less astonishment.[12]

It was this solid cadre of professional commanders, trained by war and hardship, often hand-picked by Napoleon, that made the achievements of the Grande Armée possible. It was the flair and steel of his chosen subordinates, honed by combat and shared hardships, that gave this weapon its edge.

Down through the years legend has enhanced achievements that today would be called unbelievable and extraordinary. The levels of both leadership and generalship in the Grande Armée were very high, more so the longer the odds became. Again and again, officers and NCOs led their men to the beckoning call of the trumpet and rumble of the cannon, to follow the drum and defend *La Patrie*. Valour, leadership in combat and fighting against long odds became commonplace: the one-legged battery commander at the Berezina, Captain Brechtel, having his wooden leg shot off by a Russian round shot, calmly telling his open-jawed orderly to fetch another from the battery wagon;[13] the commandant of Vincennes in the dark days of 1814 refusing to surrender until the allies returned his amputated leg; Louis Lepic chiding his Horse Grenadiers to stop 'saluting' incoming Russian artillery rounds at Eylau, as they were bullets, not turds; Lannes telling the terrified conscript on sentry duty who had just mistakenly shot at him and missed that he was sure it had been a mistake,[14] and that the sentry surely had no intention of hitting him; the alert French sentry who shot at Jean-Baptiste Bernadotte, now a former French marshal and then currently Crown Prince of Sweden and a member of the allied coalition, under a flag of truce in 1814, stating he was merely trying to apprehend a French deserter;[15] Joachim Murat riding through the Prussians at Jena leading his cavalry with only a light whip in his hand; artilleryman Alexander-Antoine Senarmont leading the artillery assault at Friedland, manoeuvring within slingshot range and destroying the Russian centre with point-blank artillery fire; Jean-Baptiste Eble repeatedly leading his frozen scarecrows into the ice-choked Berezina River to repair the rickety trestle bridges that his pontoniers had constructed on the spot and that that had once again broken under the strain of the continuous crossing; the unnamed Young Guard drum major leading a clump of Young Guardsmen through the ditch and over the wall of a redoubt at Dresden in 1813 to retake it from the allies; Michel-Marie Pacthod bellowing through the roar and mess for his National Guardsmen to once again reform with empty muskets and red bayonets against the Tsar's picked horsemen at La Fere-Champenoise; 'Père' Roguet telling his grenadiers at Ligny that anyone who brought him a prisoner would be shot;[16] another unknown Guard drum major, swinging his loaded mace at every Prussian head in range, at Waterloo leading the two battalion bayonets-only assault at Plançenoit to throw fourteen Prussian battalions out of the burning village; the kick of a heavy musket, the frenzied rush of closed columns, the excitement of cavalry breaking into the charge, manhandling artillery to 100-yard range to demolish British squares at Waterloo's ending – this was the experience of close combat and the leadership, and a very high level of generalship, that made the Grande Armée one of the greatest military organisations in military history. They suffered reverses and defeats and gained victory after victory for their Emperor, but they were never beaten.

These soldiers were hard used by the wars. Nicolas Oudinot took thirty-four wounds in twenty-three years. Lannes took ten, including one in the neck at Acre that left him permanently wry-necked. Jean Rapp was wounded so often that he was referred to as a piece of fine lace by the army. Claude-Pierre Pajol and Emmanuel Grouchy were so crippled by wounds at various times during their careers they had to be sent home. Joseph Poniatowski, wounded at Leipzig, where he had just been awarded his marshal's baton, was wounded trying to escape across the River Elster after the bridge was prematurely blown. Jean Baptiste Bessières was killed in action just as the 1813 campaign was under way and would be sorely missed by his devoted guardsmen. Guillaume-Marie Brune would be messily murdered and left to rot by a Royalist mob in 1815; Michel Ney, le Rougeaud and François La Bedoyère, among others, would be wrongly executed by the Royalists after Napoleon's second abdication. Oddly, Masséna was never wounded, but was badly hurt after Essling, commanding his corps from a carriage and four at Wagram, launching it, his terrified domestics and himself into the fire to inspire his troops. He lambasted his troops, 'Scoundrels! You get five *sous* a day, and I am worth 600,000 francs a year – yet you make me go ahead of you!'[17] Marie Victor Latour-Maubourg, another of the plethora of skilful cavalry commanders in the Grande Armée, had a leg blown off at Leipzig leading what could have been the decisive cavalry charge, piercing the allied centre and told his weeping orderly, 'What are you crying about imbecile, you have one less boot to polish.'[18]

Many fell and could not be replaced. After Lannes's death at Essling, Napoleon promoted three marshals after Wagram: Auguste Marmont, Nicolas Oudinot and Etienne MacDonald. The army subsequently dubbed them 'Lannes's small change'. Bessières was killed by a chance cannon shot in 1813, before the campaign was well begun. Desaix has already been mentioned. Louis St Hilaire was mortally wounded at Essling, having a foot blown off by Austrian artillery fire at the head of his infantry division. The heavy cavalryman Jean-Louis d'Espagne was mortally wounded leading his cuirassiers in yet another desperate charge on the field of Essling in 1809. Pierre Montbrun, probably the most skilful of Napoleon's cavalry commanders, was knocked out of the saddle by a Russian round shot at Borodino;[19] his replacement, Armand Caulaincourt's brother, Auguste was killed leading his troopers against the Great Redoubt the same day. The two *mauvaises têtes* of the artillery, Senarmont and Eble, both died before their time: Senarmont at the siege of Cadiz (oddly, the same way his father was killed at Valmy by an artillery round) and Eble, after building the bridges that enabled the Grande Armée to escape from Russian in 1812, of exhaustion with most of his gallant pontoniers after the retreat. Artillery general Baston Lariboissiere, died of exhaustion along with Eble after the Great Retreat, having suffered the loss of his carabinier officer son at Borodino.

Their reputations and abilities, along with their Emperor's, have been repeatedly sullied after the wars by their enemies and some latter-day writers. These flawed generalisations have been many and varied: Napoleon intentionally kept his subordinates in the dark as to his operational plans and method of making war; Napoleon was fortunate that Desaix died early because he was jealous of him; the French only won repeatedly because of 'their superiority in sheer pugilism'; Napoleon discouraged original thought among his generals; Napoleon's method of waging war intentionally was focused to squash initiative at the higher echelons of command; that French artillery officers were not good commanders at division or higher level. These impressions are incorrect and lump Napoleon's commanders into one group that has been underestimated since the last round was fired in 1815. Napoleon himself undoubtedly would have dismissed such foolish notions with a few characteristically caustic remarks.

What one finds is that both leadership and generalship levels in the Grande Armée were high. Certainly, the Grande Armée had its share of incompetents, but they usually did not last long. Napoleon did make some odd command choices in the latter days of the Empire, counting too much on Oudinot, Ney and Augereau, and leaving Davout bottled up in Hamburg. However, the successes by these generals on the battlefield and on campaign far outweigh their failures. As Frederick the Great once mentioned, offensive generals and those who could command independently are few in any army. This is also true of the Grande Armée. However, those with which it was blessed are among the best commanders in any age. Desaix, perhaps second in ability only to the Emperor himself, was a superb independent commander, capable of taking on any mission and successfully completing it. Conqueror of Upper Egypt, he was known as the 'Just Sultan' and imbued Rapp, Savary and Davout with his expertise in military intelligence.

Ferdinand von Funck, the Saxon staff officer who served on the Imperial staff made some interesting character-sketches of the marshals and a general or two. He stated that several of the commanders other than Davout were as strict in maintaining discipline. Murat was kind, but would not discipline his troopers for looting. Soult, Latour-Maubourg and Suchet were all strict disciplinarians, but Ney, Bernadotte and Augereau were not. Victor (properly Victor-Perrin, but he went by Victor) tried to emulate Davout, but did not have the requisite character to do so. Mortier was self-disciplined, but was an only an average commander, as was Macdonald.[20]

Masséna and Marmont were both greedy and self-serving, though Masséna had a stronger character and as a commander was more strict with his troops than Marmont was. Both of them demonstrated bad example to their troops through their lack of selflessness in their personal avarice. Masséna was burned out by 1811 and was not employed again after his failed campaign in the Peninsula. Marmont nursed grudges and imagined insults and turned traitor in 1814. Bessières had a very strong character, but was not always successful in disciplining the Imperial Guard, whose poor reputation von Funck blamed on Napoleon's indulgence for his picked veterans. Both Bessières and Nansouty punished looting and watched out for the civilian inhabitants. Von Funck admired both Cyr (properly Gouvion St Cyr) and Oudinot, but noticed that the former's frequent illnesses and the latter's many wounds inhibited their strictness as commanders.[21]

These, then, were the men who crafted the weapon that would become the Grande Armée and that Napoleon would so deftly lead on the battlefields of Europe through victory and defeat for ten years. This is their story, told through some of the battles they fought. There are victories and defeats within, and not all of the generals of the Consulate and Empire have their story told by name. Yet, it is the story of them all, and the men they led into and through the fire for over twenty years of almost constant warfare . . .

PROLOGUE

Old men forget; yet all shall be forgot,
But he'll remember with advantages
What feats he did that day... WILLIAM SHAKESPEARE

08:00 30 November 1808, Somosierra, Spain

The Emperor was growing impatient. Sitting on his horse at the foot of the winding, rocky pass of Somosierra he was waiting for Victor's infantry to outflank the entrenched Spaniards. Despite the low, hanging fog, the French knew there were three artillery batteries up the pass, and quite possibly a fourth. Supported by large numbers of infantry, the Spanish undoubtedly thought their position impregnable.

Directly behind the Emperor was his customary escort of Guard cavalry. The 3rd Squadron of the regiment of Polish Light Horse had the duty. Newly organised, these Poles had become a crack, hard-riding outfit by tough training and good leadership. It was a determined group of die-hards and champing at the bit for action.

Returning from a personal reconnaissance up the valley Colonel Pire informed the Emperor that the Spanish positions were heavily fortified and impossible to take by a frontal assault, the Spanish artillery being entrenched at the bends in the road up the pass. Irritated by this, the slow progress of the infantry, and stating emphatically that he did not know the meaning of the word impossible, Napoleon, tight-lipped with impatience, turned to the Poles and ordered the squadron commander, 'Monsieur, take it for me, at the gallop.'

Accepting the almost flippant order as a challenge, Chef d'Escadron Kozieltulski drew his sabre, turned in his saddle towards his trumpeter, and ordered '*Au trot!*' The crimson-and-white-jacketed trumpeters raised their trumpets to their parched lips at the order and as one sounded the charge and as Kozieltulski's upraised sword arm swept forward, he bellowed '*En Avant!*' and the squadron sunk spur.

The 150 Poles broke into a sharp trot, sweeping past the Emperor and his amazed staff at the salute in perfect order in a column of fours and made for the first battery at the foot of the pass. The shocked Spaniards, watched by the equally shocked French, were caught open-mouthed by this reckless and almost unbelievable action. They almost immediately opened fire and as the guns found the range, Kozieltulski's upraised sabre flashed in the sun, the trumpets again clarioned an order and the Poles broke into a canter. Round shot found the range and began tearing into the blue-clad ranks knocking over men and horses and splattering their comrades with blood and brains. Both horses and men tensed, knees grew tighter on the horses' shoulders, and as one they muscled forward, the horses answering the trumpet calls without being urged by their masters. Closing ranks as holes were torn in the column, the Poles urged their horses into a dead run, following Kozieltulski's bellow of '*Chargez!*'

The squadron charged as if it lived a charmed life, breaking into the first battery, horses jumping the line of guns, the Polish troopers sobering the gunners without quarter. Kozieltulski was shot out of the saddle, but the battle-crazed Poles sensed victory and went for the second battery at the gallop, trumpeters again blowing the charge.

The surviving officers led their troopers yard by bloody yard up the pass through intense Spanish gunfire. Spurring up the pass, the parched-throated cavalrymen roared '*Vive l'Empereur!*' as they overran the second battery, scooping up five Spanish colours as they went, one taken by a maréchal des logis-chef of the 7th Company. Bloody sabres rose and fell, more Polish saddles were emptied, horses were hit, screamed and went down, and all officers, save one, were shot out of the saddle. The Spaniards fell where they stood or ran, but intense cannonfire from the third battery fell among the Polish remnants. Led by the senior survivor, Lieutenant Niegolewski, the battle-maddened Poles regained their momentum and went for the third battery.

With their wounded lieutenant, the Polish survivors staged a wild, whooping hell-for-leather charge that hit the Spanish battery like a juggernaut, killing or scattering the Spanish defenders wherever they could find shelter from the madmen.

At the foot of the pass, sensing success, Napoleon ordered another contingent of Guard cavalry to the Poles support. Commanded by Pierre Montbrun, the squadron of Chasseurs à Cheval of the Guard spurred up the valley now littered with corpse and round shot, heralded by their sky-blue-jacketed trumpeters and echoing the Poles shouts of '*Vive l'Empereur!*'

Joining the greatly depleted Polish squadron, the Guard cavalry continued up the valley to the last Spanish battery, overrunning it and cutting down the Spanish gun crews ignoring Spanish calls for quarter. The small knot of Tzapka-topped, blood-and-gore smeared Polish cavalrymen stopped at the top of the pass as Lieutenant Niegolewski slid from his horse with his seventh wound of the day.

The chasseurs maintained a bold front, shielding the worn-out Poles. Seeing the French cavalry still ready for action, the terrified Spanish infantry threw down their weapons and fled, later taking out their vengeance on their commander by shooting him to pieces and tying his shattered body to a tree.

Eighty-three Polish casualties marked the route of the charge up the pass. One of Napoleon's aides, de Segur, who was caught up in the emotion of the moment and joined the Poles' wild chevauchee, was wounded for his trouble.

As the exhausted Poles collected their wounded and licked their wounds, the Emperor rode through their decimated ranks praising their effort and rewarding it with sixteen crosses of the Legion of Honour. Napoleon dismounted at the head of the pass to talk to Lieutenant Niegolewski and personally pinned his own cross on the near-prostrate officer, who survived to fight another day. The charge and rout of the Spanish had taken all of ten minutes.

As the army trudged through the corpse-strewn Spanish positions and past the now veteran Poles, unit after unit gave the Poles the marching salute, even the grimly silent units of the Old Guard saluting the newest unit to join their ranks. Replacing the Poles as the Emperor's escort, Montbrun joined the Emperor's relentless pursuit of the Spanish.[1]

CHAPTER I

LA FEU SACRÉ

Organisation and tactics of the Grande Armée

*Nothing should be concealed from the Emperor, either good or bad; to deceive him, even about
things that are likely to be disagreeable to him is a crime.*   BERTHIER TO LANNES

*In my campaigns Berthier was always to be found in my carriage. During the journey I used to
study the plans of the situation and the reports sent in, sketch out my plans for battle from them,
and arrange the necessary moves. Berthier would watch me at work, and at the first stopping-place
or rest, whether it was day or night, he made out the orders and arrangements with a method and
an exactness that was truly admirable. For this work he was always ready and untiring. That
was Berthier's special merit. It was very great and valuable, and no one else could have replaced
Berthier.*   NAPOLEON

10:20 10 October 1806, near Saalfeld, Saxony
The advance guard of Lannes's V Corps, the 10ᵉ Hussars, in dusty blue and
white trotted through the Saxon countryside looking for a route to, and a
crossing over, the River Saale. Suddenly, shots rang out to their front, and their
advance picket came pounding down the road towards then, one of the troopers
being held in his saddle by his comrades. Immediately whistling up a courier, the
chef d'escadron in command of the advance guard gave him a quickly pencilled
dispatch for both the corps commander and for the commander of the 17ᵉ
Légère, which was close behind them. Deploying his command, the experienced
cavalry commander trotted forward with his trumpeter and a certain trusted
maréchal des logis to see what the disturbance was about on this cool, crisp
autumn morning in what had been until a few minutes ago, a rather routine
morning for a light cavalryman.

The roar of Prussian cannon split the morning tranquillity with more finality
than the pistol and musket shots of a few minutes earlier. Rounds whistled
overhead, striking the road and ricocheting across it into a tree line, where,

thankfully, none of his troopers were. Looking at his maréchal des logis, he nodded, causing the sergeant to rein his mount around and gallop back down the road, looking for Marshal Lannes. No written communication was needed – he and the NCO had been together for a very long time and the NCO knew exactly what to do. A sizeable Prussian force had been found and they were going to have a very busy morning.

1025 10 October 1806, near Schleiz, Saxony
The sudden explosion of cannonfire caused the heads of the Imperial staff to jerk north-west all at once. Loud and completely unexpected, it was evident to even the most casual observer that the advance guard of the Grande Armée was in a fight. Lannes had gone looking for one and he had found it. Arguably the most combative general in the army, hopefully this time Lannes had not bitten off more than he could chew.

The staff, as if on cue, burst into activity. Orders were barked for couriers and aides-de-camp, escorts were gathered from the available squadron of the Ier Hussars that was the Emperor's mounted escort, as the Guard cavalry had not yet arrived. Finally, the Emperor, conferring with Berthier, dictated an order for Augereau to join Lannes by forced marches; Davout, Lefebvre, Nansouty, Klein and d'Hautpoul to move on Schleiz; Soult to advance through Weida on Gera; Jérôme to advance to Hof instead of Lobenstein. Berthier patiently took notes in his ubiquitous green notebook. When Napoleon finished, Berthier motioned to an aide, gave him quick, careful instructions, mounted his horse and followed his Emperor, with the escort of the light blue-and-white-uniformed hussars, led by a tough-looking, one-eyed, scarred lieutenant following in their wake.

The command group of the Grande Armée was galloping up the road to the north-east from Ebersdorf to Schleiz. Seeing Davout's escort, they reined in and asked for the marshal, he being in the midst of his staff, listening to the reports of a courier from the III Corps cavalry screen. Walking over to talk to the Emperor, who himself had now dismounted, surrounded by the silent protective band of hussars, the two men discussed the situation. The conclusion drawn was to order Davout to Possneck, just north-east of Saalfeld, to be ready to support Lannes if he was in trouble. Milhaud's light cavalry brigade and Dupont's division of Ney's VI Corps would be attached and go with him. Davout nodded, concurring, and headed off, calling to his chief of staff and his senior aide-de-camp, Colonel Bourke.[1]

Warfare was changing in 1792 at the beginning of the Wars of the French Revolution. Industrialisation was taking hold in Europe and new production techniques were being applied to weapons. Mass production was not only possible but being employed by the major powers. Along with technological innovations and improvements, new tactics, organisation and the command and control of armies were changing, ushering in a new era in the history of warfare. This chapter will attempt to outline how these changes affected the French armies and eventually the Grande Armée that Napoleon would command and lead in his numerous campaigns against a plethora of enemies in many different settings of terrain and climate.

The French Royal Army's gradual slide into inefficiency, defeat and ignominy that began at the beginning of the eighteenth century during the War of the Spanish Succession turned into an avalanche that hit the bottom in the Seven Years War. Neglect, a grossly overstrength and increasingly effete officer corps, petticoat influence, and a general malaise and lack of determined leadership had culminated in defeat and humiliation in central Europe at the hands of toughly disciplined British regulars and Frederick's Prussians. The French troops who were repeatedly defeated in this debacle bore little resemblance to the tough white-coats of Marshal Turenne from whom they were descended. Thoughtful officers, such as Marshal de Broglie,[2] who had performed well in Europe, and the ingenious artilleryman General Gribeauval[3] who had served with distinction during the war with the efficient Austrian artillery, were dedicated to the reform of the French army and wanted to create an instrument that could defeat the iron-disciplined Prussians on the battlefield.

The French military reformers, with vengeance very much in mind, set to work with a will. These proposed reforms generally took two forms, the first intellectual and the second practical. Theorist Jacques Guibert (1743–90) wrote and thumped on with his *Essai de Tactique*,[4] Pierre Bourcet[5] turned his genius to staff procedures and mountain warfare, while François-Jean Mesnil-Durand (1729–99) wrote and argued over manoeuvring and fighting with heavy columns.[6] The du Teil[7] brothers wrote and taught about new, aggressive artillery tactics, for which Gribeauval was labouring mightily to provide new guns and equipment with interchangeable parts that could keep up in a rapidly moving and offensive army and co-operate with the infantry on the battlefield.[8]

An underlying current of discontent flowed through the Royal Army, somewhat more purposeful than the general unhappiness that had begun to infect the French people as a whole. Thoughtful officers believed they could revitalise the army to the glory days of Turenne and his invincible white coats. Successful French generals from the late war, and there were a few, de Broglie and Gribeauval among them, saw the need for drastic changes and set out to achieve it. Training, tactics and organisation all became targets for those who wanted the French army to resume its place of pre-eminence in Europe. Some, such as Guibert, began to put their new ideas on paper.

In a military sense, disaster could be said to be the mother of invention. Officers not only wrote and argued about the best way to reform the army, but also became specific about ways to improve discipline, morale and training. The writings of older, venerated practitioners and theorists, such as Folard and de Saxe were dug out, dusted off and put to good use. Folard's ideas greatly impressed a young, unruly and talented officer from Burgundy with bad eyesight, Louis-Nicolas Davout.[9]

These writings and the subsequent arguments between the adherents to *l'ordre mince* on the one hand and the *l'ordre profond* on the other, provided food for thought. It was finally decided to launch a series of experiments to try out the new tactics of *l'ordre profond*,[10] fighting and moving in columns relying on shock action over firepower, backed by de Broglie, and compare it to the traditional linear evolutions of *l'ordre mince*,[11] backed by almost everybody else. Each system had its adherents, de Broglie himself favouring columns supported by large numbers skirmishers, others preferring to turn the French infantry into ersatz Prussians, as the only tried and true method of defeating the seemingly invincible host of Frederick.

One French officer of Prussian origin, General Johann Ernst Pirch, wanted to make the French Army into a copy of the Prussian, but there was not widespread support for this. Prussian-style uniforms, cheap and tight, were not popular. There was even an attempt to introduce Prussian-style corporal punishment into the ranks, but that was not approved by either officers or men. The experiment was an aberration in the evolutionary practice and the serious reformers soon sorted it out and got back on track.[12]

The first of the series of manoeuvres that was to test one theory against the other were to take place using the two regiments of the garrison of Metz in 1775.[13] They merely demonstrated that Mesnil-Durand's theories were plausible. More extensive testing was planned and took place in August and September of 1778 at a training area established in Normandy at Vaussieux. Forty-four infantry battalions, six dragoon regiments and a considerable artillery train were assembled, trained in the manoeuvres through August, and the tests began in earnest on 9 September, ending on the 28th.[14]

The training started with the battalions, then worked up through the regiments, brigades and divisions. The first trial had thirty-two infantry battalions organised in four divisions, each of two brigades of four battalions each. Each 'manoeuvre,' eight of them through the month of September, was designed to test linear movements of troops against that of columns, using the Règlement of 1776.[15]

Military conservatism is hard to overcome in any age, in any army. So it was in the aftermath of the experiments at Vaussieux. The proponents of *l'ordre mince* proclaimed that not only had linear formations looked much more orderly and disciplined, which they had, but they had done better against Mesnil-Durand's clumsy columns. Based on these manoeuvres the adherents of the linear school of thought won the first round.[16]

Mesnil-Durand, among other proponents of the column, de Broglie being one, was both disappointed and incensed. General Wimpfen, who was a conservative proponent of the linear system, condemned both de Broglie and Mesnil-Durand in writing.[17] The arguments were bitter and prolonged. The very capable General Rochambeau commanded one of the brigades in the series of experiments, doing very well using linear tactics and said so.[18]

De Broglie generally expressed content and satisfaction with the manoeuvres[19] but Wimpfen and other officers opposed and disagreed with him at every turn, generally attacking the manoeuvres in column in general and Mesnil-Durand in particular.[20] There were glaring errors with the columns as formed and constituted, which did show up in the manoeuvres.

Despite opposition from the conservative generals and their adherents, de Broglie still thought that Mesnil-Durand's ideas had merit, but had to be fine-tuned. The columns used in Normandy were too large and clumsy, and skirmishers in larger numbers had to be employed to protect the column, which had little protective firepower.

De Broglie also thought that some of the general officers that participated agreed with him, among them Marshal von Luckner.[21] It did impress a generation of younger officers, however, who not only witnessed or participated in the manoeuvres, but also read the related manuals and treatises.

There were flaws in the system that Mesnil-Durand was proposing, which was one reason why there was so much opposition to it (the other was undoubtedly the inherent conservatism of the officer corps – but this time the system was broken, which was evident to most, and something positive had to be done to either repair or replace it). However, the experienced de Broglie stubbornly supported it because he took the larger view, regarding it as something that could put the whole army in motion, and not just worrying about minor tactical problems that could be worked out later. There was virtue in having the experiments at all, and even the condescending comments and disagreements of Wimpfen and other critics bore fruit. The armies of the Revolution and the Grande Armée in particular all benefited both from the manoeuvres and the following bitter arguments.

Generals de Castries and de Puysegur were two other French officers who saw promise in the new tactics and were proponents of *l'ordre profond*. These two recommended a compromise between the two extremes of *profond* and *mince*, and this was gradually and generally accepted by the majority of the younger officers. De Castries favoured making the columns smaller, such as the march columns already authorised by the 1776 Règlement. De Puysegur mentioned that the smaller, more compact battalion columns were much better than the large, awkward formations that Mesnil-Durand wanted to employ.[22] These were used eventually – they could move over rough terrain quickly and to either flank if necessary, and it was relatively simple to form square against cavalry from them. This was the movement and attack formation eventually employed during the Revolutionary and early Empire period, either in a column of companies or a column of divisions.

Paul Gedeon Joly de Maizeroy (1719–80) finally seemed to sum up what was needed and attempted to end the controversy between *l'ordre profond* and *l'ordre mince*. He believed that the infantry had to move quickly and efficiently on the battlefield, and that the armies had to be able to move quickly on a strategic level. Mobility, both tactical and strategic, was the key to success.[23]

Maizeroy firmly believed that any officer who attended the manoeuvres who had an iota of common sense and experience would recognise the superiority of Mesnil-Durand's system and his arguments for its use. But he thought the heavy formations had to be changed to increase mobility and the command-and-control of the units involved – Mesnil-Durand's formations were just too big and awkward.[24]

French light troops, as we would come to know them in the Napoleonic period, were first formed in the 1740s to oppose the excellent Austrian grenzers, pandours and hussars. Both the French and the Prussians had trouble with these freebooters, who generally were not paid and had plunder-rights. They played havoc in rear areas and were expert in *la petite guerre*, 'the little war' of raids, ambushes and patrolling.[25] A French officer, François de Grandmaison, reported quite bluntly that the enemy light troops seemed to be everywhere attacking rear echelon units, convoys and small detachments, and that Austrian light cavalry raided deep into friendly territory, capturing French general officers almost at will.

At first, the French were singularly unskilled in this type of warfare, but they gradually improved: the Royal Army finally formed twelve battalions of green uniformed chasseurs à pied which eventually became the senior, famous regiments of light infantry in the Revolutionary and Napoleonic period.

The Austrian employment of Grenzers had been very effective through the Seven Years War. However, after that period, some Austrian officers wanted these excellent light infantry to become more disciplined, and the effort to give them regular discipline and organisation lessened their value and their general quality declined (even Napoleon remarked on this).[26] There were still tough, excellent troops from the Austrian military border, but their overall effectiveness dropped significantly because of high losses and from the often officious attempt to make them into something they were not.[27]

The damage, however, had been done. Austrian attempts at regular infantry being employed as tirailleurs was rarely successful, being drawn from the proverbial third rank of the linear formation, but were recommended to be those troops most able to operate successfully in open order. The Austrian General Radetzky observed that neither the Austrians nor the Russians understood fighting in open order and believed that skirmishers could only be used in a very small, limited way.[28] The conclusion that was reached was that the Austrians were not the equal of the French when fighting in open order.

The practitioners of the new French 'system' apparently did experiment with the use of the third rank as skirmishers, but probably found it unsuitable, as it was not a cohesive unit that was being deployed in open order, only a fragment of one. Hence, while the Prussians and Austrians, as well as the Russians, continued to employ this somewhat unsatisfactory solution, the French went ahead, both by accident and design, trying different methods to see which one would work, ending up with their deployed companies, battalions and regiments, which worked for them very well, and attacking with battalions in column, supported by artillery and skirmishers, becoming a system that was difficult to defeat, especially when the French commanders were skilled in the employment of combined arms, a doctrine that was taught in the excellent French artillery schools.[29]

In the hands of a commander such as Davout or Lannes, the instrument was effective and deadly. In the hands of less skilled generals, such as Oudinot or Ney, it could become clumsy and rely more on mass to win – neglecting the time-honoured application of combined arms techniques – and not on the innate skill of the subordinate officers and men who knew their business and how to apply it.

Neither the Règlement of 1776 nor that of 1791 covered the employment of massed skirmishers as an offensive weapon, nor was the use of columns in combat covered, at least not how they were going to be employed once the shooting started. The 1791 Règlement was essentially written by the adherents of l'ordre mince, and it covered in detail, complete with detailed diagrams, every possible movement for every possible eventuality up to the battalion level. When war came in 1792, shortly followed by the huge mass armies allowed by the levée en masse, there was simply no time to thump both the volunteers and conscripts into the mindless discipline required to perform and master the required, myriad movements of made necessary by the linear system of eighteenth-century warfare.

The only mention of tirailleurs, per se, in the 1791 Règlement is about using the ubiquitous third rank for flank guards when a column on the march may be threatened by cavalry, hardly a guide for how skirmishers came to be employed in mass as an offensive weapon. The 1792 provisional instruction mentions tirailleurs being used in open order against artillery gun crews, again, not what they would be used against when the Great Wars actually exploded across Europe. The bottom line with the Règlement of 1791 is that there is virtually no reference to employment of tirailleurs, at least not the way they were going to be used, at all.

Therefore, what the French commanders initially did was to get as many troops as possible, trained or otherwise, forward into the firing line and to launch them into the attack. That solution, quite simply, was open-order formations backed up by battalion columns. Initially, there were disgraceful stampedes, but the new 'system' sorted itself out. Battalion columns were handy formations capable of forward and lateral movement. They could cover ground swiftly without too much loss of cohesion. Skirmisher-fire, and the skirmishers themselves, were hard to combat by an enemy in perfect, symmetrical lines, firing away in controlled volleys on command. Their skirmisher screen, if they used one at all, was usually driven in or overwhelmed by entire battalions and regiments deployed as *tirailleurs en grandes bandes.*[30]

Sometimes French units just dispersed into open order as skirmishers, by command or not, formed into swarms and proceeded to shoot the enemy's line to pieces. As the system matured, these large numbers of skirmishers became the fire-support element of an attack on the enemy, covering the advance of a line of battalion columns, and, as the columns finally rushed for the enemy line, formed between the columns and kept shooting. These were supported by aggressively handled artillery that was hauled up to slingshot range and opened fire.

General Maximilian Foy described in detail how the French employed their skirmisher swarms. Large numbers were employed to open an action and they were given a general, vice a specified, mission. They were to harass the enemy by fire and not to become decisively engaged. They were to give way if attacked and protect themselves from artillery fire by their dispersal and also by taking advantage of any and all natural cover. The skirmishers were to look for weaknesses in the enemy front and concentrate their efforts there. They were to be continually relieved by the troops in formed order so that the fire of the skirmishers did not weaken or stop. The skirmishers' operations would actually find the weakness or weaknesses in the enemy line and the French main effort would be organised against that point. The French troops designated for the main attack would form in battalion columns and move forward, being supported by fire from the skirmishers as they attacked the enemy line in force.[31] Skirmisher swarms would also be used in economy-of-force missions, to keep other portions of the enemy line busy while the main effort took place elsewhere. Sometimes French commanders would 'form' their front line as a heavy skirmisher line and 'feed' it from the second line which was formed in battalion columns, fresh troops moving forward to take their place in the skirmish line while those who had been in action retired and reformed in the second line.[32]

Thoughtful French officers trained their troops as much as possible, from *la petite guerre*, to fighting in line, column and when deployed in open order. General Custine went so far as to establish a training school at Cambrai, staffed with a *bataillon d'instruction* that was used to train cadres from units and then sent back to help train their own units.[33]

Some commanders, such as Duhesme, would state that the French armies were composed solely of light infantry,[34] but as the fighting continued, and the troops and their officers became more skilled, attacks in line became more common.[35] However, it did become standard practice to deploy whole battalions and even whole demi-brigades as skirmishers, the afore-mentioned tirailleurs en grandes bandes.[36] Attacks on strong points were sometimes delivered in this formation, though using columns against villages and strong points was more common.

French use of tirailleurs and light infantry became so necessary to their new method of making war that they evolved into elite troops, at least being considered that by their commanders, including Napoleon. Additionally, there was a definite difference between légère and ligne units. While organisation, training and equipment were identical for both line and light infantry, there was a tradition of detached service for the légère formations, and light infantry had the right to lead all attacks.[37]

While open-order fighting might have suited the French genius for improvisation, effective employment did require well-trained troops that were aggressively and competently led. It was not a job for the uninitiated or the amateur. French commanders insisted on light infantry training, both for the *la petite guerre* and for light infantry operations on the battlefield. There was, however, no Règlement for skirmishing in the Grande Armée. There were local and corps-level instructions, such as Davout's in 1811, but an army-wide regulation was never published. It should also be noted that the light infantry tactics employed by the French did not replace the 1791 Règlement, which remained in effect throughout the period. The new tactics did, however, supplement the Règlement.

The emphasis on marksmanship was revealing and a key to the entire role of skirmishers. Napoleon thought that 'the fire of skirmishers is best of all'[38] and insisted on marksmanship training for the Grande Armée as a whole. He wrote to Marmont along the channel in March of 1804 to ensure the troops were drilled twice per week dry-firing their weapons and had target practice. Further, they were to go through the drill evolutions three times per week.[39]

The use of skirmishers in any army was not unknown before the revolutionary wars, but the unprecedented use of them on a large scale to decide issues on the battlefield, if not the battle itself, was new and innovative and had its beginnings in the camp of Vaussieux in the 1770s. As the divisions, armies and soldiers and their officers and commanders became more skilled, especially after learning hard lessons from the allies, the tactics became much more sophisticated – and this was as early as 1794.

There was still disagreement on the both the use and utility of the 1791 Règlement. Reputedly both St Cyr and Duhesme thoroughly hated it and thought there were too many useless movements in it.[40] This attitude may have come from the fact that they did not have enough regimental service before the Revolution. Lannes and Augereau were both expert drillmasters and could – and did – use the Règlement successfully in combat. Masséna as a sergeant before the Great Wars apparently could manoeuvre his regiment better than any of his officers.[41]

Generally speaking, the French attacks evolved into something along the lines of the following generalised scenario. Skirmishers would deploy in large groups, described as swarms, against the enemy line. They would use every scrap of cover and open a general fire against the enemy's tight ranks, and generally start to shoot it to pieces. As the enemy's line became unsteady and losses mounted, with an ensuing loss of control by the allied commanders, French commanders would order the supporting battalions, in compact battalion columns, forward, sometimes moving to the attack in chequerboard fashion, generally in two lines. These lines of battalion columns could cover ground rapidly without losing unit cohesion. Moving forward at the double the battalion columns went for the enemy line supported by the fire of the skirmishers. As the line of battalion columns came up to the skirmishers, the skirmishers would redeploy in the intervals between the columns continuing to fire and move forward with them.

Artillery would come forward with the battalions making a run for the enemy line. Relying on shock and the firepower of the skirmishers, the battalions in column would shatter the enemy's line at first impact, the battalions of the second line of columns exploiting the breach in the enemy line. The key to this was the continued firing of the rallied skirmishers that reformed in the column intervals and kept up their accurate, rapid fire. The charging columns had little defensive firepower and without the skirmishers were likely to be defeated.

The Grande Armée generally formed for battle in two lines of battalion columns. These were placed chequerboard fashion, so that cavalry and artillery could move up between the intervals. This also aided the difficult passage of lines, which Lannes performed under fire at Jena in perfect parade ground order.

Companies formed either into columns of companies, one directly behind the other, or columns of divisions, which was two companies abreast, four divisions deep. The same two companies always formed together. If the grenadier company was with the battalion, it was divided into two and they formed on either side of the leading division. The column of divisions was the most used, as it was the easiest to manoeuvre. There can be some confusion during the period as to army organisation and the term 'peloton'. This is commonly translated as 'platoon'. However, it was not the same as the definition used today, a tactical subdivision of a company. There was no such organisation in the Grande Armée, and peloton is either a synonym for company or a tactical subdivision of the battalion.

Up to 1808 there were nine companies per battalion: eight of fusiliers/ chasseurs and one grenadier (the third company officially becoming the voltigeur company; Napoleon had originally decided that a tenth company would be the voltigeurs, but the conversion of an existing company made more sense). After 1808 there were four fusilier/chasseur companies, one grenadier/ carabinier company and one voltigeur company.[42] Regiments originally had two battalions, then a third was added as a depot battalion. After 1808 regiments were to have four battalions, with a depot battalion, the depot battalion would have no elite companies.

Brigades were made up of two or more regiments, although a good number of brigades had only one regiment. Divisions would be made up of two or more brigades and a corps (after 1800) of two or more divisions. Divisions prior to 1800 were made up of all three combat arms: infantry, artillery and cavalry. The corps d'armée came into use in 1800 by Napoleon during the Marengo campaign. Thereafter it was the smallest formation of all arms in the Grande Armée. Divisions were now either infantry or cavalry with both having attached artillery. There was also a cavalry reserve and an artillery reserve under army control.

Training and drilling during the Revolutionary period was catch-as-catch-can, conscientious officers ensuring it was done. The most intensive period of drill was the three years in the channel camps before the Ulm/Austerlitz campaign. While the French armies had become more professional during 1798–99, they were probably at their professional best in 1805–7. The Grande Armée that marched east in August 1805 was the best Napoleon ever commanded, one-third being veterans of at least six years' service, over half of the cavalry and over forty per cent of the infantry having seen the owl and heard the elephant. The remainder were new soldiers but 'thoroughly trained and indoctrinated'.

The Grande Armée's battles would generally start with units shaking out their light infantry, either the individual battalions and regiments, or the battalions their voltigeur companies to make jarring, local attacks on the enemies positions all along the line. Behind this screen artillery would move up to support the skirmisher swarms and prepare the way for the main attack, sometimes in front of the infantry. As the battle 'ripened', the corps, or other units selected for the main attack would move into their attack positions in battalion columns prepared to advance on order. When the enemy was sufficiently 'prepped' out of the smoke and noise the infantry would come at the double, and follow the skirmishers or the artillery to the objective, smashing into the enemy's shredded infantry, rupturing their defensive line. Heavy cavalry, dragoons and even available light cavalry would quickly charge to open the breech, rolling back the now shattered shoulders of the breech back on top of the enemy's line. Supporting infantry and artillery would then advance to consolidate the victory while designated light cavalry units would pick up the pursuit.

In the Revolutionary armies, and in the early Empire, the columns most used to advance and attack were either what the Règlement called a 'column of attack' or a closed column, the difference being that a column of attack had twice as much distance between its divisions as a closed column did. The column of attack was used when coming under fire because it was harder to hit. The closed column, while easier to control, was an easy, compact target.

The columns advancing behind the skirmisher swarms would get within striking distance, close ranks and go for the enemy line at the double with a shout and with bayonets at the charge. Emerging out of the smoke of the prolonged firefight, still with supporting skirmisher fire and artillery support, would shatter the enemy line at first impact, even if suffering heavy losses, as MacDonald's large, hollow oblong did at Wagram.[43]

Sometimes, as at Friedland, Lützen, Ligny and Wagram, large concentrations of artillery would advance, or as Senarmont's corps artillery did at Friedland, conduct a 'charge,' unlimber within 150 paces of the enemy's line, and blow out their centre with rapid-fire canister, clearing the way for the infantry and supporting horsemen.

Examples can be found throughout the period of the use of French light infantry in myriad roles. The Consular Guard's chasseur company deployed in open order preceding the grenadier battalion's deployment on Lannes's right at

Marengo in 1800. Light infantry from Oudinot's big elite division assigned to Lannes provisional corps in 1807 outfought larger numbers of Russian jägers and light infantry in the forest of Sortlack, in a 'fluctuating tree to tree fight,' while delaying Benningsen's Russian field army at Friedland. Davout's light regiments, cavalry and infantry, were conspicuous in the hill fighting south of Ratisbon in 1809 during the first half of the 1809 campaign. At Moghilev in 1812, Davout's light infantry continually hovered on the flanks of Bagration's army, ambushing the Russian flanking regiments. French infantry of Lannes's V Corps at Jena fought in open order, continually shooting the Prussian lines to pieces, taking advantage of every scrap of cover and concealment while the Prussians stood in the open, in ranks, firing volleys on command. The Guard Chasseurs à Pied attacked in open order at Hanau in 1813, their brethren in the Grenadiers à Pied attacking in line to their left, both noticed by an officer in the thick of the fighting.[44]

French commanders in the Revolutionary Wars had adapted their tactics for the types of terrain in which they operated. Attacks in column line and *l'ordre mixte* (see below) were not only dictated by the skill of the officers and training level of the troops but also by any mountains, plains, forests or combinations of all of these. When the troops and commanders from the different Revolutionary armies were ultimately organised as the Grande Armée, the army as a whole benefited from all these different methods and experiences.

In the later years, formations became heavier and sometimes too heavy, for two main reasons: units and armies were becoming much larger and the large number of conscripts that had to be employed, especially after the crippling losses of the Russian campaign. Still, missions were carried out competently and battles still won: Lützen and Bautzen were won by sheer combativeness, Dresden by enthusiasm and skill. The fighting at Leipzig was determined and valorous and, apart from an ammunition shortage and the premature detention of the Lindenau bridge, it could have been an outstanding example of withdrawal under pressure. The fighting in 1814 was bitter, conscripts, veterans and national guardsmen fighting at long odds and almost winning, defeating larger allied armies time and again until finally the odds became too great.

Regiments both line and light for years had developed, organised and trained companies in each battalion as *éclaireurs*, or scouts. These were finally officially recognised by Napoleon in March 1804 for the infanterie légère and in September 1805 for the ligne battalions. These were to be outstanding soldiers, too short to be grenadiers, and they adopted various combinations of green, yellow and red as their designation colours.

They finally adopted the hunting horn as the distinctive device on shakos and turnbacks after an official, and several unofficial, rows with the grenadiers. The combination of moustaches and grenades by the *kleinen manner* was too much for the grenadiers, but it was matched with a dedicated efficiency, as when some were mounted on the backs of Polish lancers as they swam the Berezina amid the ice chunks to clear the opposite bank so that Eblé's pontoniers could start constructing their bridges.

French tactics also developed other, more flexible formations, such as *l'ordre mixte*, which consisted of battalions alternately in line and in column, preceded by skirmishers. This reportedly was Napoleon's favourite formation and was used with deadly effect, for example, by St Hilaire at Austerlitz during Soult's assault on the allied centre, and in Desaix's employment of Boudet's division at Marengo. *L'Ordre mixte* was also employed on defensive missions, also covered by skirmishers.

As the skills of both officers and men increased, so did the tendency to fight in line, both to attack and defend, although skirmishers were still employed in the covering role. A defensive line might only consist of units completely deployed *en grandes bandes*, with their individual fire the more deadly as they did take aim. The Prussians complained after Jena that the French skirmisher deliberately took aim at, and hit, a large proportion of the Prussian officers and NCOs, a complaint the British made in the War of 1812 against the Americans, terming it 'unsporting' and 'savage'.

The infantry was not the only arm of the French army that was badly in need of reform after the Seven Years War. The artillery produced a reformer of its own, and his fertile brain, and subsequent actions, completely revamped the French artillery from muzzle to cascable, introducing a new system of artillery that enabled the sweeping campaigns and the fire support needed for the army on the battlefield.

In the development of European artillery systems there was much cross-fertilisation of ideas. The French had a light artillery system as early as the 1720s, but it went by the wayside in favour of a heavier one because of the emphasis on siege warfare. The Swedes were artillery innovators, much of what they did being a great influence on the Prussians, French and Austrians. The practical Prussians developed the screw quoin (later copied by both the Austrians and Russians) as well as the limber with attached ammunition chest.

The Prussian artillery clearly was better organised and trained, and had a much more manoeuvrable field artillery, than the Austrians, whose artillery arm was still a guild in the 1740s. Based on those lessons, Prince Lichtenstein developed a new artillery system, Europe's first integrated one, by 1753 based on the Prussian field calibres of 3-, 6- and 12-pounders. The Austrians surpassed the Prussians and surprised them in the next go round (1756–63). Their excellent system lasted until the mid-nineteenth century when it was becoming somewhat long in the tooth and outmoded by 1789. Lichtenstein's reforms were thorough and far-reaching, but he was to be outdone by a French 'competitor'.[45]

Jean-Baptiste de Gribeauval designed, tested and fielded his new system by 1765.[46] He was influenced by the Swedes, the older French Vallière System, the Prussians and Austrians. He had served with the Austrians in the Seven Years War, inspected the Prussian artillery before that, and already had an established reputation as an artillery innovator and developer of ordnance as early as 1748.

Gribeauval was not the only artillery innovator France had produced. Generally speaking, the French had been at the forefront of artillery development since their first artillery school had been established at Douai in 1679. They had also fielded the first standardised artillery system in 1732, but that had only standardised calibres, not the entire system to include vehicles, and there had been no distinction between field and siege artillery. Subsequently, they had been surpassed in artillery development first by the Prussians in the 1740s and then the Austrians in the 1750s.

The artillery cartridge was invented by French artillery general Brocard in the early 1740s. Prior to that, and sometimes after if necessary, loose powder had been loaded with a ladle. The ladle was still used in an emergency but the loading of loose powder into the gun tube was a dangerous proposition on a good day.

The development of fixed ammunition probably had several 'firsts' from different countries, the inclusion of the wooden sabot instead of the traditional wadding probably being the most important component as it helped cut down the windage (the distance between the round and the inside of the bore) thus giving the piece more inherent accuracy.

Gribeauval, after being commissioned in the early 1730s, worked hard as a regimental officer and also did much scientific work on artillery matters for the first twenty years in uniform. Gribeauval had an excellent grounding as a professional artilleryman and had a knack of developing new artillery material. It was during this period that he developed his new garrison carriage (1748). Gribeauval made a deliberate decision to construct his new gun tubes at 150 pounds per pound of round to increase tube life over the lighter Prussian and Austrian tubes (which were constructed at 100 and 120 pounds per pound of round respectively). The *An XI* gun tubes were designed at 130 pounds per round. Gribeauval fielded his new weapons in the early 1760s and field-tested them in 1764. Further, they were entirely new designs innovative, manoeuvrable and deadly.

Gribeauval had made an inspection trip to Prussia before the shooting started in 1756 and after the war began was seconded to Austria to supplement their artillery arm as they were short of qualified senior artillerymen. Because of his excellent service in Austria he was promoted to general and decorated with the Order of Maria Theresa. The Austrians considered Gribeauval a 'collaborator' in their work.[47]

Upon his return to France he had working models of both the Austrian and Prussian pieces made and tested, and produced his own designs. The famous Strasbourg artillery tests clearly demonstrated the superiority of his new designs over the older Vallière pieces, and started a debate between Gribeauval and Vallière *fils* that lasted until the latter's death in the early 1770s.

Gribeauval made his field artillery tubes (using Vallière's standardised calibres of 4-, 8- and 12-pounders) longer than either Prussia's or Austria's and much stronger, so as to have a longer service life before being replaced. His gun carriages were shorter and better designed than Lichtenstein's, the gun tubes having a fixed front and adjustable rear sight. These, combined with a mandatory reduction in windage and the elevating screw, made the guns inherently more accurate than the Austrian.

It should also be noted that the Gribeauval System was not a copy of the Lichtenstein System – the gun carriages, gun tubes and ancillary vehicles were different in appearance and the Gribeauval gun tubes were entirely redesigned and constructed.

In the development of his new artillery system Gribeauval introduced the following innovations:

- stronger, better gun tubes for field artillery, with a longer tube life than either the contemporary Prussian or Austrian gun tubes.
- the *prolonge*
- the iron axle for field artillery vehicles and gun carriages
- the *bricole*
- a new moveable rear gunsight that did not have to be detached from the gun tube when firing.
- standard elevating screw.
- the Etoile mobile, a technologically advanced searcher or 'cat' to ensure gun tubes did not have internal defects.
- new artillery doctrine.
- a new garrison gun carriage in 1748.
- new, improved gun carriages for field artillery.
- gun carriages with two trail handspikes instead of the normal one to

make traversing the piece much easier.
- better trails for the piece to give it a more sledge-like appearance to enhance the use of the prolonge.
- new tools to ensure the diameter of the rounds was within tolerance and with no outside defects
- reducing the windage significantly, making it less than the AUstrian tolerances and half that of the other Vallière gun tubes.

His systems aimed to emphasise mobility and firepower. At that, he succeeded. Further, there was detailed doctrine to go along with it, and as such was taught in the excellent French artillery schools post 1763.

Gribeauval's gun carriages were designed to take in both axes of recoil – backward and downward, hence the characteristic bend in the carriage that is more pronounced than on any other Continental gun carriage. Further, two handspikes were used on the trail to aid in forward movement by the 'man team' when using the bricole. It is interesting to note that with the double handspike arrangement, one man could use it when pointing (aiming) the piece when it is in battery and preparing to fire. This was because of the excellent balance of the carriage which was taken into consideration in the design of the gun carriage.

The artillery system that resulted, and became known as the Gribeauval system, was an entirely new family of field artillery, consisting of 4-, 8- and 12-pounder guns; a new 6-inch howitzer, and the ancillary equipment to support and maintain them in the field.

Still, interchangeability was still something of a problem. There remained twenty-five different sizes of wheel and there were two different sizes of caisson, one for the 4-pounder and one for the 8- and 12-pounders. There was also the problem of 'encastrement' where the 8- and 12-pounder gun tubes had to be moved forward on the gun carriage when being made readied for firing (the howitzers and 4-pounders did not have this problem). This was necessary because of the balance of the piece, and had to be reversed when the artillery companies were on the road. For short moves on the battlefield (and undoubtedly for longer ones as neither commanders nor crews wanted to hump gun tubes all day), the gun tube was left in the firing position. Lastly, there was nowhere on the avant-train (gun limber) for the cannoneers to ride.

Captain Adye, the author of *Bombardier and Pocket Gunner*, the standard British artillery manual of the period made the definitive verdict of the Gribeauval artillery system which made a definite impression and undoubtedly influenced British artillery development:

The French system of artillery was established as far back as the year 1765, and has been rigidly adhered to through a convulsion in the country which overturned everything like order, and which even the government itself has not been able to withstand. We should therefore, conclude that it has merit, and, though in an enemy, ought to avail ourselves of its advantages. At the formation of their system, they saw the necessity of the most exact correspondence in the most minute particulars, and so rigidly have they adhered to this principle that, though they have several arsenals, where carriages and other military machines are constructed, the different parts of a carriage may be collected from these several arsenals, in the opposite extremities of the country, and will as well unite and form a carriage as if they were all made and fitted in the same workshop. As long as every man who fancies he has made an improvement is permitted to introduce it into our service, this cannot be the case with us.[48]

Other artillerymen did not refrain from joining the argument, and the du Teil brothers, two of the greatest influences on Napoleon, stressed that in a war of manoeuvre, greater mobility was mandatory for field artillery that would be assigned to the field armies, and emphasised the increased use of massed fire-power. This would eventually cause greater use of artillery, and consequently firepower for the army would be greatly increased. Aggressive French artillery-men would later use their guns literally on the skirmish line to gain an advantage, even risking the guns themselves to win.

The du Teils believed counter-battery fire to be useless and stressed that artillery should be generally used against troops. There were only two occasions that counter-battery fire should be employed: when your own artillery was taking unacceptable losses from enemy artillery fire, and when there were no infantry targets. Ricochet fire was very important and was to be used when at all practicable, as was the use of grazing fire. It should be noted that ricochet fire effectively doubled the range of the artillery being employed.

Field artillery during the Napoleonic period consisted of foot, horse and mountain artillery. The largest calibre used for field artillery was a 12-pounder. What is interesting is that the French were the only belligerents during the period to codify their artillery doctrine beyond the artillery manuals: that doctrine covered not only artillery operations, but also coordination with the other combat arms, and how artillery was to be deployed above the battery level in the field. Du Teil's *Usage* is one of these, as well as the lesson texts in the French artillery schools. It gave them an immense advantage on the battlefield.

The du Teils advocated that artillery should go into action between 500 and 1,000 yards. He also thought that more guns of light calibre massed against fewer guns of lesser calibre were more effective, if counter-battery firing could not be avoided. His theories proved to be accurate, the lighter guns being able to fire quicker than those of heavier calibre, and to keep it up for a sustained period of time. Additionally, French gunners in the wars when firing against enemy artillery would mass their fire against the enemy's guns one at a time until it was knocked out, then shift their massed fire to the next target, quite literally taking them out one at a time down a gun line. That had to be unnerving to the gunners of the next target. If the battery limbered up to displace, the objective had been achieved without more expenditure of ammunition. A battery moving or displacing cannot shoot.

These problems came to a head during 1802–3. Napoleon established an artillery committee, which included Gassendi, Eblé and Marmont, mandated to simplify artillery construction and reduce the number of calibres employed with the field armies. What came out of it was a new 6-pounder, which replaced the 4- and 8-pounders, and a new 5½-inch howitzer, sometimes called the 24-pounder. Along with these new field guns came redesigned and improved caissons, limbers and gun carriages. The committee also recommended a new 24-pounder siege gun, light enough to accompany the Grande Armée into the field, as well as a light 3-pounder mountain gun and a light 5½-inch howitzer, also for mountain work.

The greatest change undertaken by the French artillery after the introduction of the Gribeauval system was the replacement of the 4- and 8-pounder guns with a newly designed 6-pounder, of the system of the Year XI, which also produced a new howitzer, better vehicles and the militarising of the artillery train, which took place in 1800. Instead of the civilian drivers and teams that hindered battlefield mobility during the Revolutionary Wars, and sometimes abandoned them on the battlefield, Napoleon introduced the *Train d'Artillerie*, which greatly improved the artillery arm. The train was a 'highly efficient military organisation,' arranged in battalions and companies, of which one was assigned to every artillery company to move its guns and equipment. They would always take the field together and because of this long-time service together they became highly efficient and cohesive. Originally the train company commanders were sergeants, but this was later changed to lieutenants. The chef de bataillon was a captain. This worked quite well, as they were one grade lower than the corresponding artillerymen. The train troops also brought along a trumpeter, which had to have come in handy.

The *Système An XI* was never fully implemented; it was only approved by a 'split vote' among the artillery committee. The only two guns produced in any quantity were the 6-pounder and the 5½-inch howitzer. Apparently there was also a new 6-inch howitzer which was employed with the Guard artillery's 12-pounder companies.

The 6-pounder seemed like a compromise between the 4- and 8-pounder, designed to replace them both. But there were design problems with the 6-pounder gun carriage, and it was finally replaced with older Gribeauval designs that stood up to campaigning much better than the new equipment. The 8-pounder was not made obsolete, merely replaced, and the French 6-pounder was superior to the Austrian equivalent, being a much more modern gun tube, the reinforcing bands being abolished as redundant, giving the gun tube a much cleaner lines.

The older 8-pounders could still be found in Spain, where in many cases they replaced the heavier 12-pounders which were unsuitable because of the terrain and the lack of remounts for the larger gun teams required for the 12-pounder.

There was a continuing debate within the French artillery community after the approval of the Système An XI, notably by General Gassendi. A new commission established by Napoleon in 1810 and headed by experienced General Songis concluded that the An XI system was unsuitable. The decision was made to continue with the Gribeauval System and 'accommodate' the new 6-pounder field piece as an interim measure.

There was much argument over the introduction of the 6-pounder, as many of the artillery generals did not approve of it. Ruty did a study of it comparing it with the 8- and 4-pounder, and the 8-pounder was readopted as the standard after the wars. When the new Vallée System was adopted to replace the Gribeauval System in 1827–29, the two standard field artillery calibres employed were the 8- and 12-pounders.

The introduction of horse artillery in 1792 greatly increased the mobility of the French artillery, as the gunners had their own mounts. Generally speaking, they were assigned to support the cavalry, but Napoleon always tried to assign at least one battery per corps in addition to that assigned to the cavalry. Horse artillery was designed to keep up with cavalry both on the march and on the battlefield. All French horse artillery pieces were pulled by six-horse teams to increase speed and mobility.

French artilleryman Louis de Tousard in his American *Artillerist's Companion* states that

> . . . the horse artillery was formed, and, in order to give it the advantage of a superior fire to that of the other powers, eight pounders and six inch howitzers were adopted. These two calibres appear to have, hitherto, completely answered every object which was expected from them, and the ammunition required for

these dimensions did not occasion an excess of wagons, or an embarrassing weight, which, in bad roads, would follow very tardily the rapid movements which this kind of artillery is constantly performing.

Though the 8-pounder be the most preferable calibre for the general service of the horse artillery, still the twelve pounder may be employed very advantageously; for it is equally susceptible of celerity in its motions. Its weight is only 1,800 pounds [gun tube only], consequently six or eight horses, if the ground be difficult, are more than sufficient to execute, in conjunction with the cavalry or chasseurs, the most prompt and decisive manoeuvres.[49]

Not having the gunners individually mounted did cramp speed and manoeuvrability. It also increased the weight the gun team had to pull. In the Austrian service, cavalry batteries, which were not true horse artillery were supported by cavalry, not the other way round as in the French service. The British, Württembergers, Dutch and others had horse artillery which was much more mobile than the Austrian cavalry batteries. Ney praised his Württemberg horse artillery in Russia as the equal or superior to his comparable French units. The British thought the French horse artillery superior to their own.

The Austrians, on the other hand, did not have true horse artillery. They organised cavalry batteries which were employed as mobile field artillery. The trouble with the Austrian cavalry batteries was that they were not horse artillery in the truest sense of the word. Horse artillery supported the cavalry it was attached to – the cavalry batteries had to be supported by cavalry to function properly just because they were not as mobile as they could have been.[50]

As the wars progressed, artillery took over part of the skirmisher's role. This happened generally for two reasons: the declining quality of the French infantry, mainly resulting from heavy losses in Russia and in 1813, and the greater employment of artillery as a whole as it grew it strength and flexibility. Still, in 1814 French attacks were preceded by swarms of skirmishers, and at Waterloo's ending, the veteran French infantry resorted to deploying as tirailleurs en grandes bandes and, working closely with artillery that had been manhandled up to within 250 and sometimes 100 yards were gradually taking apart the remnants of Wellington's line. Unfortunately, the French right flank was gradually being overwhelmed and the entire situation caved in.

The development of French tactical doctrine was an evolutionary process that began with the ashes of disaster after the Seven Years War. Both theorists and practitioners had their input – thoughtful officers were smart enough to realise that something had to be done to correct the inherent weaknesses in the French Army that had proved fatal. The intellectual side of the argument was just as important initially as the practical side, the practical side finally taking precedence in the cauldron of combat.

To accompany the technical improvements of the artillery equipment came equally innovative doctrinal changes, inspired both by Gribeauval, who had served with the excellent Austrian artillery during the late unpleasantness of the Seven Years War, as well as by the du Teil brothers, Pierre and Jean-Pierre, who would educate and train Napoleon in his formative years as a young artilleryman.

Owing to the limitations of the Vallière System and the mental inflexibility of French commanders and tacticians, the French artillery was seen merely as a support weapon that, once emplaced on the battlefield, could influence only what was within sight and range. The du Teils wanted the French artillery to become a combat arm of influence on the battlefield, equal to its comrades in the infantry and cavalry. Consequently, they emphasised mobility, striking power and accuracy, as did Gribeauval.

Napoleon's input to the artillery arm was more than helpful. He militarised the artillery train, making it the best of its kind in Europe during the period. He also lost patience with the senior artillery staff and put them to useful work with the field armies. He was also insistent on how much artillery ammunition would be carried on campaign for each piece. Napoleon generally allocated a double *approvisionnement* (basic load) of ammunition for each gun, between 300 to 350 rounds.

While the artillery was organised in regiments, the basic tactical unit was the company, which was trained to handle any type of artillery issued to it, and was normally assigned a 'division' of guns when taking the field. Artillerymen were considered elite troops, and collected the traditional *haute* pay of elite troops. They were on the average bigger than their infantry and cavalry comrades, serving the guns being gruelling, hard work, not just in combat, but before and after, having to clean the guns, fouled by hours of firing, and maintaining the tubes, carriages and vehicles. The vehicles and carriages might appear strong and sturdy, but prolonged firing and travel over execrable roads could quite literally shake the vehicles apart. In today's parlance, the artillery arm was 'maintenance intensive'.

At the beginning of the Revolutionary Wars, the drivers and horse teams for the artillery were hired civilian drivers. This was not only awkward, it was dangerous. In the middle of a fight, the civilians might decide things were getting just a little dangerous and depart, leaving the gunners on their own to save or move their guns as best they could. This was particularly inconvenient for the new horse artillery arm, organised in 1792, which was an excellent idea and innovation, but could quickly be converted to 'foot' artillery after the shooting started.

Napoleon fixed this upon becoming First Consul in 1800. His excellent *train d'artillerie* had its own distinctive uniform and was organised into battalions. The companies were parcelled out in wartime, matching up to artillery companies and their long service together made them crack, battle-tested units. It also gave the foot companies trumpeters, which the battery commanders undoubtedly found to be very helpful, especially as their drummers might not always be available as they were on foot like the gunners.

Tactics, as developed and recommended by Gribeauval and the du Teil brothers, were taught in the excellent artillery schools. They emphasised infantry/artillery co-operation. There were, however, 'no official regulations governing its tactical employment' (although the Guard did publish some for their use in 1812). Standard operation procedures were developed by both the corps artillery commanders and the corps commanders themselves. Artillery-men generally attempted to emplace their companies on slightly elevated ground; too high an eminence would leave considerable dead ground in front of the position which could not be covered by the guns, leaving them vulnerable. Generally, overhead fire was not used with friendly troops. Fuses for shells were generally unreliable and premature detonations could cause friendly troops to turn hostile. Also, it could unnerve untried conscripts.

The tactical employment of French artillery could be considered reckless. Guns were traditionally considered to be the 'standards' of the artillery company. Their loss was as serious as losing an eagle. However, to gain a decisive advantage, guns were risked by corps and company artillery commanders, and by Napoleon himself. Guns would be 'fought to the last extremity', especially on defence. Artillerymen would engage enemy assault columns 'head on'. French commanders would seldom engage in counter-battery fire, or an 'artillery duel' if you will. Their targets were the enemy troop formations, especially the infantry. If the enemy's artillery was doing particular damage to friendly infantry and cavalry, or it was appreciably hurting their own artillery, French commanders would mass their artillery against the enemy artillery, knocking it out either gun by gun or battery by battery. This was done effectively to the Russian batteries across the Alle River at Friedland in 1807 in support if Senarmont's attack. Guns accompanied infantry attacks, horse artillery would go in with the cavalry, unlimber close to the enemy and open a brisk, accurate fire on the opposing formations. The best example of this was in the mud and mess at Dresden in 1813. The ground being too wet and muddy for cavalry to charge effectively, Napoleon doubled up his horse teams. The threat of French horse artillery induced Austrian squares to surrender.

The chaos with which the French waded into during the Revolutionary Wars was generally sorted out through much trial and error. The much-needed French reforms began with 'The theory and experimentation of the military enlightenment, represented by the Gribeauval system, the Règlement of 1791, and the tactical convictions of the generals'[51] and this wrought a revolution in how wars were fought and won. Sans-culotte generals, junior officers who had been recently promoted, and former Royal Army NCOs who clawed their way up the promotion ladder dragged, pushed and thumped their odd mixture of old Regulars, volunteers and conscripts into effective fighting units that developed the later standard of small, handy battalion columns supported by clouds of skirmishers and supported by whatever artillery was at hand. The system they finally perfected, led by former enlisted men, junior officers, and especially by a grim, quiet and studious Corsican artilleryman, swept the battlefields of Europe and enabled the Grande Armée to 'stable their horses in every capital of Continental Europe,' defeating every army involved in the coalitions against France at least once, and left a legacy of hard-won victories and an enduring tradition.

The French cavalry at the beginning of the Revolution was governed by the out-of-date *ordonnance* of 1788 and during the period really had no up to date drill or tactical manual. There was a provisional ordonnance issued in September 1804, but what the French cavalry commanders actually did was develop their own hard-hitting tactics learned through hard experience.

There were three types of cavalry: heavy (line), light and dragoons. Because of the experience of the Revolutionary Wars, and coming in a distant second to the excellent Imperial Austrian cavalry, the cavalry arm was reorganised during the Consulate period. The heavy cavalry regiments, known as *cavalerie de bataille*, only one of which, the 8th, wore the cuirass, were reduced from twenty-five regiments to twelve, which became the Ier to the 12^e Cuirassier regiments. These were armoured with a full cuirass and helmets with a horsehair plume.

Napoleon abolished seven of the heavy cavalry regiments, the men and horses being put into the remaining eighteen regiments to bring them up to strength. Six of those remaining were converted to dragoon regiments. All of the tall men, and the biggest horses, fit to carry a cuirassier and his equipment, went into the first twelve regiments. What Napoleon wanted was a heavy cavalry arm that could meet and defeat the Austrian heavy cavalry on the battlefield.

There were three additional cuirassier regiments formed later in the Empire. The 13^e Cuirassiers were formed from provisional heavy cavalry units in Spain and served excellently with Suchet in eastern Spain. The 14e Cuirassiers were formed from Dutch heavy cavalry after Holland was annexed to France in 1810. The last, the 15e Cuirassiers, was a provisional unit formed by Davout in Hamburg in 1813–14 around a cadre of the Ier Cuirassiers.[52]

The two carabiniers à cheval regiments were retained unarmoured as heavy cavalry. This lasted until the end of the 1809 campaign where these efficient, black horse regiments suffered heavy casualties. There were armoured in a full cuirass and helmet in 1810.

The French light cavalry arm consisted of hussars and chasseurs à cheval. Both were equipped and trained the same, but the chasseurs were uniformed in green and the hussars were dressed as per regimental traditions. The hussars were more showy than the chasseurs à cheval, but their functions as light horse were the same. They would be joined by six regiments of lancers in 1811. There were twelve regiments of hussars and twenty-five of chasseurs à cheval.

There were thirty regiments of dragoons, and here is where there were major teething troubles. Many of them were dismounted in 1805–6 because of a general shortage of horses and because of Napoleon's projected invasion of England before the Grande Armée had to turn east in August 1805. Some dragoon units, especially those in Grouchy's division, performed excellently in the early campaigns. However, most were sent to Spain to 'learn their trade' in 1807–8, and they became well-trained, combat-tested units that were the best cavalry the in Grande Armée in the campaigns of 1813–14.

The French cavalry was at its peak in 1805–9. Service in Spain divided the French cavalry arm and the campaign in Russia crippled it. Still, there were high deeds done and the French cavalry arm in 1815 had regained much of its efficiency after more than a year of garrison duty.

The light cavalry's mission was scouting, screening and acting as flank guards on campaign. French light cavalry units were used on the battlefield as well as the heavy cavalry. Each corps was assigned a brigade or division of light cavalry for its security, and aggressively handled light cavalry worked with their horse artillery and the infantry in combined arms operations on the battlefield. Sometimes dragoons were used to reinforce the Grande Armée's cavalry screen on campaign, and they were employed as heavy cavalry on the battlefield along with the cuirassiers and carabiniers.

The main effect of cavalry employment on the battlefield was the application of shock by disciplined, massed charges. Charges had to be tightly controlled by their commanders. Experienced commanders always employed a reserve when attacking, in order to either reinforce success or to rally on if repulsed. The 'normal' progression for a charge was to begin at the walk. The command to both draw sabres and to trot would be given at 200 to 300 yards from the unit's objective. The command to gallop would be given at about 150 yards and for the last 50 yards, the command to charge would be given and the horses would go in at the dead run.

Sometimes this was not done. Some commanders would charge at the trot for better control, especially the heavy cavalry. Others would move around the battlefield at a trot or an 'easy gait' with sabres still in their scabbards and when the commander was ready to go in the commands to draw sabres and charge would be given immediately, not giving either the enemy or his own troopers any advance warning.

When a charge was over, the unit's trumpeters would sound the rally and the unit would regroup. Cavalry against cavalry actions could be vicious, but usually did not last too long. The winner was either the unit that had the better swordsmen or whose supports got there first. Charges would be conducted in waves, one squadron following the other, or a regiment following another. Sometimes regiments would alternate squadrons when attacking. Supporting horse artillery would cover withdrawals or soften up targets before the cavalry would charge.

The two greatest developments in the French service that ripened at the beginning of the Revolutionary wars. Both of these developments were organisational and they would give the Grande Armée greater operational flexibility, a great advantage over its opponents through the course of the wars, above and beyond the operational capabilities of the allies. First, was the existence of a permanent army-level staff, echoed at corps, division and brigade levels. Second, was the development of the corps d'armée, which was a tactical and operational organisation consisting of a permanent staff, two or more infantry divisions, supporting artillery and enough cavalry to scout for it and perform security missions.

The French started experimenting with the division concept in the last years of the Seven Years War. This developed into the territorial division concept and when the Revolutionary Wars started, the French fielded divisions of all arms, which would be combined into armies. This permanent division organisation, each with their own staffs, provided cohesion and gave the French an advantage which their opponents did not have.

As early as 1795–6, some field commanders started experimenting with pulling their cavalry out of the divisions and forming either brigades or divisions of cavalry under a senior cavalryman. Napoleon certainly did this in Italy in 1796–7. This evolved into homogenous divisions of infantry and cavalry, each with attached artillery for support. Light cavalry was brigaded with light and heavy cavalry was also brigaded together.

The next logical step was the formation in 1800 in Italy and Germany of the first permanent multidivision formation, the corps d'armée. In actuality, this was a headquarters with combat units attached to it. It was assigned two or more infantry divisions with a brigade or division of light cavalry and enough artillery to support it. It was flexible, in that divisions could be cross-attached between corps and provisional corps could be deployed for certain missions. Further, the units trained and lived together and became cohesive units from long association.

This organisation gave the Grande Armée great flexibility as the corps were semi-autonomous and could operate alone and were expected to be able to fight and survive for twenty-four hours before help could arrive from other units.

The cavalry was also given a corps organisation in the Grande Armée, known as the Cavalry Reserve. It was a multidivisional system with its own staff, artillery and supporting troops, but no infantry were assigned to it. In the later Empire, cavalry corps were organised instead of the separate divisions under the Cavalry Reserve, making command and control that much tighter.

General Pierre Bourcet, from whom all modern staff organisation and functioning evolve, was the premier staff officer of his time. His work and publications mark the beginnings of the development of the modern staff system. Bourcet's importance to Napoleon's developing method of making war cannot be overestimated. From him, and the staff school at Grenoble which he established and of which he was the director from 1764–71, came the embryo from which evolved the Napoleonic staff, of which Berthier was the preeminent product.[53]

The Grande Armée did not have a permanent staff corps that the Prussians were starting to develop after the catastrophe of 1806. One had been started in the old Royal Army, but it had been abolished by the Revolutionary government as being 'Royalist', much like throwing the baby out with the bath water. A draft copy of their written regulations covering staff organisation and operations vanished with them. However, a provisional instruction could have been issued in 1791. Officers assigned to the staffs of divisions and armies in the Revolutionary armies generally had to rely on 'the advice of older officers and the expensive lessons of their own experience. Berthier, who was chief of staff of the Armée des Alpes in 1795 issued simple instructions for the operation of an efficient staff, later to be reissued to the staff of the Armée d'Italie in 1796. These were apparently derived from the draft regulations of 1788 'on which Berthier may have worked'.[54]

Louis-Alexandre Berthier (1753–1815) senior of the Marshals, was the first of the great chiefs of staff in military history. Born at Versailles of a soldier father, he was carefully brought up and trained for a career as a soldier. His father being in the select Topographical Engineers, young Berthier too entered that corps in 1766 at the age of sixteen, and was selected to accompany Rochambeau's expeditionary force to America in 1780. Assigned *à la suite* to the

Soissonnais Régiment de Infanterie, he embarked for America as an infantry captain. An eager, aggressive and valorous officer, he was 'neat and orderly in all things' and was praised, promoted and decorated for gallantry in America. Berthier was not merely a staff officer, he also served as an instructor and became an experienced officer in the field.

Returning to France from America in 1783 he went into the corps d'état major, the new permanent staff corps the French were organising, part of the reforms based on their dreadful experience in the field in the Seven Years War and the experiments conducted by officers who wanted to improve the service back to the old standards of Turenne. A new staff manual was begun, and there is evidence that Berthier had a hand in its writing; at any rate, he absorbed its lessons carefully. His other duties included testing new tactics and different types of organisations to modernise the army, as well as conducting a study of the military system of Frederick the Great. By the time the Revolution erupted and France went to war with at least half of Europe, Berthier's reputation as a talented officer was well established.

Berthier supported the Revolution, but he was considered a *ci-devant* noble as he had the Order of St Louis. He was requested for service in various theatres by a number of army commanders. He was assigned as chief of staff of L'Armée du Nord, but just as quickly he was charged with *incivisme*, and went on inactive duty. Not one to sit on his hands, he ended up as a volunteer in the Vendée. Noticing his talents, the powers that be sent him as chief of staff to L'Armée de la Rochelle. His superiors proved to be totally incompetent and somewhat cowardly. Berthier was wounded in action, Rochelle failed and Berthier went to Paris to seek a better assignment. Put once again on inactive status with the threat of the guillotine looming over him, he was recalled to active duty in 1795 as chief of staff for Kellermann. The next year he and Napoleon were paired as chief of staff and commander respectively and the partnership that would last until after the first abdication in 1814 began.

Berthier served gallantly, efficiently and loyally: he served as chief of staff in the Armée d'Italie, 1796–97, then in L'Armée d'Egypte, 1798–99, as commander and chief of staff of L'Armée de la Réserve, 1800, and as minister of war, 1800–7, and as chief of staff and major general of the Grande Armée, 1802–14. He was Napoleon's shadow, and many of his greatest accomplishments have either been taken for granted or ignored. In the course of his duties, he managed to infuriate the egotistical Swiss renegade, Antoine Jomini. Attempting to teach the young mercenary proper staff procedure when he was serving as an aide-de-camp to Marshal Ney, Jomini took it personally and for the rest of his life attempted to blacken Berthier's reputation.

Berthier had both a strong character and constitution. He could work for days without sleep, some of his subordinates once claimed he had gone thirteen days straight without any sleep at all. If true, that is quite amazing. Reputedly, Berthier would rest after a long day's ride by sitting down and writing the Emperor's orders for the next day. He was short, stocky, an expert horseman, strict, but fair, with his subordinates, methodical and modest. He took good care of the troops and officers in his charge, but put up with no nonsense and always insisted on proper staff procedures, even though he was sick and getting a little long in the tooth in 1813–14. Coignet thought quite highly of him, as Berthier had given the famished Coignet some bread to eat after Coignet's capture of an Austrian cannon at Marengo in 1800.

Berthier developed the staff procedures the Grande Armée would later use, as well as the staff system that went with it. Quite possibly he had saved the embryonic staff manual that had been with the corps d'état major in the 1780s. He also developed certain procedures later adopted by the Prussian general staff, such as having chiefs of staff of comparable organisations communicate with each other without involving their commanders to save them unnecessary headaches.

Berthier believed the chief of staff to be the central point for the head-quarters, 'the headquarters pivot'. He needed to either see or sign everything that comes in and goes out of the headquarters. The staff itself had no set hours, as it is there to serve the commander and the good of the army as a whole. When work was finished, the staff could then rest. Above all, the commander should always be told the truth, no matter how unpleasant, and whatever the consequences. Something akin to the modern military maxim, 'bad news does not age well'.

The *Grand Quartier Général Impérial*, which developed from Berthier's work in the armies of the Alps and Italy, and refined by both himself and Napoleon was an efficient organisation, tailored and suited to Napoleon's method of waging war. Berthier has been characterised by many as nothing but a chief clerk. That is as inaccurate as it is unfair. Berthier ran the staff, and, through it, he and Napoleon ran the Grande Armée. Thiebault had remarked that Berthier was the ideal chief of staff, as he relieved Napoleon of all detailed work; he was also the only person who could read Napoleon's deplorable handwriting, not the least of his many talents.

Berthier's achievements were many and frequent. He is usually underestimated by historians because he worked in the long shadow of the Emperor. Berthier commanded and organised the Armée de la Réserve and moved it across the Alps in 1800. With it, Napoleon fought and won Marengo, regaining northern Italy for France. He was responsible for the planning that moved the Grande

Armée from the channel across the Rhine and into Germany in 1805 to surprise the allies and surround Ulm. In 1812, Berthier planned and executed the huge concentration for the invasion of Russia, including all the detailed planning of moving units from the far reaches of the Empire in an orderly matter. The logistical requirements alone were seemingly insurmountable, but the Grande Armée of 1812 was the best supplied and equipped of any Napoleon ever led.

Berthier has frequently been blamed for the command and staff mess at the beginning of the 1809 campaign. Although with the Armée d'Allemagne, he was not the commander, as is often said. He was still serving as Napoleon's chief of staff. Napoleon, still in Paris, had the irritating and confusing practice during this 'transition' period of sending both letters and telegraphs to Berthier which got out of sequence because of the different speed of the two forms of communication. Berthier finally was 'politely blunt' and told Napoleon that his presence was required with the army; a measure which ended the command and staff problems.

Berthier was an aggressive and imaginative officer, whose character shone through in victory and defeat, triumph and adversity. He could rally a broken column of infantry, seize a regimental colour and lead it forward through shot and shell, as he did at Lodi in 1796; be coldly courageous at Fort Bard in the Alps in 1800; coordinate the advance of different arms as at Friedland in 1807; or, in what probably was the most important action he ever completed, pulled the wreck of the Grande Armée together in Poland at the end of the retreat from Russia after Napoleon's departure for Paris to raise another army and Murat's desertion just to go home, by persuading Prince Eugène to assume command before the situation completely fell apart and set the example 'of loyal and energetic subordination' thereby stopping the useless quarrelling between the marshals.

Napoleon himself summed up Berthier's overall worth as a soldier, and to the Grande Armée in general, referring to his absence at Waterloo, 'If Berthier had been there, I would not have met this misfortune.'

The Grand Quartier Général, or the army general staff, itself consisted of three main sections: Napoleon's *Maison*, the Grand Etat-Major General and the *Intendance*. The Intendance was the Grande Armée's administrative staff, which will not be covered in this study. The Intendance was headed by the Intendant General and was never fully militarised, much to Napoleon's chagrin, and this caused much wastage, incompetence, and plain dishonesty, to the ordinary soldier's disgust and detriment.

Napoleon's Maison, or household consisted of his personal staff which included what was referred to as the 'General Officers neat His Majesty' such as

Duroc and Caulaincourt, the Master of the Horse to the Empress, Constant Corbineau and the Governor of the Pages, Mathieu Gardane, whose billet eventually went away with the pages themselves. Also in the Maison were the *officiers d'ordonnance*, who were a junior type of aide-de-camp, headed by chef d'escadron Gaspard Gourgaud (who left a valuable memoir of the Russian campaign, disagreeing with the less than accurate one left by de Segur with a novel form of literary criticism: he called de Segur out and shot him in a duel).

The innovation of Napoleon's Maison was the creation of the General's aides-de-camp, experienced general officers, each an expert in his own branch of service, who were 'trained up in Napoleon's own school of war' and capable of significant independent assignments, from a task force of all arms on the battlefield to the negotiating of a treaty. There were generally twelve of them at any one time, but not all of them were present all the time. These men were obeyed by even the marshals and were Napoleon's eyes and ears. Their aides-de-camp, also called the 'little aides-de-camp, were employed by Napoleon when needed. These general officers serving the Emperor as Imperial ADCs were

men for all missions, leading improvised task forces to meet unexpected emergencies, massing artillery to support a decisive attack, clearing a snarled supply line, conducting large-scale reconnaissances, and sometimes handling minor diplomatic assignments. They had authority to require even marshals to hold reviews and showdown inspections so that they might examine the state of their troops. Isolated commanders trusted them to take Napoleon a factual account of their problems. They were loyal but not courtiers; they spoke the truth as they saw it and did not flatter. Napoleon gave them his trust, accepted their frankest advice and comments without rancour (if not without occasional anger), and counted them as friends.[55]

Napoleon also had an organisation, his cabinet, which was divided into three sections. The first, the Secretariat, was responsible for his correspondence and consisted of civilian secretaries, archivists and a librarian. Next, the *Bureau de Renseignements*, was a military intelligence organisation, responsible largely for strategic intelligence, which was passed on to Berthier's cabinet. Lastly, the Topographic Bureau, headed by Bacler d'Albe, who himself maintained the Emperor's situation map. This section also kept maps, plans of fortresses and files on the 'resources' of the areas in which the Grande Armée operated.

There were elements of Napoleon's *Maison Civile* which accompanied the staff to war, and generally, Maret, Napoleon's Secretary of State, Berthier's civilian counterpart, was with the army on campaign.

Berthier's organisation was the *Grand Etat-Major General*, which consisted of his own cabinet, his personal staff of aides-de-camp and the état-major general 'proper'. Berthier's cabinet, sometimes called the *Etat-Major particular*, consisted of a small group of talented and experienced staff officers generally organised in three sections: troop movements, intelligence and personnel. Monsieur Salamon was the head of the troop-movement section, and Colonel Blein the intelligence section. There were also Berthier's two private secretaries. The aides-de-camp were known throughout the army as *enfants terribles*.

Depending on the year, the Etat-Major General was headed by either one or more assistant chiefs of staff (premier aide-major general). In 1805 it was Andreossy, in 1809 it was Bailly de Monthion (interestingly, Andreossy's assistant in 1805 was Colonel Pascal Vallongue, the officer who had the responsibility after Marengo of writing the official history of the battle. He did so faithfully and had Napoleon tell him to rewrite it as going exactly as planned and to destroy all the copies of the original, and more accurate, report. He did as told, but one copy of the original survived, some say under a desk blotter). Generally speaking, this section of Berthier's staff was in three 'divisions'. The first was in charge of troop-movements, officer assignments, countersigns and general correspondence. The second division handled supply, police, hospitals and headquarters administration. The third division was responsible for prisoners of war, recruiting, deserters and military justice. Lines of communication, as they became longer and more complicated fell under a fourth division organised in 1806. As staff responsibilities grew during the wars, so did the number of divisions in the Etat-Major General. Still, the basic organisation and functioning remained.

The staff was stretched thin for the huge responsibilities if 1812, and it was worse after heavy losses in Russia for 1813. Still, Berthier helped Eugène reorganise the shattered remnants of the Grande Armée in early 1813 after Murat's desertion, and built up an effective army of about 60,000 awaiting Napoleon's arrival with reinforcements in April 1813 for the spring campaign.

On campaign, the staff moved generally in two echelons, the *Petit Quartier Général*, with Napoleon and Berthier and key staff officers, essentially what today would be called a 'jump command post' would move behind the army's advance guard. The rear echelon would move under a senior officer of the gendarmerie (something what troops today would call the 'ash and trash', or, more politely, the 'rear echelon').

There was also a *quartier général volante*, a 'flying headquarters', that would be employed from time to time that would be very small with only a few staff officers and escort, with orderlies and one senior staff officer in charge, that would advance and set up immediately behind the advanced cavalry outposts and send back all gathered intelligence to the operational headquarters. As Napoleon and Berthier were usually found with the advanced guard of the Grande Armée on campaign, staff duty was hardly a plush assignment (the chief of staff of the Guard, a general of division, was killed in action in 1807, having his head taken off by an artillery round),and losses throughout the campaigns, especially in 1809 and 1812, were particularly heavy.

Corps and division staffs and headquarters would mirror the Grand Quartier Général, although necessarily smaller. Brigade headquarters, because it had no administrative responsibilities, those being taken up by the parent divisions, appear to have been ad hoc organisations, consisting of only an aide-de-camp and a detailed officier d'ordonnance from one of its regiments. Some corps commanders, Davout being an outstanding example, used his generals of brigade much as Napoleon used his Generals Aides-de-Camp.

Staff functions at army level sometimes overlapped, and on the surface it would appear that the different section might interfere with one another, which they undoubtedly did, creating duplication of effort. There was also no equivalent of the modern operations staff, as Napoleon was his own operations officer.

While it would be incorrect to state that Berthier was Napoleon's strategic planning partner, it would also be incorrect to state that no strategic planning was done in the Etat-Major General. Berthier was the Grande Armée's major general and nothing close to a chief clerk, as he has often been unfairly described. Some of this undeserved reputation was resulted from the spite of Jomini, noted above. Unfortunately, some uncritical admirers and writers took Jomini at his word.[56]

The organisation of the French general staffs was codified in 1800 in Thiebault's staff manual. However, all Thiebault was doing was putting on paper what was already being done in practice, and had been since Berthier's work in the early to mid-1790s. The following is an example from the manual on how a general staff should be organised with the field armies:

> The first office (which might be considered as the particular office of the chief of the Etat-major-general,) would comprehend,
>
> > 1st, Everything appertaining to the movement of the troops, to prisoners of war, and to the organisation of the army.
> > 2nd, The general correspondence.
> > 3nd, The relations with the minister.
> > 4th, The making up of situations and other statements.
> > 5th, The general report of the army.

6th, The paroles and general orders.

7th, Furloughs and leave of absence.

8th, All the relations with the general, and the other chiefs of the artillery, with respect to everything belonging either personally or materially to that establishment.

The Chief of the Second Office should be entrusted

1st, With the furnishing provisions, and the distribution of them to places of war, with the active divisions, and daily allowances for the troops in motion.

2nd, With . . . remounts.

3nd, With the business relative to the modes of distributions in these places where the principal distributions are to be made, and other particulars relative thereto.

4th, With the business relative to transports, that is to say, artillery carriages, victuals and forage, with the flying hospitals and military effects.

5th, With the correspondence, and other relations with the commissaries general, inspector general, etc.

6th, With the business relative to hospitals and convalescents.

7th, With everything that relates to individuals, etc.

The Chief of the third office should be entrusted

1st, With the payment of troops.

2nd, With the contributions.

3nd, With the accounts, and particular and secret disbursements of the Etat-major general and the Etats-majors of division.

The functions of the Chief of the fourth Office might be entrusted

1st, With the secret department, such as spies, and guides, properly so called.

2nd, With the exchange of prisoners.

The chief of the fifth office should be charged with the department of topography.

The chiefs of all four offices should communicate daily with that of the first, for those articles which they have to furnish pursuant to general orders, etc.[57]

The following comments from the same manual offer insight into the organisation and functioning of the French general staff of the period:

The organisation of our Etat-major (although yet incomplete) is nevertheless worthy of admiration, and one of the greatest excellences in our mode of making war. It may be conjectured, which impulse, and effect a number of select, zealous, intelligent, and skillful officers, forming an Etat-major like ours, and intimately connected, as they are, with all the various distributions of war, may give to an army, in expediting its operations and infusing into them all possible perfections. Our Etats-majors are still, doubtless, not what they might be; but they form nevertheless the basis of a beautiful edifice, and we should solicit in aid of an organisation of so much importance, the zeal of men of genius, whose talents and experience have been called forth and augmented by war and the love of their country.

There are few places in the army, the duties of which have been less examined, determined and developed than those of the station of chief of the Etat-major-general. Yet nevertheless, this chief is really next to the commander-in-chief, the first man of an army, the person who can do most good or most mischief. The same deficiency exists relatively to Etat-majors, considered abstractly. Guibert, in the 2nd Chapter of his General Essay upon Tactics, vol. ii, speaking of Etats-majors, calls them 'immense details upon which there is nothing written, upon which there remains much to imagine, and almost every thing to reduce to principles.

It would be doubtless unnecessary to observe here, that the Etat-major general of an army never quits his headquarters. It has nevertheless happened during the campaign of Bonaparte in Italy, that through the difficulty attending his motions, the Etat-major general of this army, remained sometimes in the rear, although General Berthier had quitted it to accompany General Bonaparte in his grand operations. General Berthier was then only followed by his aides-de-camp, and adjutant-general, two deputies, and a secretary, and had nothing with him but his porte feuille. All the other general officers, or individuals employed upon the staff, together with their secretaries . . . which belonged to the Etat-major general, the papers of difference offices, and all the chiefs of administration, moved with the equipage of the headquarters, when the difficulty of their movements no longer exposed them to danger.[58]

The following material established the French general staff in French law:

This new organisation was decreed the 29th of October 1790, by a law of the national assembly, which created thirty of these officers . . . seventeen having the rank of colonel, and thirteen with the rank of lieutenant colonel.
The various steps to promotion in this particular line have been regulated and modified by different successive laws.
The number of those established by the law which created them, was further increased by different decrees, up to the epoch, when the national convention

conferred upon the executive council, the right of choosing and nominating the generals, as well as that of increasing their number according to circumstances.

The description of duties attached to these new stations has never yet been explained or made publicly known. A particular ordinance upon this subject was indeed announced, but has never yet been produced. There exists upon this subject nothing but a provisional instruction, relative to the functions of adjutant general, which was published on the 21st of June 1791, from the necessity of giving at least an idea of these functions, and laying down the principles upon which they were supported.

This instruction is to this day unknown in our armies. It is true, that it would have been insufficient, because the Etats-majors of a division, whose labours properly speaking, the necessity of existing circumstances has organised in the persons of these men, who were truly deemed the most competent to be entrusted with this charge, have unanimously felt, that they have at this day imposed upon them, duties which, in their practical detail, are more extended, more important and more capacious than those that had been originally assigned to them.

By this same instruction, the adjutants-general, for the purpose of aiding and assisting them in the execution of their functions, are permitted to associate three officers in each frontier division, and one in each division of the interior. These officers must be chosen by the general commanding the division; but upon the recommendation of the adjutant general. This association can only continue during the time of the campaign, during which these officers enjoy an addition of pay as a compensation for extraordinary service.

These preliminary, but inadequate dispositions, were according to existing circumstances and the fluctuating state of the military force, variously observed, until by a decree of the 21st of February, in the second year of the republic, the convention comprised Etats-majors in the organisation which was then established for the army.

By this regulation, four adjutants general were stationed with the chief of general Etat-major, who attaches one of these to each effective division, one to the advanced guard, and one to the reserve of each army and two assistants to each of them, determining the mode in which these latter shall be appointed.

The law of the 14th Germinal further altered one part of the regulation of that of the 21st of February, and prescribed amongst other matters, that these assistants should be selected only from the lieutenants and sub-lieutenants, excluding captains from these stations.

This latter disposition remains at this day no longer in force, although it has never been formally repealed. Thus the Etats-majors still remain the same as they were created by the law of the 21st of February in the Year I, amended by that of the 19th Germinal in the Year III, and by a resolution of the committee of public safety, which conferred the rank of chief of brigade upon all the adjutants general of the armies.[59]

Finally, Thiebault states the major purpose of the general staff:

> A general Etat-major is, as we have already observed, the central point of the grand operations of armies.[60]

Berthier also started the operational tradition, while chief of staff of the Armée d'Italie, of direct communications between chiefs of staff of different armies without either the permission or knowledge of the respective army commanders. He initiated this procedure with Reynier, also an expert staff officer as well as an excellent planner, who was then chief of staff of the Armée des Alpes. It was one of the French innovative staff procedures that the Prussians later adopted in their staff operations sometime after Scharnhorst's reforms. It made for faster communication, relieved the army commanders of unnecessary minutiae and usually worked very well.

Whatever the case, Berthier developed, obviously with Napoleon's approval and tailored to his method of waging war, an efficient, smoothly operating general staff that was the best of its time and which later became something of a model for the Prussian General Staff. It operated efficiently from 1796 to 1814, enabling the Grande Armée to conduct its sweeping campaigns across Europe, Berthier and his staff being responsible for such under-appreciated accomplishments as the movement over the Alps in 1800, the movement from the Channel to Austerlitz in 1805 and the unprecedented concentration for the invasion of Russia in 1812, including the very successful logistic preparations.

Heinrich von Brandt, who came out of Spain with the Legion of the Fistula left an interesting picture of the march from Spain to the assembly areas for the invasion of Russia in 1812. It attests to the efficiency of the Grand Quartier Général Imperial and is overlooked:

> On our part we could only admire the way in which the various stages of the march were organised. Everywhere one could see, in the smallest of details, the aura of a master perfectly obeyed. As all orders concerning troops on the march emanated from the Ministry, all the quartermasters and commissaries knew where to meet us at the various stops and the Ministry knew exactly which troops would be where and when. When we reached a halt, the quartermasters would first obtain a permit

from the commander of the place or from the commissioner and then a list of billets from the town hall and receipts for food, supplies, and wagons which they would hand over to the suppliers. Collection of the meat ration could either be individual or as a whole, but bread was always as a whole. Companies to be billeted in villages alongside the main road picked up their rations as they were passing through or were obliged to come in and get them. This organisation, imitated by each of the great powers since, worked with a precision and ease unimaginable. It was rare indeed that any complaints were forthcoming. As far as the Poles were concerned they even knew that we Frenchmen of the North preferred quantity over quality and distributed rations in accordance.[61]

Jean Rapp (1771–1821), an Alsatian by birth, enlisted in the Chasseurs des Cevennes in 1788 and was promoted to brigadier-fourrier in 1791. Two years later he was a maréchal des logis and was commissioned by 1794. He became an aide-de-camp to Desaix in 1796 and was promoted to chef d'escadron in 1798 and chef de brigade the next year. His service up to this time was with the Rhine armies and when Desaix was assigned to the Armée d'Orient, Rapp accompanied him to Egypt.

After Desaix was killed in action at Marengo in June 1800, Rapp was 'adopted' as an aide-de-camp by Napoleon. His service under the Consulate and Empire was distinguished. He organised the Mamelukes of the Guard in 1801 and was promoted to general of brigade in 1802. By 1805 he was an Imperial aide-de-camp and colonel en second of the Grenadiers à Cheval of the Guard. He led the last charge of Guard cavalry at Austerlitz that defeated the Russian Chevalier Garde and captured its commander and its horse artillery.

Many times wounded, and referred to by his comrades as a 'piece of old lace' Rapp's commands and assignments were many and varied. He commanded Davout's advance guard in 1806 for a time and made all the major campaigns of the Grande Armée. Assigned to command the city of Danzig after the disastrous Russian campaign, he conducted a successful defence until British naval rockets destroyed his supply warehouses and he was forced to capitulate. Rallying to Napoleon in 1815, he commanded on the Alsatian frontier, successfully conducting delaying actions against Schwarzenberg. Rapp always spoke his mind to Napoleon, whether or not the Emperor was inclined to listen. Stubborn and loyal, a born combat leader, he was one of the trusted inner circle that always told Napoleon the truth.

Considered a friend by Napoleon, his relations with him were 'blunt, frank, and loyal'. Rapp opposed the divorce from Josephine and the Russian campaign, and his relationship with Napoleon did not suffer from his opinions.

Anne Jean Marie René Savary (1774–1833) was another of Desaix's aides-de-camp that Napoleon 'adopted' after Desaix's death. A captain in 1793, he was a general of brigade ten years later and a skilled commander of light cavalry. He was also unusually good in intelligence work, thus willing to do Napoleon's dirty work, giving Napoleon honest and blunt advice, as well as loyal service. Promoted to general of division in 1805, he was involved in the Enghien affair and in the arrest of the Spanish royal family in 1807.

Savary had unusual skill in intelligence work which was why he was appointed as Minister of Police to replace the feckless Fouche. He greatly expanded the ministry, making it more efficient and had nothing to do the intrigue and treasonous conduct Fouche had been involved in.

Savary was also one of the Imperial aides-de-camp, as such conducting much of the negotiation with the allies prior to Austerlitz, being allowed by them to come and go without escort through their camps and lines. He was also an expert light cavalry officer who was no stranger to command at high levels, witness his excellent performance in Poland in 1806–7 when he temporarily commanded Lannes's V Corps.

Georges Mouton (1770–1835) was an expert tactician who volunteered for duty in 1791 and became an aide-de-camp to Joubert in 1798. He was with Masséna and the Armée d'Italie at Genoa in 1800. He became an Imperial aide-de-camp in 1805 and was promoted to general of division in 1807. He distinguished himself in leading the assault across the Landshut bridge under heavy fire in 1809, prompting Napoleon to quip 'My sheep is a lion' (*Mon Mouton est un lion*).

At Essling in May 1809 he and Rapp led an assault of Young Guard infantry that was delivered with such shock and violence that they defeated Rosenberg's Austrian corps and driving it from the village.

Considered one of the best tacticians in the Grande Armée, he commanded the small VI Corps in 1815, keeping the Prussians off Napoleon's right flank until the odds became too long.

Jacques Alexandre Bernard Law Lauriston (1768–1828) was another of the distinguished general officers that formed Napoleon's personal staff of aides-de-camp. An artilleryman who began his military career in military school in 1784, he was a captain by 1791 and a colonel of artillery four years later.

He became one of Napoleon's ADCs in 1800, played a prominent part in the build-up for the Marengo campaign and was promoted to general of division in 1805. Successfully defended Ragusa in 1806 and was Ambassador to Russia in 1811. A corps commander at Leipzig, he was captured after the Lindenau bridge was blown prematurely. After 1814 he remained loyal to the Bourbons.

In 1809 at the battle of Wagram, he commanded the large 102-gun battery that supported Macdonald's attack and covered Masséna's change of front.

Antoine Drouot (1774–1847) was a product of the Metz artillery school and has been described by one historian as a 'simple, honest, awkward gunner'. Graduating from Metz in 1793 he was assigned to the Ier Régiment d'Artillerie à Pied. He was promoted to lieutenant in 1794 and was assigned to the Armée de Sambre et Meuse from 1794–6. Promoted to captain in 1796 he served both on the Rhine and in Italy from 1797–9 and was assigned to Eble's staff in 1800–1. He commanded the 14e Companie of the 1st Foot Artillery from 1803–4 and was present afloat at Trafalgar in 1805. Promoted to chef de bataillon that year, he was serving on the Grande Armée's staff while being the inspector for arms manufacture at Mauberge.

Promoted to major in the 3rd Foot Artillery in 1807 and was the arms inspector for Charleville the same year. Sent to Spain in 1808, he was later picked by Napoleon that year to form the Artillerie a Pied of the Imperial Guard, leading it into Austria the next year and distinguishing himself at Wagram fighting under Lauriston. Wounded at Wagram, he was promoted to colonel in July 1809 and made a Baron of the Empire.

Drouot served in Russia, led the artillery attack at Lützen in 1813 that destroyed the allied centre, paving the way for the Guard's decisive assault. Expertly handling his guns at Hanau late in 1813, he destroyed the cavalry sent to attack him and supported the Guard infantry assaults that won the day. He accompanied Napoleon to Elba in 1814, being made the governor of the island.

Drouot was with Nord in Belgium in 1815 and was court-martialled by order of Louis XVIII after Waterloo. Acquitted, he refused a pension from the Bourbons until years after Napoleon's death. He wished to accompany Napoleon to Elba, but was refused by the Bourbons. He was both religious and highly intelligent, being dubbed the 'Sage of the Grande Armée'. He read his Bible every day. 'He disapproved always of the Emperor, but remained faithful.'

Along with their admiration for the Gribeauval artillery system, the British also admired the organisation and functioning of the French Grand Quartier Général Imperial as stated at the beginning of the English translation of Thiebault's staff manual of 1800:

The great advantages which must manifestly result from a well conducted Etat-major or staff, are acknowledged in every military country. France, however, seems alone to have to have entered fully into the system, and to have added the experiment of practice to the suggestions of theory.

This, then, is the staff fashioned by Berthier on Bourcet's beginnings and brought to maturity by both Napoleon and Berthier in the camps along the Channel before the Great Wars resumed in 1805. It was the most sophisticated general staff in history up to that time and none in other armies approached it for either organisation or efficiency. It is also the staff from which all modern staffs developed and evolved. We use its model still. The achievements of Berthier and the Grand Quartier Général Impérial have generally been overlooked, especially Berthier's value and achievements, but without them both, the great, sweeping and terribly devastating Napoleonic campaigns, both to the kings, their thrones and armies, would not have been possible.

Finally, Napoleon's judgement of Berthier's abilities is quite succinct:

> Berthier, the chief of staff, always spent the day around me in combat and the night at his desk: it is impossible to combine more activity, goodwill, courage, and knowledge. He was very active and followed his general on all reconnaissances without neglecting any of his work at the bureau. He had all the qualities of a good chief of staff. He knew topography well, understood reconnaissance detachments, attended personally to the expedition of orders, and was accustomed to briefing the most complicated movements of an army with simplicity.

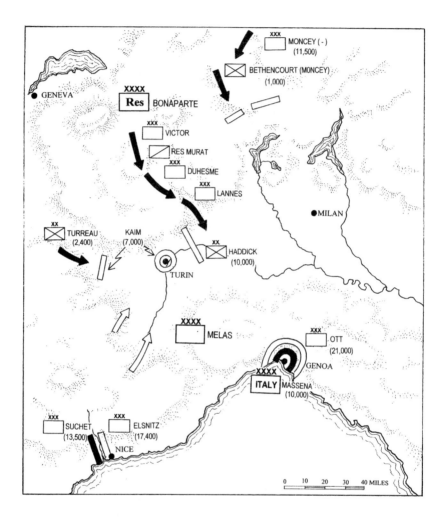

The Marengo Campaign: The French Crossing of the Alps

The main French crossing was through the Great Saint Bernard Pass. Smaller units under Turreau and Moncey crossed the Alps as shown. Melas did not understand until 19 May that there actually was a French Armée de la Réserve and that it was moving into northern Italy. By that time, the French were already at Fort Bard. Further, Melas believed that Turreau's column was the main French effort. The French would debouch into northern Italy, cut Melas's line of communication and seize the major Austrian depot at Milan, changing the strategic situation of the campaign.

CHAPTER 2

RETURN FOR GOD'S SAKE

The battle of Marengo, 1800

Perhaps I should not insist on this bold manoeuvre, but it is my style, my way of doing things. NAPOLEON

War is composed of nothing but accidents . . . there is but one favourable moment, the great art is to seize it. NAPOLEON

13:30 14 June 1800 near Torre di Garofoli, Liguria, northern Italy
The veteran infantry of the Consular Guard stood lounging in ranks as the vulgar uproar near the little hamlet of Marengo grew in intensity and rolled slowly towards them. Officers stood talking among themselves; soldiers smoked their pipes or talked to their section mates. The senior officers, Chefs de Bataillon Soules and Tortel, mounted in front of the two battalions of 'old sweats,' calmly ignored the growing conflagration, as their weary horses cropped the spring grass and swished their tails against the annoying flies. The troops, being veterans, knew what was coming. Fugitives and walking wounded had been passing them from the direction of Marengo for at least two hours.

Out of the gloom, noise and smoke from Marengo a mounted officer wearing the brassard of an aide-de-camp and a grim, somewhat panicked expression, came pounding up the road. Sweat-soaked and grime covered, a soiled bandage covering one side of his face under his bicorne, he violently reined in front of the Guard officers, panted a few words, wheeled his horse and started south on the road to Novi.

The officers exchanged knowing looks. Orders were barked to the company commanders, who in turn grabbed lounging drummers and the long roll of *'la Diane'* was boomed out by the closest tambour, being picked up and passed down the line. As if an electric current was turned on, the battalions came immediately to life, grenadiers and chasseurs checked cartridge boxes and bayonets, straightened their massive bearskins and faced up the road, even the band hustling to take its place in the column. At the command '*En Avant!*' the column stepped off into what would soon be the mouth of hell.

The Egyptian expedition had taken some of France's best regiments and senior commanders from the decisive theatre. While Napoleon was in the east, losing a fleet and having his army stranded outside Europe, the armies of the Coalition were reconquering Italy and putting *La Patrie* in desperate straits.

Widespread government corruption in France did not help the situation and Napoleon had informed that Directory that he would return if needed. He had been recalled twice, but neither summons had reached him. Informed of the situation in France and on the Continent by Sir Sidney Smith, the British ne'er do well who had helped defeat Napoleon at Acre, Napoleon turned over the command in Egypt to the grumpy Kléber and embarked with a select party of officers, slipping by British naval units in the Mediterranean and landed in France. The situation changed shortly and abruptly. Hailed as a hero because of his well-publicised victory over the Turks at Aboukir, he was sought as a 'sword' by those who wanted a quick change of government in France.

The coup was successful, but those who wished Napoleon only to assist in the coup soon found they had a new master.

1800 dawned darkly for France. The Second Coalition, even with the defection of Russia, her armies called home by an insulted and sulking Tsar, appeared to hold all the cards. Two Austrian armies were poised to invade France: Kray's large army in Germany and Melas's army in Italy. Melas was also supported by a British fleet and expeditionary force in the Balearic Islands.

Napoleon, now First Consul of France was faced with a grim military situation. Having taken control of France by a *coup d'état* in November 1799, he was still not popular in most of the French armies; in fact he was largely an unknown quantity to them. His task of defending France against the forces of the Coalition was daunting.

Napoleon had offered peace to the Coalition, knowing full well two things: first, he needed peace to consolidate and firmly establish his new government; second, that the Coalition, bargaining from a position of strength, seemed on the verge of victory and would not negotiate. He was right on both counts.

France, depleted of resources after seven years of war, her armies exhausted and without proper clothing and regular supplies, equipment ragged, and short of everything from horses to harness to shoes, was yearning for peace. Napoleon more than anyone else realised that there was one last chance to end the war victoriously. Failure in another campaign would not only be disaster for

France, but it would spell the end of his short, but promising, government.

He planned boldly.

The Marengo campaign was critical to the consolidation of Napoleon's power as First Consul and head of state. It was also vital to France's survival. It was a campaign he had to win, and he had to win it quickly. In most French armies, he was not only not very popular, he was virtually unknown. Moreau, the commander of the Armée du Rhin, on the other hand, was immensely popular with both officers and men, and could have posed a significant problem with Napoleon's consolidation of power.

Napoleon was faced with the other significant and more urgent problems of supplying the French field armies with enough replacements, supplies and ammunition to fight this next campaign. The available manpower was stretched to the limit, money was gone and the new government had not yet had a chance to make its presence felt. The threat of allied invasion was very real, even after Masséna's victory at Zurich and the withdrawal of Russia from the Coalition.

France's best troops, and some of her best field commanders, were still marooned in Egypt; the Armée d'Italie was in desperate straits; and another army had to be organised to enter the lists in northern Italy where the allied main effort was taking place under the Austrian general Melas. To organise this new army, designated l'Armée de la Réserve, Napoleon named Berthier to make it ready to debouch into Italy.

Napoleon did not take the field to organise his new army in Switzerland and around Dijon. He delayed his joining the army as late as possible, understanding that his new responsibilities as First Consul were urgent, and also that it might mask his actual intentions from the Austrians. Berthier, ably seconded by his chief of staff Dupont, was replaced as Minister of War by the capable Carnot. Napoleon began to plan the campaign, which included Moreau's Armée du Rhin, and Masséna's Armée d'Italie as soon as practicable.

Berthier's mission of organising the Armée de la Réserve began on 25 January 1800. The organisation of the army was to be kept secret, for surprise was one of the weapons that was needed for success in Italy against Melas.

My intention, Citizen Minister, is to organise a reserve army, the command of which shall be reserved to the First Consul. It will be divided into a right, centre, and left. Each of these three grand corps will be commanded by a lieutenant of the general in chief. There will also be a cavalry division commanded by a lieutenant of the general-in-chief.[1]

You will keep extremely secret the formation of the aforesaid army, even among your own office force, of whom you will ask only such information as is absolutely necessary.[2]

His instructions to Berthier were quite specific on where he wanted the army organised, and for the first time he directed that a French army be organised, not as a collection of separate divisions, but in corps d'armée[3] which from then on would be the standard French practice. On 2 April, Berthier was officially named commander of the Armée de la Réserve and Carnot as his replacement as Minister of War.

Through the entire process of planning the campaign, Napoleon finally realised that Moreau would not take orders from him. What he tried to do was to outline a plan of campaign for Moreau and make it attractive enough for him to co-operate.

Berthier informed Moreau on 25 March what was expected of him to allow the success of operations in northern Italy:

The Consuls of the Republic have decreed, Citizen General, after having considered the positions of our troops in Switzerland, on the Rhine, in Italy, and the formation of the Army of the Reserve at Dijon, the following plan of operations:

1st. That it is necessary to begin the campaign at the latest from the 20th to the 30th Germinal [10 and 20 April.

2nd. That the present Army of the Rhine will be divided into army corps and a Reserve corps. The Reserve Corps, under the command of General Lecourbe shall be composed of one-fourth of the infantry and artillery of the army and one-fifth of the cavalry.

3rd. Between the 20th and 30th Germinal you will cross the Rhine with your army corps, profiting by the advantages offered you by the occupation of Switzerland for turning the Black Forest and rendering null such preparations as the enemy may have made to dispute its gorges.

4th. The Reserve Corps will be specially charged with guarding Switzerland. Its advance guard, 5,000 to 6,000 strong, will occupy the Saint Gotthard. It will have six 4-pounders on sledge-carriages. You will have prepared some plain sledges for hauling the rest of the artillery for your Reserve Corps. You will have collected at Lucerne 100,000 bushels of oats, 500,000 rations of biscuit, and 1 million cartridges.

The first object of your Reserve Corps will be, during your movement in Swabia, to protect Switzerland against attacks which the enemy might make to invade it by way of Feldkirch, St Gotthard and the Simplon. It is known to the government that the enemy has gathered considerable supplied on the Italian lakes.

5th. The object of your movement into Germany with your army corps must be to push the enemy into Bavaria so as to intercept his direct communications with Milan by way of Lake Constance and the Grisons.

6th. As soon as this object is accomplished and it is certain that the main hostile army will be unable – even should it succeed in forcing you to fall back – to reconquer in less than ten or twelve days the ground they have lost, it is the intention of the Consuls to have Switzerland guarded by the last divisions of the Army of Reserve, composed of troops less inured to war than the organisations which compose your reserve and to detach your reserve with the elite of the Army of Reserve of Dijon to enter Switzerland [Italy] by the St Gotthard and Simplon passes and effect the junction with the Army of Italy in the plains of Lombardy.

This last operation will be confided to the General in Chief of the Army of Reserve assembled at Dijon who will consult with you and whom the Consuls will appoint.

Greetings and fraternal sentiments
Alex. Berthier[4]

Sending Masséna, a trusted lieutenant from the old Armée d'Italie of 1796–7, to command in northern Italy, he assigned him an almost impossible task. Ill-fed, ill-equipped and not ready to assume offensive operations, Masséna was expected to keep Melas's attention while the Armée de la Réserve moved into Italy over the Alps.

Napoleon to General Masséna, Commander-in-Chief of the Army of Italy, 9 April 1800
In their operations the Army of the Rhine under General-in-Chief Moreau, and the Army of the Reserve under the orders of General Berthier now assembling at Dijon, must communicate with each other and execute simultaneously and with great harmony.

The Army of the Rhine will take the field first, which will occur from the 10th to the 20th of April. It well be divided into two parts; one, about 100,000 strong, under the immediate command of General Moreau, will cross the Rhine, enter Swabia, and advance by the side of Bavaria until it can intercept, by its position, the communication of Germany with Milan by the route from Feldkirch, Coire, and the Italian bailliages of Switzerland.

The other corps of the Army of the Rhine, forming its right flank, will be about 25,000 men under the immediate orders of General Lecourbe. Its mission is first to occupy Switzerland in order to secure the right flank of the corps that is to enter Swabia, to facilitate this invasion, and to keep the enemy out of Switzerland by preventing them from penetrating by way of Rheineck, Feldkirch, the Grisons, the Saint-Gotthard pass, or the Simplon. Once this initial mission is fulfilled and General Moreau has made his way a dozen or fifteen marches from these Rhine crossings, General Lecourbe will pass with his corps under the orders of General Berthier, cross the Saint-Gotthard pass, and enter into Italy. At the same time one portion of the army of the reserve will . . . also penetrate into Italy either by the Simplon or the Saint-Gotthard, while the rest of this army will take the place of the corps commanded by General Lecourbe in Switzerland.

It is at this precise moment . . . when the troops commanded by General Berthier will have entered Italy, that you must combine your movements with his in order to attract the attention of the enemy, compel him to divide his forces, and bring about your junction with the corps that will have penetrated into Italy. Until then you will maintain the defensive. The mountains that cover you, by making the enemy cavalry and artillery inactive, will assure your superiority in this strategy, that is to say, the certainty of maintaining yourself in your positions, which up to this point, must be your true and only objective.

Any offensive on your part would be dangerous before this point because, when your army moves into the plains it would restore to action those enemy forces that are paralysed by the nature of the mountainous country you now occupy. It would be impossible to send you enough help directly to give you a decided superiority. It is from Switzerland that this help would arrive, by attacking the rear of the enemy. Once your junction is accomplished, this superiority will be decided; then the offensive will be resumed, the fortresses of Piedmont and Milan will be seized or blockaded, and the French army will emerge by its own courage from the shocking scarcities we suffer, and which we cannot effectually remedy.

If special circumstances cause the columns penetrating into Italy, either by the Saint-Gotthard and the Simplon or by one of these two passes, to reunite, they will probably total about 65,000 men, comprising General Lecourbe's column of 25,000 and General Berthier's 40,000, in which he will find nearly 6,000 cavalry and 2,000 artillery.

To debouch into Italy you will assemble the forces at your disposal in the rear as far as the Var; you will gather from those scattered from the Var to Mount Cenis all men whom you judge fit and prudent to reinforce yourself, and those who shall remain from Mount Cenis as far as Valais will form a special corps placed at the dispositions of General Berthier to facilitate his movement . . .

When your operations will have advanced to this point I will transmit further instructions . . . for the achievement of the campaign.

You know very well . . . the importance of the most profound secrecy in such circumstances . . . You will employ all the demonstrations and appearances of movement that you judge convenient to deceive the enemy about the real strategical objective and persuade him that he will first be attacked by you. Therefore exaggerate your forces and announce immense and near reinforcements approaching from the interior. Finally, you will mislead the enemy, insofar as possible, about the true points of attack, which are the Saint-Gotthard and the Simplon.[5]

Napoleon's frustration with Moreau's passive refusal to co-operate fully in the campaign made planning difficult. Accepting that Moreau would only co-operate on a limited basis and that he could not relieve and replace him with another general officer, Napoleon put his faith in himself and his two most trusted subordinates, Berthier and Masséna. The situation was grave, the campaign a dice throw. Resolutely, the plans, catch-as-catch-can they might be, went forward.

The first consul ordered General Moreau to take the offensive and enter Germany in order to stop the movement of the Austrian Army of Italy . . . The entire Army of the Rhine was to . . . cross the Rhine . . . so that the enemy will have no knowledge of it. By throwing four bridges simultaneously . . . the entire French army would cross in twenty-four hours . . .overthrow the enemy's left, taking from the rear all Austrian fortresses between the right bank of the Rhine and the defiles of the Black Forest. Those Austrian units that could escape would fall back into Bohemia. Thus the first movement of the campaign would result in separating the Austrian army from Ulm, Philippsburg, and Ingolstadt and giving our own forces possession of Wurttemberg, all of Swabia and Bavaria. This operational plan must give rise to . . . decisive events, depending upon . . . the audacity . . . of the French general.[6]

The Allied plans for their campaign was an Austrian invasion of southern France, which would be supported by an English amphibious operation along the Mediterranean coast. The first thing that had to be done was to dispose of the French Armée d'Italie. Heavily outnumbered, and in a desperate situation, it was being methodically pushed towards the Mediterranean coast by the unrelenting, but slow and methodical, Austrian advance.

The plan of campaign adopted by the allies was that the Austrian army under Kray in Germany should remain on the defensive, holding Moreau in check if possible, while the Austrian army under Melas in Italy attacked the Army of Italy along the Apennines and the Maritime Alps. By this means, the allies expected that the Austrian forces in Italy, so superior in numbers to the French, would be able with the help of the British fleet to blockade Genoa, and to drive the Army of Italy across the Var into southern France. This movement being accomplished, the purpose was that Melas, supported by the British navy and Abercromby's corps, should invade France, and attack and capture Toulon. Furthermore, the allies hoped, by adopting this plan, to receive some support from the Royalists in the south of France. If this operation succeeded, it was expected that Moreau would detach a sufficient force from the Army of the Rhine to march on Toulon for the purpose of driving back the allies: whereupon Kray could attack the Army of the Rhine, thus weakened, with much hope of success; that, in fact, he could take the offensive, force the crossings of the Rhine, and invade France.

In this calculation, no plans were made to attack the French forces in the great stronghold of Switzerland. If, however, the allies succeeded in their designs, Kray and Melas could unite their armies in France, thus cut the communications of the French forces in Switzerland, and smother them, as it were, between the two great Austrian armies.[7]

Napoleon required a tough, no-nonsense commander for the Armée d'Italie. He assigned Masséna to command it, as he was his most experienced general in independent operations and Napoleon trusted him. Further, Masséna would not hesitate to do all that might be required to keep the Austrians distracted while Reserve was organised and Napoleon began his offensive into northern Italy. In February 1800 Masséna assumed command and began operations to delay Melas and his Austrians for as long as possible and to assist the Armée de la Réserve's advance into northern Italy.

Melas attacked and surprised Masséna on 6 April. Caught unprepared by the Austrian offensive, Masséna failed to concentrate his army to meet it and by the next day the Armée d'Italie had been split in two. Masséna now commanded half of it and it was driven back into Genoa, where the British fleet supported the Austrian siege, which began on 20 April. The other half of withdrew behind the River Var by 10 May. Commanded by the able Suchet, it would hold the line of the Var against all comers.

Melas pursued Suchet and General Ott was left to deal with Masséna in Genoa. These operations had drawn the bulk of Melas' army away from what would become a French avalanche across the Alps into northern Italy and across Melas' line of communication.

Berthier arrived at Dijon on 18 April, assuming command of the Armée de la Réserve. Almost nothing was available and it had to be built from scratch. Supplies were scrounged from every corner of France. Units in France's interior and in other theatres were found and designated for it, and movement orders issued in secret to their assembly areas.

Some conscripts were sent to Dijon and officers were assigned to command them. By accident or design they became part of the deception operation to keep the formation of the Armée de la Réserve a secret from the Austrians as long as possible. Troops were drawn from Holland and the Vendée and new units were raised, as well as employing Italian units that were available. Logistical difficulties required that the troops had to be billeted over a large area, so the concentration of troops in and immediately around Dijon was relatively small. Allied spies only saw a collection of ragged conscripts and too many officers, and drew the conclusion that the Armée de la Réserve did not actually exist. Melas's headquarters reported that it was nothing but a depot of about 8,000 conscripts and invalids that had been established to make the Austrians believe there was a real French army forming there which might intimidate them into abandoning the siege of Genoa and relieving Masséna. The French deception plan was working.

Napoleon's comment on how the Armée de la Réserve was formed is instructive and also indicates the need for operational security during its formation. The correspondence is full of accounts of it being short of everything from rations to ammunition, from horse harness to the horses themselves. Napoleon's hard-riding aides-de-camp wore out horses travelling all over France and into Switzerland, doing their general's bidding and quite literally making bricks without straw.

For the crossing of the Alps, there were a few choices as to the best route. Berthier selected the Great St Bernard Pass, as that would facilitate the logistical problems facing the Armée de la Réserve. On 27 April Napoleon approved of the crossing point. While it was crossing there, other, smaller columns would cross the Alps in support and would also serve to confuse the Austrians as to which was the main crossing site. Five French columns would cross into northern Italy at the same time over a front of 115 miles. The Armée de la Réserve would concentrate at Ivrea after the crossing to continue operations against Melas.

On 1 May Napoleon learned that Masséna was besieged in Genoa. Despite this, Masséna could still maintain contact with Berthier. Leaving Paris,

Napoleon joined Berthier at Geneva on 9 May and approved of what he has done to prepare the army to cross the Alps.

For the French offensive to succeed, Masséna had to hold Genoa until at least 30 May and Suchet had to hold Melas on the Var until the beginning of June. Both Masséna and Suchet were hard pressed to accomplish their missions, and Napoleon was continually encouraging Berthier to get the army moving. Napoleon's objective in this campaign was the destruction of Melas's army. The relief of Masséna was a secondary objective. Napoleon believed that it was important, but victory in the field over Melas's army would result in the ejection of the Austrians from Italy and prevent an invasion of southern France.

However, Napoleon also believed that if he entered Italy by the Great St Bernard Pass he would get into the Austrian rear to seize their depots and cut their line of communication with Vienna. That would force Melas to turn and fight the Armée de la Réserve. That, and Melas's destruction, was the strategic goal of the campaign. In that way Napoleon would seize the initiative from the Austrians and make them fight on his terms.

The intermediate objective was the Austrian depot at Milan. All rested on Masséna and Suchet keeping the Austrians busy and the Armée de la Réserve getting across the Alps as swiftly as possible.

Lannes, commanding the Armée de la Réserve's advance guard, started his crossing on 14 May. The rest of the army followed. On the 17th Lannes seized Aosta in the pass and had cleared Chatillon on the 18th. The next day, however, the French were held up by Fort Bard, which was held by the Austrians. This was a definite obstacle and it stopped the French advance. A way found to bypass the Fort but artillery could not be taken past it. Only six guns were taken across with the army – the rest would have to wait until the fort was taken. Any artillery required would have to be taken from the Austrians. A blockade on the village was maintained by each successive unit as they moved up the pass and it was taken on the night of 21–2 May, though the fort stubbornly held out. By 22 May Lannes had cleared the pass and taken Ivrea at its southern end by a bayonet assault.

Meanwhile, on 19 May Melas had received convincing intelligence that the Armée de la Réserve was indeed in existence and was in Switzerland. He left Elsnitz in command against Suchet on the Var and hurried north, issuing orders for an Austrian redeployment to face the new French threat. Initially, he believed that the French column moving toward Turin was the advance guard but dispatches he received from Fort Bard on 24 May convinced him that the main French army was coming across the Great St Bernard.

Masséna was informed by 20 May that the Armée de la Réserve was moving south. On the 22nd, Elsnitz was attacked and defeated by Suchet on the Var line. Elsnitz had already received Melas's instructions to withdraw to Genoa, but was outflanked. Suchet aggressively pursued his prey, inflicting heavy losses – almost half of Elsnitz's command – and showed no signs of slowing his pursuit.

Masséna's troops were barely subsisting in Genoa. They had conducted an outstandingly grim defence of the city, but there was no food and the inhabitants were starving. Finally, on 31 May, he agreed to a parley with Ott, but would not capitulate. Ott was forced into accepting terms favourable to the French, and Masséna evacuated on 4 June. The city was Ott's, but Masséna's army was free to serve again once they were within the French lines.

With the exception of one division, the French were concentrated around Ivrea, the crossing completed, by 26 May (the bulk of the French artillery, still held up by Fort Bard, would not reach Ivrea until 5 June). Meanwhile, Melas had ordered the Austrians to concentrate at Alessandria on 31 May. On 2 June the French took Milan, which was full of supplies, arms and ammunition, and advanced to the line of the Po. The Austrians were attempting to concentrate against this new French threat, but the French crossed the river on the night of 7–8 June, even though the river began to flood.

Across the Austrian line of communications, Austrian couriers were being intercepted and Napoleon was reading Melas's mail. Using this information, Napoleon ordered the army forward with the Austrians hustling to meet them. Lannes and Victor defeated Ott at Montebello on June, and the French continue to advance, hunting Melas's army.

On 9 June Napoleon, who had remained in Milan because of urgent political issues that needed to be addressed, rejoined the army. Desaix arrived from Egypt two days later, and Napoleon reorganised the army to give Desaix the command of a corps. The next day some French artillery arrived from Ivrea.

The situation that the French now faced can only be described as confused. There was no contact with Melas, and the intelligence gleaned from all sources gave three possible locations for Melas's army. The Austrians could be in Alessandria, still north of the Po, or off to the south around Novi. Lapoype was ordered north of the Po, and Desaix with only one of his two divisions was sent towards Novi. The rest of the army was on the Marengo plain, east of Alessandria. When it bivouacked on the evening of 13 June, Napoleon left its emplacement to his two corps commanders, Victor and Lannes. They were careless of their dispositions and worse with their local security. Across the Bormida River in Alessandria, Melas was preparing a very nasty surprise.

The Marengo 'plain' was not what it first appeared to be. Both Lannes and Victor found it crossed by trails, creeks and fields, making reconnaissance

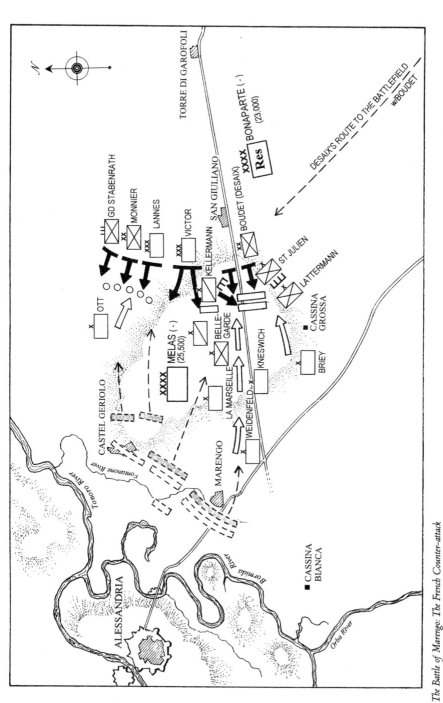

The Battle of Marengo: The French Counter-attack

The initial French positions are shown as dotted lines. This map shows the execution of the French counter-attack led by Desaix with Boudet's division. This was the decisive action of the day, and it should be noted that the French had become completely disengaged from the Austrians and were able to rally and support Desaix with every available man and gun. Marmont's artillery position is shown as well as Kellermann's decisive counter-attack, both in support of Desaix, who was killed in action leading Boudet's division.

difficult. There was little fighting on the 13th. The Austrians abandoned the village of Marengo in something of a hurry. The French did find that the Austrians had constructed a pontoon bridge north of their fortified bridgehead, but the Austrians moved it into the bridgehead later, afraid that the French might either take it or destroy it. By evening, all of the Austrians were back across the river.

Melas and Zach, his chief of staff, planned to strike from the bridgehead on the morning of the 14th. Napoleon thought otherwise, believing that the Austrian abandoning of Marengo and the east bank of the Bormida meant that Melas did not want to fight. That attitude apparently permeated the French army encamped on the plain.

At 08:00 on the morning of the 14th, one of Murat's aides-de-camp reported to Napoleon that the Austrians were stirring and it looked as though they were getting ready to attack. Napoleon disagreed and ignored the warning. At 09:00 Melas's advance guard struck Victor's forward division under Gardanne. Unhappily surprised, Victor's corps was roused by the firing to find that the Austrians were swarming out of their bridgehead and mounting a full offensive.

This initial attack pushed Gardanne back to Marengo and the Austrians formed line of battle behind this fight and attacked with their bands playing them into the fight and regimental colours waving above the lines of white coats. Gardanne fell back somewhat rapidly, running into Victor's other division under Chambarlhac that was trying to form up behind Fontanone Creek. The superior Austrian artillery went into action, overwhelming what French artillery was on the field, and Chambarlhac ran from the field in a panic after his orderly was killed by Austrian cannonfire.

In the middle of this mess, Lannes formed his corps in line of battle behind Victor. The smoke and noise of the battle urged Napoleon into action around 10:00. Before that, he still was adamant that this was not a major Austrian attack. He mounted and went forward to see for himself and the gravity of the situation was made quite clear. Victor was fighting for survival and Lannes was attempting to form to support him. Monnier and the Consular Guard were ordered forward at once and aides were sent to Lapoype and Desaix to recall them to support the main army.

Off to the south, Desaix halted before crossing the Scrivia and continuing his advance on Serraville. The growing evidence of gunfire and smoke towards Alessandria convinced him to send an aide, Savary, with a detachment of cavalry to reconnoitre Novi. Savary returned with bad news: the Austrians were there, and Desaix immediately dispatched him to Napoleon to inform him. He waited in place for Savary to return with a decision. This delay undoubtedly saved the Armée de la Réserve.

Lannes had formed on Victor's left and the fighting on Victor's front was desperate and bloody. Victor's two divisions were intermixed, as were his brigades and regiments. His losses were heavy, but four Austrian assaults on Marengo were bloodily repulsed. The Austrians deployed more units to their left and Ott took Castel Ceriolo 1400, outflanking Lannes. Both Victor and Lannes had to start withdrawing, or they would be overwhelmed.

At this point Monnier arrived on the field opposite Castel Ceriolo. He was given the mission to recapture Castel Ceriolo, but botched his attack. He committed his demi-brigades piecemeal, failing to stop the Austrian attack. Ott continued to advance despite Monnier's presence, and the Austrian follow-on unit under Vogelsang retook the village as it advanced. Defeated and outflanked, Monnier started to withdraw to conform to Victor and Lannes and to avoid being overwhelmed in turn.

Around 14:30 the Consular Guard infantry arrived on the battlefield. Its overall strength was about 800 all ranks. It, or perhaps part of it, was first employed in bringing up ammunition to Victor's beleaguered troops.

> Our cartridges were giving out and we had already lost an ambulance when the consular guard arrived with eight hundred men having their linen overalls filled with cartridges; they passes along our rear and gave us the cartridges. This saved our lives.[8]

However, a 500-man battalion commanded by Soules was committed on Lannes's right flank to buy time for the defeated French to break contact with the Austrians and reform. For thirty minutes this small unit fought outnumbered against the victorious Austrians. French accounts have it standing in square and repulsing at least three cavalry charges before withdrawing.

> Then our fire redoubled and the Consul appeared; we felt ourselves strong again. He placed his guard in line in the centre of the army and sent it forward. They immediately held the enemy, forming square and marching in battle order.[9]

> The foot grenadiers of the consular guard now came up, in the same state they have always been beheld on the parade. They formed up in the most orderly manner, in subdivisions, and advanced against the enemy, which they met with not a hundred paces from our front. Without artillery, without cavalry, to the number of five hundred only, they had to endure the brunt of a victorious army.

But, without considering the smallness of their numbers, they kept advancing, and forced everything to give way in their passage. The lofty eagle hovered everywhere around them, and threatened to tear them to pieces. The very first bullet which struck them laid three grenadiers and a fourrier dead on the ground, being in close order. Charged three times by the cavalry, fusilladed by the infantry within fifty paces, they surrounded the colours, and their wounded, and, in a hollow square, exhausted all their rounds of cartridges; and then, with slow and regular steps, fell back and joined our astonished rearguard.[10]

One French eyewitness states that it withdrew in order after heavy casualties. An Austrian account maintains that the Guard infantry was caught in line from behind by Austrian cavalry under Frimont and destroyed. What is clear is that this battalion suffered heavy casualties, around 280 to 300, and then withdrew with its survivors, and its colours, intact. This action lasted approximately thirty minutes.

The brutal fighting died down as the French retreated all along the line. It had been a long and bloody fight, and the Austrians had finally been victorious all along the front. Melas, exhausted and hurt, turned the pursuit over to his chief of staff, General Zach, and rode back to Alessandria.

This respite allowed the French to break contact around 15:00–15:30. Napoleon was seen by Coignet as they retreated.

Looking behind, we saw the Consul seated on the bank of the ditch by the highway to Alessandria, holding his horse by the bridle, and flirting up little stones with his riding whip. The cannonballs which rolled along the road he did not seem to see. When we came near him he mounted his horse and set off at a gallop behind our ranks.[11]

The Austrians did not begin their tardy pursuit until around 16:30, allowing the French to break contact and begin to sort out the mess that had resulted from the retreat. Cavalry was not available to conduct a roaring, driving pursuit that would have ruined Napoleon and the Armée de la Réserve. The Austrian cavalry did not have the tradition of acting in mass, and much of it had been either wasted or defeated by the ubiquitous Kellermann during the fighting. Instead, they took their time allowing the French to withdraw and partially reform.

12:00 14 June 1800, northern Italy, along the banks of the Scrivia River
The long columns of Boudet's sweat-soaked, panting infantry division route stepped through the northern Italian countryside, passing dry vineyards and

dusty villages in the hot June sun. Commanded and led by Desaix, newly returned from Egypt, they proceeded on the mission assigned them by the First Consul – to seek out and destroy, if they could find them, any Austrians between Alessandria and Novi.

Riding uneasily and hearing the roar of a major battle behind them growing in intensity off to the north-west, Desaix ordered his subordinates to halt the thirsty column and rest the bedraggled infantrymen yet again. He had a bad feeling that they were going in the wrong direction and that there were no Austrians ahead of them, only behind them as the noise of a very large battle obviously proved. As the troops dropped their packs and fell out alongside the rutted excuse for a road, Desaix beckoned to Rapp and Savary, his aides-de-camp. He sent Rapp hustling forward to their intended objective to check just one more time for any Austrians 'out and about'. He ordered Savary back towards Alessandria to tell the First Consul, again, that they had found nothing, nor were they likely to. The two aides exchanged long looks – they had already done this once today. Napoleon was proving more stubborn than usual

Down the road from Terra di Garofoli, a hard-riding horseman was seen pounding towards them, causing Rapp to rein in his horse violently before he went off toward Novi again. Ignoring everyone except Desaix, the sweat-stained, blood- and grime-streaked officer, a bandage thrown over a wounded eye, handed him a simple dispatch from the First Consul. Desaix saw the shock and despair in the simple, scratched out note: 'Return, For God's Sake!' Realising his instinct was correct, he reacted at once. Not wasting a minute, Desaix turned to Boudet and ordered him to fall in the division and head back the way they had come. Boudet called out for his chief of staff and the demi-brigade commanders. Shouted commands rang down the length of the column. NCOs trotted down the column kicking men awake who had dozed off, dragging others to their feet. The infantrymen humped their packs, fell in and checked their arms and ammunition, thoughtful ones checking to see if they still had their bayonets. It was going to be another forced march with a big fight at the end of it. At least the Austrians, undoubtedly a lot of them, had been found.

Subordinate commanders were swiftly given their marching orders. They joined their demi-brigades and quickly briefed their staffs and chefs de bataillons. Orders were barked out, drums began to pound la Diane, the long roll, and the 9ᵉ Légère, as was customary for légère regiments, hustled to the front of the column. It would not do to have the division led into a fight be a ligne demi-brigade. Some things just were not done, no matter how desperate the situation.

Calmly turning to Boudet and his chief of staff, after sending Savary pounding up the road with the First Consul's courier to tell him they were coming, Desaix informed them of his intent to return to reinforce Napoleon and ordered them to lead the division as quickly as possible across country, guiding themselves on the smoke and roar of the fighting. He and Rapp were going to ride ahead to see the First Consul. He would meet Boudet and his troops on the battlefield. As Desaix and Rapp galloped off, Boudet placed himself at the head of his division and led off at the double, the file closers, as usual, having to run to catch up.

Desaix, after receiving Napoleon's recall order, moved across country using the smoke from the battlefield as a guide. He arrived before 17:00 and grimly told Napoleon that the battle was lost, but there was time to start and win another one before darkness set in. Boudet's division would spearhead the counter-attack and would be supported by all available units from Lannes and Victor.

Boudet's division was formed in front of the village of San Giuliano. Kellermann's cavalry was formed on Boudet's left and Marmont massed all of the artillery he could find on Boudet's right flank. The remainder of Reserve formed on Boudet's right flank: Victor, Lannes, Monnier and the Guard infantry. By 17:00 the French were ready and the Austrians advanced to meet them.

The Austrians were met by infantry volleys at a hundred yards and Marmont's artillery firing point-blank canister. The leading Austrian brigade took heavy casualties and went to the rear in something of a hurry. The unit behind them, Lattermann's grenadiers, maintained their formation while Austrian artillery deployed on both flanks. The Austrian artillery fire forced the French 9e Légère back, and the Austrian grenadiers continued their advance. In the middle of this crisis, Desaix led the rest of Boudet's division forward at the charge and was shot out of the saddle and killed.

However, Marmont and Kellermann rose to the challenge. Marmont had followed the 9e Légère forward. He immediately unlimbered and fired into the grenadiers, stopping their advance. Kellermann roared out of nowhere, riding over and through the grenadiers, sweeping 1,700 of them up as prisoners, and capturing Zach, the Austrian chief of staff in the bargain. Kellermann spotted the Austrian cavalry on the enemy's left flank and with a wave of his sword and a shouted command, echoed by the brigade's trumpeters, the victorious French cavalry swung around to the charge yet again. The Guard cavalry, led by Bessières, joined the wild chevauchee splattering Austrians in all directions.

Boudet rallied his division and charged, and the Austrians who were not killed, wounded, or prisoners went to the rear. Melas's victory started to collapse. Ott, who was attempting to support the Austrian main attack and envelop the French right flank, found himself facing a resurgent French army that was manoeuvring to fight him. Outnumbered and without orders, he extricated his units and fought back to the bridgehead. Fighting petered out all along the front around 21:30 after the last surviving Austrians were back in their bridgehead.

Marengo was a long, drawn-out and bloody fight. Napoleon had been surprised and his generalship was not better than average. Until 11:00 he was too unconcerned with events on the battlefield and it almost cost him the battle. French losses were 5,835 and the Austrians tallied 9,402. Melas's army, however, lived to fight another day, and the war would continue until the overwhelming victory of Hohenlinden in December brought a peace favourable to France that would lead to the Peace of Amiens two years later – perhaps 'the proudest peace in French history'.

Jean Boudet (1769–1809) started his military career as a dragoon in the Régiment de Penthière in October 1785. In 1792 he was a lieutenant in the 7e Bataillon de Volontaires de la Gironde, and became Lieutenant Colonel of the 1er Battaillon des Chasseurs in December 1793. He served at the siege of Toulon and on Guadaloupe. Promoted to general of brigade in 1795, he returned to France in 1799 and was given command of the 3e Division de l' Armée de Batavie under Brune in October 1799. Assigned to the Armée de la Réserve in 1800, he was given command of an infantry division which ended up in Desaix's corps after that officer returned from Egypt and joined the army.

Boudet's division delivered the decisive counter-attack at Marengo, where Boudet was wounded and Desaix killed in action. Thereafter, Boudet was assigned to the Haitian expedition and returned home to France in September 1802. He served both Victor and Marmont as division commander and was assigned as such to Marmont's II Corps in 1805. He served at Colberg in 1807 and in 1809 commanded a division in Masséna's IV Corps rendering yeoman service at Essling. At Wagram Boudet was careless on the army's left flank and lost his artillery to an Austrian offensive and was driven into the old French bridgehead, being covered by Reynier.

Boudet was an outstanding division commander and was present at some of the most desperate battles of the Consulate and Empire. Steady and competent without being brilliant, he could be relied upon to perform his duty with his troops well in hand.

Auguste-Frederic-Louis Viesse Marmont (1774–1852) was a fellow artillery officer and one of Napoleon's oldest friends. Marmont graduated from the Metz artillery school in 1793 and became Napoleon's aide-de-camp at Toulon. When Napoleon was put in prison briefly after Toulon, Marmont took another assignment and only rejoined Napoleon after the latter was released (Andoche Junot, another ADC at the time, stayed with Napoleon during this trying period). Marmont was a colonel by 1797 and a general of brigade the next year. Sterling service at Marengo won him promotion to general of division that year. He was appointed artillery inspector-general in 1801 and was instrumental in getting the new artillery Système An XI approved to replace the Gribeauval System, though it was not completely implemented due to the exigencies of the service and the almost constant warfare through 1815.

Marmont was not on the first list of marshals, which annoyed his well-developed ego, but he was given command of II Corps of the Grande Armé in 1805 and was assigned as military governor of Dalmatia after Austerlitz, where he remained until summoned north to join with the Armée d'Allemagne for Wagram. He was finally promoted to marshal in 1809.

He was in Spain from 1810–1812 and relieved Masséna. He did much to revitalise that hard-used army and manoeuvred expertly with Wellington until the latter found a weakness and attacked, defeating Marmont at Salamanca. Severely wounded, Marmont missed the Russian campaign, but commanded the VI Corps in Saxony in 1813.

Marmont was an excellent officer, commander and artillerymen. An able administrator as well as a tactician, his service as military governor in Illyria from 1805–9 was outstanding. He was better educated than most of his fellow marshals, but there was a sense of his being unappreciated which allowed him to listen to convincing scoundrels such as Talleyrand to soothe his ego. His performance in France in 1814 was droopy and uninspired and he was convinced to turn traitor by Talleyrand and his own ego, by turning over his corps to the allies thus hastening the return of the Bourbons. His ducal title, Ragusa, was turned into a verb, raguser, which means to lie, cheat and betray because of his treachery. Napoleon's comment was succinct: 'The ingrate. He will be much unhappier than I.'

François Etienne Kellermann (1770–1825) was the son of the marshal, the hero of Valmy. He was in the diplomatic service in 1791 but was back in the army by 1793. Promoted to colonel in 1796, he was with the Armée d'Italie and was made a general of brigade by Napoleon. Famous for the outstanding handling of his cavalry brigade at Marengo in 1800, especially for the decisive charge he led at exactly the right moment in support of Desaix. He was promoted to general of division for his service there.

An excellent cavalry commander, he was also frequently involved in scandals during the career, which were always forgiven by Napoleon because of Marengo. He served in Portugal and Spain, but missed Russia as he was ill. He commanded a cavalry corps at Waterloo and at Quatre Bras, committed unsupported by Ney with only a single cuirassier brigade, penetrated the allied centre.

Louis Charles Antoine Desaix (1768–1800) according to Napoleon was 'the best balanced of his lieutenants' and if he had not been killed in action at Marengo undoubtedly would have been a marshal. He was a sous-lieutenant at the beginning of the Revolution and by 1793 he was a general of brigade. The next year he was promoted to general of division and met Napoleon while on a visit to northern Italy that year. He accompanied Napoleon on the Egyptian expedition, conducting an expert campaign in Upper Egypt, being dubbed 'The Just Sultan' by the natives.

He returned to France in 1800 and immediately joined the Armée de la Réserve, that army being reorganised to give him command of a corps. An excellent tactician and strategist, he had an unusual understanding of intelligence operations, which he impressed on Davout, Savary and Rapp. He was probably the most skilful general in the Rhine armies. His death at Marengo, where his decision to slow his march south and his prompt return to the battlefield, undoubtedly saved the day – and Napoleon's career.

A man of high character and well-educated, his one object in life was to serve his country. Marmont said of him that 'Nobody was braver – bravery of the modest sort which did not attach the price of being noticed. Man of conscience before all; man of duty, severe on self, an example to others, his kindness tempered his severity . . . esteemed by all who met him.'

Napoleon's comments on Desaix deserve to be retold. Also mentioned is Kléber, whom Napoleon admired and who was left in command in Egypt when Napoleon returned to France. He was assassinated by an Arab fanatic on the same day as the battle of Marengo.

> Of all the generals I ever had under me, Desaix and Kleber possessed the greatest talents – especially Desaix; as Kleber only loved glory inasmuch as it was the means of procuring him riches and pleasures, whereas Desaix loved glory for itself, and despised everything else. Desaix was wholly wrapped up in war and glory. To him riches and pleasure were valueless, nor did he give them a moment's thought. He was a little, black-looking man, about an inch shorter than I am, always badly dressed, sometimes even ragged, and despising comfort or convenience. When in Egypt, I made him a present of a complete field-equipage several times, but he always lost it. Wrapped in a cloak, Desaix threw himself under a gun, and slept as contentedly as if he were in a palace. For him luxury had no charms. Upright and honest in all his proceedings, he was called by the Arabs the Just Sultan. He was intended by nature for a great general. Kleber and Desaix were a loss irreparable to France.[12]

Certain aspects of the pivotal battle of Marengo in 1800 which was so critical to the survival of both Napoleon and France are as interesting as they are controversial and have arisen because of the care Napoleon took to have the history of the battle 'preserved' for posterity to have gone exactly as planned. As we have seen, that is not the case.

First, the famous Bulletin should be addressed. Napoleon never intended the Bulletins as history.

> The Bulletins were after-action reports, directed as much at civilians as at the Grande Armee. On the whole they were fairly accurate; the Twenty-Ninth Bulletin, issued on his return from Russia, made no bones about the Grande Armee's immense losses, though it did blame them all on the weather. They usually exaggerated enemy losses and understated French casualties. Also they sometimes failed to give credit to various officers and units who felt they should have received honorable mention. In time a soldier who trifled with the truth might be said to lie like a Bulletin. Napoleon, however, never intended them as history.[13]

Napoleon's attitude upon taking up position in the vicinity of Marengo was interesting in that he did not believe the Austrians would attack from Alessandria. He left the security arrangements for the army, especially Lannes's and Victor's corps, to the local commanders and failed to inspect himself or even check with his subordinates. Local security and reconnaissance were worse and the French bivouacked generally where they stopped for the night. The Austrian attack on the morning of 14 June was a surprise both to Napoleon and his commanders. In fact, Napoleon was not convinced that a major attack was taking place until late in the morning when he rode forward to see for himself.

There were at least two 'official' reports on the battle of Marengo. The first, which used eyewitness interviews as well as French and Austrian reports, was a generally accurate account of the battle. It was written by Colonel Vallongue of the Dépôt de Guerre. Vallongue did his professional best and was an excellent staff officer who later served with the Grand Quartier Général Impérial in the 1805 campaign. This first report, issued in 1803, was initially approved by Napoleon. Interested in making Marengo a minor epic and as going exactly as planned, he later ordered this version destroyed and officially rewritten.

The obviously harried Colonel Vallongue complied, producing the corrected version in 1805 (which was again fiddled with by Napoleon on St Helena). Interestingly, one copy of the 1803 report was saved by a clerk, supposedly found under a desk-blotter, and that has been used to give us a generally accurate account of the battle. Napoleon was very concerned with the performance of Monnier's version, and this was one of the major areas for the official rewrite in that Monnier's 'manoeuvre' on the Austrian right flank was intended and successful. As we have seen, Monnier committed his division piecemeal and, although the individual units performed well enough, Monnier was defeated and forced to retire along with the rest of the army. For that failure, Napoleon relieved him as well as other commanders in the Armée de la Réserve. This is interesting in itself because Napoleon's normal practice for his subordinates that performed poorly was to give them another chance. This is a definite indicator that Marengo was very important to Napoleon and that it was a very 'near-run thing'.

> The passage of time can play tricks with men's memories; and, even when participants wrote down their impressions soon after the battle, it must be recognised that the vast majority of them could have possessed only the haziest of ideas about what took place a small distance away form their own narrow and smoke-obscured sectors. Similarly, it is a well-known fact that two neighbouring eyewitnesses of the same historical phenomenon will rarely agree on all the details of what both observed at close quarters. From the mass of depositions assembled by the Depot de Guerre in the years immediately after the battle, however, and the many detailed analyses that have been made by generations of distinguished military historians over the last century and a half, it is possible to paint a credible picture of the events of the battle of Marengo.[14]

CHAPTER 3

THE EMPEROR MAKES WAR WITH OUR FEET

The encirclement at Ulm, 1805

When once the offensive has been assumed, it must be sustained to the last extremity. NAPOLEON

In peace, there's nothing so becomes a man as modest stillness and humility; but when the blast of war blows in our ears, then imitate the action of the tiger. SHAKESPEARE, HENRY V

09:00 23 October 1805, Ulm, Bavaria
They were the handpicked marchers and killers of the Grande Armée and their glistening, perfectly ordered ranks were drawn up outside the Bavarian city of Ulm. Veterans of a dozen campaigns and countless fights, these Grognards had repeatedly fought and defeated the best troops in Europe and their efforts had humbled proud royal houses. Drawn from every unit in the army, they were truly a *corps d'élite*.

Uniformed in their full dress of dark blue habit-veste, white breeches and gaiters, white, pipe-clayed belts and topped by the gigantic bearskin with brass eagle plate, red cut-feather plume and white cords and flounders, the Grenadiers à Pied of the Imperial Guard stood motionless under the gaze of the feared and respected commander, Dorsenne, to witness the surrender of the Austrian army of the 'unfortunate General Mack'.

It had been an amazing campaign. The seven corps d'armée, Cavalry Reserve and Imperial Guard of the Grande Armée led by the Emperor had marched, manoeuvred and fought wherever and whenever hostile forces had been found. In four weeks of relentless marching and manoeuvre without fighting a single major engagement, the Emperor had cut off and surrounded an entire Austrian army and forced it to surrender.

Unfortunately, the Austrian Archduke with them had escaped, but out of the entire crop of archdukes promoted to general, only the Archduke Charles was

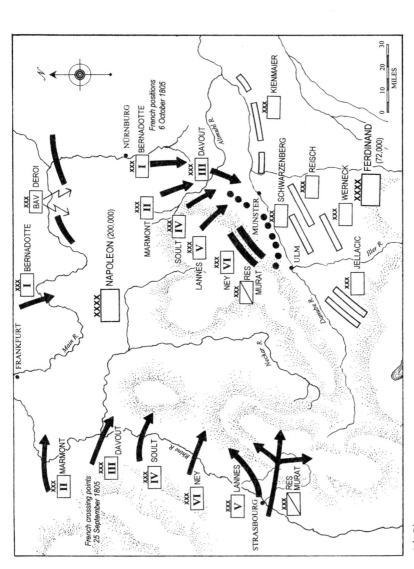

Ulm: The Crossing of the Rhine

The French made it to the Rhine from the English Channel in twenty-nine days. They left their camps on 27 August and the first elements, Lannes's V Corps immediately followed by the majority of the Cavalry Reserve crossed the Rhine on 25 September. Napoleon had decided to turn east on 23 August. Between then and the time that Lannes crossed the Rhine the French cavalry screen had been formed on the Rhine beginning on 24 August; officers went into Germany incognito to reconnoitre the area of operations, and spies in various disguises, peddlers, travellers, horse dealers, wandering fiddlers, or dancing masters', who would find information and supporters who would be helpful to the Grande Armée.

worth a *sou*, and he was in Italy facing his own problems, namely Marshal Masséna and the Armée d'Italie. Unfortunately, too, in the eyes of these scarred veterans, even though there were plenty of nasty little fights with Austrian units desperate to escape the French trap, the Imperial Guard had remained in reserve, always a grim presence, but never a deciding factor. They had done their share of marching, but the Grenadiers had not fired a shot. The Grumblers, as Napoleon had realistically nicknamed his veteran Guard infantry, viewed this as shame and insult, as they yearned for action and envied the ligne units having all the glory and excitement.

As the veteran grenadiers looked on, Mack and his staff were offering their swords as tokens of their defeat and capture to Napoleon and his retinue. The massed Imperial Guard, not only the grenadiers, but the Chasseurs à Pied, Grenadiers à Cheval and the ubiquitous Chasseurs à Cheval were all present in full dress, their swords and bayonets ensuring the continuation of their Emperor's reign. In front of the grenadiers, along with their colonel, Dorsenne, stood gigantic Drum Major Senot, his uniform dripping gold lace, his *chapeau* topped by a tricolour plume. All eyes of the Guard were on him, as his upraised mace would signal the call 'To the Emperor'.

In the ranks of one of the grenadier companies, one veteran nudged the ribs of the grenadier next to him and murmured, 'The Emperor now makes war with our feet, not out bayonets.' His comrade, also scarred from some long-forgotten engagement, sagely nodded his agreement, both men maintaining a perfect alignment and position of attention as they patiently waited for the next word of command from their company commander and the massive mace of Drum Major Senot.

The rupture of the Peace of Amiens on 18 May 1803 brought continued war to Europe. Great Britain and France had reached an impasse. Great Britain could successfully wage naval warfare against France, whose navy was at best second rate, but could not alone wage war against France on the Continent of Europe. France could not defeat Great Britain militarily unless she could actually get at her, and that meant invasion. England had not been successfully invaded since 1066 when William, Duke of Normandy, had crossed the Channel and killed the English King Harold at Hastings.

Faced with this strategic situation, Napoleon began concentrating troops and equipment along the Channel in six large camps in June 1803, which have been collectively dubbed the 'Camp de Boulogne' and ordered the building of an invasion flotilla based on Boulogne. This army, christened Armée des Côtes de l'Ocean, was intensely trained from its inception and grew into the Grande

Armée, officially named so in August 1805. The 'camps' were called corps d'armée with numerical designations, the camp commanders becoming the respective commanders of the corps.

The British were anxious to get the Grande Armée off the Channel coast. The threat of invasion was real. Naval raids on the Boulogne flotilla had not been successful, Nelson being twice defeated by French Admiral Latouche-Treville in attacks on the *Flotilla Nationale*.

As Great Britain would do time and again as the 'allies' paymaster' during the period, she raised the Third Coalition against France, inducing Austria and Russia to attack France from the east to draw the recently christened Grande Armée away from the Channel coast and into central Europe. The Austrians and Russians obliged.

The Grande Armée of 1805 was the finest Napoleon had ever led.[1] In organisation, administration, training, morale and leadership it was the best army of the period. The army had nearly three years of training and was led by senior commanders who had earned their stars on a myriad of battlefields and had survived by skill and luck. Almost all of the officers and NCOs were combat veterans, but only a third of the rank and file were. Only about three per cent of the personnel were veterans of the old Royal Army. While a good proportion of the veterans had volunteered or been conscripted during the wars of the Revolution, most of the veterans had entered the army in 1799–1800. About half of the cavalry and over forty per cent of the infantry were veterans, but the new soldiers were excellently trained and were more than prepared to go on campaign.[2]

When loosed upon the coalition in August 1805 the Grande Armée began a long, hard road that would finally end up a decade later on sodden Belgian fields fighting two allied armies, followed by defeat, retreat, abdication and the revenge of Royalists who either had not heard the proverbial shot fired in anger or had served against France. Along that road were hard-won victories and famous fights, and the hard-earned reputation as a tough, professional force that had earned their enemies' respect even in defeat. The Grande Armée's drums might have been stilled in June 1815, but they were still remembered and feared long after their time was past.

The Ulm campaign was unique in that there was no battle of Ulm. There was plenty of fighting during the campaign, large-scale rearguard actions and small-scale, but no less vicious, battles such as Haslach and Elchingen, but the main effort was at Ulm where the Austrians under Ferdinand and his chief of staff Mack (properly Mack von Leiberich) were finally cornered and surrendered.

The Grande Armée was organised in seven corps d'armée, a Cavalry Reserve and the Imperial Guard. They were pulled off the Channel in late August.

Napoleon, realising that Admiral Villeneuve could not achieve what he wanted against the Royal Navy, and the fact that there were armies organising and marching against him from Austria and Russia, decided on 23 August to go east.

The next day the French cavalry screen began to form along the Rhine. On the 25th, Murat and two of Napoleon's jack-of-all-trades Imperial aides-de-camp, went incognito into Germany on a reconnaissance mission. The two aides, Generals Bertrand and Savary, were particularly well suited for this mission. Bertrand was an expert engineer and Savary had unusual skill in intelligence work. On the 27th, the Grande Armée began its march from the Channel.

Ahead of it and in front of its cavalry screen another movement was taking place. Napoleon was expert in his application and use of intelligence and counter-intelligence. A steady stream of intelligence-gathering 'personnel' preceded even the Napoleonic cavalry screen of hussars and chasseurs à cheval into the theatre of operations. French intelligence agents and spies were already in Germany disguised as a myriad of professions and ne'er-do-wells, 'peddlers, travellers, horse-dealers, wandering fiddlers or dancing masters' were ahead of the advance guard of the army seeking information on the enemy. As the light cavalry patrols of the cavalry screen advanced, these spies would be waiting for it, ready with information Napoleon and his staff needed to continue operations. As a system it was quite effective, affording Napoleon continuous up-to-date intelligence data on the enemy – and usually the commander with the best intelligence wins.

The Austrians began their offensive on 2 September. It was not until 13 September, however, that Napoleon, still in Paris, learned of it. France and Austria severed diplomatic relations on 20 September and Napoleon left Paris on the 24th. Already massed on the Rhine, the Grande Armée crossed into Germany on the 25th.

Mack believed that the French would cross the Rhine and then enter the Black Forest, the traditional invasion route into Germany from France, and begin operations there. Both Murat, with most of the Cavalry Reserve. and Lannes's V Corps crossed the Rhine and gave the impression that was the route chosen by Napoleon to invade Germany. It was merely a feint which the Austrians bought. Bernadotte's I Corps, Marmont's II Corps, Davout's III Corps, Soult's IV Corps and Ney's VI Corps (from north to south) were racing south to the Danube to seize the crossings there. Davout, Soult and Ney were deep in Germany by 30 September. Lannes and Murat joined them, and this avalanche descended upon Donauworth on the Danube on 6 October, surprising the Austrians and threatening to cut their communications with Vienna.

The Austrians had no idea what the French were really up to as their light

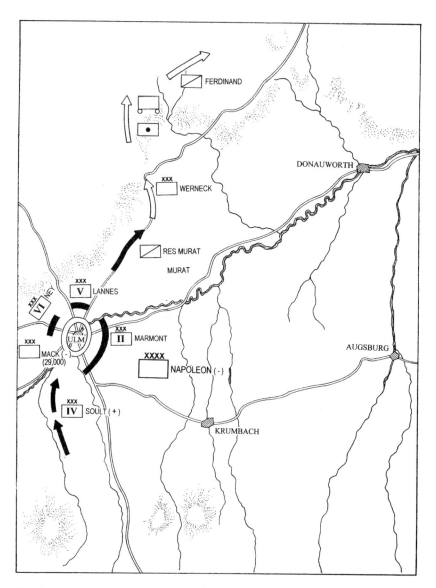

Ulm: The Investment

This is the investment of Ulm by the French which forced Mack to surrender. At this phase of the campaign there had been much fighting in the French rear areas between detachments, with much ensuing confusion. Mack had recognised Napoleon's manoeuvre for the encirclement of the Austrian army, but generally was not supported by the Austrian subordinate commanders, a good portion of whom left with Ferdinand when the archduke decided to escape northwards.

cavalry had failed in their security mission. They simply had not found the French and had been fooled by Lannes and Murat in the Black Forest. The Austrians had not concentrated to meet any threat until 3 October and were dispersed in a cordon to cover all the exits from the Black Forest. When warned that Murat had withdrawn his cavalry from that area, Mack ordered a concentration around Ulm, south of Donauworth on the Danube.

There was no urgency in the orders or procedures for the army and the concentration was proceeding lackadaisically when the French flooded into Donauworth. Ferdinand and his staff went into mental convulsions, but Mack, realising that Napoleon was attempting to cut his communications with Vienna and was close to accomplishing that mission, planned to counter-attack the French boldly as they crossed the river. He was overruled by Ferdinand, who had the support of his other subordinate generals, and a retreat was ordered. The tone of the campaign had been set.

By 5 October the French had not established definite contact with the Austrians. However, the main Austrian forces in the area were located in the Ulm area. This information had been gleaned from both friendly civilians and Austrian prisoners.

On 7 October Napoleon arrived in Donauworth. He firmly believed that the Austrians would just retreat, wanting to do anything to protect their communications with Vienna. Over-optimistic regarding Austrian intentions, as he had been in the Marengo campaign in 1800, Napoleon made several thumping errors.

First, he overestimated the French marching rate and, as the weather had turned nasty with icy rain and snow, some units were unable to reach their objectives when expected. His aggressive corps commanders got in a terrible traffic jam near Eichstadt, slowing the march further. Second, he expected a fight on the River Lech on the 9th that never materialised, as he completely misread the strategic situation. Last, he believed the Austrians to be massing in and around Augsburg and ordered Soult, Davout, Marmont and the Imperial Guard to march for Augsburg to meet the expected enemy concentration.

What actually happened was that Ferdinand, with his army in and around Burgau, ready to advance to the east on 9 October, was frightened into ordering another retreat, this time to the south, to avoid the French who were on his line of communication. Mack was thoroughly disgusted and issued a counter-order for an advance north to cut Napoleon's communications. He believed Ulm was a very strong position with ample supplies and ammunition. Ready to comply after the confrontation, the Austrian commanders' resolve wilted when they heard that d'Aspre had been surprised and destroyed near Gunzberg.

On hearing the news, Ferdinand demanded either a northward advance or a retreat through the Tyrol. Mack ordered that the army return to Ulm to reorganise for the rest of the campaign. Mack was somewhat disheartened by the behaviour of the senior Austrian generals. Ferdinand, though nominally in command, did nothing to support Mack's efforts in and around Ulm or to discipline and encourage his senior commanders. Even though there was little or no French action on the 10th, the Austrians remained in the Ulm area accomplishing nothing except to convince Napoleon that they were there in strength, passively awaiting their fate.

Napoleon was finally convinced of the Austrian strength and position by two things: reliable reports from Davout and information from the captured d'Aspre given during his interrogation by the French. He also convinced himself, wrongly, that the Austrians were about to retreat south through Memmingen. Mack intended to fight and that fact would lead to the hardest fighting of the campaign.

Thus Napoleon ordered Ney to invest Ulm. Both Lannes and Murat were to support Ney, and Napoleon thought there were enough troops between Ney and Lannes to handle anything the Austrians might have in mind.

Napoleon's misreading of the situation and obtuse troop handling by Ney and Murat caused Dupont's infantry division became isolated on the north bank of the Danube. Arriving at Haslach at around noon on 11 October Dupont ran into Schwarzenberg and Reisch. The surprise was mutually unpleasant and the Austrians outfought Dupont, ran his trains out of town and drove him against the town. In a tight spot, alone and without orders and dangerously out-numbered, Dupont led his men in a savage fight that lasted until darkness. Withdrawing to Albeck after dark, he retreated in the direction of Brenz after midnight, even though he had just received orders to move to Gunzberg by Ney.

Mack was wounded in the fight and, because of command failures, the victorious Austrians failed to destroy Dupont. However, they did capture his orders, which revealed the complete disposition of the VI Corps, and using this information Mack planned boldly to continue operations north of the Danube to link up with the Russians who were moving tardily to their support. This movement would also put them in the French rear with an excellent opportunity to do to the French what Napoleon had done to them.

The Austrian commanders were more weary than their troops. They dithered, to Mack's frustration, and the opportunity passed. The fight at Haslach had given Napoleon a clear view of the situation and he ordered a concentration around Ulm to trap the Austrians there. Marmont and Soult were ordered west towards Ulm with Davout and Bernadotte still facing eastward across the old Austrian line of communication. No one would interfere with Napoleon and his dealing with Ferdinand and Mack.

On the night of 12–13 October, French outposts facing Ulm captured an Austrian courier with all of the Austrian dispositions and positions, showing strengths and commanders. Napoleon reinforced the troops on the north bank and in a neat little fight took Elchingen and its bridge from Reisch. Ney's first attack on the bridge had resulted in failure. That and his responsibility in Dupont's isolation and near-destruction brought an Imperial 'I want a report,' spurring Red Michael to greater efforts.

It was now Mack's turn for errors in judgement. Rumours of problems in France coupled with seeing what he wanted to see from French troops movements convinced Mack that Napoleon was giving up the campaign and heading home. The situation could not have been further from the truth. Napoleon was investing Ulm, setting a deadly trap for the Austrians.

Ferdinand did understand the situation and his reaction was to run northward with an escort, ostensibly to 'deprive the French of the glory of capturing a Hapsburg'.[3] Some of the senior Austrian commanders thought it a good idea, including Schwarzenberg, and deserted their commands to accompany Ferdinand. Ferdinand asked Mack to go with them, but he refused. The following inglorious scuttle ensured Ferdinand's desired escape and caused confused fighting in the French rear, but did not affect the overall situation for the main Austrian army in the least.

Focusing on the matter at hand, Napoleon completely invested Ulm by the 15th and sent a surrender demand to Mack. Mack attempted to fight and hold out, but his remaining subordinates refused and the Austrians, led by 'the unfortunate General Mack' surrendered on the 20th. The French captured at least 50,000 Austrians — an entire Austrian army went into captivity. Without fighting a major battle, Napoleon had won his first campaign as Emperor with the feet of his Grande Armée.

Pierre Dupont de l'Etaing (1765–1840) started his military career in 1784 as a sous-lieutenant in the Legion de Marlebois in the Dutch service. He transferred to the Dutch artillery in 1787 and served there until 1790. He was nominated by Rochambeau as a sous-lieutenant in the 12th Demi-Brigade in July 1791 and was a captain by 1792. When General Dillon was attacked by the mob, Dupont was wounded defending him, demonstrating admirable courage and character.

A chef de brigade by 1793 he was assigned to the Armée du Nord. Promoted to general of division in 1797, Dupont was later assigned as the chief of staff of the Armée de Reserve to Berthier in 1800. He fought well at Marengo and later negotiated the Convention of Alessandria that followed the victory.

He served with the Armée d'Italie from 1800–1801 and in August 1803 was assigned as the commander of the Ière Division of the VI Corps under Ney. He fought at Haslach and Durrenstein, and his conduct and reasons for fighting at Haslach are still something of a puzzle. His performance at Friedland in June 1807 was superb, advancing on his own initiative and defeating the infantry of the Russian Guard.

Assigned as an independent commander in Spain the following year, he completely mismanaged his campaign in southern Spain and capitulated at Baylén. His subsequent conduct was disgraceful, he and his senior officers brokering their return to France while abandoning their men to a cruel imprisonment that only ten per cent survived. Court-martialled and convicted, he was made destitute and imprisoned, later being employed by the Bourbons as their first Minster of War, one of the incidents that precipitated Napoleon's return.

It appears, then, that wherever their generals allowed the Austrian troops to fight, they fought well; and it would be a very rash, and a very false opinion, to impute the misfortunes of war to them. In that, as well as in all former instances, the Austrian army distinguished itself by its courage, its devotion to the cause, its constancy in supporting unheard of privations, and by its implicit obedience. It was at Ulm that these brave troops, victims to the conduct of M. Mack, were subjected to that heart-breaking fate which was the destruction of the German army. But, at Ulm, many regiments that had not fired a single shot were obliged to surrender, in consequence of the operations pursued, and in pursuance of orders given by that M. Mack, who talking of death, yet feared to die.[4]

CHAPTER 4

SOUTHERN SORROWS

The battle of Maida, 1806

Five thousand men were enough to thrust 6,000 or 7,000 English into the water. REYNIER

Steady light infantry. Wait for the word. Let them get close. KEMPT

12:00 4 July 1806, near Maida, Calabria, southern Italy
The attack had been a disaster, the veteran Ière Légère literally falling apart under the deadly fire of the British infantry. The regiment had actually disintegrated into a mass of fugitives and fled before the British infantry's lowered bayonets. The regiment's losses had been very heavy.

General Reynier sat his horse among his small staff, having given his orders for the army to retreat and regroup, calmly puffing on his pipe to the amazement of his staff. His chief of staff was issuing coordinating instructions to the surviving officers, but losses, again, had been very heavy and not just in the Ière Légère. Reynier, taciturn and somewhat cold, and not a man to question at a time like this, looked on without any expression on his face as the officers discussed what had to be done to rally the defeated army to continue operations against the British. After this disaster, it might be a long campaign.

Certainly, the Emperor would not be pleased. War with Prussia was looming on the Empire's horizon, and failure in a secondary theatre was not a pleasant thing to consider. Reynier was already on Napoleon's bad side for his attitude in Egypt in 1800, but you could not tell what the Swiss-born General was thinking behind those clever eyes of his and the blank expression on his face as he sat his horse and puffed on his pipe.

Reynier's uniform was filthy and sweat-soaked, and he had to be as exhausted as the rest of his staff, but you could not tell by looking at him. As the chief of staff finished and the questions died down, General Reynier took notice of them and nodded his head to the left, leading off to follow the army to its new

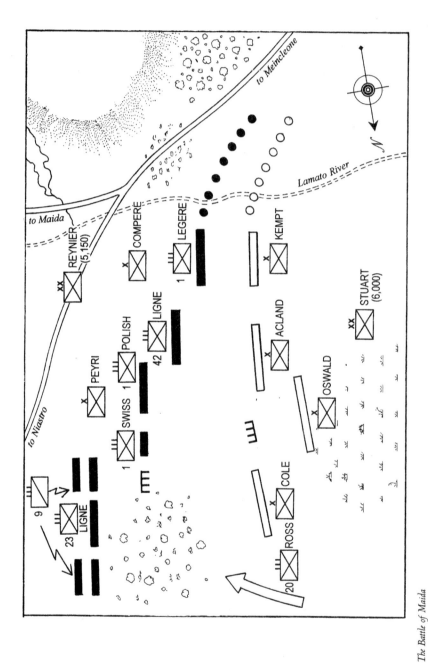

The Battle of Maida

The French attacked the British right in line and were bloodily repulsed, virtually sealing the British victory. Reynier is said to have sat on his horse calmly smoking his pipe, which was entirely in character. Reynier attacked sloppily, without combining skirmishers as his fire-support element to cover his main effort. He paid for his mistake by seeing his division routed.

assembly area. As the officers dutifully followed their chief, more than one wondered what Reynier's expression would be when he received the dreaded summons from Napoleon, the 'I want a report' that ended his correspondence when he was displeased. Undoubtedly, Reynier's expression would not change one bit. He had disagreed and stood up to Napoleon before.[1]

The battle of Maida was a meeting engagement between relatively equal forces of French and British troops in southern Italy. Strategically, it had little meaning, as the British expeditionary force that landed in Italy from Sicily was too small to have any lasting impact in the area and re-embarked for Sicily soon after the battle. Tactically, it really had little to offer for study, but it was a harbinger of things to come and a lesson for the French of the dangers of the firepower and steadiness of British infantry. Reynier lost the action because he was overconfident, had little but contempt for his enemies, and he did not prepare or support his attack with large numbers of skirmishers which could have caused the British no end of trouble, as they had in the 1790s in Holland.

Reynier was unfortunate in that he, and the troops he commanded at Maida, clearly underestimated the deadly, close-range hitting power of British infantry in an open-field engagement. British firepower was murderous, and British infantry had been noted as tough, grim and grudging opponents on European and American battlefields as far back as 1066 when William the Conqueror remarked that he had never met such infantry.

On 29 June 1806 the British expeditionary force under General Sir John Stuart set sail from Messina, Sicily, for the Italian mainland. The naval force was commanded by that erstwhile adventurer, Sir Sidney Smith, and the squadron anchored in the Gulf of St Euphemia on 30 June. Landing in Calabria, southern Italy, the next day, the troops came ashore unopposed except for a detachment of Polish troops who did not give them much trouble.

Nor did the French oppose the landing of any naval units. It should be noted that the ubiquitous Royal Navy gave the British nearly unchallenged strategic mobility during the Napoleonic Wars. Yet British amphibious expeditions were not always employed as expertly as they might have been.

The British force was composed of approximately 5,200 troops organised in three (some sources say four) infantry brigades under the command of Wroth Acland, Lowry Cole and John Oswald. The detached light infantry companies were commanded by James Kempt. The British had no cavalry to scout for them or screen them, but did have four field guns, two mortars and ten mountain guns. After getting his division ashore, Stuart, an uninspired commander at best, sat on the beach for three days to see what the French might do.

Reynier, the French commander in the area, arrived in the vicinity on 3 July. He had two brigades of infantry, a horse artillery company and a small cavalry regiment available for operations against Stuart. Reynier probably had in excess of 6,000 men available and with him at Maida. Some were veteran French regiments which had distinguished themselves in previous engagements. There were also Swiss and Poles among his infantry units, troops that should perform well. The battle would take place the next day, with both sides more than ready for an engagement.

Both commanders knew of the other's presence in the area and at dawn on the 4th, they had their troops stand to and prepare to advance. Between 06:00 and 07:00 the British moved along the beach for about nine miles until they reached the mouth of the River l'Amato. There, they turned to move inland. The French were on the high ground facing the plain upon which the British were to advance. Seeing the British advancing from the beach, Reynier had his army move down from the high ground and debouch on to the plain and form for battle.

At 08:00 the British were clearly advancing from the beach inland. They took up positions with the river on their right. On the other side of what was a glorified stream was a tangle of bushes and low growth, into which Stuart deployed some of his light troops. The rest of the command formed in line of battle with Kempt's light troops on the right, followed in order down the line by the commands of Acland, Oswald and Cole. Ross, with the 20th Foot, was not as yet on the field. The artillery was emplaced between Cole and Acland.

The French formed for battle with the Ière Légère on the left facing Kempt, then the 42nd Ligne, the Poles, the Swiss and the 23e Légère on the far right. The cavalry was between the Swiss and the 23e Légère. The horse artillery took position to the right of the Swiss along with the horsemen.

Both armies advanced in echelon, the British from the right and the French from the left. The British were in line and ready for battle when Reynier attacked, the redoubtable Ière Légère advancing in line against Kempt. Interestingly, neither side had deployed skirmishers to their front. What happened next is one of the most interesting and short combats of the Napoleonic period.[2]

When the advancing Ière Légère was within range, the ominous command 'Ready, Present!' rang out from the stoic red line standing in the hot Italian sun like a brick wall. At the bellowed 'FIRE!' the red wall exploded into a blaze of well-directed musketry and the Ière Légère staggered as if by a body blow. There are different accounts as to how many times Kempt's troops actually fired into the Ière Légère. It was at least twice. Almost immediately, Kempt ordered the British infantry to charge into the smoke and carnage, and the Ière Légère became nothing but a horde of fugitives, many of them being bayoneted while trying to run.

The English remained with ported arms until the 1st légère came within half a musket shot; they then opened a tremendous fire, which did not at first stop the charge, but when the columns were only fifteen paces from the hostile line and could have broken it by one more thrust, the soldiers of the 1st turned their backs and ran to the rear . . .[3]

The battle was neither over nor won yet by the British. The 42e Ligne was also advancing to the right of the Ière Légère, but they were met by the same devastating musketry as the French light infantrymen had been. As the Ière Légère had been routed, the 42e Ligne 'conformed' to their 'manoeuvre' and withdrew as well. Reynier's main attack had failed.

The British advanced from their centre to support Kempt's pursuit on their right, and in front of this determined advance the discouraged Poles left the field in something of a panic. Reynier did rally the Swiss, and French artillery fire and the presence of the French cavalry caused heavy casualties on Acland's troops. These actions stopped the advance of the British centre.

Reynier, seeing that there was now a gap in the British centre because Acland had advanced and the British left was still in its original position, ordered the 23e Légère on the French right to advance. However, the 23e was already in a firefight with Cole's command, which was starting to get in a bad way. French light infantry were manoeuvring through the brush and scrub on the British right flank, supported by their own cavalry, endangering the British left flank.

On to the battlefield, fortuitously positioned to support the desperately fighting Cole, marched the 20th Foot commanded by Robert Ross. This regiment ably supported Cole, relieved the pressure to Cole's left flank, and forced the 23e Légère to disengage. To all intents and purposes, the battle was over. Stuart, who had done little actual fighting, had won for himself a neat little victory over a superior French force, quite literally shooting it to pieces. The French fled the battlefield, the exhausted British remaining to sleep on the field.

British losses were 237 killed and wounded, all ranks. The French losses were at least 2,000, all ranks. A more lopsided outcome could hardly be imagined. British discipline and firepower, and Reynier's underestimation of his enemy, had been the main causes of the French defeat. Reynier had failed to take advantage of his numerical superiority or of his cavalry. While actually outnumbered in artillery, he nevertheless did not employ his army to the French advantage. He failed to deploy skirmishers in any numbers for his main effort, which might have both negated the small British superiority in artillery and actually done what that system was designed to do, shoot the enemy's line to pieces to prepare it for a decisive assault. Further, he also failed to use his artillery to any advantage, such as support the main effort by the Ière Légère and the 42e Ligne. Finally, Reynier did not use the terrain to his advantage. He gave up the high ground in order to fight the British on their terms, and whatever advantage he could have gained after descending from the heights was given up in his overwhelming desire to get to grips with an enemy he grossly underestimated.

On the British side Stuart was a nonentity. Had their roles been reversed, Reynier, or any other French commander for that matter, would have at least attempted to pursue a beaten enemy. Arthur Wellesley, later the Duke of Wellington, certainly would have, but as was to be shown time and again, Wellesley was not an average general. Stuart, because of his inactivity won merely an 'ordinary' victory, and one from which the French almost immediately recovered.

The battle was won by Stuart's subordinates, who took advantage both of the assets they had on hand and by letting a numerical superior enemy come to them. The traditional steadiness of the British infantryman was indeed a major factor in the victory, but the intelligently handled 23e Légère was giving Cole more than a little trouble. If the French had been handled better tactically, the British might have had a very long day.

Jean Louis Ebenezer Reynier (1771–1814) was Swiss and has been described as 'an admirable soldier but a difficult individual'. He was an honest and taciturn Protestant who held most of the marshals in contempt and was not a man to insult as he was also a deadly duellist. He enlisted as a private in 1792 and by 1795 was a general of brigade with an established reputation. He was promoted to general of division the next year and became Moreau's chief of staff. Blunt and outspoken, he also favoured being alone and quiet.

He was a friend of Desaix and was with him on the Egyptian expedition. Reynier's victory at El Arish won praise from Napoleon. He also got on Napoleon's bad side by recommending evacuation of Egypt. He commanded the Lobau garrison in 1809 and saved Boudet's division from being destroyed on the French left flank. He served well and successfully in Russia, and he usually did better with foreign than French troops.

Napoleon valued him as a planner: 'Reynier was a man of talent, but better fitted to [plan the operations of] an army of 20,000 or 30,000 men, than to command one of 5,000 or 6,000.'[4] Courageous, quick-witted and with an excellent sense of terrain, he commanded a corps in 1813, but was captured at Leipzig when the Lindenau bridge was blown prematurely. Alexander offered him a Russian commission, which Reynier contemptuously turned down. He died in France of exhaustion. Napoleon wrote to Clarke while in the midst of the almost hopeless 1814 campaign, 'I am surprised that nothing has yet been done to honor the memory of General Reynier . . . a man who served well, was an honest man, and whose death was a loss for France and for me.'[5]

Bugeaud's excellent narrative of British volley fire, and the discipline that produced it, from his experience in the Peninsula against those same British could have been describing the firefight at Maida with the 1st Légère:

The English generally occupied well-chosen defensive positions having a certain command, and they showed only a portion of their forces. The usual artillery action first took place. Soon, in great haste, without studying the position, without taking time to examine whether there were means to make a flank attack, we marched straight on, taking the bull by the horns. About 1,000 yards from the English line them men became excited, called out to one another, and hastened their march; the column began to become a little confused. The English remained quite silent with ordered arms, and from their steadiness appeared to be a long red wall. This steadiness invariably produced an effect on our young soldiers. Very soon we got nearer, crying 'Vive l'Empereur! En Avant! A la baionette!' Shakos were raised on the muzzles of muskets; the column began to double, the ranks got into confusion, the agitation produced a tumult; shots were fired as we advanced. The English line remained silent, still and immovable, with ordered arms, even when we were only 300 yards distant, and it appeared to ignore the storm about to break. The contrast was striking; in our innermost thoughts we all felt the enemy was a long time in firing, and that this fire, reserved for so long, would be very unpleasant when it came. Our ardour cooled. The moral power of steadiness, which nothing can shake (even if it be only appearance), over disorder which stupefies itself with noise, overcame our minds. At this moment of intense excitement, the English wall shouldered arms; an indescribable feeling would root many of our men to the spot; they began to fire. The enemy's steady, concentrated volleys swept our ranks; decimated, we turned round seeking to recover our equilibrium; then three deafening cheers broke the silence of our opponents; at the third they were on us, pushing our disorganised flight.[6]

From the British side, Ensign Joseph Anderson of the 78th Foot wrote:

As soon as these formidable French columns came sufficiently near, and not till then, our lines were called to 'attention' and ordered to 'shoulder arms'. Then commenced in earnest the glorious battle of Maida, first with a volley from our brigade into the enemy's columns and from our artillery at each flank without ceasing, followed by independent firing as fast as our men could load; and well they did their work! Nor were the enemy idle; they returned our fire without ceasing, then in part commenced to deploy into line.[7]

CHAPTER 5

THE COMBAT ENDS FOR LACK OF COMBATANTS

The battle of Auerstadt, 1806

The III Corps would always be worthy of the confidence of their sovereign and that it would be for him, in every circumstance, that which the X Legion had been for Caesar. DAVOUT TO NAPOLEON

Le miserable Ponte Corvo. DAVOUT, 14 OCTOBER 1806

11:00 Hours 14 October 1806, south-east of Hassenhausen, Saxony
The smoke and roar of the battle to the division's front was a growing crescendo that seemingly threatened to swallow them whole. They knew they were marching into a fight, but not to face the dreaded main Prussian army. Frantic, hard riding couriers and even harder-faced aides-de-camp had pounded up and down the road towards Hassenhausen all morning, and General Morand had hustled the division down the same road since dawn.

At the head of the column of Morand's Ière Division of Davout's III Corps, the panting 13e Légère sweated under their heavy packs as they hastened to the vulgar uproar in front of them. They realised the rest of the corps was engaged with the Prussians. They also knew the situation was undoubtedly desperate — why else were their officers urging them on at this speed?

Orders barked out at the head of the column, and the lead companies of the Ier Bataillon shook out as skirmishers in open order. So, it was to be that way, was it? As they double-timed down the road, men reached back to pull cartridge boxes closer round to their hips for easier access. Others touched bayonets to ensure they were still there. Still others spat and wiped their sweat-streaked faces as they rushed towards the smoke and roar of what would be for some of them, their last battle. The rookies among them were visibly upset, fresh-faced conscripts and downy-cheeked sous-lieutenants alike, yet their young faces were set and determined. At least Davout had ensured they were well trained and could shoot. They still had no idea what kind of hell they were walking into.

As they reached the battlefield, they saw their comrades off to their right, at least one division formed in squares fighting off clouds of Prussian cavalry. Cannon on both sides belched fire and death, ordered volleys of musketry from the Prussians and the more individual fire of their comrades in Gudin's and Friant's divisions threw clouds of smoke over the battlefield.

Morand's divisional artillery clattered past, trumpeters and drummers playing them into action, both instruments clear through the noise. Battery commanders mounted on skittish horses were waving their swords and bellowing commands, the foot artillerymen double-timing to keep up with the gun teams. Team horses snorted in the early morning dust, sometimes tripping, but gathering themselves up with their drivers urging them on with a word and sometimes a whip. Guns and limbers followed by ammunition caissons slid around bends in the road, oblivious to the hustling infantrymen now on either side of the one good thoroughfare.

More commands were barked by their regimental and battalion commanders, and swiftly and expertly each light infantry company, urged on by their NCOs, each battalion led by their chef, deployed as skirmishers until the entire regiment was in a thick skirmish line, meant to cover the division front while the other four regiments behind them deployed to fight.

The companies and battalions of the 13e Légère shook out in skirmish order along the entire front of the division. Company commanders took their places behind their deployed companies, with a handy reserve of ten to twelve picked men and their company cornet, to enable the company to rally if necessary and to control their skirmishers. Smart company commanders had kept their drums when ordered to turn them in – the cornet was a very weak-sounding instrument and not as martial as the drum. Every company had one cornet, but those who kept the drum used it, undoubtedly to the chagrin of their company drummer who had to lug it around to keep up with his more lightly accoutred company commander.

The companies moved forward on the left flank of what they later discovered was Gudin's division. Muskets started to bark all along the line as the lead companies ran into, or rather, went after any hostile Prussians. The other four regiments of their division, all ligne, deployed in column behind them. Suddenly, as if on cue, the voltigeur companies of the ligne battalions were shaking out as they had done, behind them, deploying in open order to replace them along the division front. The *kleine manner* were an efficient, aggressive and cantankerous lot, ready to fight with musket and bayonet or fist and wine bottle as the occasion demanded, undoubtedly because they were all so short – light infantry with an attitude. They hustled to catch up with the now deployed 13e

Légère, replacing them covering their own battalions. Chasseurs in the centre companies of the légère regiment started shouting at the newly arrived voltigeurs that it took more than *haute* pay to make a light infantryman, getting quick, nasty looks in return. That argument would have to be settled later.

Orders were again barked, cornets blew and drums beat away, and the companies and battalions reassembled and shifted to the left flank of the division, to screen it from any hostile Prussian movement. Companies and battalions moved off with the fluid ease of veterans, some chasseurs turning for one last insult to the ligne's voltigeurs before being cuffed along by their NCOs

On the far left flank of the regiment, one dapper, veteran company commander, in a light cavalry colpack with a green and yellow plume and yellow bag decorating it, calmly nodded to his company first sergeant. The redoubtable, veteran NCO shouted a few concise orders, and the company began to shift smoothly and expertly to the left. Satisfied, *monsieur le capitaine* spoke a few quiet words to his drummer, and the two of them trotted off to rejoin the company reserve.

After Austerlitz and the treaty that followed, Napoleon set out to turn the western German states, who feared encroachment from both Prussia and Austria, into an organisation that would be both friendly to France and a buffer for her eastern marches. What resulted was the Confederation of the Rhine, an important military ally to the French Empire and under Napoleon's protection. Pledging by treaty troops to the mutual defence of the Confederation and Empire, Napoleon's allies were both promoted and given more territory.[1] Further, Napoleon stayed out of the internal affairs of the member states, though the armies of these states were reorganised along French lines which both made it easier to operate with French formations on campaign and in combat and modernised the respective states' armies.

Prussia bristled at the French control of western Germany. She had her own designs on the German states, and that did not include either their alliance with France or their expansion. This French 'interference' was one of the main causes why Prussia chose to go to war with France in late 1806.

Prussia was ill prepared to fight a modern war. Her army was the inspired shadow of Frederick the Great's triumphal army of the Seven Years War. Training standards were low, much of the army was on furlough for the majority of the year, and her generals were too old. What was worse, they scoffed at French fighting techniques and firmly believed that the Grande Armée was no match for the Prussian army.

In preparation for the war against Prussia, Davout received the following order from Berthier at 04:00 on 7 October:

The Emperor orders, Marshal, that you move your headquarters during 7 October to Lichtenfels. Your 1st Division will bivouac around that town; your two other divisions between Bamberg and Lichtenfels in such a way that tomorrow, the 8th, your corps can be concentrated in order of battle in front of Kronach in a position to support Marshal Bernadotte, who should reach the Saale on the 9th.

I inform you that the right of the army, leaving Amberg, will occupy Bayreuth on the 7th and will be at Hof on the 9th. It is composed of the corps of Marshals Soult and Ney.

The centre will occupy Kronach. It will move via Lobenstein. It is composed of your corps, that of Marshal Bernadotte, of most of the reserve, and the Imperial Guard . . .

The left, leaving Schweinfurt, is ordered to Coburg, and from there to Grafenthal; it is composed of [the corps of] Marshals Lannes and Augereau.

Headquarters is at Bamberg. It will be at Lichtenfels on the 8th and at Kronach on the 9th.

The III Corps moved out, led and screened by its corps cavalry under Vialannes, and by 10 October had reached Schleiz. The day before Murat, with elements of the Cavalry Reserve and the I Corps light cavalry, had fought a sharp action with the Prussians at Schleiz and driven them away.

After reaching Schleiz and bivouacking, elements of the III Corps were dispatched to reconnoitre towards Saalfeld, where a sharp action was fought by Lannes and the V Corps against the Prussian advance guard under Prince Louis. The Prussians were badly defeated and Prince Louis was killed in action by a French hussar sergeant from the 10e Hussars.[2]

The next day III Corps marched on, taking up a post five miles past Auma at Mittpollnitz. Napoleon decided to begin to manoeuvre the Grande Armée to its left. Napoleon's plan of campaign was to make contact with the army in a compact, flexible formation, preceded by its cavalry screen, and be able and prepared to manoeuvre and fight in any direction. Napoleon dubbed this formation his 'battalion square,' and it was both compact and flexible, being able to be manoeuvred by the Emperor as a good battalion commander would on the battlefield.

Napoleon manoeuvred to his left because there had been no appreciable enemy forces encountered by the right-hand column. Davout with the III Corps and Bernadotte with the I Corps were now going to hook to their left and continue the movement to contact. On 12 October Davout was ordered to Naumberg which the leading elements of III Corps reach on the 13th.

The Prussians were in a state of confusion and indecision. The defeat and

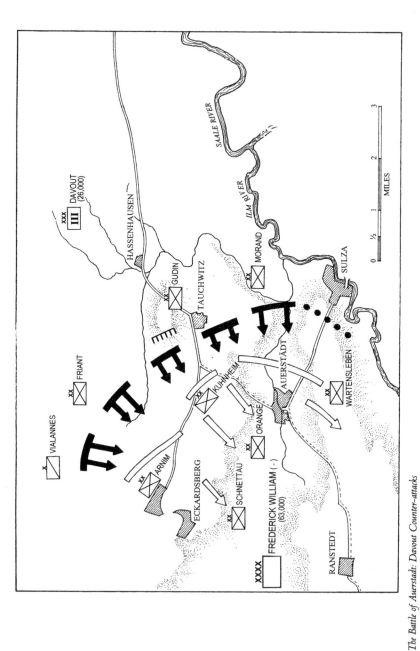

The Battle of Auerstädt: Davout Counter-attacks

This map illustrates the last phase of the action with Davout's III Corps executing a double envelopment of the main Prussian army. Both armies arrived on the field piecemeal, commanders on both sides feeding their troops in as they arrived. Davout, unlike Brunswick (who was mortally wounded) and Frederick William (who hesitated to assume command after Brunswick was hit), had command of the action from the first shots. His performance can only be classed as masterful. The thoroughness with which the III Corps had been trained, the innate toughness of the troops (one-third of whom were conscripts with less than a year's service), and the outstanding leadership displayed at all levels of the corps make this a 'model engagement'.

death of Prince Louis at Saalfeld greatly disheartened the Prussian commanders. Any thoughts of aggressive offensive action were forgotten, and the
decision was made to withdraw to the north. On 12 October the Prussians
achieved a concentration of sorts around Weimar but the army was disorganised
and the troops did not know how to forage for themselves.

On the 13th it was decided to withdraw north: Brunswick's command would
leave in the morning, covered by Hohenlohe and Ruchel, to link up with Württemberg's command on the Saale; Ruchel was instructed to wait for Saxe-Weimar.

Napoleon believed he faced the main Prussian army at Jena on 14 October.
Unknown to him, Brunswick's withdrawal put him on a collision course with
Davout and Bernadotte. Bernadotte's refusal to support Davout, and his blatant
disregard of the orders to do so, put Davout in considerable danger. Davout
would have to face Brunswick alone.

At 03:00 on 14 October Davout received Napoleon's order to advance on
Apolda via Auerstadt. The order's postscript, by Berthier, directed the following:
'If Marshal Bernadotte is with you, you will be able to march together, but the
Emperor hopes that he will be in the position indicated to him, that is,
Dornburg.'[3] Davout wasted no time and immediately sent Bernadotte a written
copy of the order. Bernadotte refused to remain with Davout and chose to
execute his interpretation of the order and march to Dornburg. This was either
a deliberate refusal or an amazing act of disobedience. As it turned out,
Bernadotte and I Corps took no part in either Jena or Auerstadt. Bernadotte
coldly left Davout and III Corps on their own to face whatever enemy would be
in front of them.

At 06:30 14 October Davout was on the road to execute the orders received
in the early morning hours. Gudin's 3e Division marched first and his advanced
units seized the defile at Hassenhausen through which the rest of the corps
would have to pass. There was a fog in the area before dawn and the ground was
not the easiest to fight over. The area past the Saale River, which was unfordable,
was mostly a high plateau and it was crossed by small streams and ravines, as
well as sunken roads. There were many small villages in the area which could be
used as ready-made strong-points. To the north it became more undulating,
being dotted with small hills and stands of trees. The left bank of the Saale was
covered with trees and was steep. For the skilful commander who could make
ground fight for him, it was good defensive terrain. For one who was not, it
could become a death-trap.

Davout dispatched one of his aides-de-camp, Colonel Bourke, with a detachment of the Ier Chasseurs from the corps cavalry brigade on a reconnaissance of
the area in front of III Corps. Davout knew there were Prussian units in the area,

but he did not know how many or in what strength. Bourke ran into Prussian cavalry in the fog and snatched a few prisoners, with which he returned to Davout.

Davout hustled Gudin to the battlefield, as the Prussians were racing from the opposite direction. Blücher was en route with his cavalry and Schmettau was already on the field with at least part of his division. Gudin seized Hassen-hausen and became engaged all along the line as his regiments came up. As Blücher arrived, Gudin's division formed square to resist the masses of Prussian horsemen. In a line of squares, Gudin's infantry defeated charge after desperate Prussian charge, Blücher leading furiously from the front. Wartensleben's and Orange's divisions arrived, and the pressure against Gudin increased.

At 08:30 Friant arrived just as Gudin's hard-used division began to buckle under the pressure. Forming on Gudin's left, Friant drove one of the Prince of Orange's brigades from the village of Spielberg, and Gudin's left, now being secured by Friant's arrival, could shift his left flank units to reinforce his depleted centre.

Davout's corps cavalry, with the exception of the two squadrons of the Ier Chasseurs à Cheval that had been with his advanced guard, was late. He had already employed his corps gendarmerie detachment to overrun and capture a Prussian artillery battery, but the absence of his corps cavalry was puzzling to the corps commander. Vialannes finally arrived on the battlefield at 09:00.[4]

Shortly thereafter, Brunswick, who was now on the field, ordered Schmettau and Wartensleben to make a coordinated attack against Gudin's division. In the fighting that ensued, Brunswick was mortally wounded, shot through both eyes, and Schmettau followed his chief with a mortal wound. The attack fell into disorder and failed. However, Orange's division was successful in its advance against Gudin's left flank, which began to give ground. Hassenhausen was abandoned by the French, but at the crisis Morand's division came onto the field at the double time, led by the 13e Légère.

Morand drove in hard, easing the pressure on Gudin and shattering Wartensleben's division. Blücher's cavalry, which had rallied after its failure against Gudin, again charged, but Morand expertly drove them off. King Frederick William, who had assumed command after Brunswick's fall, frantically ordered Blücher's infantry and the infantry of the Prussian Guard against Morand, both of which failed. Frederick William then snatched at least part of Kuhnheim's division and ordered it against the victorious Morand. As none of the attacks were properly coordinated and generally were without proper artillery support, they were also defeated.

The fighting was desperate on both sides. The French were steadily getting the upper hand. With all three of his divisions on the field, Davout was ready to assume the offensive against the Prussians.

Since Brunswick's fall, Frederick William had been the de facto commander of the main Prussian army. However, he stayed on the Prussian right flank and made no effort to take command of the army. He displayed admirable coolness and bravery in the field under fire, but his non-comprehension of the situation doomed whatever chance the Prussians had of defeating III Corps.[5]

By 13:00 the Prussians were beginning to fall apart. After defeating the last Prussian counter-attack against him, Morand pivoted on his right flank and outflanked the Prussians, taking their entire line in enfilade. Friant defeated Orange and kept hold of the village of Spielberg. Pivoting on his left, he took the Prussian left in the flank and his fire interlocked with that of Morand, using artillery and infantry to wreak havoc with the now unorganised Prussians.

Gudin's exhausted survivors surged forward and the Prussian line started to break up, units and individuals heading for the rear and any place of safety. The divisions of von Arnim and Kuhnheim, under the control of Kalkreuth, advanced and attempted to stop the surging French divisions, but they too were driven from their positions and started to break up as they went to the rear.

By 16:30 the Prussians were in full retreat, many units not being able to rally. The French infantry was exhausted and finally were stopped by Davout to the south-west of Eckartsberg. The jubilant French corps cavalry, three regiments of chasseurs à cheval, continued chasing the Prussians until 19:30 and halted in the vicinity of Buttstadt.

It had been an overwhelming victory for the III Corps and its chief, Davout. But the price had been heavy. Of the 26,000 men available to III Corps at Auerstadt, almost 8,000 had become casualties. Gudin's division had lost approximately 3,500 men. However, the Prussians were thoroughly defeated and broken. They had suffered a loss of 12,000 killed and wounded, 3,000 prisoners and 115 guns. Davout had not only held his position against 63,000 Prussians but had gone on the offensive and executed a double envelopment of the main Prussian army.

1700 14 October 1806, near Jena, Saxony
The Emperor gazed upon the disintegrating wreck of what he had thought was the main Prussian field army. What was passing for a rearguard was being overrun by jubilant elements of the Cavalry Reserve and the VI Corps light cavalry being led by Murat who was brandishing a riding crop above his head instead of his sabre. The exhausted, panting French infantry were rapidly chasing the broken Prussian counterparts, supporting artillery hurriedly limbering up to follow.

Marshal Berthier, the army's major general and chief of staff, and his assistants were busily writing and issuing orders for the immediate pursuit of the broken Prussians. The marshal's aides-de-camp were galloping off in all directions delivering orders to hustle the designated units along.

Fresh units who had not been engaged were rapidly outpacing those that had. The Emperor was becoming increasingly convinced that he had not engaged the main Prussian army, but where was it?

17:30 14 October 1806 near Hassenhausen, Saxony
Standing on the smoke-shrouded battlefield near the tiny hamlet of Auerstadt with the surviving members of his staff, Marshal Davout, commander of the III Corps, surveyed the wreck they had made out of what had been the main Prussian army. The chasseurs à cheval of his corps light cavalry were wading into the horde of Prussian fugitives that were collapsing in rout before his severely depleted and exhausted infantry. The Prussians had finally sensed they were in a trap. Colonel Bourke, Davout's senior aide-de-camp, busily scribbled the marshal's dispatches for the Emperor, while a nervous medical attendant hurriedly dressed his wounded arm. Trying to hold the paper and write at the same time, Burke grimaced at the none-too-gentle ministrations of the orderly.

Pausing to take the jubilant salute of his gendarme detachment, which had just charge, overrun and captured a Prussian artillery company, Davout greeted the commander of his 3rd Division, General of Division Gudin. Slightly wounded, filthy and sweat-streaked, Gudin's division had formed the rock-hard point of manoeuvre for the rest of the corps during the first, critical hours of the engagement, and had suffered the heaviest casualties.

Taking his friend's hand in gratitude, Davout ensured the first of his couriers, among them Colonel Bourke, were sent off to report to the Emperor. Under his breath, but heard by Gudin and Bourke, he roundly damned Bernadotte, 'that damned Ponte Corvo', for failing to come to his aid when he undoubtedly could have. Maybe the Emperor would have him shot, which would undoubtedly have the approval of the entire III Corps.

03:30 15 October 1806, the Emperor's bivouac, near Jena, Saxony
Out of the early morning mist towards the Imperial bivouac, commonly called the palace by the ubiquitous Guardsmen on duty, pounded one of Davout's couriers from Auerstadt, Colonel Falcon. Passing through the always alert duty squadrons of the Imperial Guard, Falcon was passed through and delivered his dispatches to the escort commander and awaited the Emperor's pleasure.

Taking the dispatch from the immaculately turned out Guard officer, Napoleon ripped open the sealed envelope and was somewhat surprised by what he read: III Corps, alone, had met and defeated the main Prussian army, over twice the strength of Davout's corps. Napoleon looked at Colonel Falcon suspiciously and remarked, 'Your marshal sees double'. Receiving an incredulous, raised eyebrow look in return from the shocked aide, Napoleon grinned. He knew few dared question the stern marshal, and all, including Vandamme, did his bidding.

Long minutes passed in grim silence, until the arrival of a second courier from Davout arrived, bearing another dispatch that removed all doubt about the first.

Turning to Berthier, Napoleon issued brief, succinct orders for the start of the pursuit, Berthier taking them down in his green notebook. Orders were given, horses gathered up and a new wave of aides-de-camp set off searching for the commanders to give the Emperor's new instructions. Satisfied, Napoleon offered Colonel Falcon some snuff, bade him good morning, sat down in his chair near a large fire, and promptly went to sleep.

What followed was the most relentless and complete pursuit of the Napoleonic period. The retreating and demoralised Prussian army was hunted down by the Grande Armée and either destroyed or captured. Prussian fortresses meekly surrendered to handfuls of French cavalry. Stettin surrendering to Lasalle's bluff was an outstanding example. The French captured 140,000 prisoners, 800 field guns and 250 flags. In three weeks of campaigning, the Prussian army was all but destroyed. There were still units in East Prussia, and these would serve well and usefully, especially at Eylau and the siege of Coburg, but the army that Frederick the Great had inherited and maintained no longer existed.

Berlin was taken without a fight, the city fathers turning the city over to the French meekly. Units started eastward to face the Russians, as they were still marching westward and were not attempting to either negotiate or quit. Other units continued to pursue the Prussian units that had not capitulated. The last of them, Blücher's, were finally cornered in the old Hanseatic city of Lübeck, and after attempting, and failing, to escape, surrendered.

Further, the civil population succumbed to the French in an orderly and subservient manner. Towns and cities were easily occupied and order maintained by the French. The city fathers of Berlin met the leading French elements with the keys to the city. Old Prussia had been quickly and for the most part quietly occupied.

Napoleon's gratitude and appreciation for Davout and the III Corps was evident from the following proclamation to the unit as a whole:

Generals, officers and non-commissioned officers of the III Corps, I have gathered you here together to tell you in person that I am satisfied with your splendid conduct at the battle on October 14. I have lost brave men; I regret their loss as if they were my own children, but they died on the field of honour as true soldiers. You have rendered to me a great service in this particular circumstance; it has been particularly the brilliant conduct of the III Corps of the army which has produced the results you now see. Tell your men that I have been satisfied with their courage. Generals, officers, non-commissioned officers, you have acquired an everlasting right to my gratitude and favour.

Louis Nicholas Davout (1770–1823) was quite possibly the most skilled of Napoleon's marshals. His titles, Duke of Auerstadt and Prince of Eckmuhl, were for battles he won on his own. Davout was from an old Burgundian military family of whom it was said that when a Davout was born it was akin to drawing a sword from its scabbard.

Davout was one of two marshals who started their careers as cavalry officers, Grouchy being the other. He began his road to the marshalate at the Royal Military School at Auxerre in 1780. He was a graduate of the Military School of Paris where he began two years of advanced study in 1785. His first assignment was to the Royal Champagne Cavalry Regiment.

With revolutionary fermentation spreading like a cancer in the French army, Davout was in sympathy with the Revolution and was expelled from the army. He enlisted in the volunteers and quickly came to the command of a battalion and came through the first battles with a growing reputation for efficiency. Davout opposed Dumouriez attempt to turn his army against the French government, actually being the officer who ordered the troops to fire on the soon-to-be exile. He was promised promotion to general of division because of good service along the northern marches and in the Vendée in 1793, but he resigned from the army because political fanatics were intent on driving all former nobles from the army.

Upon returning home, both Davout and his mother were unjustly imprisoned, but he was recalled in 1794 as a general of brigade and sent to the Rhine armies. He met Desaix, who thought very highly of him and took him with him to Egypt, both of them returning together, Davout by this time a firm supporter of Napoleon. Promoted to general of division in 1800 he was given command of the Grenadiers a Pied of the Consular Guard. Davout also married Aimée Leclerc, sister to General Victor Leclerc, the 'blonde Bonaparte'.

Appointed as a marshal in the first promotion, Davout was given command of what would become the III Corps. He always led the best-trained and equipped troops in the Grande Armée, and III Corps usually got the hardest assignments because of it. Davout held the outnumbered right flank at Austerlitz, fought and defeated the main Prussian army at Auerstadt the next year, and delivered the main attack at Eylau the following February. He missed

Friedland, but was given command of all the troops remaining in Germany after Tilsit and did not go to Spain.

Davout's rare appreciation of intelligence and counter-intelligence work, and especially his use of his light cavalry, enabled him to give sufficient warning of the impending Austrian offensive in 1809. He played a major part in the Ratisbon phase of the campaign, missed Essling because the French bridge to the north bank was destroyed before he could cross, and was one of the main reasons Napoleon won at Wagram.

Davout was an excellent tactician and strategist and had the strongest character among the marshals. Honest and incorruptible, he was also an excellent administrator. As such, he supervised the creation of the Grande Duchy of Warsaw and the creation of the Armée du Nord was his doing in 1815. His loyalty to Napoleon was unquestioned, to his own, and his family's, hurt. He carried a miniature of his lovely wife on campaign with him around his neck and sent her presents from the countries in which he lived and campaigned.

Davout was strict with his subordinates, stricter with himself, and always took responsibility for his subordinates' mistakes if they had acted according to his instructions. His relationship with Napoleon was one of frankness and blunt loyalty. Never a courtier, and not caring for those who were, he never lost an engagement. He always ensured his men were fed and properly equipped, and he permitted no looting. He treated inefficient administrative officers harshly; dishonest ones he had shot. His soldiers nicknamed him 'The Just'.

He served well in 1812, defeating Bagration outnumbered at Moghilev in July, and his I Corps was the best-equipped to ever serve in the Grande Armée. Assigned to defend Hamburg in 1813, he held it against all odds, only surrendering after Napoleon's first abdication and not submitting until a bona fide representative from the French government confirmed Napoleon's abdication. Snubbed by the Bourbons for his epic defence of Hamburg, he had to defend himself against bogus charges by them after his return to France. Clearing himself easily, he refused to swear any oath of loyalty to them, holding them in contempt both as the royal family and as men.

Davout rejoined Napoleon immediately after the latter's return and was made Minister of War, which undoubtedly was a waste of his military talent, but Paris was held under his firm hand and the shenanigans of the year before did not take place after Napoleon went north.

Ferdinand von Funck, Saxon orderly officer and aide-de-camp, left this interesting sketch of the Iron Marshal:

Of the Marshals, Davout was the only one who always maintained strict and exemplary discipline, and, however much his despotic rule was the curse of every country he occupied, history will in due course do justice to his virtues. Above self-seeking as his character was, he never took the veriest trifle for himself or his establishment. He made prompt payment for everything beyond what was due him as a Marshal for his big household and staff, and enforced the same conduct on the generals subordinate to him. He kept his supply officers strictly to heel. He never accepted table money or presents of any kind himself, and was careful to see that none of his subordinates did. He wrung the requirements of his forces sternly and inexorably out of the provinces, but he was equally inexorable in punishing every high-handed exaction; and a crust of bread thrown away might easily have a death sentence for its sequel. The provinces in which he held command always felt secure in his incorruptible sense of discipline. But his suspiciousness, that made him see an enemy of the Emperor in every non-Frenchman and always scented conspiracies, and his blind devotion to Napoleon, whose orders he carried out with relentless severity, made him hated everywhere.[6]

Heinrich von Brandt, who was interviewed by Davout early in his career, left this account of the 'Iron Marshal':

Upon my arrival in Warsaw I was sent for by order of the governor, to whom I was introduced after being kept waiting an inordinate amount of time. Marshal Davout was then at the prime of his life (thirty-eight years), and was a man of medium height with a robust complexion and lively, intelligent features despite being prematurely bald – something which tended to accentuate a look of severity.

After describing how he had been grilled in the interview by the marshal, von Brandt continued, 'He dismissed me there and then. I later understood that he took this kind of tone with all young officers in the same position as myself.'[7]

Davout, whose temper was violent when aroused, is described again by von Brandt:

In the middle of the ceremony it was announced that some cuirassiers had broken into the shops and were pillaging the lace just as they would a town taken by storm. Marshal Davout sent one of his aides, and those responsible were arrested, taken before a court-martial and shot the next day. But this regrettable incident was the final straw for Davout, who had already been rankled by various other such incidents. Ina general review, held on 12 July, he lost his temper and vented his spleen on a [Dutch] regiment in Compans' division which had been reduced from a strength of four battalions to just a few hundred men despite not having fired a shot. The marshal bawled at the officers and had the regiment march past the rest of the troops with its musket butts in the air. This was a harsh chastisement and unfair, as those who had resisted the temptation had been punished rather than those who were in fact guilty.[8]

Charles-Antoine-Louis-Alexis Morand (1771–1835) was elected captain in the 7e Bataillon des Volunteers du Droueys in 1792, being promoted to Lieutenant Colonel later that same year. His service from 1792–97 was with the Rhine armies and was sent to Italy in 1797 with Bernadotte's division. He was prompted the chef de brigade of the 88e Demi-Brigade in 1798 and general of brigade the next year. He was with Desaix, and later Friant, in Upper Egypt from 1798 to 1801.

He was a brigade commander in Soult's IV Corps in 1805, and was transferred to command Cafferelli's old division in III Corps in 1806. From then until after Russia he served Davout, not always happily. However, he was an excellent division commander and served loyally and ably.

1813 found Morand in Saxony in Bertrand's IV Corps, later commanding its remnants in Mayence from late 1813–14. Morand rallied to Napoleon in 1815, commanding an Old Guard infantry division in Belgium and also serving as an Imperial Aide-de-Camp.

Louis Friant (1758–1829) enlisted in the Gardes Français in February 1781, becoming a corporal of grenadiers in 1782 and rising to sergeant by 1787. 1798 found Friant as a corporal fourrier in the Paris National Guard. By 1792 he was Lieutenant Colonel of the 9e Bataillon of it. Assigned as chief of staff to Scherer in July 1794, he was promoted to general of brigade the next year. He was in Bernadotte's division in 1797 and was transferred with that division to the Armée d'Italie, where he commanded an infantry brigade. He went with Desaix to Egypt, serving as a brigade commander.

After Desaix's departure from Egypt, Friant became commander of the division in Upper Egypt and served well for the rest of the campaign. He returned to France in 1801 with the rest of the 'Egyptians' and served as Inspector General of Infantry from 1801–3. That year he was transferred and given a division in what was to become the famous III Corps under Davout, who was Friant's brother-in-law. Friant made all the major campaigns with III Corps through 1809, being known as one of the 'three immortals (along with Gudin and Morand) after Auerstadt in 1806.

He remained in Germany with Davout after Tilsit and again after Wagram and was again a division commander for Davout in the I Corps that went into

Russia. Assigned to the Old Guard in early 1813, he commanded a Young Guard division in Saxony in 1813 and the 2d Old Guard division in Belgium in 1815. He served under Mortier in 1814. He was wounded in the Guard's last attack at Waterloo.

Friant was an excellent infantry commander and had a knack of leading foreign troops. One of the best division commanders in the Grande Armée, his service was marked with distinction and loyalty. He and his division are famous for their forced march to Austerlitz from Vienna in time to support Davout's effort on the French right flank.

Charles Etienne Gudin de la Sablonnière (1768–1812) was a nephew of General Etienne Gudin, to whom he was an aide-de-camp in 1793. He attended the Ecole Militaire de Brieene and was a gendarme supernumerary in the Garde du Roi in 1782. By 1784 he was a sous-lieutenant in the Artois Régiment de Infanterie, which later became the 45e Ligne. By December 1793 he was a chef de bataillon and a chef de brigade in June 1795. The next year he was chosen as chief of staff to St Cyr and was promoted to general of division in 1796. He was promoted to general of division in 1800.

Gudin was assigned to the troops that were to become the III Corps in 1803 and made all of the major campaigns with Davout (III and I Corps) for the remainder of his career. Justly famous for his performance and conduct at Auerstadt, being the first of Davout's divisions on the field, he was killed in action at the battle of Valutino in 1812. Close to Davout, he was greatly missed and for the first time since 1806 the 'three immortals' were no longer in the field together.

Jean-Baptiste Jules Bernadotte (1763–1844) was the only marshal to retain a crown after the wars, and he accomplished that fact by turning on Napoleon and his native land. He enlisted in the Régiment Royal-Marine when he was seventeen and was first sergeant eight years later. Promoted to lieutenant in 1791 he was a general of division by1794.

An ambitious, scheming, distrustful and unreliable comrade, Bernadotte had the ability to have others do his dirty work. He was also tall, courageous in action and a competent tactician. He also was capable of acts of moral courage, as in 1790 when he protected his commanding officer from a Marseilles mob.

He was assigned with his division to the Armée d'Italie in 1797 and Desaix thought him impressive. In 1799 he was sent as Ambassador to Vienna and left in a hurry as he was run out of town. He was also briefly the Minister of War until just as quickly fired and placed on inactive status.

Bernadotte commanded the I Corps in 1805–7 until he was wounded and replaced by Victor. He served credibly at Austerlitz, but his performance on the day of Jena and Auerstadt was treacherous, spending his time marching between the two battlefields and not becoming engaged. His men did not even have to clean their weapons. He definitely disobeyed orders and did not support Davout. His slowness in marching southward, said by him to be following the intent of his orders, ensured that he would not be engaged at Jena either, though there was time and opportunity for either course of action.

Employed in 1809 as commander of the Saxons, he commanded limply, was insubordinate and was relieved and sent home by Napoleon. Bernadotte was approached by the Swedes to become the Crown Prince to their fading Royal family. He accepted and the Swedes thought he was a loyal henchman of Napoleon. Bernadotte instead realigned Sweden with her traditional enemy, Russia and became one of Tsar Alexander's clients.

He re-entered the lists against Napoleon in 1813, was cautious enough with his Swedes so as to not incur excessive casualties, and was not trusted by his allies. He hoped to also become King of France after Napoleon's first abdication, but that was a pipe dream.

Davout's expert handling of his corps at Auerstadt enabled him to take apart the main Prussian army and rout it. He almost accomplished the same thing at Eylau. His epic defence of Hamburg made him famous, and his name a synonym for loyalty and steadfastness. He was the personification of the French term *Feu Sacré*, the sacred fire, which was the ultimate desire to win or not come back.

While Waterloo may be the most studied battle of the Napoleonic Wars, the Jena–Auerstadt campaign might be the least understood. The Prussian army was greatly feared by Napoleon, and there are many indications that Napoleon did not want this war with Prussia. The Prussians had a reputation second to none from the Seven Years War, so why did the Prussians lose, and lose so completely and quickly?

Much has been written and more analysis has taken place, possibly, on the campaign of 1806 in Saxony between the Grande Armée under Napoleon and his veteran commanders and the Prussian/Saxon army under the Duke of Brunswick and his well-intentioned king, Frederick William III, than on any other Napoleonic campaign, with the exception of Waterloo. It has even been analysed as a campaign study in the course on the history of the military art at West Point.

It is generally agreed that the Prussians had antiquated and aging generals, and that is usually submitted as the main reason for their defeat at the hands of the French. That is only one of the reasons for the disaster that took place in October 1806 when, in three weeks of manoeuvre, battle, and unsparing pursuit, the Prussian army was completely destroyed, except for a few units that were stationed in East Prussia.

Gerhard von Scharnhorst, the former Hanoverian artillery officer who became the greatest of Prussia's military reformers both before and after the debacle of 1806, was particularly blunt on this point after the campaign, stating the Prussian officer corps did not know how to command (he was also quite succinct on the shameful conduct of fortress commanders who surrendered to inferior numbers of aggressively led and commanded French troops).[9]

An interesting incident that occurred a week before Jena will illustrate the full import of Scharnhorst's frustration when trying to reason with Prussia's recalcitrant nobility. In early October 1806, the Duke of Brunswick received indications that the Grande Armée was moving north toward the Thuringen Forest as Scharnhorst had foreseen. Captain Muffling, a member of Scharnhorst's staff section, was sent on a hasty reconnaissance to confirm this alarming news. Observing the French army in Ansbach, he noticed 'the ease of movement of their infantry'. Three days later Muffling reported to Prussian headquarters that all French company officers 'were of foot with packs on their backs, while our battalions require 50 luxury horses!' According to Muffling, General Ruchel responded: 'My friend, a Prussian nobleman does not walk.'[10]

Scharnhorst made the point that French junior officers marched with the troops and carried their own packs. Russian and Austrian officers also walked. Scharnhorst was adamant that Prussian infantry officers share their men's hardships and that meant that they walked and carried their own kit. He further stated that Prussia could not afford a horse for every officer.[11]

Moreover the point was made that the Prussians, and their Saxon allies, required regular issues of food, fodder and even firewood, and this placed an undue burden on the supply system. It was recommended that levying contributions and at least attempting to live of the land if necessary be used. As the troops were not used to this type of campaigning, during the Jena campaign they frequently went hungry and cold.

The Prussian failure was a combination of factors: the outmoded tactics and organisation of the Prussian army, its staff organisation and functioning, and the failure to organise, train, employ light infantry, even though urged by such officers as Scharnhorst to do so.

The Prussian army that marched off to defeat and disaster at Jena and Auerstadt was the relic of Frederick the Great's allegedly invincible army. One of the main causes for the Prussian defeat at Jena is that the army was still built and organised on mid-eighteenth-century policies, and that half of the personnel in 1806 were mercenaries.

Frederick was responsible for the decline of the Prussian army after the Seven Years War. The army as he had inherited it had native Prussians outnumbering foreigners by two to one. Frederick's goal was to reverse that ratio and that native cantonists should not be more than three per cent of the native adult male population of Prussia.[12]

Further, between 1751 and 1786, the year of Frederick's death, the number of foreigners in the Prussian army grew continually until by 1786 almost half of the army was composed of foreigners of various nationalities.[13]

The Prussian system of conscription was supposedly universal, but in fact many native Prussians were exempt from military service, among them artisans and the entire upper classes, and the burden of military service fell on the farm workers and the peasants. Even many of these were only required to serve two months out of the year and were furloughed to ensure that large landholders, on whose land these men worked, were not inconvenienced. Thus the Prussian army was only at anything approximating full strength during peacetime in April and May.[14]

Recruiting foreigners was expensive, and the foreigners had to be watched as they were prone to desertion. The foreigners were in reality nothing but 'cannon fodder', used to do nothing but fill the ranks of the Prussian regiments.[15]

The effects of Frederick the Great's practices increased towards the end of his reign and were continued by his successors. The numbers of mercenaries in the army continued to grow, the efficiency declined and Frederick the Great's insistence on nobility for his officers resulted in the middle class officers being discharged at the end of the Seven Years War. It was, though, the practice of extended furloughs that greatly reduced the efficiency of the army, and the training and cohesion of the army subsequently suffered.

Recruit training and the Royal Manoeuvres were reduced to the bare minimum. Training was inadequate and overall efficiency decreased exponentially. Further, the furlough system was finally extended to the native Prussian professionals in the ranks. The army was only together for a period of from four to ten weeks per year.[16]

In this general deterioration the much-vaunted officer corps was affected fully as much as the rank and file: 'the flower of Frederick the Great's officer corps was killed off in the Seven Years War'.[17] Frederick's rigid exclusion of bourgeois officers from the army after 1763 not only deprived the army of talented and experienced officers but imposed a military burden upon the native nobility which it could not bear alone. The net result of this was that commissions had to be given to foreigners with noble patents and, although many distinguished officers came to the Prussian service in this way – including Scharnhorst, who was ennobled before his admission to the Prussian army in 1801 – many less-than-qualified personnel came as well.

Some progressive officers, such as Scharnhorst who had transferred from the

Hanoverian service and who had seen action against the French in the Revolutionary Wars, however, did note the changes that had been introduced by the French, some intentionally and some quite by accident. Some were because of experimentation due to the defeats in the Seven Years War. One of the more interesting comments Scharnhorst made was that the French had learned from their repeated defeats in the Seven Years War. Further, he was convinced that if the Prussians did not adopt the French innovations in tactics, organisation and administration, the Prussians would fail.[18] Some of the new ideas were from theorists, many of them soldiers themselves, who advocated change in both organisation and tactics. Some were practical, wanting better artillery, and some were innovative, who wanted co-operation between the different arms on the battlefield to be a matter of practice, institutionalising it so it would be uniform, standard operating procedure if you will, as in the French army as a whole.

While the composition of the army was not the sole reason for defeat in 1806, it was a major contributor. The Prussian army was not a cohesive fighting force and, because of the cost-cutting policies of furloughing much of the army for ten months of the year, neither was it a well-trained force, used to working and training together. In large part, the enlisted men were not known by their officers, and they were not toughened to the rigours of campaign because of the furlough policy.

In 1806, the Prussian light infantry arm consisted of twenty-four battalions of fusiliers and one Jäger regiment, which was commanded by Colonel Yorck. While these troops had been trained in the light service, the fusiliers were still, doctrinally, to be held in massed formation most of the time, with only some of the unit deployed in open order, and never were they to be deployed as a complete unit, as the French habitually did with their light infantry, and their line infantry as well when the tactical situation called for it. The jägers were tactically hamstrung in 1806, and Yorck's influence as their commander considerably reduced, by the unit being parcelled out among the Prussian divisions throughout the campaign.[19] Some units, had, however, been trained 'in the French manner' and did well.[20]

Consequently, during Grawert's division-sized attack against Verzehnheilegen, there was little light infantry available to support it and the Prussian line battalions, with very few exceptions, were not trained in open-order tactics. They met the French, who were deployed in open order and taking cover in the village, walled gardens and in the terrain to either side of the village. Stopping inside musket range to dress ranks and come on line, all four of Grawert's line regiments stood in the open for over two hours volleying on command against the French, causing little harm, while the French infantry's aimed fire shot the Prussians to pieces. Losses were particularly heavy among the Prussian officers and NCOs.[21]

Lannes's infantry, Grawert's opponents, had displayed a tactical finesse and expertise throughout the battle. Lannes's divisions fought in line and battalion column, advancing to the attack in both, both formations being covered by swarms of light infantry which paved the way for the French attacks. 'Lannes corps moved forward, partly in line and partly in column, the whole front covered as usual by dense swarms of skirmishers.'[22] The Prussians could not penetrate the thick skirmisher screen, though at both Jena and Auerstadt, skirmishers were sometimes driven back by determined Prussian infantry attacks. The open-ordered French infantry always returned to their main objective once the Prussian attack was spent or driven back — to continue fighting in open order firing on their own against the tight Prussian ranks, inflicting heavy losses and paving the way for French infantry assaults. There were apparently little or no light infantry available to screen or skirmish for Grawert, and his troops stood in the open to be shot down methodically in large numbers by the better-deployed French infantry.

Lannes also performed the very difficult passage of lines straight out of the 1791 Règlement when his first line was running low on ammunition. Passing the second line through the first, and the attacks, continued unabated on the Prussian infantry. It was a virtuoso performance by both the French commanders and their troops.

Gerhard Scharnhorst (1755–1813) and other far-thinking Prussian officers, such as Karl Freiherr von dem Knesebeck and Ludwig Wilhelm von Boyen, attempted reforms in the period 1801–5, going so far to form what would now be called a 'think-tank' for the modernisation of the Prussian army. This *Militarische Gesellschaft* met in Berlin and produced many worthwhile papers on the tactics, organisation and administration of the period. It was an uphill fight, however, and gaining support among the greater majority of Prussian general officers was difficult, if not impossible.

What is also interesting is that the Prussians did not perform very well in any engagement or conflict from 1763 to 1807, when Lestocq's small Prussian corps and Gneisenau's defence of Kolberg drew admiration and results.[23] Even the Prussian army's performance in the War of the Bavarian Succession, the so-called 'Potato War' in which there were no engagements of note, was dismal.

Scharnhorst and his colleagues both had enough combat experience among them and had seen the French on the battlefield and on campaign to understand that new methods of warfare, from tactics to army organisation and administration, were being employed successfully by the French. Furthermore, their leadership were fully schooled in its application, mostly on the battlefield.[24]

The French employment of light infantry was of the most interest to

Scharnhorst and others who wanted to improve the Prussian army. Knesebeck mentioned that he had witnessed at least six engagements where the French had deployed all of their infantry in open order and were able to gain an advantage against their more rigidly deployed opponents.[25]

The writings of such officers as Knesebeck undoubtedly helped in the formation and improvement of the Prussian light troops and infantry tactics, as well as hasten the military reforms that were badly needed after Jena and Auerstadt. Scharnhorst, Boyen, Knesebeck and others were adamant on the need for the Prussian officer corps to be both educated and introspective. Scharnhorst himself further believed that it was in the light service that officers learned the most. The light infantry could teach promising young officers how to operate independently and develop skills that could be used when they became senior officers.[26]

Even among the reformers, though, opinions differed on the training and use of light infantry. Knesebeck believed that line and light infantry were too different to be combined and that they had to be organised and trained separately. Even after witnessing the French employment of line and light infantry, he was still convinced that they were two different entities. Scharnhorst differed greatly in this aspect of light infantry employment, believing that the French light infantry were the key to their success on the battlefield.[27]

Captain Ludwig von Boyen, later to be War Minister after Waterloo and who attempted to sustain the gains of the Reformers in peacetime after the danger had passed, was the author of a paper supporting the use of line infantry as light infantry if necessary, as the French employed infantry. Boyen believed that any infantry unit might encounter situations on the battlefield that could only be solved by using open order tactics or by fighting *en tirailleur*.[28]

However, Knesebeck, as well as Scharnhorst, Boyen and the others, believed that both the Austrians and Prussians could learn much from the employment and fighting ability of the French light infantry. Scharnhorst's opinion on the French ability to not only use light infantry, but combined arms employment, especially between infantry and artillery, was decisive on the battlefield.[29]

One of the things that deeply impressed Scharnhorst and other progressive Prussian officers was the ability of the French light infantryman, or tirailleur, to act on his own initiative, while still fighting and operating as part of a team.[30] From the available evidence, neither the Prussian senior leadership, nor for that matter the Austrian or Russian equivalents, believed that infantry operating in open order as part of a larger whole, or on their own could be an effective battlefield asset. All three generally believed that the numbers of Jäger or other light infantry in their own armies were sufficient. Scharnhorst, on the other hand, did not agree that German jägers and fusiliers were the same as the French light infantry. Heretically, he believed the French light infantryman to be superior to his German, and Prussian, counterparts.[31]

Scharnhorst, from both experience and personal observation, believed that the infantry should fight in a much less rigid and geometric manner, combat now being a much more fluid, rambling business, where individual initiative, on the part of both the officer and enlisted man could have decisive results.

In the higher levels of the Prussian service this was tantamount to heresy, as the famous Prussian drill, harsh discipline and controlled volley fire were thought to be able to overcome any obstacle on the battlefield. Additionally, many Prussian officers thought that the French were simply going through a process that was just a fashion that would eventually pass, and that warfare would revert to what it had been, with the Prussian method supreme and copied by all.[32] They failed to see that warfare itself had changed and that, as the Bourbons were to learn in 1814, the clock cannot be turned back. Scharnhorst and others had figured this out on their own.

Further, Scharnhorst fully believed that the 'physical ability and high intelligence of the common man enables the French tirailleurs to profit from all advantages offered by the terrain and the general situation, while the phlegmatic Germans, Bohemians and Dutch form on open ground and do nothing but what their officer orders them to do.'[33]

Much, if not most, of what Scharnhorst and company talked about and recommended came to fruition, but only after the disaster of 1806. Major Karl Anton Count de la Roche-Aymon, a French émigré officer in the Prussian service stated in 1808:

At the start of the Revolutionary Wars, the French government decided to introduce new tactics ... Instead of the line they chose the column...regular fire was exchanged for the tirailleur system, and thus the basic elements of the French victories were formed ... Now the corps and divisional commanders no longer recognise the existence of terrain dangerous to them; they only know more or less favorable ground on which they are able to fight at any time.[34]

Finally, the competent and intelligent Prince August, who served well at Auerstadt in command of a grenadier battalion stated that the military theorists of the eighteenth century 'recognised the advantages offered by an intelligent combination of line and light infantry. The French were the first to carry out this excellent idea on a large scale from which arrangement they derive important advantages'.[35]

The bottom line, though, was that 'In the Prussian army the introduction of light infantry battalions and company sharpshooters was undertaken in too formalistic a manner to achieve the same results' that the French achieved in their light infantry units as well as their line outfits.

In conclusion, the Prussian army missed the lessons of the French Revolutionary Wars. Generally unwilling to modernise to new tactical systems, such as having a general staff capable of relieving the commander of all detailed work and a flexible tactical and operational organisation, doomed them to failure in 1806. They were amply warned, but the harbingers went unnoticed or ignored.

Some reform was attempted. Staff functioning was improved, more light infantry were raised and trained, and the army organised, shortly before the campaign opened, into permanent divisions. However, the staff was neither as large nor as efficient as Berthier's in the Grande Armée.[36] The divisions organised were divisions of all arms, which the French had abandoned in 1800 in favour of the corps d'armée system. Light and line infantry were not integrated and their functions remained separate, as this brief study has demonstrated. The French system was not understood, and the Prussian infantry went into combat unprepared for modern warfare.

The campaign of 1806 ended with the near-complete destruction of the 'long-feared' Prussian army. The Prussian generals had fought that campaign with an army that was the remains of what Frederick had put into the field in the Seven Years War. However, there was no Frederick to lead or inspire it in 1806. The Prussian leadership was too old, too pedantic, and indecisive. Frederick William was the nominal commander, but he failed to rein in his bickering generals, and, when he did have the chance to assume command of the main Prussian army at Auerstadt after Brunswick's mortal wounding, he remained in action on the left flank, 'displaying great bravery' and winning the respect of his troops, but displaying no comprehension of what was happening across the field as a whole.

What this tells us is that the military and tactical conservatism of the Prussian leadership kept the level of training at that of the Seven Years War, and that new tactical innovations, such as the French employment of skirmishers in large numbers as a decisive element in the attack, were either ignored or overlooked. Scharnhorst agreed with this assessment. Most Prussian officers were unwilling to either allow line infantry to fight in open order, or to employ their light troops in the proven French method. This outlook would definitely change after 1806.

CHAPTER 6

LET US GO AMONG THEM

The great cavalry charge at Eylau, 1807

It would be better for us if he were less brave and had a little more common sense. SAVARY
ON MURAT

*An army can march anywhere and at any time of the year, wherever two men can place their
feet.* NAPOLEON

10:00 21 February 1807, near Preussich-Eylau East Prussia
In the days of the old Royal Army, they, like gentlemen, had not fought in the
dead of winter. They had gone into winter quarters to sit out the worst weather
and they would attempt to enjoy themselves while doing it.

The Emperor never allowed minor details, such as the weather, to get in his
or the Grande Armée's way. General Lepic, commander of the Grenadiers à
Cheval of the Imperial Guard was undoubtedly more concerned about the
Russian artillery and what they might do to his regiment before they could get
into action on this very cold February day. His shivering trumpeter, behind him
and to his left, continually rubbed the mouth-piece of his brass instrument with
his gauntleted hand to keep it from freezing so his mouth would not stick to the
metal when and if the time came to sound the next call.

In front of them the Russian army finally stood to fight. The troops were
eager to get at the Russians, if for no other reason than to get a warm bivouac.
The night before there had been a lively brawl between the half-frozen troops of
Marshal Soult's IV Corps and the Russian advance guard which had taken up
residence for the evening in the tiny village of Preussich-Eylau. The engagement
served no other purpose than to secure even semi-adequate shelter against the
elements for the night, no matter what the Imperial staff said or thought. They
were usually wrong, anyway. Soult's men had won, and a good thing it was, too.

As Lepic motioned to one of his officers, the artillery duel between the outnumbered French guns and their Russian counterparts increased in intensity. Simultaneously, Augereau's VII Corps began to advance through the falling snow against the Russian centre. Originally sheltered from observation behind some low hills, the massed ranks of Augereau's troops, led by the sick marshal, his battered *chapeau* tied to his head by a ragged bandana, began to deploy in the face of the gradually worsening snow storm and the more lethal Russian artillery bombardment.

By accident or design, Russian artillery fire began to find the range and fall among the usually stoic Grenadiers à Cheval. Occasionally one would find a target and hit home. Men and horses would scream and go down, bits and pieces of them hitting men to either side of the victims and staining the snow bright red. Witnessing their comrades being knocked from their saddles by round shot or pinioned beneath dead or dying mounts, the troopers began to chafe from taking casualties and not being able to hit back.

Eventually, they began to duck as incoming rounds whistled over the formation. Lepic became mildly enraged. His grenadiers 'saluted' no one, especially not the Russians. Turning in his saddle and shouting in his usual parade ground voice he chastised his troopers with the command, 'Heads up, by God! Those are cannon balls, not turds!' The shocked and amused cavalrymen immediately forgot or ignored the imminent danger from the Russian artillery rounds and sat their horses at attention, their chuckling NCOs going about their business of dressing ranks.

The Napoleonic Wars mark the epitome of the evolution of the cavalry. Throughout the period, ever-increasing swarms of cavalry were employed in a myriad of missions and never before had Europe seen such an impressive array of cavalrymen pass by. Very rapidly, as both the size of armies increased and the skill of commanders in the use of the mounted arm grew, large formations of cavalry were organised for both operational and tactical missions. Cavalry regiments were formed into brigades, those brigades eventually into divisions, and sometimes cavalry divisions were organised into cavalry corps.

The most famous of these cavalry formations was the Cavalry Reserve of the Grande Armée, which would itself be comprised in the later empire of a number of cavalry corps. From 1805 to 1807 the Cavalry Reserve was commanded by the flamboyant Joachim Murat, whose ability to deliver mass charges, leading from the front, became legendary.

Joachim Murat (1767–1815) is usually considered the '*beau sabreur*' of the period. He commanded the Grande Armée's Cavalry Reserve in the campaigns of 1805–7 and again in 1812 and 1813. However, he never learned to care properly for his men nor his mounts and this was never more apparent than in 1812 where his ignorance and negligence ruined the French cavalry.

One of Murat's problems was that he had too little regimental service, and so missed out on learning the rudiments of the profession of senior officer. Murat was a somewhat scruffy enlisted man in a French cavalry regiment, transferring to the Garde Constitutionelle in 1792 but was unceremoniously discharged the next month under cloudy circumstances.

He returned to his original outfit and was promoted to chef d'escadron late in 1793, but was involved in intrigue against his commanding officer. His regiment was posted to Paris in 1795 and he was given the mission on the night of October 4–5 of seizing the guns that gave General Bonaparte the upper hand and fired the 'whiff of grapeshot' and saved the French government from a Royalist coup. Murat became Napoleon's aide-de-camp when Napoleon assumed command of the Armée d'Italie, and Murat 'more or less' promoted himself to colonel.

Murat married Caroline Bonaparte, thus becoming part of the Bonaparte clan. He also had the ability to animate and move forward masses of men and led in person. He went with Napoleon to Egypt and supported his brother-in-law in the 1799 *coup d'état*. Promoted on the first list of marshals, he was given command of the newly constituted Cavalry Reserve, with a good chief of staff to keep him out of trouble.

A superb combat leader, Murat led the Cavalry Reserve with panache and dedication from 1805–7. He was at his finest at the head of his massed squadrons, sometimes charging, as at Jena, with nothing but a light whip in his hand. Other times, as Elzear Blaze noted, he always came back with blood dripping from his sabre. The huge massed charge at Eylau was probably his greatest achievement.

Murat was not a tactician and had no idea of strategy, but, as Odeleben noted in 1813, Murat 'threw himself into the midst of the enemy in the strongest sense of the word'. Savary's comment in 1807 was more telling: 'It would be better for us if he were less brave and had a little more common sense.'

The Russian campaign depressed him and he deserted his post after Napoleon left for Paris without designating a successor. If it were not for Berthier insisting on Eugène taking command, the disaster would have been even worse.

First given Cleves-Berg to rule, Napoleon then gave Naples and a crown to Murat, Napoleon's brother Joseph being 'transferred' to Spain as its new king. Murat was sincere in his kingship, tried to rule well and his implementation of law and order, as well as honest government, were not appreciated by some of his new subjects. He was also bullied by his wife who finally convinced him to turn traitor in 1813 to keep the crown. Murat was a good comrade, kind to prisoners and defeated enemies. He was also generous and open-handed, and he had aided people who were on Napoleon's bad side, as Josephine also had.

He turned to Napoleon again in 1815, but his inept performance ended in front of a Neapolitan firing squad after trying to regain his kingdom.

Murat's performance as a cavalry commander gradually improved through 1805–7 and his best performance was undoubtedly in the great French cavalry charge at Eylau, where he led over 10,000 veteran cavalrymen against the centre of the Russian line that had just destroyed Augereau's VII Corps.

Murat's lack of experience on the regimental level meant he needed a good staff, especially a good chief of staff. In that category, he was ably seconded in the Cavalry Reserve by General Belliard, who was chief of staff of the Cavalry Reserve from 1805–7 and again in 1809. An excellent cavalryman and premier staff officer, Belliard was exactly the man that Murat needed to ensure that the men and horses in the divisions were well taken care of and managed. Belliard was one of the unsung heroes of the Grande Armée.

Auguste-Daniel Belliard (1769–1832) is justly remembered for his excellent work as chief of staff. Keeping track of Murat must have been a major endeavour in itself. A junior officer in the Ier Bataillon de Volontaires de la Vendée, Belliard had service as a staff officer from 1792–3 and was promoted to chef de bataillon in 1793. Suspended from the army that July, he volunteered for the 3e Chasseurs à Cheval a year later.

By 1795 he was adjutant general and chef de brigade. He was in the Armée d'Italie under Napoleon, being chief of staff to Serurier, and was promoted to general of brigade after Arcola. With Desaix in Egypt, he returned with the Armée de l'Orient after the French defeat. He was chief of staff to Murat from 1805–8 and again in 1812. Service in Spain from 1808 to 1811 was followed by the command of a cavalry division in 1814.

Rallying to Napoleon in 1815, he served as Napoleon's personal liaison with Murat in 1815 after Napoleon's return, but apparently Murat did not take either his advice or Napoleon's instructions on what to do with his (Murat's) precarious position as King of Naples.

Jean Joseph Ange Comte d'Hautpoul (1754–1807) entered the army as a gentleman cadet in 1771 and belonged to an old but poor family from Gascony. Poorly educated, he commanded the 6e Chasseurs à Cheval who stood by him in 1793 when the Revolutionary government tried to purge him as a noble. Shouting 'no d'Hautpoul, no 6e Chasseurs' his troopers refused to give him up, forcing the revolutionary hotheads to crawl back to Paris and feed some other unfortunate to the guillotine.

He was an outstanding combat leader, but found criticism when it was reported that he rated his subordinate unit's efficiency more by the commander's cravat than what they could actually accomplish. Courageous, leading with dash and panache, d'Hautpoul commanded a cuirassier division from 1805–7, leading it into the frozen hell of Eylau and dying there in the snow and cold.

Eylau was a unique battle for a number of reasons. First, it was fought in the dead of winter in one of the worst possible places – eastern Europe. Second, it marked the destruction of one of the original corps d'armée of the Grande Armée that had been so successful in 1805 and 1806. Third, it demonstrated that properly led, Prussian troops could still perform well and was a foreboding of 1813–14. Last, the losses incurred by the Grande Armée were staggering. Any other army of this period that suffered losses of this magnitude might well have fallen apart. Bennigsen's Russian army after Friedland certainly did. It is a testament to the training, discipline, organisation and leadership of the Grande Armée that it not only remained a cohesive unit on the field that day, but it recovered to be ready in the spring to again resume the offensive.

After the stunning success of the 1806 campaign against Prussia, the war continued against the Russians and the Prussian remnants in Poland and East Prussia. The fighting was savage and the weather and terrain were worse. Casualties mounted from both enemy action and sickness, and making war on the eastern edge of Europe was more than difficult. Napoleon's problem was massing enough troops in the decisive sector and bringing Benningsen's army to engage in a decisive battle.

Snow covered the ground where the battle took place and the rivers, lakes and ponds were frozen over. On reaching the battlefield on 7 February, the French drove in the Russian outposts and Soult attacked Bagration's Russians and drove them out of the village of Preussich-Eylau, gaining for his cold and miserable troops shelter for the night.

8 February dawned cold and dark and the Russian cannonade began as soon as the sun started to appear over the horizon. French artillery replied and one of the most bloody and hard-fought battles of the period began in earnest.

The previous evening Murat and Soult attacked and outflanked the Russian Bagration, whose troops held the hamlet of Preussich-Eylau. The most probably reason for Soult conducting what was essentially a night operation was to take Eylau for the night as shelter against the extreme cold. Bagration was driven out of Eylau after several hours of fighting, Soult's IV Corps settling in for the night, licking its wounds.

Bennigsen had 60,000 troops on the field, Napoleon somewhat fewer. As dawn crept over the snow-covered horizon, no more than 45,000 French

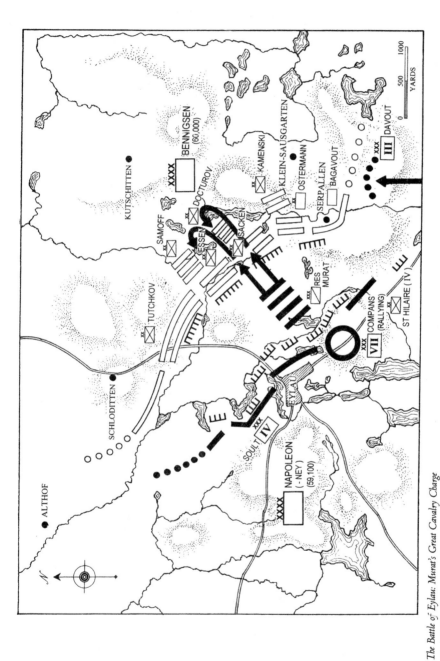

The Battle of Eylau: Murat's Great Cavalry Charge

Murat led his cavalry forward in a column of divisions, Grouchy leading. This attack ruined the Russian centre, and combined with Davout's flank attack that was just starting when Murat led off, nearly crushed Bennigsen's army. Lestocq's timely intervention, by accident or design, outflanked Davout, who was driven back to a line about 500 yards north of Klein-Sausgarten. Davout rallied his corps, counter-attacked and gained back some of the lost ground, and was nearly back in Kutschitten when the fighting ceased around 22.00 hours.

veterans were in line of battle, though Davout was coming up quickly on the French right. The Russians had massed their artillery in three large batteries along their front. One of seventy pieces was directly across from Eylau. To its right there was a battery of sixty guns and to the left of another of forty. More artillery was in reserve.[1]

The French were not only outnumbered but outgunned, and the artillery duel was intense. Russian artillery fire was not accurate, but the sheer mass of incoming artillery rounds caused considerable casualties amongst Soult's corps.[2] However, much of the French army was under cover and this helped to minimise casualties. The Russians of all arms, on the other hand, were exposed to the massed fire of the expert French artillery and suffered greatly from their more accurate fire.[3]

Napoleon wanted to finish this as quickly as possible. Night came early in the winter and the weather was starting to turn bad. He would not wait for Ney to arrive and, as Davout's corps was forming for their flank attack, he wanted the French main effort to be a coordinated one. Augereau's VII Corps was given the mission of attacking the Russian centre.

Until Davout could get his corps to the field by forced marches and begin his attack of the Russian left flank, all Napoleon had available on the field was Augereau's VII Corps, Soult's IV Corps, Murat's Cavalry Reserve and the Imperial Guard.

Also heading for the battlefield from the north were two forces, one of which would be decisive for the outcome of the battle. Ney's VI Corps was pursuing Lestocq's Prussian command, both about the same size at around 10,000 men. Lestocq was marching desperately for Eylau, trying to be kept from being drawn into a major engagement with Ney. It was a running fight between the two almost the entire way to the battlefield, the Prussian finally outpacing his French opponent. Lestocq marched for Eylau at 08:00 with Ney not far behind. It was a race to see who could reinforce whose army first.

The Russians failed to take Windmill Hill at around 09:00, and shortly after Davout's flank attack began, slowly building up momentum and chewing up Russian units one after the other, steadily taking ground into the Russian rear. At 10:00 Napoleon ordered Augereau forward against the Russian centre.

Augereau, sick, but refusing to go to the rear and tying his hat to his head with a large handkerchief so he would not lose it, led his corps off into the assault. A huge snowstorm broke as the divisions stepped off, a violent wind blowing snow into the face of the advancing French. For all practical purposes, this blinded the French advance. Augereau's troops advanced into the teeth of a mass of artillery fire that was described as 'murderous'. To compound problems, his attack strayed off to his left and into the bombardment of friendly artillery. As if this were not enough, Russian cavalry attacked and Augereau's corps was decimated. This attack a failure and Davout's not yet gaining offensive momentum, it looked as if French fortunes on this field were dim.

Eylau is known for one of the most famous cavalry charges of the period. Murat had on hand and available for employment four cavalry divisions. One division of cuirassiers was commanded by d'Hautpoul and three divisions of dragoons were commanded by Grouchy, Klein and Milhaud. Faced with seeming disaster, Napoleon maintained his calm and presence of mind and coolly turned to Murat and ordered him to take his cavalry forward.[4] Murat acknowledged the order and he and his aide-de-camp, Captain Manhes, turned their horses and trotted off to join the Cavalry Reserve. Murat placed himself at the head of approximately 10,000 horsemen and led off into the snow in a column of divisions.[5]

Seemingly coming out of nowhere, the mass of French cavalry drove all before it in one of the most magnificent charges in military history. Murat certainly had his faults as a cavalry commander. On this field, however, he carried forward by sheer force of personal example a mass of cavalry that defeated the Russian cavalry that was cutting Augereau's troops to pieces and shattered the Russian centre, trampling the Russian first and second lines and forcing Bennigsen to commit his reserve to try and stop it.

Grouchy's driving attack struck the spent Russian cavalry like a juggernaut, splattering Muscovite horsemen in all directions and getting them away from the retreating French infantry. Grouchy, leading his men from the front, had his horse shot out from under him, but was remounted by a faithful aide-de-camp. Rallying his troopers, Grouchy again led them forward, supporting his committed first brigade with his second. His personal leadership and example were outstanding.

Milhaud led his division against the Russians in and around the village of Serpallen, forcing the Russians there to evacuate to the rear.

Murat, appearing out of nowhere in front of Grouchy's division, personally led them in a wild chevauchee against the Russian cavalry in the centre of their position. As his division wheeled to the left, Grouchy and Murat expertly led the victorious division against the Russian cavalry that advanced to meet them. With a whoop and a holler, the French dragoons, along with d'Hautpoul's cuirassiers who linked up with Grouchy on his right swept up the slope to the Russian masses. The shock had to be terrific. The Russian cavalry, whose advance was slow and methodical and lacked the dash and élan of the French attack, were overwhelmed by the dragoons and cuirassiers and driven back on their own infantry.[6]

Fresh Russian cavalry joined to mêlée, and Grouchy's dragoons were finally checked by this new onslaught. The cuirassiers, however, maintained both their formation and their momentum and swept all before them. Big men on big horses, they pressed their attack and broke the Russian line and overran a portion of their artillery cutting down the gunners who tried to stand and swept on. They broke the second line of Russian infantry and found themselves unsupported in the Russian rear.

There the Russian reserves – horse, foot and guns, met them near Anklappen, 2,500 yards from Murat's starting point. The situation was critical. Grouchy appeared to be checked and Milhaud was not within supporting distance. D'Hautpoul's division, now without their hard-riding commander who was mortally wounded in the snow, was apparently cut off from all support.

Bessières, the only man in the army who maintained his hair long and powdered in the old style, suddenly appeared out of nowhere with the cavalry of the Guard, trampling any and all Russians that stood in his path. Overrunning infantry and artillery, the two Guard cavalry regiments cut the cuirassiers loose, and they all wheeled and started to cut their way home.

Some cuirassiers and grenadiers à cheval got cut off by Cossacks and were roughly handled, but most got away and overran all in their path. Lepic, the commander of the grenadiers a cheval was actually called on to surrender by a Russian cavalry officer. His answer was to rally his troopers and fight his way out. He later told the Emperor that there was no way he would surrender; he'd die first.[7]

The driving attack by the French cavalry ruined the Russian centre and used up their reserves. It was also undertaken at heavy loss. Between 1,500 and 2,500 of the French horsemen were casualties, but the attack had shaken the Russian commander and convinced him that Napoleon was far from beaten. He had no idea how heavy the French losses were from Augereau's repulse and the Russian artillery bombardment.

To the north, Ney received Napoleon's order to rejoin the main army. Murat had gone forward around 11:00. Now the main effort was on the French right flank where Davout's almost irresistible assault was gaining momentum and the Russians were massing every available man and gun to try and stop it. The combination of Murat and Davout were too much for Bennigsen's troops. Davout, with his three divisions in line and ably supported by his corps cavalry under Marulaz, steadily outfought his opponents and drove in the Russian left flank. Russian units were literally falling apart and becoming intermixed. Many were heading for the Königsberg road and the Russian rear, wounded and 'survivors' alike, and the bloodbath was taking the shape of another decisive victory before the vagaries of war robbed the French of the fruits of their day's labour.

At 14:00 Lestocq reached the village of Althof, not far from the Russian right flank. With Ney rapidly approaching, Lestocq left a rearguard in Althof and marched for the Russian left flank which was being held by nothing but good luck. Attacking from march order, Lestocq by chance enveloped Davout's right flank, forcing the marshal to halt his advance and reorganise. This action saved the Russian army from encirclement and disaster.

The rest of the fight was between the Prussian and Russians under Lestocq and Davout. Suffering heavy losses which would amount to a third of the troops in III Corps by the end of the action, Davout not only stabilised the situation, but counter-attacked, again driving the Russians and their Prussian reinforcements before him. By the end of the action he had retaken much of the ground he had lost and the Russian line was at right angles to its original position. Nightfall and exhaustion had ended the fighting.

Ney reached Althof at 19:00, swallowing the rearguard left to delay him. By 20:00 he had taken Schlodditen and cut the Königsberg road in Benningsen's rear. However, believing himself not strong enough to hold there for the night, Ney withdrew to Althof, later repulsing an attack at 22:00 by Bennigsen. Bennigsen, looking at the French bivouac fires believed himself to be almost surrounded and ordered a withdrawal. Many of his subordinates protested, telling him he had just won a victory. His losses had been very heavy and most of his Russian units were in a mess. There were few men remaining around the colours and the only cohesive units he really had left were those in Lestocq's command. He had been outfought continuously all day by the French and was in no mood to either hold his ground or fight again the next day. Additionally, he was almost out of ammunition with no reserves to resupply his units. He ordered a withdrawal. The Russians began withdrawing at 24:00, the Prussians two hours later.

Soult reported the Russians leaving the battlefield around 03:00. Davout also reported them withdrawing on his front. He was seen with his ear to the ground listening for signs of the Russians pulling out. Napoleon knew his losses were very heavy. At least 20–25,000 French were casualties and there was nothing to show for it. It had been a long and hard fight, but the Russians had got away. There would have to be another campaign to defeat them and it would take a rested and reinforced Grande Armée to do it.

CHAPTER 7

LET NOT ONE ESCAPE

The battle of Friedland, 1807

It is very advantageous to rush unexpectedly on an enemy who has erred, to attack him suddenly and come down on him with thunder before he sees the lightning. NAPOLEON

The ideal army would be the one in which every officer would know what he ought to do in every contingency; the best possible army is the one that comes closest to this. I give myself only half the credit for the battles I have won, and a general gets enough credit when he is named at all, for the fact is that a battle is won by the army. NAPOLEON

06:00 14 June 1800 near Posthenen, East Prussia
The wry-necked,[1] tough-looking French general officer was watching the Russian divisions cross the pontoon bridges over the Alle and make their way through the streets of the little town of Friedland, deploying on the near side of the town facing the troops he was commanding. Why the Russian commander was crossing the river to come after him was mystifying to the Gascon, but crossing they were and his corps would have to hold them in place until Napoleon could arrive with the main body of the Grande Armée.

On the far side of the Alle, Russian batteries were going into position to cover the crossing and the deployment. The Russians had a mania about the number of guns they deployed. They had as many assigned to a division as the French assigned to a corps. Perhaps it was a practice they had developed to make up for their inaccurate shooting. More massive bombardments, even if their aim was a little off, could make up in volume what they lacked in accuracy.

The general had sent couriers off at a gallop to Napoleon to let him know the situation. If he could hold on to the Russians and keep them on the left bank of the Alle long enough for Napoleon to ride to the rescue, so to speak, then the anticipated battle with Bennigsen and his army could take place. Tough as Eylau had been in February, and the general had not been present at that one, he had no doubt what the outcome of a fight here would be.

The terrain was excellent and the developing Russian position was going to be split by a significant water obstacle. There was a large forest on the right which would be an excellent assembly area to mass for an attack on the Russian left flank. The general had ordered light troops into that forest and he could see them hustling to occupy it before the Russians were fully deployed.

There did not seem to be any urgency on the Russians' part. Perhaps they thought he would withdraw when he found out how many of them there were were in the field. If that were the case, Bennigsen would be disappointed. The general would hold his positions as long as he possibly could. He was confident he could hold through the day and it would take the Russians some time to destroy his corps. If not, it would take them some time to withdraw. The siting of their pontoon bridges was amateurish — all three fed into Friedland, which was itself tucked into a neat little bend in the river, ensuring that troops crossing them would feed into a bottleneck. Not a place from which to withdraw easily.

Lannes's whole command had yet to reach the field, but his subordinate commanders would be driving their troops forward if they had to. Even though this was a newly organised provisional command, the general had a reputation as a tough commander and a violent temper when roused to fury. He was confident that his corps would be on the field when needed. That being done, the general shut his glass and motioned to his immediate staff to follow him. The corps command group trotted smartly after their commander. Marshal Lannes, commander of the Reserve Corps of the Grande Armée wanted a closer look at his enemy.

The war begun by Prussia against the French Empire in the autumn of 1806 had flowed into Poland, mud and misery against the Russians and Prussian remnants after the destruction of the Prussian army at the battles of Jena–Auerstadt. The French pursuit that followed was ruthless; Prussian fortresses and prisoners being scooped up wholesale. Only units in East Prussia escaped the disaster. The Russians belatedly came to the aid of their defeated allies, which led to a bitter winter campaign in the miserable wastes of eastern Poland and East Prussia. It culminated in a vicious pounding match at Eylau in the bitter cold and snow in February 1807. Both armies, exhausted and suffering heavy casualties, went into winter quarters to retrain and refit.

Napoleon once again demonstrated his terrible genius for organisation, drawing units from secondary theatres to return the Grande Armée to fighting efficiency. Replacing commanders killed or disabled, the toughness of the Grande Armée reasserted itself, commanders ensuring their units were ready for campaigning in the spring and inspections from the Emperor. The armies again took the field in the spring and, after hard, indecisive campaigning, Bennigsen, the Russian commander, shoved his head into the tactical sack at the little village of Friedland on the River Alle. Crossing the river to engage and destroy the French corps of Marshal Lannes, Bennigsen thought he could quickly dispatch Lannes and recross the Alle without becoming decisively engaged. Knowing that Napoleon was within supporting distance with at least three corps, Lannes sent aides galloping off with messages for help and waged an expert delaying action to fix Bennigsen in place.

Bennigsen reached Friedland at 23:00 13 June. He immediately had his pontoniers throw three bridges across the Alle leading into Friedland, condemning any and all troops that went across the river into a bottleneck that would retard any withdrawal. By 24:00 part of Bagration's command was across the river as well as two other infantry divisions and Galitzin's cavalry command. These troops slowly went west from Friedland and by 03:00 were in a tactical brawl with Lannes's troops.

Lannes's advance guard reached the village of Posthenen around 01:00 24 June almost directly west of Friedland running into and splattering the Russian outposts they encountered in all directions. They immediately advance to the outskirts of Friedland. By 02:00 Lannes was in a position to see the Russians crossing the river in strength and prepares to fix them, sending aides to Napoleon to request all available support.

Lannes summoned all of his corps forward as quickly as possible as more Russians cross the river. Lannes at no time has anything near numbers parity with Bennigsen, but as an experienced advance guard commander and an expert tactician he knew how to take advantage of the ground to support his dispositions.

Grouchy arrived by 06:00 and assumed the role of chief of cavalry for all mounted units that were on the field.[2] He placed most of it on the French left around the hamlet of Heinrichsdorf and from there waged a cat-and-mouse game with the Russian horse that outnumbered him. Uvarov attacked around 06:00, but was outfought and outclassed by Grouchy, securing the French left flank for the time being.

Bennigsen attempted to take the forest of Sortlack on the French right flank. Lannes had made a great show of the strength he did not have, completely duping Bennigsen so as to force him into a fight there where the terrain and the skill of the French light infantry would minimise the disparity in numbers.

The open-order fighting in the forested area on the French right flank favoured the French. Better skirmishers, and better led, they fought the Russians

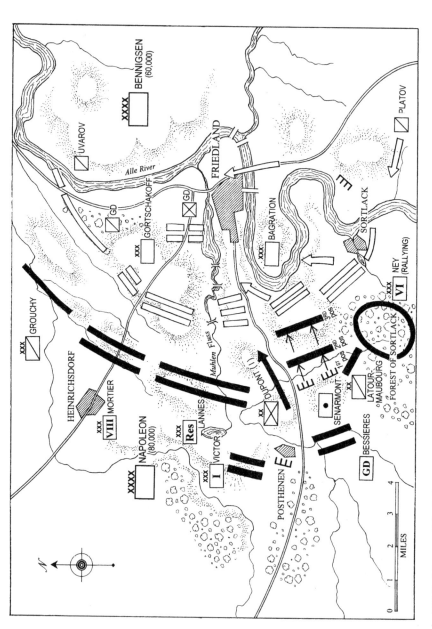

The Battle of Friedland: Senarmont Takes the Initiative

This is the situation during Senarmont's artillery attack and his destruction of the Russian centre. Ney had been repulsed and counter-attacked. Bagration's outnumbered command was either dead on the field, driven into the river, or into the Friedland bottleneck where it became a target for French artillery. On the French left, Grouchy had 'held the whip hand' all day, masterfully keeping the large numbers of Russian cavalry off the French infantry and from getting around the flank and into the French rear.

from tree to tree, gully to gully, and held their own against great numbers of frustrated Muscovites, who would almost push the French out of the forest, then be outflanked and driven out themselves.[3]

By 07:00 elements of Mortier's VIII Corps were arriving to support Lannes and by 07:45 Lannes had all of his infantry committed. At 09:00 Bennigsen attempted a major attack against the French left flank. Grouchy was up to it, cleverly using his reserves to repulse the Russians, and the Russian flanking attempt failed. After this failure, Bennigsen allowed the fighting to degenerate into nothing but an artillery duel, which suited Lannes, who needed time for reinforcements to arrive.

With never more than 26,000 men, Lannes forced Bennigsen to commit progressively more troops across the Alle to defeat him. Showing a bold front, and shifting troops where needed to stop Russian advances, especially in the forest of Sortlack on the French right, Lannes held Bennigsen in place until the French had massed 80,000 troops on the left bank of the river. Bennigsen was trapped and had to fight. Having thrown all of his pontoon bridges at or near the bottleneck of the village of Friedland, Bennigsen had unwittingly trapped his troops on the west bank.

Napoleon arrived at 12:00 and could not believe his good fortune. There was no way that Bennigsen could get his army out of the trap he had put himself in.

Napoleon's plan was to hold with his deliberately outnumbered left flank, employing Ney's VI corps to deliver the decisive attack on the French right. Ney's preparations were masked by the forest of Sortlack. Victor's I Corps would hold the centre, with Mortier's VIII Corps and the Guard in reserve. As Murat was at Heilsberg, Grouchy acted as chief of cavalry. Grouchy would particularly distinguish himself here, holding the French left very skilfully while outnumbered, ruining what some of the opposing Cossacks thought to be a good day. The Emperor wanted to destroy the Russians, not a repeat of Eylau.

At 16:00 both Victor's I Corps and the Guard infantry arrived on the battle-field. Ney was already present, and both Lannes and Mortier was in position. The signal for Ney's attack, three artillery salvoes from the guns in position behind Posthenen, was fired at 17:00.

Ney's corps debouched from its forested assembly area, the two infantry divisions formed abreast in closed columns. Latour-Maubourg's cavalry division was in direct support. Ney cleared the woods, but failed or refused to deploy, making his divisions compact targets for the numerous Russian artillery on the right bank of the river. Russian cavalry charged the heads of Ney's two divisions while artillery raked them unmercifully. This was too much for VI Corps: except for three regiments that formed square, the rest bolted for the rear.

As Ney's attack fell part, one of Victor's infantry divisions, commanded by Dupont, advanced on the Russian centre without orders. Senarmont, Victor's chief of artillery, supported this advance with twelve guns, six on either flank of Dupont's division and, deeming them insufficient, immediately requested permission from Victor to advance with the remaining twenty-four that belonged to the corps. Permission granted, he quickly organised the artillery companies into two fifteen-gun batteries, keeping six in reserve behind Posthenen. Placing his two batteries on either flank of Dupont's division, he rapidly outpaced the sweating infantry and proceeded to attack the Russian centre on his own.[4]

The artillery companies clattered past Dupont's panting infantrymen, the foot-artillery gunners running to keep up. Trumpets blaring at Senarmont's barked order, the artillery broke into a charge. Another order barked, trumpets again sounding a call, and company commanders' raised sabres flashing in the sunlight, the artillery companies wheeled into position and began to unlimber. Company commanders' sabres again swished in the June sunlight as they directed their guns into position and shouted their first fire order. Trumpets blowing 'Action Front!' and the well-trained artillery horses responded without any direction from their drivers. Panting, sweating gunners caught up with the now halted gun teams, horses and men out of breath with both excitement and tension. Calloused hands of the gun crews grasped handspikes and gun trails and the heavy carriages were lifted from their limbers by the grunting gunners. Trails were swung round and the guns manhandled into position by sweat and muscle. More trumpet calls, the rush of gun teams and the two fifteen-gun batteries rapidly advanced by successive bounds towards the Russian centre.

Russian artillery fire screamed overhead as the first French rounds went down range. The gun companies began to take casualties, but the crew drill never slackened after the first order to open fire. Senarmont's artillery batteries were aiming for the mass of infantry in the Russian centre and the vulgar uproar from the Russian counter-battery fire was ignored, regardless of casualties to men and horses. Not satisfied with the range, Senarmont ordered his artillery forward by bricole and man-team, to save the horse teams on limber and caisson. Moving rapidly forward, the inaccurate Russian artillery fire slackened for a moment as the range changed and at 150 yards from the Russian centre the terrain narrowed so that both French batteries had to combine into one.

As the action 'ripened', Senarmont once more closed the range, advancing to within 120 yards of the Russian centre. Round after round of solid shot and canister poured into the steady Russian infantry, who neither took cover nor tried to manoeuvre. They stood as if on parade, literally shot to pieces. For twenty minutes Senarmont's artillery pounded the Russian centre, killing or maiming 4,000 men, and completely destroying it.[5]

Dupont supported Senarmont's advance, meeting the infantry of the Russian Guard and defeating them in a bayonet fight. Their cavalry attempted to take Senarmont's large battery in the flank, but the quick-witted artilleryman ordered a change of front and his gun companies to load with canister. As the picked cavalrymen of the Russian Guard broke into a charge two vollies of canister hit their closely packed ranks and destroyed their charge.[6] It was noted during the action that Senarmont's gunners 'calmly awaited their approach'.[7]

The initiative was clearly in French hands. Ney reorganised his defeated corps and led them to attack the Russian left flank. Again supported by Latour-Maubourg who defeated the Russian cavalry on this part of the field, Ney's assault pounded the Russian left flank so badly that it began to run for the bridges in Friedland. Ney's artillery went into action against the Russian batteries across the river, keeping them off Senarmont's back and finally silencing them.

Back in the middle of the field, the action was shaping up into another overwhelming French victory. Dupont's infantry pressed on after defeating the Russian Guard infantry and advanced on Friedland and the Russian bridges. Senarmont sent six guns to accompany Dupont's continuing advance, while the main battery supported other French infantry which had joined the general advance. Displacing forward once again, Senarmont brought his companies forward so that his guns could sweep Friedland's streets clear of any Russian attempt to rally. Repeated Russian attempts to re-form were denied by accurate artillery fire and French infantry. Benningsen's army was rapidly falling apart, Russians either being killed outright or driven into the river. Few of them knew how to swim.

On the French left flank, Grouchy, who was chief as Murat was not present, expertly handled his horsemen to keep the more numerous Russians off the French flank. His use of terrain and his tactical ability were masterful and clearly demonstrated what well-handled, but outnumbered, cavalry could do in a tight tactical situation. He mouse-trapped the Russian horse, feigning retreat and then turning on them at his advantage, routing both Cossack and regular Russian cavalry in turn.

The fighting petered out by 22:30. Russian losses were very heavy. At least 11,000 dead littered the battlefield and there were at least 7,000 wounded, but the number of recorded casualties has to be too low. Eighty guns were taken by the French. The French had lost 1,732 killed, 9,108 wounded and 55 prisoners. The fighting had been intense and bloody. Bennigsen was ruined as a commander, his reputation and self-confidence shattered. He had been bested in three out of three major engagements by Napoleon and undoubtedly had no desire to face him again. Even when he inflicted heavy losses on the Grande Armée, as he had at Eylau, they kept coming on for more. Much of the Russian arms and equipment had been lost at Friedland, and the army lost confidence in both itself and its commanders. Despite the exaggerated claims in Bennigsen's after action reports, Tsar Alexander sued for peace.

Four French officers distinguished themselves at Friedland: Jean Lannes, Emmanuel Grouchy, Senarmont and Pierre Dupont (see chapter 2).

Jean Lannes (1769–1809) was the only Gascon among the marshalate of the First Empire. A troublesome youth from Lectoure, he was remembered as a rascal by his fellow townspeople when home on leave from the army, even after winning his general's stars. Characterised by one historians as 'd'Artagnan's successor,'[8] if Lannes had not been an real character of the period, he would have had to be invented by a novelist.

Lannes literally came out of nowhere, ill-educated (he was taught to read, write and do basic arithmetic by one of his brothers who was a priest), bad-tempered and full of fight. Apparently, his first military service was in his home district's volunteer battalion which elected him a sous-lieutenant. He first served with Augereau on the Spanish frontier and was transferred to the Armée d'Italie where he met Napoleon. Lannes was a colonel. By 1797 Napoleon had promoted him to general of brigade and to general of division in 1799.

Lannes was the ideal advance guard commander: aggressive and careful at the same time, and continually improving his military education. He thirsted for knowledge and continually improved throughout his career. By the time of his death in 1809 he was in the top rank of the marshalate in generalship and was a grievous loss to both the Grande Armée and to Napoleon. The three Wagram marshals that were promoted in 1809 after his death, Marmont, Oudinot and Macdonald, were dubbed by the army as 'Lannes's small change'.

He served gallantly and well in Egypt, fought mightily at Montebello and Marengo in 1800 and was given command of the V Corps which he commanded from 1805 to early 1807. Falling ill, he turned over command of the corps in Poland to Savary and when he had recuperated he was given a provisional corps which he led with skill and dash at Friedland.

Sent into Spain, he demonstrated a talent for siege warfare, substituting careful siege operations for costly frontal assaults and reduced Saragossa, forcing its surrender. Summoned north because of Austria's invasion of Bavaria, he first commanded a provisional corps and then the II Corps, fighting stoutly at Essling until mortally wounded by a chance cannon shot.

Lannes continually improved during his career and learned to control a violent temper. Described by Desaix (who had also seen Ney in action) as 'bravest of the brave, young, fine appearance, well-built, face not very pleasing, riddled with wounds, elegant',[9] he was always at the head of his troops. Marbot's tale of him at the taking of Ratisbon arguing with his aides-de-camp who would take the ladder to the walls first after two failed attempts is typical. Morand's troops, exasperated, probably went forward a third time, successfully and led by the two aides, to stop the spectacle. A superb advance guard commander, alert and dangerous, he won the actions at Montebello and Saalfeld on his own, and his delaying action at Friedland was a recognised masterpiece. He displayed a talent for effective siege warfare in Spain at Saragossa and handled his corps expertly in Austria in 1809. His death irreparably hurt the Grande Armée. His loss was never made good. He could not be replaced.

The ubiquitous Pole, Heinrich von Brandt, left two excellent character sketches of Lannes during the second siege of Saragossa:

That same evening at a particularly exposed point…I came across Lacoste, the General of Engineers, in deep conversation with a man in an unadorned green coat and not wearing a sword. The two of them were studying the city through their telescopes without paying the slightest attention to the bullets and round shot . . . The man with Lacoste was . . . the marshal himself. He eventually seemed to realise the danger they had placed themselves in and said out loud, 'They've seen us, come on.' I could contemplate at leisure the handsome but severe Lannes . . . at Tudela.[10]

It is only really during sieges, especially sieges . . . that junior officers and soldiers are put into close contact with their superior officers . . . Lannes and Junot, above all, attracted our attention. The former often did the rounds of our positions and seemed everywhere, always asking questions or recommending some course of action. He was always confident and had an extraordinary courage that bordered on audacity. I remember when this marshal…perched himself on a rooftop and began to follow the movements of the enemy through a telescope. He soon found himself a target for sharpshooters hidden in the ruins of the convent and began to attract their shots. Lannes immediately grabbed a musket and fired back with such effect that the enemy responded with a shell which killed a captain of engineers right next to him. Lannes finally came down off the roof, and looked, to all appearances, as though nothing had happened.[11]

Alexandre-Antoine Hureau de Senarmont (1769–1810) was both one of the best artillery commanders of the period and one of the characters of the Grande Armée. His father had been an artilleryman and had prepared his son well. Senarmont was commissioned into the 2ᵉ Régiment d'Artillerie in 1785 from the Metz Artillery School and by 1792 he was a captain.

Present at Valmy, he also served in numerous sieges and was promoted to chef de bataillon in 1795. His service was mainly with the Rhine armies and in 1800 he was chief of staff to Marmont, making the Marengo campaign.

Promoted to general of brigade in 1806, he served with the Grande Armée from 1805–7 and commanded Augereau's artillery at Eylau. Transferred to the same job in I Corps, his service at Friedland was exemplary and he not only introduced a new school of artillery tactics, but they were emulated throughout the Grande Armée. Senarmont himself used them again at Ocana in Spain, where he was also caught by Spanish guerillas, who thought they had a soft and easily taken target. Senarmont's gunners destroyed the guerilla attack, saving their guns and winning the fight.

Senarmont was promoted to general of division in 1808 and all of his subsequent service was in Spain. He was killed in action at the siege of Cadiz.

Emmanuel de Grouchy (1766–1847) was one of the most skilful cavalry commanders in the Grande Armée. He entered the army in 1780 at the Strasbourg artillery school, but by 1784 he was a captain in the cavalry. He retired from the service involuntarily in 1787 but volunteered his services in 1791. He was promoted, first to colonel and then to general of brigade in 1792, but was forced out of the service that year because he belonged to the 'old nobility' but by 1794 he had been reinstated.

He was badly wounded and captured at Novi in 1799, exchanged the next year and served as an infantry division commander in the Armée du Rhin. He distinguished himself at Hohenlinden in December 1800. He proved himself an excellent cavalry commander, administrator and was honest and respected by his troops. He was one of the most-wounded marshals, being wounded twenty-three times in his career. Much of his service during the Empire was with the Armée d'Italie, serving ably in 1809.

He was a cavalry division commander with the Grande Armée in 1806–7, distinguishing himself at the head of his dragoons at Eylau, where he was badly wounded. By 1812 he was a cavalry corps commander, but was disabled for 1813. In 1814 he again distinguished himself as a hard-riding cavalry commander, remaining loyal to his Emperor when other senior officers grew discouraged and quit.

He was made a marshal upon Napoleon's return from Elba and served well as the commander of the Cavalry Reserve. He was given command of the force that pursued Blücher after Ligny and turned cautious, failing to support the Emperor at Waterloo. Subsequently, his performance was no less than brilliant, defeating Thielmann at Wavre and getting his command back to France intact, undefeated and ready to fight. He is one of the most underrated of Napoleon's commanders and it has been only recently that his true worth has been noticed.

Friedland was an example of Napoleon's generals winning the battle for him. Apparently Napoleon did not intervene in the handling of the battle. Grouchy operated on his own on the left flank, while Senarmont definitely used his own initiative to attack the Russian centre with artillery alone. This was the first time in the history of warfare that artillery was used as the decisive arm on the battlefield where it was the supported, rather than the supporting, arm. Artillery had come of age as a combat arm.

Lannes's actions delaying Bennigsen and keeping him both occupied and on the wrong side of the river was an outstanding feat. He never had more than 26,000 men, while Bennigsen had at least 60,000 at his disposal. There really is no satisfactory reason for Bennigsen to cross the Alle in the first place. His doing so and the inexpert placing of the pontoon bridges, all in the same area and badly sited, doomed the Russian army into a trap once Napoleon and his main force arrived. Napoleon was actually shocked and surprised that Bennigsen had actually done it.

Pierre Dupont's conduct, both in leadership and generalship, was exemplary. He proved himself to be a general of execution who could keep his wits in a crisis and a tight situation. He was a fighter, as he had also proved at Ulm. At Friedland he also proved he could think for himself without higher direction. Napoleon noticed this and gave him an independent command in Spain, with which Dupont promptly disgraced both himself and the Grande Armée at Baylén in 1808.

CHAPTER 8

THE WHOLE ARMY WOULD NOT BE TOO MUCH

The battle of Essling, 1809

A general's principal talent consists in knowing the mentality of the soldier and in winning his confidence. And, in these two respects, the French soldier is more difficult to lead than any other. He is not a machine to be put in motion but a reasonable being that must be directed.
NAPOLEON

A leader is a dealer in hope. NAPOLEON

14:00 21 May 1809 near Aspern, Austria
The bloody close-quarter fighting had raged all afternoon and the heavily out-numbered French had repeatedly defeated the mass of Austrians who were trying to drive them into the Danube. General Molitor and his worn-out infantry division had held the army's far left flank in the now ravaged village of Aspern and his survivors, 'the rump,' for they could be called nothing else, were settling down for an uneasy night. They were exhausted and their only relief could come from across the Danube to their backs and their only lifeline over the swollen, raging river was the tenuous pontoon bridges which could break at any time.

Molitor surveyed the terrain to his front and knew the white-coated Austrians would try another assault. Boudet's infantry division in Essling had also suffered crippling losses, but they still held as well. The Austrians would probably attack again in conjunction with another effort to break the bridges. Quickly motioning to an aide, Molitor sent a message to the units on his left flank to be alert for any type of floating object that could have been launched by the Austrians against the bridges.

A weary company of voltigeurs, or what was left of it, was ordered to the river bank and posted to watch for any floating 'projectiles'. Badly mauled in the fierce, no-quarter fighting, the surviving officer its youngest sous-lieutenant, the exhausted light infantrymen trudged to the river and set up their picket. The NCOs ordered the best swimmers to strip in case of an emergency. Almost immediately, the sentries spotted a huge floating mill sweeping downstream towards the bridge between the island of Lobau and the north bank of the river. Without orders from the amazed sous lieutenant, the voltigeurs leaped into the river and frantically swam towards the mill.

Reaching the massive structure, the wet and weary light infantrymen managed to beach the awkward object. Making their way back to their company position, the exhausted swimmers collapsed on the bank, as their comrades arrived to assist them. After hot soup and *eau de vie*, the company returned to their positions and resumed their seemingly endless watch of the raging river.

The campaign of 1809 in Austria was the first conducted by Napoleon after the invasions of Portugal and Spain. Napoleon's incursion into the Iberian Peninsula was probably a result of Napoleon's overconfidence at this continued success, which was undoubtedly beyond his wildest expectations. This misadventure however did not turn out in either the short or the long run to Napoleon's advantage. In the long run, it 'established' a second front that would drain the Grande Armée throughout the rest of its existence and also keep field commanders, badly needed elsewhere, involved against the British, Spanish and Portuguese. In the short term, it led to another war with Austria that was not of Napoleon's doing.

There were two French invasions of Spain. The first was done on the cheap with half-trained troops who were not prepared to campaign. The result of this first invasion was the Spanish revolt and the disaster at Baylén. Noting himself as the architect of failure, Napoleon's second army of invasion was carefully prepared. The Grande Armée in Germany was deactivated and troops moved towards the Spanish border. Given attachments of engineer troops as they crossed the Spanish frontier, this second invasion juggernaut fought the Spanish as they met them, splattering Spanish armies one after the other into rout and destruction. England's expeditionary force under the able, unlucky Sir John Moore was chased to the coast and run out of the Peninsula, its commander killed.

Davout was left in command of a 90,000-man army in Germany, which included all of the heavy cavalry and was built around his III Corps under its veteran commanders. It provided a stabilising influence for the newly established Confederation of the Rhine as well as enabling Davout to oversee the development of the recently christened Grand Duchy of Warsaw. Davout being Davout, he also set up a highly efficient intelligence network to keep an eye on Napoleon's defeated enemies. It was to prove fortuitous.[1]

Austria wanted revenge for her repeated defeats in 1797, 1800 and 1805. The Hapsburgs also wanted their lost territory back, especially in northern Italy. Since the 1805 disaster, the Archduke Charles, Austria's ablest general and army commander, had worked tirelessly to improve the Austrian army. New drill regulations were written and put into effect, the artillery was strengthened and modernised, the general staff organised on more modern lines and the French-inspired corps d'armée system implemented. Francis wanted to strike as soon as practicable; Charles wanted to wait until they were ready. The opportunity presented by the Spanish war was too irresistible to pass up and, without a formal declaration of war; the Archduke Charles led an army of a little over 200,000 men in an invasion of France's ally, Bavaria.[2]

From the outset, things went wrong. Even though Charles announced he was coming to 'break their German brothers' chains' the reaction in the territory of the Confederation was one of unity with France and to fight against the Austrians. Davout, using his excellent espionage system and far-ranging cavalry patrols, worked out what the Austrians were up to. Napoleon, instead of being completely surprised, knew what was coming and prepared for it. Still, in many ways it was an improvised campaign.

Davout's command was more than ready, but the troops in Spain, along with most of the commanders there, had to stay. The Imperial Guard was ordered to Germany, as were some commanders such as the irreplaceable Lannes, but Napoleon would fight this campaign with an army composed of thousands of untried conscripts, a huge Confederation contingent and Davout's command. Named the Armée d'Allemagne, this army would have teething troubles, but after a victorious first half of the campaign would shake down into an excellent army accustomed to victory.

The Austrians moved slowly and the French concentration proceeded at a frenetic pace. What could have been a disaster, with the French scattered, Napoleon still in Paris dictating in the most confusing manner to Berthier in Germany what he wanted done by both courier and telegraph, was an opportunity missed by the Archduke. Opportunity lost is opportunity gone forever: the Austrians were repeatedly defeated in the first half of the campaign in the area around Ratisbon along the Danube. Being outmanoeuvred and outfought repeatedly by Davout and his veterans, the German contingents of the Confederation and the newly organised French corps led by Lannes and Masséna, the Archduke finally withdrew towards Vienna and advised his Imperial brother to sue for peace.[3]

Francis refused. The French pursued the Archduke and through skill and good fortune, Charles got the abused Austrian army away and on the other side of the Danube from the French. This time, the bridges across the Danube were destroyed, though Vienna was again taken, again with its huge arsenal intact. Napoleon, his eye ever on his single objective of destroying his enemy's army, needed to get across the Danube to get at Charles.

After several false starts, feints and combats, the French were across the Danube near Vienna when Molitor, who commanded a division in Masséna's IV Corps, seized the Lob Grund and bridge construction began behind him. The next day Austrian outposts cleared the rest of Lobau Island, which would become decisive as the campaign continued. Charles found out the next day about the progress of the French bridge construction and started to mass his army to move against the French bridgehead. On 20 May the bridge was completed and Lasalle and Molitor crossed to the north bank between the villages of Aspern and Essling.

This operation was a hasty river crossing. Napoleon wanted to get across quickly and attempt to catch Charles inland from the river. Because of this, the usual precautions, such as pounding pilings upstream from the bridge to protect it from devices launched upriver, were not used. Napoleon was taking a calculated risk. The stakes were high. If he could get enough troops and guns across quickly and defeat Charles decisively, the war was over. If not, the French might be in for a very long day. He did not want to fight with a river at his back. However, the Austrian reaction was quicker than he had expected, with the Austrians concentrating and marching to the crossing site by 20 May.

Essling (as the French called it; the Austrians referred to their victory as Aspern) was the first time since 1796 that Napoleon was defeated on the battlefield. Having defeated the Austrian offensive in the area around Ratisbon, which Napoleon later referred to as the actions of which he was most proud in his career, the Grande Armée pursued the Austrian army under the Archduke Charles back towards Vienna.

At 17:00 on 20 May, the main bridge was broken by a vehicle sent downstream by the Austrians just after Marulaz's first squadron crossed the river. The bridge was repaired by 03:00, but it was certain that Charles knew what was afoot and eight critical hours were lost during which troops could have crossed to build up French combat power on the north bank. The clock was ticking and not in Napoleon's favour.

By midnight both Masséna and Lannes were on the north bank and at dawn Napoleon was across conducting a reconnaissance of the immediate area. Masséna, who had climbed into the church tower in Aspern, reported Austrian bivouac fires to the north. The old smuggler could bet that there was going to be a fight for the bridgehead and there was no room for the French to

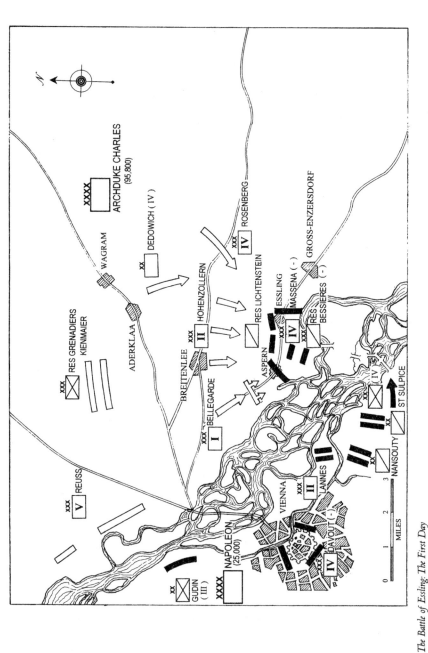

The Battle of Essling: The First Day

This map shows the situation on the first day with the approach of the Austrian army under Charles. The French are still crossing the Danube and have occupied the villages of Aspern and Essling. The only infantry available for the French effort belongs to Massena's IV Corps, and the French centre is held by Bessières with elements of the Cavalry reserve and the available corps light cavalry. The French are greatly outnumbered and are hustling troops across the temporary, hastily built bridges as quickly as possible. Charles missed a great opportunity to drive the French into the river on the first day of the battle, which would not be the more desperate of the two day fight. 'The Danube, and not the Austrians, defeated us.'

Napoleon, surrounded by several of his officers, distributes the Légion d'Honneur to the deserving.

Napoleon I, Emperor of the French (1804–15). An expert artilleryman who became one of the great captains of history had arguably the greatest gathering of military talent to ever serve one man. Without his general officers, Napoleon would not have achieved as much as he did.

The *Légion d'Honneur*. This coveted award was given to deserving men, military and civilian, who loyally served France and the Empire. It was awarded both to Frenchmen and their allies.

This *sabre d'honneur* was awarded to Lieutenant Aune, the 'second grenadier of France' for valour on the field of battle. Lieutenant Aune was the colour-bearer for the Grenadiers à Pied of the Consular Guard at Marengo and brought the colours off the field.

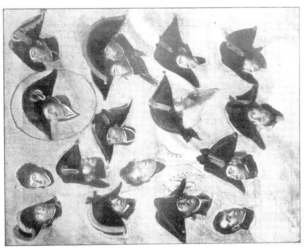

This panorama shows the commanders of the Grande Armée as they left the Channel camps for Germany and the Ulm and Austerlitz campaigns in 1805.

General Louis-Lazare Hoche, recognised by Napoleon as 'a true man of war'. He constantly improved throughout his career, noted as being humane in the Vendée. The son of a groom, he enlisted in 1782, was a captain in 1792, and got his stars a year later. Unfortunately, he died suddenly in 1797.

Marshal Louis-Nicholas Davout, the famous 'Iron Marshal' but known by his troops as 'The Just'. He was probably the best of the marshals in both talent and character, and was never defeated.

General Jean Rapp, one of Napoleon's Imperial Aides-de-Camp. Many times wounded, he organised the Mamelukes and led the last charge of the Guard Cavalry at Austerlitz.

Louis Charles Desaix, the ablest general of the Rhine armies, and Napoleon considered him 'the best balanced of his lieutenants'. He conducted a model campaign in Upper Egypt and was known as 'the Just Sultan'. Davout was his protégé.

Left: Emmanuel Grouchy, one of the ablest cavalry commanders in the Grande Armée. His achievements, notably his superb handling of the cavalry at Friedland in Murat's stead, and his participation in the great charge at Eylau, are usually forgotten because of his failure as an independent commander in 1815.

Right: Louis Charles Saint-Hilaire, who was known to be 'without fear and without reproach' was one of the best infantry division commanders in the army. He was admired, both as a man and a soldier, by all with whom he came in contact. Napoleon first met him at Toulon in 1793 and considered him a friend and hero. He was mortally wounded at Essling in 1809. If he had survived, Napoleon probably would have made him a marshal.

Left: General Claude Pajol, one of the plethora of talented light cavalrymen of the Empire, is justly famous for his galloping of the Montereau bridge in 1814 with his conscripts converted into ersatz cavalrymen. His aide-de-camp, Colonel Biot, believed seasoned horsemen could not have done it.

Andre Masséna, former NCO of the Royal Army, was an outstanding soldier, though possessed of the desire to loot for his 'little savings'. He was immensely talented, but needed a good chief of staff to keep him honest. Napoleon admired him, gave him hard assignments, and did not realise that when he was on his way to Spain in 1810 he was burned out.

Michel-Marie Pacthod was the commander of one of the two small National Guard divisions that distinguished themselves in 1814 at La Fere-Champenoise. Forced to surrender to save what was left of his men, he was saluted by his Russian opponents and his proferred sword was refused acceptance by the Tsar.

Prince Eugène de Beauharnais, Josephine's son and Napoleon's stepson. Napoleon thought more than highly of Eugène, making him his Viceroy in Italy, where he ruled in the Emperor's name fairly and honestly. He constantly improved as a soldier, performing well in 1809 and brilliantly in 1812, 1813, and 1814. He stayed loyal in Italy when he was encouraged, by Murat among others, to turn on Napoleon. He is the most underrated general officer of the period.

Joachim Murat, the dashing cavalryman who commanded the Cavalry Reserve in 1805–7 and again in 1812. He frequently led his horsemen with nothing but a light whip in his hand, but Coignet noticed that he always returned from action with a blood-stained sabre. Napoleon's brother-in-law, he betrayed the Emperor and fought against him in 1814.

Jean Lannes, the paladin of the marshalate and Napoleon's friend. An ideal advance guard commander, Lannes was an outstanding combat leader and an excellent tactician. His delaying action at Friedland in 1807 was one of the best performances of the period. An expert drill master (along with Massèna) he performed the difficult passage of lines under fire at Jena in 1806. He was mortally wounded at Essling in 1809.

Louis-Alexandre Berthier, Napoleon's 'indispensable marshal'. The first of the great chiefs of staff in history, and undoubtedly the premier chief of staff of his day, he was Major General of the Grande Armée and was obeyed by the corps commanders, unlike his Prussian counterpart Gneisenau.

Nicholas Jean-de-Dieu Soult, named 'Iron Hand' by the troops, and a strict disciplinarian and an excellent administrator, though he had an eye for religious art, no matter who owned it. He did not like being reminded that he owed anyone anything, and might react oddly if reminded of the fact.

Etienne Nansouty was a tough, reliable cavalry commander who missed the great day at Eylau, but did more than his assigned duty on many another field. He commanded the Guard cavalry in 1813–14 and died before Napoleon came back to France in early 1815.

Laurent Gouvion Saint-Cyr was an outstanding staff officer and commander, but 'waged war with the detachment of a chess player' and made no attempt to gain the affection of his troops. Tough and reliable, an excellent tactician and strategist, he was nicknamed 'the Owl'.

This is a Russian's-eye view of the charge of d'Hautpoul's cuirassier division at the battle of Eylau. This was the only French cuirassier division present on the field. The remainder of the French cavalry that charged were dragoons or the Guard cavalry. This is one of the most famous and successful cavalry actions of the period. It was launched on Napoleon's order after the defeat and destruction of Augereau's VII Corps. (courtesy Keith Rocco)

The remnants of Augereau's VII Corps, attempting to fight their way back to the French lines, were assailed by a mass of Russians. Here, one of his regiments makes a stand against the Russian infantry. General Compans rallied 3,000 of Augereau's survivors and put them in line of battle by the end of the day. (courtesy Keith Rocco)

Francois Kellermann, son of the marshal, was an expert cavalryman and contributed mightily to the victory of Marengo with his timely charge in support of Boudet's division at the beginning of the French counter-attack. He also wrecked two Austrian cavalry brigades during that day. (courtesy Keith Rocco)

Opposite top: This is the uniform and equipment of a typical French cuirassier from 1805–12. This is how the cuirassiers of d'Hautpoul's division would have looked at Eylau in February 1807. (courtesy Keith Rocco)

Opposite below: This is the charge of the Empress's Dragoons (Dragoons of the Imperial Guard) at Montmirail in 1814 (courtesy Keith Rocco)

This is a rendition of the beginnings of the attack of the Old Guard at Waterloo. The Middle Guard was not reactivated in 1815, and all eight of the Grenadier and Chasseur regiments belonged to the Old Guard. Ney, 'Red Michael' and the Emperor are also pictured here. (courtesy Keith Rocco)

This excellent painting by Keith Rocco clearly demonstrates the problems artillery could have in roads 'six feet deep in mud.' This is the Artillerie à Pied of the Imperial Guard at Sezanne in February 1814. Grouchy's horse artillery had similar problems with the roads at the battle of Champaubert. (courtesy Keith Rocco)

General Cambronne was one of the Guard infantry commanders at Waterloo and supposedly uttered 'le mot de Cambronne' at the battle's ending. Whether he did or not, undoubtedly someone did — 'Merde!'

Tribute to Caesar: This is the beginning of the famous charge at Somosierra in 1808 by the 3rd Squadron of the Polish Light Horse. A full description of the charge is in the Prologue. (courtesy Keith Rocco)

Kellermann's jubilant horsemen return with trophies captured from the Austrians at Marengo during their famous charge. (courtesy Keith Rocco)

manoeuvre. It was going to be slow going and it was going to get bloody.

Austrian cavalry was on the field and Lasalle could not penetrate their screen, which inhibited the gathering of battlefield intelligence. Boudet's infantry division of Masséna's corps and Legrand's crossed to the north bank by 09:00. The rest of Marulaz's command as well as d'Espagne's cuirassier division got across, but the bridge was again broken as the last cavalryman reached the north bank. By 15:00 there would be less than 25,000 French troops on the north bank to face over 95,000 Austrians.

At 14:30 the tardy Austrian avalanche poured from the north. Four corps, the Austrian cavalry reserve and the reserve grenadiers manoeuvred across the Marchfeld, but the attack was not coordinated. Charles could improve organisation and training, but he was poorly served by his senior subordinates. Hiller and Bellegarde (VI and I Corps respectively) attacking along the river got into a traffic jam that delayed their attack and gave the French a breather. Molitor deployed in and around Aspern and then was able to hold it against the two Austrian corps. Lichtenstein, commanding the Austrian cavalry went against the French centre along with Hohenzollern's II Corps. Bessières, a better cavalryman and commander, skilfully outfought the Austrian cavalry and stopped Hohenzollern's straggling advance. Rosenberg led his IV Corps against Essling, but Boudet held stoutly, fighting as well as at Marengo.

Lannes was sent into Essling to take command of Boudet's division and Rosenberg was stopped after his 16:30 attack. One of Rosenberg's divisions under Dedowich tried again around 18:00 but was stopped cold. Austrian artillery, however, dominated the battlefield. The French had only ninety guns on the field, the Austrians almost 300. The French fought gamely, but their artillery was outfought and outshot.

Charles rallied Hiller's and Bellegarde's commands around 19:00 and led them against Masséna and Molitor in Aspern. The Austrians took the village, ejecting the French and Germans that grimly tried to hang on to it. The fighting was bitter, with no quarter being asked nor given. Molitor was finally driven from the village. His temper up, Masséna took two regiments from Legrand's division and led them back into the flaming village, set afire during the intense fighting. These outfits took most of the village back, but could not drive the Austrians out of the church or cemetery. The fighting petered out around 20:00. The French were in a desperate situation which was punctuated in a note from Berthier to Davout, who was still on the south bank requesting 'all available troops and ammunition'. Berthier scribbled 'The whole army would not be too much' on the bottom of the note.

The bridges had been repaired around 15:00 on the 21st. During the night

Lannes command, the II Corps, crossed the bridges along with the Guard infantry. There were occasional breaks in the bridges during the night but these were relatively minor and were repaired quickly and efficiently. Davout was to cross to the north bank after these units passed.

The Austrians mostly remained out of contact with the French during the night. Charles might have thought he had won and that Napoleon would withdraw. He was mistaken. Fighting erupted in Aspern around 03:00. Small outpost scuffles grew in intensity and finally annoyed Masséna, who attacked at 05:00 and drove Hiller out of the village. At the same time, Rosenberg finally stirred and and half-heartedly attacked Essling, but this was of short duration and nothing came of it.

Napoleon's plan for the 22nd was for Lannes to attack the Austrian centre, clear the bridgehead while doing so, giving Davout room to cross and deploy to support the main effort. That would hopefully pin the Austrians against the Danube in two halves, allowing the cavalry to exploit the breakthrough and pursue another broken Austrian army.

Lannes attacked at 07:00 with three divisions (Tharreau, Claparede and St Hilaire) in echelon. Because of the lack of manoeuvre room, Lannes's initial formations would have to be large and deep – perfect targets for the skilful Austrian artillery to hammer. However, the French advanced with élan and skill and fought forward grimly under unrelenting and accurate artillery fire. St Hilaire had a foot blown off and was mortally wounded, but Bessières supported Lannes with his cavalry, driving off the Austrian cavalry and forcing the artillery to limber up and displace.

In the middle of this terrible fighting, the infantry of Hohenzollern's II Corps started to fall apart and it looked as though another decisive French victory was shaping up in the carnage. Charles launched himself into the middle of the mess and in a display of courage rallied the Austrian infantry. That done, he ordered infantry from both flanks to reinforce his centre. For over an hour the fighting was intense and unrelenting, but the Austrians finally stopped Lannes. Davout was needed to finish off the exhausted Austrians, but news came that at 08:00 the bridge was broken irreparably and Davout could not cross.

At 09:30 Napoleon ordered Lannes to withdraw almost back to his line of departure. Sensing success and the possibility of driving the French into the river, the Austrians attacked the defeated II Corps, but each assault was defeated by the grim French infantrymen. Both the French infantry and artillery conserved ammunition to meet the coming crises and the fighting in Aspern intensified once again. Four times the Austrians took the village and four times the French and Germans came roaring back into a raging inferno to take it back.

Rosenberg tried one more time against Essling. His determined assault swept Boudet's depleted division out of the village. Boudet and some of this survivors took refuge in the huge granary on the outskirts of the village and held it against all comers. Napoleon, seeing the danger, ordered Mouton, one of his personal aides-de-camp, against the village with three battalions of the Young Guard. Mouton's fanatical assault drove out the Austrians, but they counter-attacked and trapped Mouton's battalions. Rapp was sent with the remaining two Young Guard battalions to rescue Mouton.[4] He broke through to him, but instead of withdrawing as ordered, the two generals counter-attacked and drove Rosenberg's entire corps out and away from the village, rescuing what was left of Boudet's troops and holding the French right flank.[5] Finally the Austrians had enough and the main effort once again became the centre.

There, Colonel Smola,[6] the outstanding Austrian artilleryman of the period, Hohenzollern's chief of artillery received permission to mass almost 200 guns against the French. The Austrian artillery literally blew the opposing French gunners off the field. The II Corps took heavy casualties in this bombardment, including Lannes who was mortally wounded. Some of them started for the bridgehead, but the Old Guard infantry shrugged them off, forcing them to stay, and displayed admirable discipline under intense, accurate Austrian artillery fire.

Jean-Roche Coignet was present in the ranks of the Old Guard infantry and the version he tells leaves nothing out:

> A second cannon ball struck the drum sergeant. One of my comrades went immediately and took off his stripes and epaulets and brought them to me. I thanked him, and pressed his hand. This was only a prelude. To the left of Essling the enemy planted fifty guns in front of us. I felt an urgent call to relieve nature, but it was strictly against orders to move a step towards the rear. There was no alternative but to go forward of the line, which I did; and, having put down my musket, I began operations with my behind to the enemy. All at once a cannon ball came along, ricocheted with a yard of me, and threw a hail of earth and stones all over my back. Luckily for me I still had my pack on, or I should have perished.
>
> Picking up my musket with one hand and my trousers with the other, black and blue behind, I was on my way back to my post when the major, seeing the state I was in, came galloping up. 'What's this . . . Are you wounded?' 'It's nothing major; they wanted to wipe my breech for me, but they didn't succeed.' 'Ah! Well, have a drink of rum to pull you together.'
>
> He took a flask in a wicker case from his pistol holster, and held it out in front of me. 'After you, if you please.' 'Take a good pull! Can you get back alone?'

'Yes' I answered. He galloped away, and I moved off again, with my musket in one hand and my trousers in the other, bringing up the rear, and was soon back in my place in ranks. 'Well, Coignet,' said Captain Renard, 'that was a near thing.' 'It was, sir; their paper's too hard, and I couldn't use it. They're a lot of swine.' And then followed handshakes all round with my officers and comrades.

The fifty guns of the Austrians thundered upon us without our being able to advance a step, or fire a shot. Imagine the agony we endured in such a position, for I can never describe it. We had only four of our own guns in front of us, and two in front of the chasseurs, with which to answer fifty. The balls fell among our ranks, and cut down our men three at a time; the shells knocked the bearskin caps twenty feet in the air. As each file was cut down, I called out, 'Right dress, close up the ranks.' And the brave grenadiers closed up without a frown, saying to one another as they saw the enemy making ready to fire, 'The next one's for me.' 'Good, I'm behind you; that's the best place; keep cool.'

A ball struck a whole file, and knocked them all three head over heels on top of me. I fell to the ground. 'Keep cool,' I called out; 'close up at once.' 'But sergeant, the hilt of your sabre is gone, your cartridge pouch is half cut off.' 'That's nothing; the battle is not over yet.'

There were no gunners left to work out two pieces. General Dorsenne sent forward twelve grenadiers to take their places, and bestowed the cross on them. But all those brave fellows perished beside their guns. No more horses, no more artillerymen, no more shells. The carriages were broken to pieces, and the timbers scattered over the ground like logs of wood. A shell fell and burst near our good general, covering him with dirt, but he rose up like the brave soldier that he was, saying, 'Your general is not hurt. You may depend upon him, he will know how to die as his post.' He had no horse any longer; two had been killed under him. How grateful the country ought to be for such men! The awful; thunder continued. A cannon ball cut down a file of soldiers next to me. Something struck me on the arm, and I dropped my musket. I thought my arm was cut off. I had no feeling in it. I looked, and saw a bit of flesh sticking to my wrist, I thought I had broken my arm, but I had not; it was a piece of flesh of one of my brave comrades, which had been dashed against me with such violence that it had stuck to my arm. The lieutenant came up to me, took hold of my arm, shook it, and the piece of flesh fell off. I saw the cloth of my coat. He shook my arm, and said to me, 'It is only numbed.' Imagine my joy when I found I could move my fingers! The commander said to me, 'Leave your musket and take your sabre.' I have none; the cannonball cut the hilt off it. I took my musket in my left hand.

The losses became very heavy. We had to place the Guard all in one rank so as to keep up the line in front of the enemy. As soon as this movement had been made, a stretch was brought up on our left, borne by grenadiers, who deposited their precious burden in our centre. The Emperor, from the top of his pine tree, recognised his favourite, left his post of observation, and hurried to receive the last words of Marshal Lannes, who had been mortally wounded at the head of his corps. The Emperor knelt upon one knee, took him in his arms, and had him carried over to the island; but he did not survive the amputation. This ended the career of that great general. We were all filled with dismay at our great loss.[7]

Elzear Blaze, an admirer of General Dorsenne, the commander of the Old Guard infantry on the field, left this account of the kind of commander Dorsenne was:

There are men, however, who, gifted with an extraordinary strength of spirit, can cold-bloodedly face the greatest dangers. Murat, bravest of the brave, always charged at the head of his cavalry, and never returned without blood on his sabre. That can easily be understood, but what I have seen General Dorsenne do – and never have seen it done by anyone else – was to stand motionless, his back to the enemy, facing his bullet-riddled regiment, and say, 'Close up your ranks,' without once looking behind him. On other occasions I have tried to emulate him. I tried to turn my back to the enemy, but I could never remain in that position – curiosity always made me look to see where all those bullets were coming from.[8]

The Old Guard stood and took it, closing their ranks under Dorsenne's watchful eye as men were hit and went down. Bearskin bonnets flew into the air to mark the spot where the infantrymen were mown down by Austrian solid shot, but the Old Guard infantry withdrew not a step. It was the reason they were there.

The Austrian cannonade was devastating to the French. Still, the Austrians failed to take advantage of it. While it was skilfully conducted by Smola, it was men killed and maimed to no purpose, for the Austrians did not advance against the French centre. They had had enough. The fighting stopped around 16:00.

Napoleon ordered a withdrawal after having a discussion with Berthier, Masséna and Davout. The army would withdraw to Lobau, which would become an armed camp. The toll in senior officers in this action was very heavy. In addition to Lannes and St Hilaire, the outstanding cuirassier commander, d'Espagne, was killed leading his troopers against the Austrian centre. All three would be sadly missed. The ranks were growing thinner.

French casualties were between 19,000 and 20,000. The Austrians lost more, Charles stating 23,400. Napoleon had lost his calculated risk. However, it is quite possible had the bridges held and Davout had made it across, outnumbered or not the French would have won. As they stated, 'The Danube and not the Austrians defeated us.'

Andre Masséna (1758–1817) was a Sardinian who enlisted in the Royal Italian Regiment, part of the old French Royal Army and rose to sergeant major in 1784. He left the service in 1789 because he could no longer be promoted because of the prohibitive policies of the French government on non-nobles.

Apparently, he became a smuggler of some repute, after having married and 'settled down' after his discharge. When war came, however he enlisted in a volunteer battalion and two years later he was a general of division. Napoleon met him in 1795 when he was assigned to the Armée d'Italie as its artillery commander and Masséna was a division commander. When he returned in 1796 as the army's commander, Masséna was professional enough to subordinate himself to his new, and somewhat inexperienced, commander.

An extremely skilful commander, he made his own reconnaissances and was also, like Lannes and Augereau, an expert drill master. It was said that as a sergeant major he could drill his regiment more proficiently than the regimental commander.

Masséna was a superb commander at any level, sharing his men's hardships when necessary, leading from the front, being an excellent tactician and strategist. Head and shoulders above most of the other marshals as a commander (except probably Davout and Suchet and possibly Lannes) Masséna was one of the best generals in Europe during the period. However, he did need a good chief of staff as he was a careless administrator.

He served with Napoleon in Italy, being at the forefront of nearly every major action of the campaigns. He remained in Italy and Switzerland when Napoleon embarked for Egypt and finally defeated the Russians and Austrians with a masterful performance in the Second Battle of Zurich in 1799.

On the first list of marshals, he commanded the Armée d'Italie in 1805 in a generally lacklustre performance, but in 1809 with the Armée d'Allemagne, he commanded with his old skill and enthusiasm, performing superbly at both Essling and Wagram. Sent to Spain to deal with Wellington, he had trouble with his subordinates, especially Ney whom he relieved and sent home and ultimately failed against Wellington. This was the end of his active service.

Masséna was a man of superior talent. He generally, however, made bad dispositions previous to a battle, and it was not until the dead fell around him that he began to act with that judgement which he ought to have displayed before. In the midst of the dying and the dead, of balls sweeping away those who

encircled him, then Masséna was himself – gave his orders and made his dispositions with the greatest sang froid and judgement . . . By a strange peculiarity of
temperament, he possessed the desired equilibrium only in the heat of battle; it
came to him in the midst of danger. The sound of the guns cleared his ideas and
gave him understanding, penetration, and cheerfulness. He was endowed with
extraordinary courage and firmness. When defeated he was always ready to fight
again as though he had been the conqueror.[9]

Louis-Vincent-Joseph le Blond Comte de St Hilaire (1766–1809) began as a
cadet in the Régiment de Conte-Cavalerie in 1777 and volunteered for the
Aquitaine Régiment de Infanterie, which later became the 35ᵉ Ligne, in 1781. He
was promoted to sous-lieutenant in 1783 and was a captain in 1792. The next
year he was a chef de bataillon and in 1794 was promoted to chef de brigade. In
1795 he won his stars as a general de brigade. His service was in Italy and was with
Suchet in 1799–1800. He was promoted to general of division in 1799.

St Hilaire became one of Soult's division commanders in the redoubtable IV
Corps, taking part in the assault on the Pratzen at Austerlitz in 1805. He served
with Soult through 1806 and 1807, acquiring the reputation as a solid soldier
and tactician. A superb combat leader, St Hilaire was held in high esteem by
Napoleon and had he lived he probably would have been made a marshal.

Remaining in Germany with Davout after Tilsit, he did not serve in Spain,
but was part of the reinforced III Corps that began the campaign of 1809.
When the Armée d'Allemagne was reorganised after the Ratisbon phase of the
campaign, St Hilaire's division was transferred to II Corps under Lannes and St
Hilaire was mortally wounded, along with his commander, at Essling.
Universally admired as both a soldier and as a man, his death was a severe loss to
the army and to his comrades.

Jacob-François Marola dit Marulaz (1769–1842) was one of the characters
of the Grande Armée. His first service was as an *enfant de troupe* in the Esterhazy
Hussars in 1778. He was a brigadier fourrier in 1791 and was promoted to
maréchal des logis the next year, closely followed by promotion to lieutenant in
October of the same year. In 1794 he was a chef d'escadron and after being
promoted to chef de brigade commanded the 8ᵉ Hussars for thirteen years. He
was described as 'a good-looking man without refinements, outspoken and
tough; an intrepid sabreur and a stubborn disciplinarian'.

His service during the wars of the Revolution was with the Rhine armies and
was at Second Zurich in 1799 and the Armée du Rhin in 1799–1800. A
general of brigade and cavalry brigade commander in 1806 with the Grande
Armée, he served as Davout's cavalry commander in 1806–7, usually being

'chewed-on' by Davout to correct his spelling in his reports. Marulaz served excellently and remained in Germany after the Grande Armée was deactivated and many went into Spain and Portugal.

He was Masséna's cavalry commander in the IV Corps of the Armée d'Allemagne in 1809 and after Lasalle was killed he took command of his division as well as his own. Wounded seriously at Wagram, he was thereafter inactive, but was fit enough to defend the city of Besançon in 1814 against all odds until after Napoleon's abdication, still refusing to let any Austrians pass through the city after the shooting stopped.

Popular history has Marulaz killing the Marquis de Sorans in a duel after the wars, hence becoming Mayor of Filain for fifteen years.

Gabriel-Jean-Joseph Molitor (1770–1849) was a simple volunteer in the 4e Bataillon de la Moselle in 1791 being promoted to captain the same year. He served with the Rhine armies during the period and was promoted to chef de bataillon in 1793, chef de brigade in 1795 and general of brigade in 1799.

With the Armée du Rhin in 1800, Molitor was a very competent officer who was usually assigned to secondary theatres, the exception being one of Masséna's division commanders in the IV Corps in 1809. He distinguished himself at Essling, along with Boudet.

Masséna was familiar with Molitor, as both had been in the Armée d'Italie in 1805. 1806 found Molitor a division commander in Dalmatia. In April 1807 he was designated as the Governor of Pomerania and took part in the siege of Stralsund. With the IV Corps in 1807, he was acting commander of that formation in December 1807.

He served in the Campaign of France in 1814 and rallied to Napoleon in 1815. He served under Rapp on the eastern frontier against the Austrians.

Jean-Louis-Brigitte d'Espagne (1769–1809) was a heavy cavalryman of note, daring, resourceful and always leading in person. He enlisted in the Dragons de la Reine (later the 6e Dragons) in 1787 and was promoted to brigadier (corporal of mounted troops) in 1788. By 1792 he had risen to the rank of maréchal des logis-chef. He served in the Armée du Nord under Rochambeau, Luckner and Dumouriez and he was commissioned a sous-lieutenant in 1792. By the end of the year he was a lieutenant colonel.

The next year he was an adjutant general, chef de brigade and was promoted to general de brigade in 1799. With the Armée du Rhin, he commanded the carabinier brigade in d'Hautpoul's division. He was a brigade commander in Montrichard's division at Hohenlinden in December 1800. He was promoted to general of division in 1805.

That year he was the commander of the 4e Division of the Armée d'Italie and then transferred to the command of a light cavalry division. Transferred to the Grande Armée in central Europe, he commanded a division in Masséna's VIII Corps, but was back in Italy with the Armée de Naples in 1806. During anti-partisan operations in Naples, he captured the famous Fra Diavolo.

After Eylau in 1807 he was ordered to join the Grande Armée in East Prussia from Italy. Now commanding the 3rd Cuirassier Division, his division was transferred north with him. After Friedland and Tilsit in 1807, he stayed with the Armée du Rhin under Davout while other troops hiked off to Spain and Portugal. He again commanded the 3rd Cuirassier Division in the campaign of 1809, at the head of which he was mortally wounded at Essling.

CHAPTER 9

REAP THE WHIRLWIND

The battle of Albuera, 1811

The honour of a general consists in obeying, in keeping subalterns under his orders on the honest path, in maintaining good discipline, devoting oneself solely to the interest of the State and the sovereign, and in scorning completely private interests. NAPOLEON

Great extremities require extraordinary resolution. The more obstinate the resistance of an army, the greater the chances of success. How many seemingly impossibilities have been accomplished by men whose only resolve was death! NAPOLEON

10:00 16 May 1811 near Albuera, Spain

General Latour-Maubourg, commanding Marshal Soult's cavalry was sitting at the head of his squadrons on the French left flank watching Girard's attacking French infantry being taken in flank by British infantry and artillery fire and starting to melt away under the pressure. He also heard the cheers of the British infantry as they started to sweep forward to clinch their victory.

Unfortunately for them, they were either ignoring his cavalry division or they could not see it from where they were positioned because Girard's infantry was in the way or because of the smoke that hung over the firefight on this hot, sticky Spanish spring day. It looked as if the British were advancing in line without skirmishers and they were not being supported by any cavalry. They would deeply regret this last move.

Turning to an aide-de-camp, Latour-Maubourg told him very carefully what he wanted done. The aide was to go to the commanders of the 1st Lancers of the Vistula and the 2e Hussars and tell them to advance along the ridge against the flank of the British infantry brigade that was now very much in the air. He asked the aide to repeat back the order and then repeated it again to ensure the young officer had it right. Then with a pat on the back, he sped the young man on his way.

Many minutes later, Latour-Maubourg saw the aide pounding back the way he had come and the trumpet calls behind him told him that his instructions had been delivered. The two light cavalry regiments were swinging into column and moving to advance against the British along the slopes of the ridge as they had been instructed. They were apparently still unnoticed by the British brigade commander.

Latour-Maubourg was satisfied as the two light cavalry regiments smartly moved off. That British general was about to get a severe lesson in light cavalry tactics if he lived to remember it.

Albuera is unique among the Peninsular battles in that although the troops were assigned to Wellington's command, those that were engaged in the fighting were detached from Wellington's main army and under the command of British Marshal William Beresford. It is unique in other areas as well. British losses in the battle were unusually severe despite the fact that the allies enjoyed a comfortable numerical advantage over the French, although Beresford's army contained not only British troops but the excellent Portuguese, Wellington's famous 'fighting cocks', plus a considerable number of Spanish troops. One of the unusual features of Albuera is how well Zayas's Spanish division performed, standing in line and slugging it out with veteran French troops, who were no doubt as surprised at that fact as the British and Portuguese were. The Spanish contributed significantly to Beresford's bloody success.

In early May 1811 it became obvious that the allies needed to take the fortress of Badajoz. Wellington entrusted Marshal Beresford to undertake that task and that general invested the fortress and began siege operations. The siege did not progress well, thanks to the inefficiency of British siege operations as well as an aggressive defence.[1]

Soult made the decision to march to relieve Badajoz and assembled an army of approximately 25,000 men for that purpose. This was in itself not a cohesive force, but something akin to a 'task force' made up of available units that had not recently been serving together as an army in the field. Upon hearing that Soult was marching to the relief of the fortress, Beresford was forced to lift the siege and seek to meet Soult in battle.

The French were ready enough on 10 May and they marched at midnight for Badajoz. It was not until 12 May that Beresford received word that Soult was heading for him and the fortress: there was something of a scramble to reorganise for field operations and to march to meet Soult away from the city. British and Spanish cavalry made contact with the French on the 13th sent word to Beresford.

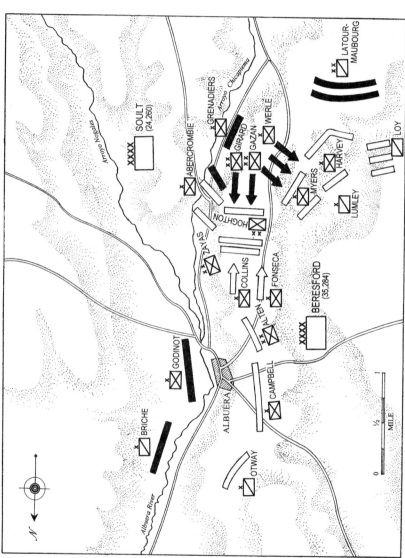

The Battle of Albuera

Soult outgeneralled Beresford in the opening stages of the battle, feinting at Beresford's centre and then making the main effort on the allied right flank. Ultimately, however, the French attacks, bitterly pushed forward, were defeated in some of the heaviest infantry firefights of the period. The Spanish manfully stood up to the contest, Colborne's British infantry brigade was caught in line from the flank by a French cavalry attack and wrecked, but the victory, bloody though it was, went to Beresford. Both sides lost about the same in casualties, but it was harder on the French as they were outnumbered on the field.

On 15 May Beresford reached the village of Albuera, which is a major road junction. Through it run the roads to Badajoz, Santa Marta, Talavera, Almendralejo and Valverde. The 'River' Albuera runs from the north to the town and then branches into two other watercourses, the Chicapierna and the Nogales. None is a serious obstacle and though some of the ground on what was to become the battlefield is described either as a ridge or high ground, most of the terrain is relatively flat and it is good cavalry country.

Neither army arrived intact in the Albuera area and both commanders waited for their outlying units to catch up. The protagonists arrived in the area from opposite directions, Beresford from the north-west and Soult from the southeast. Beresford based his initial tactical dispositions on the belief that Soult would make his main attack at the village of Albuera. Thus he made the village his centre, leaving his right flank in the air and his left in some orchards. His front was over two miles long and was not particularly strong nor well-sited.

Soult, an astute tactician, saw the weakness of Beresford's position immediately and planned to attack the village, but that was to be only a feint to hold the British in position. With the main portion of his army, the infantry divisions of Girard and Gazan and Latour-Maubourg's cavalry, he planned to envelop the allied right flank.

The manoeuvre worked well and Beresford was completely taken in, though some of his subordinates were not. The French under Godinot did attack the village and there would be fighting there for the duration of the battle, but it was merely a secondary attack that was not intended to be successful. If it was, and the village taken and held, that would be an added advantage.

On the allied right flank, Gazan's and Girard's infantry advanced under cover of woods and terrain, but they were seen by an alert aide-de-camp as well as by British cavalry patrols. The information was hurriedly passed to Beresford, who, fortunately for the allies, was convinced of its accuracy and ordered units to shift to the allied right flank. They would be just in time before the French avalanche hit.

Led by Latour-Maubourg's cavalry, who brushed aside the Spanish and British cavalry who tried to stop him, the French infantry attacked in heavy formations, designed to break through an opposing line by shock. Girard was leading, with Gazan's division following in four regimental columns, over 8,400 infantrymen ready to engage the Spanish under Zayas. French horse artillery, commanded by General Ruty, and skirmishers swarmed over the area, but the Spaniards manfully stepped up and met the French volley for volley, desperately holding their ground until the troops shifting from the British left could come to their support.

Men fell to the accurately murderous close range musket fire, troops in the rear ranks stepping up over the wounded and dead to take their place. In the north, Stewart's division was hotfooting to the sound and smoke of the firefight. Stewart's leading brigade, four British battalions under Colborne, tore into the flank of Girard's division, attacking in line and ably supported by a battery from the King's German Legion. Initially, the French manoeuvred to return the fire to their flank, but soon the French infantry had had enough and began to waver. Just as the British were about to deliver a final volley and charge with bayonets, a thunderstorm broke over the combatants, drenching everyone in a torrential rain.

All of this had not gone unnoticed by the alert and aggressive Latour-Maubourg. Seeing the British infantry brigade advance in line to the meet the French infantry, they left their flank in the air. Quickly whistling up an aide-de-camp, the French cavalry commander ordered the Lancers of the Vistula Legion and the 2nd Hussars to charge Colborne's brigade which was still in line, shrouded with smoke, and a tempting target for an attack by cavalry, if the cavalry could advance without being noticed. It was a calculated risk on Latour-Maubourg's part, but his decision would be fortuitous for the French.

The two light cavalry regiments manoeuvred expertly around the growing noise of the firefight and positioned themselves on Colborne's open flank. As the command '*En Avant!*' was bellowed by regimental commanders and French trumpets blew the charge, a vicious storm broke over the battlefield masking the cavalrymen going for the unsuspecting British infantry, whose muskets were now useless, at the dead run.

The two French regiments, 800 strong, burst like a thunderclap on to Colborne's flank and began to tear up the British brigade, rolling it up back on to itself. In one of the most devastating cavalry charges in history, the French horsemen destroyed a fine brigade of British infantry at first impact. The first battalion that was hit, the 1st Battalion, 3rd Foot, was swallowed whole and virtually ceased to exist as it was overrun by the jubilant horsemen. The next two battalions in line were also virtually destroyed, the 2nd Battalion, 48th Foot and the 2nd Battalion, 66th Foot. Only the last battalion, the 2nd Battalion, 31st Foot was able to form square and save itself. The British infantrymen fought back as best they could and the fighting around the colours was savage and brutal. Many infantrymen were cut down, some by the grim Poles after surrendering, and several of the brigade's colours were taken by the French horsemen. For good measure, the supporting artillery battery was captured by the light horsemen. Colborne's brigade was destroyed as a combat unit.[2]

To add insult to injury, Zayas's Spaniards were fired on by friendly troops in the confusion. The Spanish fired back, and it was only by the personal bravery of Beresford's military secretary, Major Robert Arbuthnot, who recklessly exposed himself to the musketry of both the Spanish and English infantry, that both sides ceased fire.

Latour-Maubourg's cavalry had done great damage to the British, but the battle was not over. Latour-Maubourg had to rally his troopers after their wild chevauchee, during which the two regiments probably lost twenty-five per cent of their strength. While this was occurring, the other two infantry brigades of Stewart's division came on to the field and an immense firefight developed, which was said by many to be the most devastating during the long war in the Peninsula.

Further, Soult did not realise, because of the same thunderstorm, what his cavalry had accomplished; by the time he was informed what had happened, the advantage gained had passed. British General Lumley did attempt to come to Colborne's aid and counter-attacked with four squadrons of cavalry, but it was too late to stop the heavy casualties.

Girard and now Gazan were hotly engaged in a firefight with the infantry brigades of Hoghton and Abercrombie. The infantry was literally fighting toe-to-toe, exchanging volleys and individual 'fire at will' at point-blank range. Werle's French brigade came to the support of Girard and got into a firefight with the British Fusilier Brigade, which had, in its turn, advanced over ground swept by French artillery fire. The British were in line, maximising the number of muskets per unit, while the French units, though outnumbering their opponents, were in deeper formations unable to bring their superiority of numbers to bear. The terrain was restricted and the senior British infantry commanders were able to manoeuvre to get the French infantry in crossfire. The fighting was unusually savage and the casualties were enormous. It was a case of who would outlast whom, and in this aspect the British infantry was victorious. Having suffered crippling losses the French had had enough, and troops started to drift away and the torrent became a rout. The British maintained their position, but their units had also suffered appalling losses and had indeed 'fed death' on this grim field. Both armies were fought out and had had enough.

With the repulse and defeat of Girard and Gazan, the battle was over and Soult was smart enough to recognise it as such. He had fought a numerically superior enemy and outmanoeuvred him. He had nearly outfought him. The French withdrew behind a strong rearguard and the allies were too beat up and exhausted to pursue. The siege of Badajoz would have to be abandoned, at least for the moment. The British had won again tactically, but it was nearly a strategic defeat.

Losses were extremely heavy on both sides. The allies had lost a total of 5,916 and the French 5,332. While the total numbers of casualties were remarkably even, it hurt Soult's army more as they had 10,000 less to begin with. It was the bloodiest day of the Peninsular War.

When Wellington heard the news of Albuera, he was appalled. He could ill afford to lose that many of his British troops and he probably never forgave Beresford for mismanaging the battle, at least to Wellington's mind. His comment to Beresford to 'write me down a victory' sounds like frustration and some grief at the heavy losses.

Nicolas Jean de Dieu Soult (1769–1851) established a reputation as the 'finest manoeuvrer in Europe' because of his steadfast performance at Austerlitz in 1805, commanding the French main attack that shattered the allied centre.

Soult enlisted in 1785 and was a sergeant by 1791. He was sent to the volunteers as an instructor and was promoted to lieutenant the next year. He served under, and was trained by, Lefebvre and Masséna and by 1799 he was a general of brigade. With Masséna in Genoa, he was wounded and captured during a sortie and held in Alessandria and was there during the battle of Marengo. Imaginative, aggressive and ambitious, he earned the nickname of 'Iron Hand' which the troops under him swore was richly deserved.

The command that he built into the IV Corps was well-trained, Soult being noted as a careful and thorough organiser and trainer. He served with the Grande Armée from 1805–7 fighting stoutly at Austerlitz, Jena, Eylau and Heilsberg. Sent into Spain, he was defeated in Portugal, performing an expert withdrawal saving his army. He pacified Andalusia so well that French personnel could go along the streets unarmed and unescorted.

In Saxony in 1813, he briefly understudied Berthier, but was sent back to Spain after the disaster at Vittoria and his service there was excellent, fulfilling the Emperor's faith in him and fighting, and almost winning, the last battle of the war.

He replaced Dupont as Minister of War during the first restoration and there are suspicions that he was working for Napoleon's return while in that office. Rallying to the Emperor upon the latter's return from Elba, he was selected as Berthier's replacement and probably made more mistakes while chief of staff of Nord than Berthier had done in his entire career.

Marie Victor Nicolas Marquis de Latour-Maubourg (1768–1850) was a skilled cavalryman and one of the best cavalry commanders in the Grande Armée. A noble and a lieutenant in the King's bodyguard in 1789, he was a colonel the next year and went with Lafayette when that prima donna went over to the allies that year. Latour-Maubourg was imprisoned by the allies until 1797.

He served in Egypt and made general of division by 1808. His service was always conscientious and outstanding and he was revered by the Germans that served under him in 1812. An excellent division and cavalry corps commander, it was Latour-Maubourg's light cavalry that charged out of a sudden rainstorm at Albuera in 1811 that overran and wrecked, all but annihilating, a British infantry brigade, scooping up four of their colours.

He was severely wounded at Leipzig, after having pierced the allied centre with his heavy cavalry. His wounding, and the failure of Murat to support the breakthrough, wasted Latour-Maubourg's efforts. He was inactive thereafter, having lost a leg. An excellent cavalry commander, he was a good tactician and an excellent combat leader. His loss in the 1813 campaign was a severe blow to the cavalry arm of the Grande Armée.

CHAPTER 10

ONE LAST RIVER
TO CROSS

The crossing of the Berezina, 1812

I know you Swiss. For the attack Frenchmen are brisker. But if it comes to a retreat we can certainly count on your courage and cool headedness. ST CYR[1]

Ordinary men died, men of iron were taken prisoner. I only brought back with me men of bronze. NAPOLEON 1812

18:00 25 November 1812, Studenka, the Ukraine

The weather had broken again and it was getting colder. That made the Artilleryman's task more difficult as the river was wider and deeper because of the sudden thaw. The orders from the Emperor eight days before to destroy all unnecessary vehicles convinced the Artilleryman that the situation was beyond desperate.

However, his calculated disobedience not to burn his last two field forges, two coals wagons and six caissons full of vital equipment had undoubtedly been correct. His pontoniers had grumbled about carrying extra loads when he had ordered them to carry a tool and extra clamps, but he did not care. This was important – on it would be based the survival of the army.

General Eble, chief of the pontoniers of the Grande Armée, or what was left of it, grimly surveyed the panorama in front of him. The River Berezina loomed out of the fog and snow and the existing bridges had either been destroyed or taken by the Russians. And all of the fords were being watched. Three separate Russian armies were rushing to trap Napoleon's remnants. Eble knew it was now up to him and his tough, independent pontoniers to bridge this last obstacle or the Grande Armée would be hopelessly trapped deep inside Russia and the survivors would then be sent to Siberia to count trees.

Behind him, his exhausted survivors trudged through the snow and slush, literally falling to the ground asleep. They were dead on their feet but could be allowed little rest. There was too much work to do.

Summoning his immediate subordinates, he ordered them to organise the men into working parties in two shifts. Each shift would work at intervals in the freezing river or on the bank building the trestle bridges the Emperor had ordered to be built. Additionally, he ordered that the village of Studenka be demolished to provide most of the raw material for the bridges. Eble felt badly about driving the poor peasants out to the mercy of the weather, but it could not be helped. Already, the two field forges were being stoked into life to forge the needed iron work. Hearing the roar of gunfire behind him, he knew the rearguard under Victor and Davout was already at grips with the pursuing Russians. He wondered how those two marshals were getting along. Probably like a house on fire. Neither liked the other, Davout for good reason. He also knew that speed was essential in the bridge-building operations.

Briefly conferring with Chasseloup, the army's chief engineer, Eble decided on his course of action. His pontoniers would have to build both of the bridges necessary. The engineers' task had been to build a third bridge, but Chasseloup did not have enough men left to get up an interesting card game. The construction in the freezing, ice-laden water was up to Eble and his scarecrows. Motioning to a waiting maréchal des logis-chef to rouse the first weary shift, he led the way to the steep river bank and the cold, black water beyond.

The greatest campaign that Europe had seen since the Mongol invasions swept across Asia and into Europe had begun with the invasion of Russia by the Grande Armée in June 1812. Crossing the River Nieman hoping to catch and trap the Russian field armies close to the border, the Emperor was continually frustrated as the Russian armies eluded his grasp.

Though there was no comprehensive Russian plan to draw the French deeper into Russia, repeated withdrawals accomplished just that. Napoleon finally found the main Russian army under Kutusov ready to fight near Borodino, just west of Moscow, in September. However, even though Kutusov was mauled and huge losses inflicted on the Russian army, as well as on his own force, Napoleon did not achieve the battle of annihilation he had hoped for.

Kutusov and his army escaped, fleeing towards Moscow. In the end, they abandoned Russia's traditional capital to the French, but its capture proved a hollow triumph. The Tsar refused to negotiate while the French remained on Russian soil, which was surprising, since Alexander was not known for either physical or moral courage. French losses, especially in horses, had been horrific. Attempting to resupply the army had been an immense undertaking and, despite all the care that Napoleon had taken in that regard, it was largely a failure.

The supporting allied armies on the French flanks under Marshal Macdonald, General Reynier and the Austrian commander, Prince Schwarzenberg, had also achieved victories in the field, but they had not proven to be decisive.

Napoleon dithered in Moscow, undoubtedly stayed too long with no decision in sight, and finally ordered the army to begin to withdraw westward in mid-October.[2] The French line of march, after several false starts, was along the same route by which they had come. Picked clean of supplies and fodder, this route could not support the army for long and the French were also encumbered by an immense amount of baggage, much of it loot.

Growing numbers of troops left the ranks, abandoned their weapons and equipment and looked to themselves. Worse, many officers did the same. The growing indiscipline was allowed to continue almost unchecked, which further slowed the retreat. The dreaded Russian winter usually set in by mid-November, and this time the Emperor had cut it just a little too short. Most of the remaining horses starved to death or were killed for food and the plight of the main army became desperate.

When winter finally blew in at the beginning of November, there was even more difficulty finding forage for the remaining understrength horses that survived. This led to creative foraging by some of the remaining units who still had mounts and horse teams. Some actually went into the Russian lines at night, searching for fodder, and brought back rations for their mounts sometimes with a Russian prisoner for good measure.

Kutusov and the Russian main army were having just as hard a time as the French.[3] Gingerly trailing the Grande Armée, Kutusov did not want to get drawn into another general engagement with Napoleon. Recent defeats, such as Maloyaroslavets, had demonstrated that the Grande Armée under its veteran commanders was still deadly. Nothing was more dangerous that a hurt and cornered wild animal and Kutusov was more than content to leave the Grande Armée alone. Seemingly hopelessly trapped or cut off French units, such as both Ney's and Eugène's corps, either fought their way through the Russian masses or bypassed blocking forces to finally rejoin the main body. Nothing the Russians did actually attempted to stop the French retreat. One eyewitness likened the Guard wading through a snarling knot of Cossacks to a warship sailing through a fleet of fishing trawlers, all guns firing, cutting down the irregulars who did not melt away at first contact.

Swarms of Cossacks trailed the French, picking off stragglers, but always stopping to loot and staying away from formed bodies of troops, especially if they had artillery. The Cossacks were a nuisance to the French, but were generally worthless in a stand-up fight. They were even worse at collecting information desperately needed by the Russian field commanders.[4]

The Cossacks did come into their own the worse the weather became. Hardy frontiersman used to the elements, they continued on where regular Russian light cavalry perished and they were fatal to unwary stragglers or small detachments that were not alert and ready to fight.

Kutusov, amazingly enough, frequently lost contact with the French, even when deep in Russia and enjoying a large superiority in light cavalry. Their maps were notoriously inaccurate and they frequently became lost inside their own country. However, the Russian secondary armies under the command of General Wittgenstein and Admiral Tshitshagov were rapidly closing in from the flanks in an attempt to cut the French off from home. Tshitshagov was bee-lining it for the little town of Borisov on the Berezina River, the last major obstacle the French would face before reaching the Nieman, Poland and safety.

Rear area detachments were alerted to the main army's situation and warning orders given to be prepared to join the main army on the march. Victor with the IX Corps and Oudinot with the II Corps began to move towards the main army and the rendezvous at the Berezina. Their respective commands were made up of more foreign elements than French, but they had not been as hard used as the formations in the main body.

On 17 November, the main army finally reached Orsha. Disorganised, exhausted and out of supplies, the troops were almost at the end of their rope. Fortunately for the French, the administrative staff was efficient and went to work with a will issuing needed supplies and ammunition to the army from march column. Many of the stragglers rejoined their units. Troops who had lost or thrown away their weapons were re-armed from the well-stocked arsenal; artillery companies were re-armed with guns and ancillary vehicles.[5] The army came away from Orsha probably in the best shape since Maloyaroslavets. What the troops really needed, however, the Emperor could not give them. One or two days' rest would have done wonders for the exhausted troops, but Napoleon could not stop the retreat even for twenty-four hours. Fear of being cut off deep in Russia nagged at Napoleon's mind and he immediately ordered the corps commanders to rouse their exhausted men and to resume the retreat.

In an attempt to make the army more mobile and give available horses to the artillery, Napoleon ordered all excess vehicles to be burned. To set the example, Napoleon destroyed his personal papers and extra vehicles and insisted that the corps commanders follow suit. Some troops would not let go of their loot and many commanders failed to enforce the Emperor's command to inspect their troops for loot and unnecessary loads in their packs.

Unfortunately, Napoleon also ordered that the pontoon train be burned over the protests of its commander, General Eble. Eble, a hard-bitten horse artilleryman, commander of the pontoniers of the Grande Armée, vigorously protested but was overruled by Napoleon.[6] Apparently complying, Eble ordered the vehicles burned, but saved two field forges, six artillery caissons full of equipment and tools, as well as two wagons full of charcoal. He also had his pontoniers each carry a tool and clamps.

Eble was one of the characters of the Grande Armée. Tall and balding, described by Bernadotte as 'having the appearance of an ancient Roman', he was taciturn, tough and competent. A strict disciplinarian, he frequently would slap any reluctant gunner or pontonier who would not obey him. Deeply revered by the rank and file, it was said he could make both artillery and pontonier units 'out of the most unpromising material'. He made few friends, but those he did make, such as Masséna's ADC Pelet, were devoted to him. He referred to the troops he commanded as 'my comrades'.

Eble was born in Lorraine in 1758, his father was an NCO in an artillery regiment. Enlisting at the age of nine, he was a true *'enfant de troupe'*. Commissioned in 1785, he soon proved to be an expert artilleryman and made a name for himself as a horse artilleryman in the early part of the Revolutionary Wars. By virtue of his performance, he became a general of brigade by 1793 and was promoted to general of division in 1808.

Upon the creation of the kingdom of Westphalia, Eble became Jérôme's Minister of War ostensibly to keep Jérôme out of trouble. His expertise was almost immediately put to the test. He organised the new Westphalian army, despite Jérôme's amateur interference, and quelled the revolt of some of its pro-Prussian elements in 1809.

Eble served under Bernadotte in 1805 and was with Masséna in 1810. Highly prized by Masséna, he became good friends with Masséna's senior ADC, Pelet. Admired by all, he was not widely liked and chose his friends carefully. Those who were close to him were devoted and life-long friends.

When the French pontonier arm was formed during the early Revolutionary Wars from Rhine River bargemen, they were an independent and unruly lot. When they finally came under the command of Eble that changed for the better. It speaks volumes for Eble's leadership and command abilities, as well as for his character, that these tough soldiers were taught 'the profession of arms' and became a highly disciplined and expert outfit.

Eble was responsible for building the bridges at the Berezina that enabled the Grande Armée to leave Russia. He died, sick and worn out, along with most of his pontoniers, at Königsberg at the end of the retreat. Because of his outstanding performance and leadership, he was made a count of the Empire, but this honour was received by his widow.

While the main army was going through Orsha, Victor and Oudinot closed on Borisov, Victor being pursued by Wittgenstein. Having loaned one brigade of his corps cavalry to Bavarian General Wrede and his VI Corps, Oudinot promptly ordered its return on 17 November. Located north-west of its parent command, its commander, Corbineau, immediately moved out across country to rejoin II Corps.

Skilfully manoeuvring across potentially hostile countryside, Corbineau fought off one band of Cossacks who tried to trap them through the use of a clever ruse. The Russian irregulars found the experienced French light horsemen too big a bite to swallow. Further on they chased another Cossack outfit from the village of Kostitza, giving them a quick, rude lesson in light cavalry tactics. The Polish lancer regiment in the brigade got in some quick revenge against their traditional enemy and granted no quarter.

Reaching the Berezina on 21 November, Corbineau was searching for a ford when he was informed by friendly civilians that there was one near the hamlet of Studenka on the eastern bank of the river. The brigade crossed the river at midnight on 21–22 November. Keeping a tight formation as they crossed, the brigade still lost between twenty and seventy troopers to the current and floating ice. The Berezina, about a hundred yards wide, was no more than two to three feet deep, except for a twenty- or thirty-foot stretch in the middle of the river. A sudden thaw in the next few days would both widen and deepen the river, compounding the French bridging operations. Noting the location of the ford, Corbineau moved south to rejoin Oudinot.[7]

The main French army continued its trek west from Orsha. Its fighting units consisted of the Imperial Guard, Davout's I Corps, Ney's III Corps, Eugène's IV Corps, Poniatowski's V Corps and Junot's Westphalians (VIII Corps). Altogether, there were approximately 25–30,000 serviceable troops still with the colours. Following these formations was a mass of approximately 40,000 stragglers. There were between 250 and 300 usable guns with the army.

General Bronikowski commanding the Minsk garrison had moved northwards to contact the main army. He seized and occupied Borisov, along with its bridge over the Berezina. His security, however, was lax and he failed to fortify either his position or the bridgeheads. He was surprised and driven out of the town, losing the bridge to Tshitshagov on 21 November. The commander of one of Bronikowski's Polish regiments forded the river with his regiment in order to avoid encirclement.

Rochechouart the ubiquitous Royalist stated that Bronikowski had 'hardly 2,000 men to oppose to 30,000 Russians' and 'not merely had he not organised any defense. He had not even tried to put up any resistance, which anyway

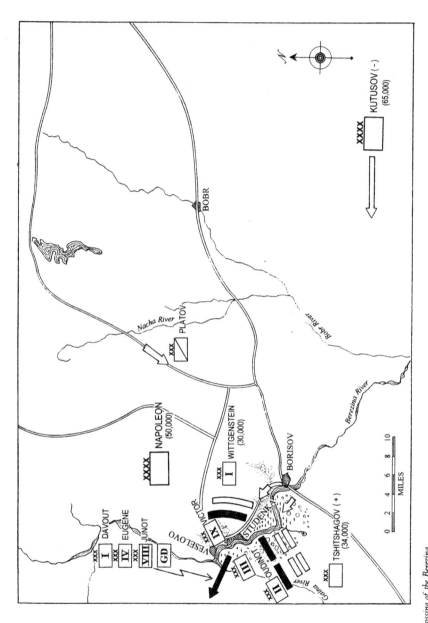

The Crossing of the Berezina

The French crossing of a river, building two bridges while doing so, is one of the most outstanding examples of the innate fighting ability of the Grande Armée. Outnumbered, seemingly trapped by two hostile armies, with a third approaching, Napoleon attacked across the river, his troops held the opposing bank against repeated Russian counter-attacks while the French rearguard under Victor kept Wittgenstein from crowding in on the crossing. Partouneaux's infantry division was captured by Wittgenstein, but the army got across the river and escaped.

would have served no purpose. Why had not he foreseen our army corps' march? Why had not he sent out a few scouts, if only to know what Prince Schwarzenberg was doing and where he was . . . ?'[8]

Guillaume de Vaudancourt suggested that Bronikowski 'had drawn up no plan of retreat, given no orders, so most of the garrison troops, without either a general or any orders, had moved mechanically toward the main army, which by this time we knew was retreating.'

Dombrowski's well-trained and conditioned Polish division arrived and attempted to reverse the situation, but they failed against the Russians.[9] Napoleon was informed of these events by 23 November and ordered Oudinot to seize a crossing of the river between Veselovo and Berezino. He was also ordered to inform Imperial Headquarters of the proposed crossing site as soon as possible so the army could move in that direction without losing too much time.

Dombrowski was described by Major Everts of the 33rd Ligne as 'very simply dressed in a middle-class overcoat, with a wretched cap on his head, but on his chest the great star of the Order of Poland, surrounded by a brilliant escort of Polish lancers. The general's tall stature, together with a certain dignity and his way of speaking . . . made a good impression.'

Vaudancourt's description of the conduct of Dombrowski's troops could be taken to describe the conduct of the Grande Armée in the coming operation: 'He did so in good order. The valorous Poles crossed the bridge in closed ranks and sustaining the enemy's reiterated attacks. Dombrowski took up a position immediately behind Borisov on the high ground on the river's left bank. The enemy tried in vain to dislodge him and night put an end to the fighting. Thus was lost the bridge over the Berezina.'[10]

Oudinot immediately and efficiently carried out his mission, the first time in the campaign he actually commanded well. About this time, a slight thaw set in, melting some of the ice in the marshland on the west bank of the Berezina opposite Studenka. It also temporarily ruined the already bad roads compounding the mobility problems for both armies.[11]

Lorencz succinctly recorded the choices Oudinot had as to which crossing to choose or recommend to Napoleon: 'We had three crossing points reputed to be fordable: Oukholoda, two miles downstream; Stadkov, one mile upstream; and lastly Studenka. We had these points reconnoitered as far as the night's darkness permitted. We found them all guarded. Anyway, the first two were too easily seen by the mass of the enemy's forces to tempt Marshal Oudinot, who never varied in his preference for the last.'[12]

Tshitshagov had by now pushed his advance guard under the French émigré

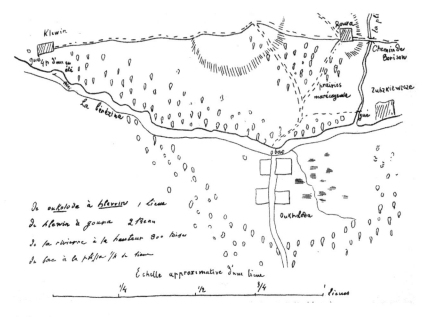

Sketch of the reconnaissance at Oukholoda, sent on the 24 November to Oudinot. This series of sketches clearly demonstrated the magnificent effort Oudinot and his subordinates put into preparing the Studenka bridgehead. That along with the expert deception plan were key to the success of the operation.

General Lambert across to the east bank of the river looking for the French. For reasons known only to Tshitshagov he also shoved his trains and army headquarters across the river, clogging Borisov with wagons and carriages that were not needed. The narrow streets were now blocked to artillery and formed bodies of troops.

Oudinot's advance guard under Corbineau, who by now had rejoined Oudinot and informed him of the ford at Studenka, slammed into Lambert's unsuspecting troops six miles east of Borisov on the Smolensk road. Over-running the lead elements, he routed the surprised Lambert inflicting some loss in a short, sharp engagement. The jubilant light cavalrymen chased the Russians back into Borisov and the traffic jam. Bursting into the town on the Russians' heels, the two chasseur regiments of Castex's brigade bypassed the wagons and went for the Borisov bridge. Dismounting to charge the bridge, the chasseurs shot down the Russians who were hastily trying to set fire to the bridge.

A Russian grenadier battalion counter-attacked across the bridge from the west bank and threw the chasseurs back, enabling other Russians to set fire to the bridge. The fire spread quickly and the frustrated chasseurs watched helplessly as three-quarters of the bridge collapsed into the river. The bridge that Napoleon was counting on to get out of Russia was now destroyed.[13]

Corbineau had captured the Russian trains and headquarters baggage, including meals that had been prepared for staff officers in Borisov. One thousand Russian prisoners had also been taken. The supplies found in the wagons by the eager chasseurs were distributed swiftly and with order. Warned against hiding any unauthorised loot, the half-starved troopers were inspected by their NCOs before mounting up and departing. Any forbidden goods were confiscated and unceremoniously thrown into the snow at the side of the road. Corbineau mounted up and immediately reported to Oudinot that the Borisov bridge had been destroyed.[14]

Rochechouart's comment of the action was quite succinct: 'Of the advance guard of 6,000 men with 12 guns, only about 1,000 and two cannon had re-crossed the bridge. All the rest had been dispersed or captured.'[15]

Corbineau's hard-riding brigade was now dispatched northward from Borisov to find and occupy two fords for the army. The Studenka ford was already known. Another found closer to Borisov (which had been used by Bronikowski on 21 November). Sending word to Oudinot, Corbineau was now given command of a task force consisting of his won brigade, an infantry regiment and all of Oudinot's pontoniers, and sent to Studenka to hold the ford.

At the same time, Oudinot cleverly set up a deception operation on the east bank to confuse the Russians as to the actual crossing site. Other units were sent to other known crossing sites and to be within sight of the Russians. The units selected energetically carried out their missions and completely fooled Tshitshagov. The ever-increasing mass of stragglers that came into the area helped in the deception.

Swallowing the proffered bait, Tshitshagov pulled off to the south toward Berezino, convinced by Oudinot' demonstrations that the French would cross below Borisov. Massing below Borisov, Tshitshagov confidently awaited the expected French crossing attempt. Unfortunately for the French, he had the presence of mind to detach a strong infantry division under Tschaplitz to remain near the Studenka ford.

Off to the north-west Victor was having problems of his own. Being outnumbered by Wittgenstein, he was nonetheless waging an aggressive delaying action, but the execrable condition of the Russian roads was hampering his mobility. A dangerous opponent in a tight corner, Victor expertly continued to withdraw towards the Smolensk road, keeping Wittgenstein off Napoleon's flank. On 25 November came the summons to join the main army.

The Emperor ordered Oudinot to cross the river at Studenka and fortify the west-bank bridgehead against the expected Russian reaction to a French crossing. Oudinot had wisely chosen the Studenka ford instead of the one near Veselovo. The Studenka ford was less well known and the Russian division there was paying more attention to Veselovo. The Russians had amateurishly left an outpost at the Studenka crossing point, but were not there in strength. One good shove and the French would have their bridgehead on the west bank. Additionally, the Russians watching Studenka were not especially vigilant, the French crossing being expected much further to the south.

The terrain in the vicinity of Borisov and Studenka is open and rolling, with low hills and ridges dotting the countryside at regular intervals. The entire landscape is pockmarked with heavy forests of native pine. The eastern bank is somewhat higher than the west bank, giving the French excellent fields of fire to cover a river crossing. There is considerable marshy area west of the river which is impassable to vehicles in the spring and summer. Twenty-two bridges linked a causeway through the marshes. This was a vital objective for the French to seize after crossing the river. If the Russians did it first, they would have to fight their way out and across the frozen marshes.

The previously mentioned thaw initially caused Napoleon and his subordinates some concern. By 25 November, though, winter had returned, freezing the marshes. Without the aid of the weather it is quite likely the Grande Armée would have lost its artillery.

Eble and Chasseloup finally arrived in Borisov at 04:30 that day. They were notified that Oudinot was near Studenka, and after a brief reconnaissance both officers proceeded to find the marshal. Reaching there by early evening, they met with both Oudinot and Murat. The army's cavalry commander was morose and contributed little, but Oudinot quickly and efficiently briefed them on the situation.[16] Oudinot's sketches of the Berezina were accurate, to the point and are a great reference for the operation.[17] They decided to build three bridges, Eble two and Chasseloup one. Eble would build one each for the infantry and vehicles. Trestle bridges had to be constructed as the pontoons had been burned at Orsha. Trestle bridges were considered an engineering specialism, but the pontoniers had the necessary skills to construct them. Napoleon also reached Borisov on the 25th and saw that Oudinot's troops were taking shelter in the buildings of the town.

During the discussions, it became apparent that the engineers did not have the equipment to build their bridge. Eble had enough for his two, so the engineers were assigned to him and the number of bridges reduced to two. Plans were finalised and the pontoniers, engineers and Bouvier-Detouches' sailors, assigned to Eble, began tearing down the village of Studenka for bridging material. There were seven pontonier companies available to build the bridges.

The remaining engineers would construct the trestles for the bridges and the sailors would construct and man the rafts needed to finish the bridge in the middle of the river.[18] Virtually every structure in the village was torn down to provide material for the bridges. French working parties laboured continuously to assemble the needed material. Field forges coughed into action and all of the needed ironwork was forged in place. The clanging of blacksmith hammers rang through the pine forests, harbingers of the fighting to come.

Through the long cold night the bridge trestles, twenty-three for each bridge, were constructed as quietly as possible. No one wanted the drowsy Russian pickets to become suspicious. There was little or no movement on the west bank and no Russian officer was curious enough to find out what was going on over there. When dawn broke the night's handiwork was hauled to the riverbank. Construction parties briskly trotted to the river's edge from their covered positions behind the bank lugging the trestles with them. Piling by piling, the posts were pounded into the soft mud of the river bed, the troops gradually becoming immersed in the freezing water. When they could no longer touch bottom in the centre of the river, rafts were constructed to float the men and tools into the deeper water. To stabilise them, they were anchored to the riverbed.

Eble, 'deeply revered', worked alongside his men, going into the water with every shift. Those frozen from the water went back to fires and dry clothing and whatever food and drink that was available.

The rest of the army was on the move. Those designated to cross first moved into their assembly areas. Mortier's Young Guard was ordered into Borisov, its two divisions commanded by Delaborde and the deeply respected 'Pere' Roguet. The bulk of Oudinot's corps had displaced to Studenka, leaving detachments along the river to maintain the deception operation. Victor withdrew to the Smolensk road, but found it hard going, the roads being worse than in Poland in 1806–7. He continuously had to re-route his artillery and trains to make sure they did not get stuck in axle-deep mud and so have to be abandoned. These problems were compounded by the thaw that slowed every vehicle of both armies, wearing out the already exhausted horse teams. The gaunt, gallant animals would sometimes finally collapse in their traces and could not be coaxed back to their feet.

Even with all the problems the French encountered, Wittgenstein made no attempt to crowd in on Victor's withdrawal, growing more hesitant as time passed. This gave Victor the opportunity to link up with Davout, the army's rearguard. They continued on together, burning any bridges over streams and creeks to further retard the already slow Wittgenstein.

Victor was shocked at the appearance of Davout's corps.[19] The once magnificent regiments had been the best in the army, on a par in discipline and training with the Imperial Guard. They were now ragged, hungry and had sustained heavy losses. Victor now realised that the situation was desperate.

There had been no contact with Kutusov's main body in days. His initial pursuit had degenerated into an amateurish and hesitant blind probe. He definitely did not want to fight the Grande Armée again. Neither Wittgenstein nor Tshitshagov would receive any assistance during the coming fight from Kutusov and that was probably deliberate on Kutusov's part. In actuality, Kutusov only wanted the French to leave Russia and was personally afraid to meet the Emperor on the battlefield again.[20] Platov did show up in the area, but any meaningful support from the old Russian did not materialise. Platov and his Cossacks demonstrated nothing but the ability to rob, abuse and murder defenceless French stragglers that they came across and captured.

For the coming fight available Russian forces numbered approximately 75,000 of all arms against no more than 49,000 French and allies. There were approximately 30–40,000 French stragglers strung out along the line of the Berezina.

By the afternoon of the 25th, Napoleon had arrived and expertly conducted a thorough reconnaissance of the Borisov area, making himself as conspicuous as possible. Always accompanied by his faithful escort of Guard cavalrymen, he undoubtedly was spotted by the Russian outposts on the opposite side of the river. This reinforced the Russian impression that the French would cross below Borisov. He and his master of horse, Caulaincourt, even ventured out on to the ruined Borisov bridge for a better look across the river.[21]

Napoleon's remark at the success of Oudinot's deception operations was typical of him. 'I've fooled the Admiral! He thinks I'm at the spot where I've ordered the feint attack. He's hurrying off to Borisov.'[22]

Tshitshagov had apparently ignored Kutusov's warning of operating against Napoleon in the field, wryly remembered by Rochechouart, a Royalist who was serving with the Russians against his own countrymen: 'You have to do with a man as clever as he is cunning. Napoleon will make a demonstration that he is going to cross at one point, to draw your attention to it, while most likely doing it on the other side. Prudence and vigilance!'[23]

After midnight, the Emperor departed for Studenka, wanting to start crossing the river on the night of 25–26 November. The overall situation of the army was desperate. If the Russians could effectively oppose and defeat the river crossing, the Grande Armée would be trapped deep in Russia between two hostile armies and within striking distance of a third. The Emperor, his immediate subordinates and every private realised this and were prepared for an all-out effort. Napoleon told his staff and commanders: 'If we succeed in crossing the Berezina I shall be master of the situation, for the two fresh corps and my Guard will suffice to defeat the Russians.'[24] Of course, the two 'fresh' corps were relative. With that, all relied on Eble.

Napoleon was observed by Captain Rosselet waiting impatiently for the bridges to be completed. 'I saw him at close quarters. His back was resting against some trestles, his arms were crossed inside his overcoat. Silent, having an air of not paying attention to what was going on, only fixing his glances from time to time on the pontoniers a few paces away, sometimes up to their necks amid the ice floes, busy placing the trestles, which they seemed to have the greatest difficulty in fixing deeply, while others, as soon as they were in place, were laying the planks on them.'[25]

Père Roguet noticed Napoleon testing the planks as they were laid on the bridges and Captain Begos of the 2nd Swiss Regiment heard Napoleon impatiently talking to Eble 'It's taking a very long time, General. A very long time.' Eble replied to him: 'You can see, Sire, that my men are up to their necks in the water, and the ice is holding up their work. I've no food or brandy to warm them with.' Napoleon's reply of 'that'll do' ended the conversation.[26]

Still, Napoleon's troops had faith in him and his innate abilities as a commander. 'In such critical circumstances we still had faith in his genius. On his way back, his reconnaissance over, he passed close to us. We thought he seemed more satisfied. He was chatting and gesticulating vivaciously with his generals. We could not hear what he was saying, but we realised he was congratulating himself on having lured the Admiral into making a mistake. Shortly afterwards a double battery was set up on the hillock the Emperor had just left. And we were allowed to go up there to see the march past of the enemy whose rearguard frequently kept turning round to keep an eye on our operations.'[27]

Dawn on the 26th saw the Emperor personally supervising the emplacement of Oudinot's artillery on the ridge behind Studenka. This large battery would give fire support for the crossing and seizure of the west bank of the river. Colonel Chevau's forty-four guns were brought into battery by their exhausted gun teams, unlimbered and laid by their gun crews. They immediately opened fire and swept the opposite bank with accurate suppressing fire as Polish lancers of the 8th Lancer Regiment gave a cheer and splashed into the river, swimming their horses to the opposite bank. Each trooper carried a voltigeur behind him and as they gained the opposite bank the light infantry dismounted and together the voltigeurs and lancers 'went Cossack hunting'. Follow-on units came across dead Cossacks, all of whom had been shot in the head.[28]

During the fighting, General Rapp remembered when one of the artillery company commanders, a Captain Brechtel, 'who did the whole campaign with a wooden leg which did not prevent him from mounting his horse', was hit by a Russian round shot in that very leg, carrying it away and knocking the intrepid artilleryman to the ground. Helped to his feet by one of his gunners, he ordered him to fetch a spare leg out of 'wagon number five' and he continued to give his fire orders to his battery by holding on to a vehicle wheel, strapping on the spare when the gunner brought it back to him.[29]

As soon as the advance guard disappeared into the woods on the west bank, 300 infantrymen were immediately shuttled across on Eble's rafts. The personnel 'running' the shuttle service were Bouvier-Detouches's sailors.

Behind this screen, Eble began constructing two 105-yard long bridges at 08:00. The bridging sites were staked out, soundings taken and the pontoniers, engineers and sailors worked continuously in water up to their shoulders for hours at a time, setting in the pilings for the bridges. The pilings never received proper foundations because of the mud, but the trestles went in nonetheless. After the bridge planking was hammered into place, straw was spread across the roadbed to cut down on vibrations as the bridges were crossed. Eble knew the rickety structures would eventually collapse through prolonged use, but there was no time to make them permanent and therefore more sturdy.

The Emperor repeatedly checked on the construction, distributing bottles of wine to ease some of the cold and numbness of the troops working in the water. There was very little dry clothing to change into and hypothermia was the real danger to the men in the water: it caused most of the casualties from the I^e Bataillon des Pontonniers, the men's clothing sometimes freezing to their bodies. Baron Fain, who witnessed their unceasing and selfless work, remarked that they 'braved the cold, fatigue, exhaustion, even death, they're working ceaselessly, water up to their shoulders. The death they must find under the ice floes is not less the death of brave men for that.'[30]

The first bridge was completed by 13:00. Immediately Oudinot's troops poured across followed by Dombrowski's Polish Division. Doumerc's cuirassier division led their horses over the rickety structure accompanied by horse artillery, which ignored the efforts of Eble's men to slow them to a walk.

Napoleon had remarked that Oudinot would be his 'locksmith' for the crossing operations and Oudinot would fight with skill and valour before he took another of the thirty-four wounds suffered during his career. As he was about to cross, Napoleon told him to take care. 'Don't go over yet, Oudinot. You'll only get yourself captured.' Oudinot turned to the troops he was leading and said: 'Among them, Sire, I'm afraid of nothing.'[31]

Continuous cheers of 'Vive l'Empereur' echoed through the pine forests as the troops crossed the bridges. The Swiss, ready to cross under their general, Merle, halted near the bridge for a moment and Napoleon had a brief discussion with Merle. 'Are you please with the Swiss, General?', asked Napoleon. Merle replied 'Yes, sire. If the Swiss attacked as sharply as they know how to defend themselves, Your Majesty would be content with them.' One of the Swiss officers proudly recalled that Napoleon's reply was 'I know they're a good lot.' The same officer remarked that when the Swiss crossed the rickety bridge they 'sent up a ringing cheer for the Emperor'.[32]

The 1st Swiss Regiment, however, regretfully had to leave Colonel Raguettli behind at Borisov and some of them offered to stay behind to help him. The redoubtable commander told them 'Gentlemen, other duties call you. You must attend to them first, and if you manage to get across – as I hope you will – we'll soon see each other again.'[33]

These reinforcements beefed up the bridgehead and set up blocking positions on the west bank behind which the rest of the army could continue westward after crossing. Dombrowski's advance guard flushed out surviving Russians, seeing either dead bodies or the backs of their enemies as they withdrew. Oudinot sent Corbineau west to secure the causeways. Then, he turned on Tshaplitz.

Oudinot swiftly attacked the now isolated Russian division and sent it reeling southwards, shattered by the leading elements of his corps at first impact. The Swiss, Poles and Germans who made up the bulk of II Corps skilfully chose their defensive positions for the Muscovite avalanche they all knew would be coming. When Tshitshagov found out about Tsaplitz's defeat, he realised that he had been duped by the French and he gathered in his outlying units and immediately set out for the Studenka crossing. With any luck, he might be able to stop or delay the crossing until support from Wittgenstein and Kutusov appeared on the east bank.

Eble's numb and shivering men had finished the bridge by 16:00. Skilfully deploying his working parties on both sides of the river, it made the inevitable repair work that much quicker. Eble also attempted to persuade the stragglers to cross between the formed units. The French, however, had never been particularly adept at traffic control.

Told to cross at a walk to relieve wear and tear on the fragile bridges, most cavalry and artillery units ignored the orders and crossed at the trot, shaking the trestles dangerously which led to further breaks in the bridges which stopped traffic altogether. Most of the stragglers were more than content to stay around their bivouac fires on the wrong bank of the river and completely ignored Eble. Some did take his advice and rushed the bridges when the opportunity presented itself. Sometimes the movement degenerated into a blind rush. When this took place, they had to be cleared at bayonet-point as the formed units were badly needed to help defend the bridgehead.

A crisis developed at 20:00 as three sections of the trestles collapsed into the river. Eble scraped up one of his exhausted shifts from their relatively warm bivouac areas and led them into the river to repair the break. In the freezing cold, hands so numb that they could not feel the tools they were using, the exhausted troops repaired the bridge in three hours. Eble, soaked to the skin, reopened the bridge to the waiting traffic.

Through the entire crossing and desperate fighting, aides-de-camp and staff officers time and again made their way between the two halves of the army carrying orders or dispatches for their respective commanders. They either crossed the bridges, which was very difficult if they had to return to the east bank, or they had their horses swim the river.

Oudinot prepared his defence and also corduroyed the roads leading through the frozen marshes to make them more passable for guns and vehicles. Ney's corps and Claparede's elite Polish division now crossed the bridges to reinforce Oudinot. Junot's Westphalians and Victor's newly arrived IX Corps now moved into Borisov. Davout still acted as the army's rearguard and was eight miles east of Borisov. Contact with Wittgenstein was completely broken and nobody on either side knew where Kutusov was.

The 26th passed into the 27th and the reinforced main army was still crossing the two bridges. At 02:00 both bridges collapsed, whole sections of the bridges falling into the freezing water. Once again, Eble aroused his sleeping troops and went to work in the darkness and cold.

Bodies of both men and horses were beginning to stack up in the river, caught between the bridge pilings and the vehicles that had toppled from the bridge. Some said you could walk across the river on the bodies and not get wet and undoubtedly some did. Baron Larrey attempted to return to the east bank to help the wounded and stragglers but found the bridges nearly impassable with the press of bodies. Suddenly, he was seized by strong, helpful hands and literally pulled across the bridge to the east bank. Highly respected by all ranks, he was aided in his mission of mercy by those he had helped on past fields.

The bridges were repaired in four hours and the traffic resumed to the west bank. At 16:00 one of the bridges broke again but was repaired and serviceable by 18:00.

Napoleon ordered Victor to assume the rearguard from Davout, Victor's corps being larger and fresher. Davout's survivors then passed across the bridges, in excellent order. Victor swiftly moved ahead to Studenka and assumed an excellent defensive position on the same low ridge that had been occupied by Oudinot's artillery as it covered the initial crossing. He organised a rear slope-defence and waited for Wittgenstein and whoever else might be coming.[34]

To ensure the Russians would not crowd in on the army's withdrawal, Victor detached Partenoux's division as his rearguard, leaving a place in his line for it when Partenoux finally arrived. Unfortunately, Partenoux became lost in unfamiliar terrain at night and stumbled into Wittgenstein. Partenoux and his staff were captured early in the fighting and the division was mauled and surrounded. One battalion managed to break out and join the main body, the remainder of the division was captured.

As Eugène, Davout and Junot, now on the west bank, proceeded in good order along the western causeway, the Guard crossed the bridges to the west bank. Roguet's fusiliers and Delaborde's tirailleurs and voltigeurs established defensive positions around the village of Brili. The Emperor crossed with the Guard and established his headquarters in a few crude huts in Zanivki, dubbed by the Guard as 'Miserovo'. Curial's Old Guard division mounted Guard at the 'Palace'.[35]

Under a full head of steam and righteous anger at being fooled by the French, even after having been warned of such a possibility, Tshitshagov rushed headlong into Borisov from the south and there came to a screeching halt. This time, he knew he had the French dead to rights. Large numbers of the Grande Armée were obviously preparing to cross in this vicinity. He set his engineers to repairing the Borisov bridge in order to have lateral communications with Wittgenstein and to be able to cross to the east bank if necessary. Unfortunately for the Russians, he was fooled again. The mass of stragglers combined with the formed units waiting to go north to Studenka gave him the impression that the main French crossing would be at Borisov. More time was wasted while his subordinates were being defeated. He did send Langeron northward with a reconstituted advance guard to find Tshaplitz.

Langeron found two completed bridges flooded with Frenchmen crossing the river. He also ran into Tshaplitz's shattered division running to the south. The French were showing a bold front on the west bank. Langeron immediately sent work to Tshitshagov and rallied as many of Tshaplitz's troops as he could. Counter-attacking without waiting for Tshitshagov, he was soundly beaten by Oudinot. During this action, Oudinot was shot out of the saddle and was replaced by Ney.

Mortier's Young Guard was committed to cover the Vilna road and the Guard artillery went into action. Duelling with larger but less expertly handled guns, they slowly gained the upper hand. The mauled Russians were forced to withdraw out of range.

Arriving with his main body in the vicinity of Brili, Tshitshagov was determined to break through to the bridges. Finally communicating with Wittgenstein, the two Russian commanders planned a coordinated attack on the Grande Armée from both sides of the river the next day.

On the east bank, Victor sat on his ridge. The loss of Partenoux's division was a severe blow. Napoleon was furious, but he sent the Baden contingent back across the river to reinforce Victor. Because of the congestion on the bridges they had to leave their artillery behind, but Napoleon established a large battery on the west bank to support Victor's stand. An Old Guard contingent was also dispatched to Victor, which greatly boosted morale in the IX Corps. Victor planned his battle, the Russians licked their wounds and slept, and Frenchmen and allied troops continued to cross the river in the darkness.

Dawn on the 28th brought heavy snow and increasing cold. It also brought 42,000 howling Russians against Ney. The far left of his line, against the river, was held by four regiments of grimly silent Swiss. The hardy Swiss defeated assault after assault, standing firm, their solid red ranks pouring steady volleys into the advancing Russians, defending their eagles with bayonet, musket butt and fists. One eagle was taken and retaken three times, but their line held. The close-quarter fighting was savage and brutal.[36]

Before the action the Swiss regiments were awarded the Cross of the Legion of Honour for those deserving of it. The 1st Swiss Regiment received thirteen, the 2nd, 3rd and 4th eight, six and six, respectively. 'It all looks very pretty. If we were at home one could just be proud of it, but we aren't there yet. There'll be many empty shakos before then' one of the Swiss officers remarked.[37]

At about 09:00 the Russian round shot started passing overhead of the Swiss in their position on the far left flank of the French position to hold the bridges. 'We couldn't understand how we could have been standing so near the enemy without any outposts. Now we heard heavy cannon fire in the distance; and to our right musketry seemed to be coming closer. An orderly officer came galloping up from that direction: 'Our line's been attacked!'[38]

The 3rd and 4th Swiss Regiments were firing repeated volleys, solid as a red-brick wall and 'fighting without budging'. Russian numbers were steadily being reinforced on the Swiss front, the Muscovites rightly deciding that if the Swiss were overrun the bridges could be taken. The Russians' 'firings becoming livelier. Suddenly we're thrown back, we retreat some fifty paces.' Swiss commanders are bellowing through the noise and mess 'Forward!' and 'Everywhere the Charge is beaten. We're flung at the enemy, cross bayonets at point blank range.' The Swiss hold the line, mowing down the Russians with steady musketry as their numbers dwindle and fight with bayonet, musket butt and fist, refusing quarter or to retreat. 'Slowly, the Russians retire, still firing.'[39]

Between Russian assaults the Swiss sing hymns, the sound of which floated back across the river, heard by those on the right bank, preparing to cross. The 1st Swiss Regiment finally deployed *en tirailleurs* and all four regiments were running low on ammunition. 'On both sides the firing was murderous. It was not long before General Amey and several staff officers had been wounded and several killed, among them our commandant Blattmann. A bullet went through his brain. General of Brigade Canderas and his adjutant had fallen too; a round shot had taken off the latter's head.'[40]

The fighting was desperate defending the bridgehead. Russian dead were stacked in front of the Swiss position and Swiss officer losses were very heavy. 'The intrepid Fribourgeois Vonderweid fell, shot through the throat, dying two days later.[41]

The losses are so heavy that, as Fezensac grimly noted, even the Swiss were losing some ground. 'Only three weak battalions placed on the road – all that was left of I, III, and VIII Corps – served as their reserve. For a while the fight was sustained; under pressure from superior forces II corps was beginning to sag. Our reserves, hit by rounds hot at ever closer range, were moving towards the rear. This movement put to flight all the isolated men who filled the wood, and in their terror they ran as far as the bridge. Even the Young Guard was wavering. Soon there was no more salvation except in the Old Guard. With it we were prepared to die or conquer.[42]

So many Russians were shot down that the dead formed a breastwork in front of the Swiss position. 1,200 Swiss casualties out of 1,500 engaged marked their stand in the snow and cold.[43]

Napoleon was seen during the heaviest fighting sitting 'on a little white horse, surrounded by his whole staff. There he was, in the midst of a very well-nourished fire, as calm as at the Tuileries. He had . . . a singular habit. Each time musket balls or a round shot whistled in his ears, he shouted: 'Go past, rascals!'[44]

The Guard artillery went into action, steadily firing on command, supporting their infantry. The Young Guard assaulted Thsitshagov's right flank, Berthezène's brigade enveloping the Russian position and started to roll up the flank. The battle was at its crisis, casualties on both sides were heavy and suddenly, out of the snow-choked pine forest, Doumerc's cuirassier division, all 400 of them, crashed into the Russian left flank, inflicting 600 casualties and capturing 2,000 more. Captain Legler of the Swiss contingent saw them: 'The brave cuirassiers of the 4th and 7th Regiments, who were standing only 1,000 paces away from us, had seen the enemy too. We clearly heard the word of command: 'Squadrons, by the left flank, March!' As soon as the cuirassiers had crossed the road they went into the attack. The Russians had all but had enough.[45]

Across the river on his hard-held ridge Victor awaited the Muscovite onslaught. Wittgenstein's first amateurish attack, delivered later than agreed, was surprised by Victor's reverse-slope defence and was literally blown off the ridge. Grim, no-quarter attrition followed, but Victor had no choice, plugging gaps in his line with units drawn from other sectors of his line, ejecting every Russian penetration. His cavalry commander, Fournier, was wounded and out of action, but his brigade, made up of the Baden Hussars and the Hesse–Darmstadt Chevaux Légers, counter-attacked in a magnificent, near-suicidal charge.

Launching themselves into the midst of the Russians, they met and broke the Russian cuirassiers that were sent to stop them. When they returned to Victor's lines, barely fifty remained of the 350 that began the charge. They had, however, restored the French centre and knocked the Russians back on their heels yet again.

Victor's left flank was finally enveloped, more by accident than design, but this momentary Russian advantage was overwhelmed by accurate supporting artillery fire from across the river. Wittgenstein, defeated at every turn by Victor, was more than happy to let the French withdraw around 21:00 on 28 November. Skilfully extracting his exhausted survivors Victor completed his withdrawal by 07:30 on 29 November.

The mauled Russians could, or would, do nothing else to impede the French crossing. Defeated on both banks of the river, and not supported by Kutusov, they could really do nothing else but watch the French cross and continue westward. Napoleon and the army were greatly heartened over the success of the operation, one that is usually pictured as nothing but a mass exodus by a disorganised army. As Berthezène succinctly put it 'It has been said that the bridges presented a hideous spectacle . . . due to the crowding and confusion . . . In reality, the crossing of the Berezina in the face of the enemy was a very large military undertaking that reflects further glory on the army and its chief.'[46]

Ordered to burn the bridges at 07:30 on the 29th after Victor had safely crossed, Eble first tried once again to rouse the apathetic mass of stragglers that still populated the east bank. While the majority would not move, Eble delayed the bridges' destruction until 08:30. Finally, reluctantly, he gave the order and the remnants of his battalion scampered across the patched bridges and lighted the fires that soon consumed the whole rickety mass. At least, for a while anyway, the conflagration might have kept the stragglers warm. About 10,000 of them never crossed and were captured and sent to die in a Russian pen, some of them to 'count trees' in Siberia.

The French II and IX Corps suffered fifty per cent casualties. At least 10,000 Russian dead littered the battlefield. The wounded and missing are unknown as are the numbers of Cossacks that perished. Surprisingly, few French guns were lost. The only ones that were abandoned were those that were stuck in the ford. It was less than a company's worth.[47] In the Guard, someone was heard to say that if the French had been presented with the opportunity the Russians had at the Berezina, not one Russian would have escaped.

Clausewitz gave the definitive denouement to the crossing:

> There was never a better opportunity to force the surrender of an army in the open field. Napoleon had to rely for the most part upon the reputation of his arms; and he made use here of an asset he had been accumulating for a long time . . . Because the enemy was afraid of him and his Guard, no one dared face him. Napoleon capitalised on this psychological effect, and with its assistance worked his way out of one of the worst situations in which a general was ever caught. Of course this psychological force was not all he had. He was still supported by his own brilliant strength of character and the peerless military virtues of his army, not yet destroyed by the greatest of trials. Once out of the trap, Napoleon said to his staff; 'You see how one can slip away under the very nose of the enemy.' Napoleon in this action not only preserved his military honor, he enhanced it.[48]

> In more senses than one, Napoleon had snatched an outstanding victory out of his worst defeat, The Grande Armée might be dying on its feet, but neither winter, hunger, rivers, nor overwhelming odds in men and guns could halt it. It trampled them underfoot and went on.[49]

Besides the incomparable Eble, three officers in particular distinguished themselves at the Berezina: Oudinot, for his outstanding feint and deception operations during the period leading up to the crossing and his astuteness in recommending the Studenka ford to Napoleon; Victor for his resolute rearguard stand against Wittgenstein; and Ameil for his leadership and innate ability as a light cavalryman early in the operation. Eble's skill and leadership were exemplary in building the bridges, maintaining them under execrable conditions and for leading each shift of his men into the river to repair the frequent breaks. Eble should also be noted for his compassion in continually attempting to get as many of the stragglers to cross the bridges before he had to burn them and for postponing the time for burning them to the last possible moment.

Nicolas-Charles Oudinot (1767–1847) had served in the Royal Army before the Revolution, but had been discharged and returned home. He joined the

National Guard with the coming of war and established a reputation as an outstanding leader of fighting men and a more-than-competent infantry officer. Promoted to general of brigade in 1794, he was a general of division and chief of staff to Masséna in 1799.

Oudinot 'attracted' projectiles and bladed weapons of all types and was wounded thirty-four times during the wars. Leading an assault in 1805 he was struck in the mouth by a spent round, lost some of his teeth and turned bellowing to his men that the enemy were bad shots. Wounded three times in Russia, he was increasingly ineffective during 1813–14, but his service at the Berezina was outstanding.

In 1803 he was given command of the big elite division, Grenadiers Réunis, unofficially known as 'Oudinot's Grenadiers' and made a name for himself leading it, especially during Lannes's delaying action at Friedland in 1807. Friends with Davout, the pair allegedly spent nights in Poland drinking and shooting out candles with their pistols for diversion.

Auguste-Jean-Joseph-Gilbert Ameil (1755–1822) was, according to Marbot, the best light cavalrymen in the Grande Armée, if not in any European army. The son of a lawyer, he started his military career as a grenadier in the Paris National Guard becoming a chef d'escadron in the 5e Chasseurs à Cheval by 1799. In May 1792 he was a sous-lieutenant in the 10e Bataillon du Infanterie Légère and was promoted to full lieutenant on 4 February 1793. By September of that year he was a captain and the adjutant major of the battalion.

He served in Holland in 1799 and Germany in 1800–1, and became the major of his regiment on 19 October 1805. He served with the Grande Armée from 1805–7, went into Spain in 1808 and was with Montbrun's light cavalry division assigned to Davout's III Corps in Germany in 1809. He was appointed as colonel of the 24e Chasseurs à Cheval on 12 June 1809.

In Russia he won his stars on 21 November 1812 at the onset of the Berezina operation. In 1813 he was a brigade commander and served through 1814. Rallying to Napoleon in 1815, he was again a light cavalry brigade commander. He was proscribed by the Bourbons after Waterloo and imprisoned.

By his own reckoning during his career he participated in seventy-eight battles, 126 combats, over 800 skirmishes and four sieges. He had twenty-five wounds and had thirty-three horses killed under him.

Claude-Victor Perrin (1769–1841) was commonly referred to as 'Victor'. He started his military career as a musician (but not a drummer as legend has it) in an artillery unit and was a proficient trumpet player, rising to *trompette d'harmonie*, or first trumpet in his unit. He bought his discharge in 1791 but, thoroughly fed up with being a civilian, when war loomed on the horizon he re-enlisted in a volunteer unit. Almost immediately, he was promoted to sergeant and was a chef de bataillon the next year.

Promoted to general of brigade in 1793 he served on the Spanish frontier and in Italy. Napoleon promoted him to general of division in 1797. He served well at Marengo in 1800 as a corps commander, fighting stoutly on the French left until almost overwhelmed, earning a sword of honour for his outstanding service.

An excellent organiser and instructor, using realistic field exercises he developed men who were well drilled and trained to shoot well. Victor was not on the friendliest terms with Napoleon and he had a reputation for being an unreliable comrade and a difficult subordinate. He allowed his troops to pillage, even in France, as long as they performed in combat. He allowed general excesses that the other marshals would punish. There has been much speculation over his nickname, '*Beau Soleil*'. Victor having a bad temper, perhaps it meant a firework that went off in all directions at once. The description is apt and very French.

As a tactician, he won battles on his own in Spain at Ucles and Medellin and his outstanding rearguard fight at the Berezina in 1812 helped saved the crippled Grande Armée. His use of reverse-slope tactics there undoubtedly demonstrated that he could learn from his opponents as he had faced, and lost to, Wellington in Spain.

His superb performance at Friedland in 1807 won him his marshal's baton. His service in 1813 was excellent, but his plume drooped in 1814 and at times his performance was disgraceful. Relieved once by Napoleon for incompetence, he begged forgiveness, swearing to fight in line with a musket if necessary. Napoleon gave him another command, but he did not remain loyal after the campaign and ran with the Bourbons into Belgium in 1815. After Waterloo he helped purge the French army of officers thought to be hostile to the Bourbons.

These words by Captain Coignet neatly sum up the opinion of one of Napoleon's 'men of bronze'.

> Providence and courage never abandon the good soldier . . . Never punished, always present at roll call, indefatigable in all the marches and countermarches; I took whatever came without complaint.

CHAPTER 11

MARCH OR DIE

The battle of Dresden, 1813

To look over a battlefield, to take in at the first instance the advantages and disadvantages is the great quality of a general. FOLARD

Just as lightning has already struck when the flash is seen, so where the enemy discovers the head of the army, the whole should be there, and leave them no time to counteract dispositions. GUIBERT

04:00 15 August 1813, Dresden, Saxony
The horse artillery company had been standing to arms since 03:00. The guns had been checked and rechecked by the chiefs of section and then by the company officers. Harness leather and trace chains had been examined carefully for signs of stress and wear, unserviceable portions having been carefully replaced. The company farrier had personally checked the remounts that had been issued the previous evening when the company rolled into Dresden ahead of Victor's II Corps. The familiar sound of horseshoes striking cobblestones, sometimes causing bright sparks in the wet night, had marked his path through the company. A badly shod horse was the last thing the company commander needed.

They knew they would be going into action early that day, as the fighting the previous day had been without result. The allies had been knocked back to their line of departure, but the Emperor wanted to finish them off. At least that was the rumour from the ammunition train. The new horses would come in extremely handy, as it had been raining for hours and the churned up ground beyond the city walls was probably nothing but a slough of mud. How they were expected to manoeuvre and keep up with Pajols's cavalry was beyond them.

The senior NCOs were conducting yet another endless inspection of the company's guns and equipment. Snorting horses came awake in the pre-dawn darkness which was punctuated by the light of the NCOs' lanterns. Sleeping cannoneers and drivers who were dozing on their mounts were roughly awakened, some by being grabbed by the ubiquitous NCOs, some by simply falling of their horses in a clatter of equipment and curses.

Some of the drivers were recent replacements, veterans to a man, but some had been wounded in the hand and were missing one or two fingers. How they were supposed to control their horse pairs with crippled hands only *le bon Dieu* would know.

Their company commander, quietly walking along the company column, was a hard man. A veteran of Spain and Russia, he was strict, but fair, and had a violent temper that a few of them had seen from time to time. *Monsieur le Capitaine* had learned to control it, but sometimes it erupted with a violence that made the most hardened veteran wince.

Monsieur le Capitaine was finished with his inspection and was not standing and talking with his two young sous-lieutenants, both of whom had just joined the company, along with his maréchal des logis-chef. Observing the growing activity in the park, all four men nodded as if to say it was just about time to get going. Off to the side, the company trumpeter held his commander's mount as well as his own. It seemed as though he never left the capitaine's side.

In April 1813 Napoleon's rebuilt Grande Armée started east to confront the Prussian and Russian armies in Saxony. Built around conscripts and veterans from Spain, along with a solid cadre from the remnants of the army that went into Russia, whom Napoleon referred to as his 'men of bronze', Napoleon was ready to confront another coalition that had been raised against him.

Joining Eugène's Armée d'Elbe in Germany, Napoleon fought and won two battles against the Russians and Prussians at Lützen and Bautzen. The allies had attacked the French at Lützen and were mauled. Without an effective cavalry arm, however, the Emperor was unable to pursue effectively. Meeting again at Bautzen, Napoleon planned an envelopment of the entire allied army, but Ney, entrusted with the manoeuvre, botched it, and the allied army escaped.

The allies had lost twice and suffered crippling losses. They requested an armistice, which Napoleon reluctantly agreed to. Both sides needed to rebuild after the spring battles, but the armistice benefited the allies more than it did the French.

The joker in the pack in the summer of 1813 was Austria. Nominally an ally of France, Austria had been negotiating with the allies since the broken remnants of the Grande Armée had been straggling back into central Europe. Even though there was an Austrian corps under Schwarzenberg with the Grande Armée, Austria, under the expert diplomatic manoeuvres of her foreign minister, Prince Metternich, dithered and manoeuvred for Napoleon's destruction after the magnitude of the Russian disaster became known.

Meeting ostensibly as a mediator between Napoleon and the allies in Dresden in July 1813, Metternich had no intention of honouring the Austrian treaty with France. He gave Napoleon a list of Austrian demands which amounted to Napoleon's surrendering most of his Empire and the disbanding of the Confederation of the Rhine, knowing that Napoleon would refuse. The talks were a failure, and Austria, who already had an agreement with the allies, openly joined the war against France.[1]

Faced with this new strategic situation, Napoleon, undaunted by the odds mounting against him, prepared for the renewal of hostilities. Blücher, commanding the Army of Silesia, openly violated the armistice and began hostilities on his own. Napoleon, intent on facing and destroying Blücher, had to leave that theatre in command of Macdonald, as his southern flank was being threatened by the newly christened Army of Bohemia under Schwarzenberg. Dresden, his Saxon ally's capital, was in danger of being captured by Schwarzenberg's allied army and the XIV Corps under St Cyr, who was preparing for its defence, was not sufficient to hold the city against a determined allied offensive.

Napoleon sent Colonel Gourgaud, who was his senior *officier d'ordnance*, on a fact-finding mission to Dresden and on his return he told Napoleon that St Cyr could not hold out against a serious allied attack for anywhere near twenty-four hours.[2] Gourgaud, competent and reliable, was listened to by the Emperor, who immediately ordered Victor's and Marmont's corps to march for Dresden and Latour-Maubourg's cavalry corps and the Imperial Guard were ordered there immediately. Vandamme's I Corps, which was in the vicinity of Pirna, south-east of the city, was alerted.

Dresden on the Elbe River is divided into the Altstadt and Neustadt districts, the first being on the east bank, the second on the west bank of the river. Further, the Friedrichstadt suburb of the Altstadt was north of the Weisserwitz River. To the south-east of the city was a huge Great Garden, which was walled and an excellent defensive position. St Cyr had five redoubts, numbered consecutively I to V, constructed south of the city, as well as a *flèche* along the river on the eastern side of the Altstadt.

All five were outside of the city limits. In relation to the Great Garden, redoubt I was north of it and south of the *flèche* along the river, redoubt II was on the northern corner, covering the Pirna Gate and redoubt III was directly west of it, facing directly south. None of these three fortifications was mutually supporting. Redoubt IV, facing south-west, had much dead ground in front of it, thus restricting its fields of fire. Redoubt V was close to Weisserwitz River, which bisected the battlefield and was a major obstacle for lateral troop movement.

The entire front, round the Altstadt from the west clear around to the south-east, was dotted with small, stoutly constructed villages that provided ready-made strong-points for either army. The road network from Dresden in any direction was good. However, major roads connecting these for lateral movement were poor and the weather would make a major impact on this action. Last, the Landgraben, a large drainage ditch to the south-east, was also a major obstacle to manoeuvre.

The allies invested Dresden completely on the west bank of the Elbe. Schwarzenberg had over 150,000 Austrians, Prussians and Russians under his command and St Cyr's position was dire. The marshal established an outpost line forward of the redoubts and other defences, using the southern corner of the Great Garden as part of it.

Schwarzenberg's offensive started at 05:00 on 27 August. St Cyr, fighting desperately against almost overwhelming numbers of allied troops, fought gamely, expertly using the terrain to his advantage. The Prussians and Russians captured almost three quarters of the Great Garden by 11:00, but could not force the French out. The redoubts and the *flèche* all held. St Cyr's outpost line had been driven in by 11:00, but no key positions had been taken, and French artillery, inside Dresden and across the Elbe, had ruined the allied offensive. The battlefield became quiet, awaiting the allies' next move.

Schwarzenberg organised his main attack. The signal for a general advance would be a three-gun signal which would also trigger a general artillery bombardment to cover the advance. The allies would launch a concentric attack all along the front, hopefully overrunning the outnumbered French and smothering any further attempt at resistance. The main attack was scheduled for 16:00.

However, Napoleon had arrived in Dresden at 09:30. With him came two Guard corps under Ney and Mortier, along with the Old Guard and the Guard artillery and cavalry. Latour-Maubourg also arrived. Murat, who was finally present from his intrigues in Naples, was placed in command of Pajol, St Cyr's corps cavalry commander and Teste's infantry division, detached from Vandamme's I Corps. Marmont and Victor had not arrived and were pushing hard for Dresden.

Napoleon's arrival brought the French strength up to 70,000, including St Cyr's XIV Corps. Napoleon inspected the defences of the city, took a good look at the allied positions and began to organise his counter-attack. As per his usual practice, after conferring with St Cyr he left him alone to conduct his defence of the city.

Upon finding that Napoleon and the Imperial Guard had arrived in Dresden, the allied headquarters went into mental convulsions. Alexander 'recommended' that the army retreat immediately.[3] This caused a heated argument with the

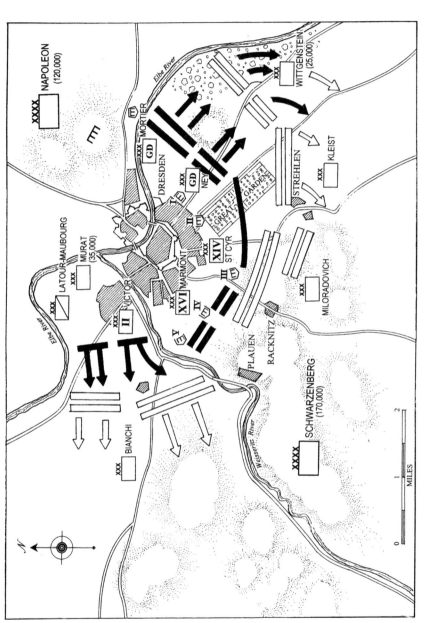

The Battle of Dresden: the Second Day

The second day of the battle of Dresden had a reinforced Grande Armée attacking the allies while still outnumbered. The allied left flank was completely destroyed or taken, and most of St Cyr's original position outside Dresden was retaken. Napoleon planned for another day of battle on 28 August, but the allies had had enough and withdrew.

usually quiet Frederick William over what should be done. The allied sovereigns ordered Schwarzenberg to hold the assault while 'options' were 'debated', which took an inordinate amount of time. Before the inefficient allied general staff could get the orders written and distributed to the subordinate commands, the signal for the main attack was sounded, the allied artillery opened up all along the front and the allied offensive 'launched itself'.

As the overwhelming numbers of allies surged forward in every sector, St Cyr's desperate corps battled for its life. The Great Garden was finally taken by Wittgenstein at heavy cost. Redoubt III was taken by the Austrians and Redoubt IV ran out of ammunition. Redoubt V, however withstood all assaults, supporting the defence with accurate artillery fire. St Cyr fought desperately to hold his positions. Vicious local counter-attacks for the time being either stalled the allied advance or retook lost positions, but St Cyr had to commit all his reserves to stave off being overrun.

Waiting for the exact moment, Napoleon struck. Mortier attacked the allies in the Great Garden and trapped Wittgenstein in a Cannae-like envelopment. Redoubt III was retaken by a Young Guard drum major who rallied fifty infantrymen and led them into the ditch, up and over the parapet and fought hand-to-hand until supported by other Young Guardsmen who stormed the redoubt from the rear.

Ney's assault in the centre of the line was so vicious that it swept all before it and forced Schwarzenberg to commit his reserve grenadiers to stop it. All along the line the allies were driven back and out of the positions they had captured with the exception of a corner of the Great Garden (which was abandoned later that evening) and a few of the small villages along the front. The weather had turned wet, soaking the battlefield and making movement off the roads for artillery and cavalry more than difficult.

The French had fought magnificently at odds of two to one. The allies, probably knowing that both Victor and Marmont were en route, decided against withdrawing and planned to stand on the defensive on the 27th, surrendering the initiative to Napoleon and the French, a fact that would definitely be acted on.

Marmont and Victor arrived in Dresden bringing French strength up to 120,000. French losses had not been heavy, so preparations were made for a counter-offensive on the 27th. The weather worsened overnight, and Napoleon realised that the mobility of his artillery would be a decisive element in the fighting. Horses and harness were found to increase the horse teams of the artillery, making them as mobile as possible, even in the off-road muck that would be a feature of the fighting the next day.

Napoleon apparently wanted to execute a double envelopment of the entire allied army. He wanted to take and hold the two key road networks from Dresden to the south, which would inhibit an allied withdrawal. Victor and Latour-Maubourg, under Murat's command, were on the French right. Marmont and St Cyr held the French centre, and Ney and Mortier with their Guard corps were on the left. The only units kept in reserve would be the Old Guard infantry and the Guard cavalry's escort squadrons. The Guard artillery was assigned to Ney and Mortier.

By 06:00 Napoleon was ready and Ney and Mortier launched a series of attacks on the allied right that cleared the woods along the Elbe and forced Wittgenstein back, giving the two French corps room to manoeuvre. Murat launched his assault at 06:30 and shattered Bianchi's command. Victor's corps advanced on the left along the Weisseritz, overrunning the Austrian positions, who after Marmont had seized the bridge over that river at Plauen, were trapped on the wrong side of the river. The Austrians either ran, were killed, or they were driven into the river.

The ground was so sodden and muddy that, while the cavalry could manoeuvre, they could not move faster than an trot. The French artillery again became a decisive arm. When Austrian infantry formed square, the French cavalry halted, stayed in formation and waited for their supporting artillery to come up, unlimber and open fire. The situation for the Austrian infantry became so desperate that they started to surrender as soon as the French artillery showed up, emplaced and lit their port-fires. Bianchi's force was entirely destroyed. 15,000 prisoners were taken. The remaining 9,000 were either killed or had run and could not be found or rallied. The fighting on the French right was over by 15:00.

The entire allied army had been driven back, losing all of their hard won objectives from the fighting on the 26th. Still, they held together, except for Bianchi's command. Napoleon considered that there would be more fighting on the 28th and he planned to destroy what remained on the allies. French artillery was still active, firing continuously to destroy the villages to their front. During this cannonade, Alexander was almost hit by French artillery fire. Moreau, who had joined the allies from his exile and acting as a military advisor to them at Dresden, was hit and mortally wounded.[4]

The battle, however, was over. The allies had had enough. Orders were given to withdraw during the night and Napoleon's plans for a 'great battle' on the 28th were now useless. The allies had suffered more than 38,000 casualties. French losses were less than a quarter of that total. Dresden was one of Napoleon's greatest victories, won against long odds in the rain and mud of a German summer.

The Emperor gave orders for the pursuit of the allies and couriers galloped south to warn Vandamme. A successful pursuit would destroy Schwarzenberg, perhaps capture the allied sovereigns with the Army of Bohemia and perhaps end the war. The pursuit started out well. Napoleon, however, did not remain with his subordinates and a repeat of 1806 was not to be. The French pursuit slackened and Vandamme, isolated and trapped at Kulm by the allies, lost half his corps in the hard fighting and was captured. St Cyr failed to support Vandamme, which gave the allies a badly needed success, and the war would now continue. The failure of the pursuit allowed Leipzig to happen.

Laurent Gouvion St Cyr (1764–1830) was an extremely intelligent, no-nonsense commander who studied the art of war 'with the detachment of a chess player' and displayed military talents of his own throughout his career. He volunteered in 1792, but his skill as a draftsman and engineer saw him assigned to staff duty and he was promoted to general of brigade in 1793. The next year saw him a general of division.

His service in the Revolutionary Wars was with the Rhine armies, but was in Italy in 1799 and he helped to pick up the pieces after the disaster at Novi. Again in Germany in 1800, he was the commanding officer of the Armée de Naples from 1803–6 and was in Spain from 1808–10 where he was relieved for 'leaving the army without permission'.

In Russia in 1812, he won his marshal's baton for excellent service at Polotsk. A loner and virtually uncaring whether he was liked or not, he was not a dynamic leader of men and did little to inspire his troops, though he took good care of them. After the victory of Polotsk, he characteristically retired to a virtually solitary existence in a local monastery, failing to inspect his troops after their performance or even to visit the wounded. He next commanded a corps in 1813 and played a decisive part in Napoleon's victory at Dresden in 1813. His failure, however, to support Vandamme in the pursuit that followed definitely helped Vandamme lose at Kulm. He later surrendered Dresden when trapped there with Lobau.

St Cyr was not an inspiring troop commander and probably had too little troop duty after entering the army. He was an excellent commander and more than capable to command independently. He was dubbed 'the prudent one' by one of his colleagues and his army nickname was 'the Owl'. An excellent staff officer, he was a careful student of his profession who was more skilled than many of his comrades. He stayed loyal to the Bourbons after the first abdication and tried to organise resistance to Napoleon after his return from Elba.

Étienne Marie Antoine Nansouty (1768–1815) attended the Brienne military school and before the Revolution was a member of the Maison du Roi, being a captain in the Grey Musketeers. Nansouty was well educated, from a noble family, an excellent horseman and one of the better unit commanders in the Grande Armée.

Surviving the purges of the Revolution, Nansouty was a general of division by 1808 and commanded a cuirassier division, leading it with skill from 1805 through 1809. Commanding a cavalry corps in 1812, he commanded the cavalry of the Imperial Guard in 1813–14 and was famous for the cavalry charge at Eckmuhl in 1809.

Nansouty lacked the dash of some of his contemporaries, but was steady and reliable, if somewhat too careful of his troopers lives. When his regimental commanders decided to have the men of his division cut off their queues while Nansouty was on leave, he was incensed upon his return and placed the colonels under arrest. Realising, after his temper had calmed down, that having them in this state would not grow the queues again, he relented, the whole action being rather silly. He was rude and sarcastic to his subordinates and was not the man for a 'do or die' cavalry charge. Still, he was efficient, an excellent commander, steady and reliable. He died during the first restoration.

CHAPTER 12

MUD, BLOOD AND VICTORY

The Campaign of 1814 - the battles of Vauchamps,
Champeaubert, and Montmirail

A general in the power of the enemy has no orders to give. Whoever obeys him is a criminal. NAPOLEON

I have had a better three days. BLÜCHER

09:30 14 February 1814, on the Montmirail–Corrobert road, east of Vauchamps
The smoke and roar of the battle was steadily moving eastward, which meant that Napoleon was driving Blücher's army before him. Grouchy was leading Bordesoulle's and St Germain's cavalry to the north of the fighting along a parallel track to try and get in front of Blücher's battered divisions to cut them off. It was hard going now that they were turning eastward off the road to cut across country and save time. It was doubtful that the horse artillery companies would be able to keep up in the mud and muck, but it was more important to get in front of the retreating allies. They were fighting on French ground now and to be defeated on their home soil was unthinkable. *La Patrie* was definitely in danger and it was up to them to defend it, with whatever means at hand.

In one of the accompanying horse artillery companies it was becoming almost hopeless. The mud was deep and thick and it was clinging to gun and limber wheels like hardened mortar. The gallant horse teams were pulling with all their remaining strength and gunners were desperately dismounting, throwing their reins to the horse handlers and grabbing gun and limber wheels to help the almost exhausted horse teams pull the guns through the muck. It just could not have frozen last night, now could it? Then they could slip and slide along the frozen mud but at least they might have been able to keep up with the cavalry, which was grimly passing them, nodding to the gunners and encouraging them to pull harder. Their commanders were not allowing them to help, though the troopers dearly wanted to, as the artillery was needed ahead. Every cavalryman was needed to meet Blücher's troops and the gunners would have to fend for themselves.

Their company commander had spoken to Grouchy himself as he had passed by offering encouragement. Monsieur le capitaine was now pulling with the gun crew of the lead piece, cursing for all he was worth – he was a master of profane language. He was like that – never afraid to get dirty and he loved his guns. He had undoubtedly forgotten more about artillery in general and gunnery in particular than anyone else in the company, including the maréchal des logis chef, would ever know. He was old for his grade, but solid. He would never quit. He was one of the Emperor's 'men of bronze' from Russia.

Next to him, his young trumpeter was leading the company commander's horse and staying out of earshot, so as not to become the object of monsieur le capitaine's ire and frustration. Those in the company that had served with the company commander for some time respected and trusted him, but his outbursts could rival Vesuvius in intensity when he was not happy – and he was not happy today. He wanted to be in on the kill and it looked like they were not going to make it. But no one in the company, from maréchal des logis chef to the youngest neophyte gunner were going to tell monsieur le capitaine that. None of them had the least desire to be knocked silly across a gun trail.

After Leipzig Napoleon withdrew from Germany, taking as many troops as possible back into France. The Bavarian general, Wrede, attempted to stop the French at Hanau, but was badly defeated. He had expected to sweep up French remnants and stragglers, but found himself facing Napoleon and the Imperial Guard.[1]

Napoleon did not expect the allies to invade France as early as they did, but they crossed the Rhine before the new year and for once Napoleon did not strike first on campaign. French commanders, notably Victor and Marmont, half-heartedly attempted to slow down the allied advance, but their efforts were minimal. Mortier, on the other hand, did more than his assigned duty and he would be remembered for loyalty and efficiency for his part in the 1814 campaign.[2]

The 1814 campaign in France is noted for Napoleon reverting from the Emperor Napoleon to the younger, tougher General Bonaparte once again. With few resources, no allies and the armies of the Coalition closing in on France, the campaign has been described as desperate and by being conducted on a shoestring. It has also been described as brilliant. Napoleon was poorly served by some of his subordinates, brother Joseph (worthless in any emergency be it foreign or domestic), Augereau and Oudinot among them, and by Marmont

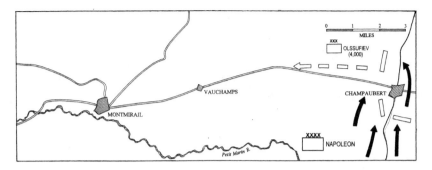

The Battle of Champaubert
Champeaubert was the first victory in the 'week of miracles' of February 1814. Here, Napoleon attacked Olsuffiev's Russian corps of Blücher's Army of Silesia that had been left unsupported by Blucher and destroyed by the French.

turning traitor at the end of the campaign. Four actions will be covered in this chapter: the battles of Champeaubert, Montmirail and Vauchamps from 10–14 February, where Napoleon came within a hair's breadth of destroying Blücher's Army of Silesia, and the fight at Montereau on 18 February, famous for Pajol's almost uncontrollable cavalry charge with his conscripts which shattered an allied army corps. Last, one hopelessly gallant action by two small National Guard divisions at La Fère Champenoise will be used to illustrate the frustration, mud and misery that the campaign of 1814 had to be for the Grande Armée.

The overall situation at the beginning of February 1814 was grim and not in France's favour. Eastern France had been overrun, and Victor and Marmont were sulking, not pressing the allies enough as they withdrew westward. Ney did nothing but sit on his hands. Mortier, on the other hand, fought a superb eighteen-day delaying action from Langres to Bar-sur-Aube, slapping the allied units he faced back into reality and winning success after small success. He was prepared to go to the wall for his Emperor and, if the other marshals had exercised half the energy and skill that Mortier displayed, much of the quick allied successes in eastern France would have evaporated and the populace might have taken heart and stood up to the invader earlier than they did.

Blücher was the most aggressive of the senior allied field commanders.[4] Losing at Brienne but defeating Napoleon on French soil at La Rothière on 1 February, he now considered the campaign swiftly coming to a positive conclusion for the allies. His overconfidence and complete misreading of the situation would almost destroy his army.

On the night of 9–10 February, Blücher left Olssufiev's corps alone and isolated in and around Champaubert. Seeing the opportunity and accurately

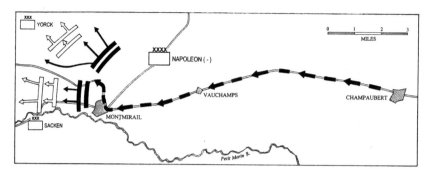

The Battle of Montmirail

After destroying Olsuffiev, Napoleon went after Sacken and Yorck, two more of Blücher's corps. They were defeated by an outnumbered Napoleon and promptly retreated in an attempt to rejoin Blücher. Both corps suffered heavy losses and just barely escaped being destroyed in detail.

informed by his cavalry of the Russian's isolated position, Napoleon pounced on him and destroyed his corps in a short, vicious tactical brawl, the French infantry fighting as men possessed.

Blücher heard the noise of the short fight to westward and ignored it, unwittingly leaving his unlucky subordinate to his fate. Napoleon wanted to continue his attack on Blücher and manoeuvred his army westward to deal with two other corps of the Army of Silesia, under Sacken and Yorck.

Aides went galloping with orders for the army's units to concentrate and at 19:00 on 10 February Nansouty and the Guard cavalry marched for Montmirail. The remainder of the army followed at 03:00 the next morning. Yorck and Sacken were not together and Sacken was the first of the two to get a nasty surprise on the morning of 11 February, running into Napoleon west of Montmirail. Napoleon outmanoeuvred Sacken, whose one tactical move in the fight was an attempt to attack Napoleon's centre which failed with heavy losses. The French were actually outnumbered, but were tearing Sacken to pieces when Yorck arrived tardily at 15:30. Napoleon was between the two corps, but Yorck's arrival saved Sacken's remnants. Mortier counter-attacked and drove Yorck northwards towards Chateau-Thierry and away from Sacken's exhausted remnants. Sacken finally escaped through the woods northwards to join Yorck, and Blücher, again happily ignorant of the desperate straits his subordinates were in, sent orders for the two corps to head for Reims, on the other side of the River Marne.

On the 12th, Napoleon continued his attack against Sacken and Yorck. With Ney in the lead, the French hustled the two allied corps commanders across the Marne, almost destroying both corps. Yorck and Sacken were lucky to still be in

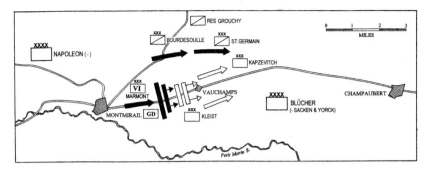

The Battle of Vauchamps

Napoleon's target was the destruction of Blücher's Army of Silesia. Blücher advanced westward on Champaubert hoping to surprise Napoleon in the rear. Instead, he was expertly delayed by Marmont until Napoleon could countermarch to his support. What resulted was a nasty surprise for Blücher, who immediately retreated. He had seen the Guard's bearskins, knew Napoleon was attacking and that his plan had failed. Blücher was severely punished in a running fight that almost resulted in the destruction of his army.

existence when they reached the other bank. That luck would have run out if Macdonald had supported Napoleon. If he had marched rapidly, Macdonald could have trapped and destroyed the remnants of the two corps. As it was, Sacken and Yorck had lost over 7,000 men, more than twenty guns and most of their trains were on the wrong side of the Marne. French losses were approximately 2,500.

Napoleon was to get one more try at Blücher. Napoleon sent word to Marmont, left in the vicinity of Montmirail, that he wanted him to lure Blücher there. Skilfully enticing Blücher to attack him, Marmont took a position west of Vauchamps; the Prussian advance guard under Zieten, confident of victory, attacked Marmont, whose position was deceptively strong. Zieten's attack was careless and his right flank was in the air. As soon as he became decisively engaged with Marmont, Grouchy hit his right flank like an avalanche, rolled it up and left Zieten's men either casualties or fugitives.

Blücher found the horde of fugitives somewhere east of Vauchamps. He also saw the bearskin bonnets of the Old Guard, panicked and ordered the army to retreat. Initially, the Army of Silesia retreated in excellent order, keeping their artillery and trains on the one good road between Montmirail and Champaubert. The infantry were in closed masses in the fields on either side of it. Napoleon and his Guard pursued mercilessly. Drouot, in command of the Guard artillery, massed his guns against the marching masses of infantry, each salvo making deep impressions in the heavy formations, the allied march route being marked by mangled corpses.

Nansouty repeatedly led charge after charge against the allies and was repeatedly repulsed, but the successive shocks began to wear down the allied infantry and the orderly retreat started to degenerate into a rout. The retreat went through and past Champaubert, and Blücher had no idea that Grouchy was leading his cavalry along a parallel route to his north in order to intercept and cut off his retreat. Grouchy's horse artillery could not keep up and kept bogging down in the mud, but Grouchy's troopers pushed on without it, and once past Champaubert swung south and cut off Blücher's line of retreat. Undoubtedly, if Grouchy's artillery had been able to keep up, Blücher would have been destroyed.

Blücher was undaunted with French cavalry to his front and Napoleon pursuing to his rear. He more than anyone else knew that if he were caught between these two forces, not many would get out. He did not want to see a re-enactment of 1806 and drove his men against the French. He finally fought his way clear, leaving a Russian division as a rearguard in Etoges. His losses had been heavy. More than 7,000 casualties, sixteen pieces of artillery and most of his trains littered the Montmirail/Champaubert road. He failed to extricate the Russians in Etoges on time and they were destroyed by Marmont around 20:30 that day.

Edouard Adolphe-Casimer-Joseph Mortier (1768–1835), the tallest of the marshals at six feet six inches whose name means 'mortar' in French, was said to have 'a short range' but it is doubtful that was said within earshot. Well educated and fluent in English, he volunteered in 1791, was duly elected captain by his fellows and was a colonel by 1795. Promoted to general of division in 1799 and was employed by Napoleon in minor independent commands or with the Imperial Guard. Occasionally, he would be assigned to command a provisional corps as he did in 1805. A competent general, he was cordial, easy-going and a good comrade. He was also clean-handed and an excellent leader of men, as witness his performance outnumbered at the battle of Durrenstein in 1805.

He served well in Switzerland in 1799 and occupied Hanover in 1803; he fought and defeated the Swedes in 1807, commanded the Young Guard in Russia in 1812 and served well in 1813–14. He was noted for his loyalty in 1814 and rallied to Napoleon in 1815, being assigned to the Imperial Guard again, but came down with a painful illness and he asked to be relieved.

Pierre Baste (1768–1814) was originally a sailor and came from the French Merchant Marine. He transferred to the navy and was an ensign in 1793. He served in the Caribbean and the Mediterranean and was taken prisoner by the English at Toulon in 1795. He served in the naval flotilla that supported Napoleon's Armée d'Italie on both Lake Garda and in the lakes around Mantua.

As part of the Egyptian expedition, he served at Aboukir and the defence of Malta. After returning to France he was promoted to lieutenant de vaisseau and was in Santo Domingo from 1802–3, then, promoted to capitain de frigate on 24 September 1803, he was assigned to the Boulogne flotilla the next year.

Assigned to the Grande Armée in 1807, he was with Dupont at Baylén and became a prisoner when Dupont capitulated. He later escaped and made his way back to French territory. He was appointed the commander of the Sailors of the Guard on 11 April 1809 and was promoted to Contre-Amiral in 1811. Subsequently, he was transferred to the army and became a general of brigade and commanded a Young Guard brigade in 1813. He was killed in action at Brienne, the site of Napoleon's first military school, in early 1814 and was greatly missed.

Claude-Pierre Pajol (1772–1844) was one of the most skilful of Napoleon's senior cavalry commanders. 1791 found him as the sergeant major of the Ier Bataillon Volontaires de Doubs and he was a sous-lieutenant the next year. A grenadiers lieutenant in 1793, he became aide-de-camp to Kléber in 1794 and captured an Austrian standard at Quithe on 8 November 1794. The next year he was captured and in 1796 after his release he was promoted to chef de bataillon.

Transferring to the cavalry, he was a chef d'escadron in 1796 and went to the 4e Hussars in 1797. He was chef de brigade of the 23e Cavalerie in 1799, being posted to the 6e Hussars that same year. He served in the Armée d'Italie in 1799 and in the Armée du Rhin the next year. With the Grande Armée from 1805–7 he rose steadily, being one of Montbrun's subordinate commanders in 1809. He stayed with Davout's command in Germany after Wagram, serving him in Russia in 1812.

He served competently in Saxony in 1813 and was brilliant in 1814 taking the Montereau bridge with his raw troopers and scattering an allied army corps once across. He was assigned as a cavalry corps commander in 1815 and was with Grouchy in his pursuit of the Prussians after Ligny.

07:00 18 February 1814, Montereau France
The small group of horsemen trotted ahead of the main body of ragged, ill-equipped cavalry to gain a better view of the enemy situation. Cursing the circumstances of their presence here, the weather, the allies and whatever else came to mind, General Pajol, himself already wounded in an earlier action, surveyed both the terrain to his front and his 'command'. The city of Montereau and its huge bridge presented no great problem. His 'command' and the allied army corps holding Montereau most certainly did.

Grievous losses in the two previous campaigns had reduced the French cavalry arm to a shadow of its former self. Shortages of all kinds, from weapons to harness and saddlery, and especially of veteran troopers and cadres, had hampered the effectiveness of the Grande Armée in 1813 and was a definite factor in the Saxon campaign ending in defeat and retreat.

All this Pajol contemplated as he turned to his aide-de-camp, Biot, and told him to alert the column. They were going into Montereau at the gallop, and woe to anyone who tried to stop his raw troopers. Only death or a brick wall would succeed in that, for once they started their charge, they would not stop until a force beyond nature forced them to.

The faithful Biot trotted back to the 'command' leaving his chief to look and ponder at the bridge they were going to cross. They would see about the allied troops holding the city after they negotiated the first obstacle. Wearily, Pajol turned his mount and followed his aide's path and could see that Biot was already supervising the orders from his chief.

On 18 February, an allied army corps occupied the strategic city of Montereau and controlled its vital bridges. The French needed to retake the city and the use of the bridges. It was not an easy assignment, but there were enough troops and artillery present to take both the city and the bridges.

The Prince of Württemberg commanded the allied troops occupying the city and he had been ordered by Schwarzenberg to hold against the French at all costs until 18 February. The Prince had organised a strong position on the north bank of the Seine River. Pajol arrived with his cavalry on 17 February, but could do little against the infantry and artillery that were arrayed against him.

Victor arrived at 09:00 the next day and attacked sloppily, with little finesse, and took a series of bloody repulses. Napoleon withdrew Victor, putting Gérard's corps in his place and Gérard methodically massed his artillery against the allied positions. As the Guard artillery was pulled into position under Drouot, the French gained artillery superiority over the allied guns and launched a coordinated attack around 15:00 that seized the key to the allied position on their ridge. The Prince knew he was beaten and attempted an orderly withdrawal and disengagement. The quick-witted Pajol, sensing the opportunity led his untrained, conscripts on their equally untrained and wild mounts against the allies, and galloped the bridge over the Seine overrunning screaming allied infantry who could not get away from the wild chevauchee fast enough. The charge, by now uncontrollable and virtually unstoppable, continued through the town and Pajol led them to the other bridge over the Yonne, splattering shocked and amazed allies in all directions.

Not to be outdone, the Imperial staff and their cavalry escort joined in the attack and galloped along the Bray road, led by Marshal Lefebvre, to support and follow up Pajol's romp. Afterwards, it was admitted that well-trained, but more circumspect, cavalry probably could not have conducted a charge like Pajol's raw troopers did, not only taking the city and both strategic bridges, but ruining an allied army corps in the bargain.

15:30 25 March 1814, near La Fere-Champenoise, France
The National Guardsmen of Pacthod's and Amey's two tiny divisions had been attacked by Russian cavalry and horse artillery in the plain near the town of La Fere-Champenoise at 10:30 that morning. Since then, formed in six squares and without supporting cavalry or artillery of their own, they had marched and fought against increasing long odds, attempting to reach their objective and safety. Barring that, all hoped against all hope that support would come to their aid from somewhere.

The National Guardsmen, in their Gallic blouses and sabots, but with bloodied bayonets washed in the gore of the Russian cavalrymen, had exceeded their commanders' expectations. Not only had they stayed in formation, but they had outfought the Tsar's cavalrymen at every turn. Closing ranks like veterans when great holes were torn in them by point-blank artillery fire, the Frenchmen had fought savagely against the ever-increasing numbers of their enemies, who were arriving on the field smelling blood, akin to a shark feeding-frenzy.

Cartridge boxes now empty, bayonets bent and broken from constant use, their commanders bellowing through the smoke and mess to either march or form square, young boys and fathers of families repulsed charge after charge and could not be broken by overwhelming numbers of men and guns. Pacthod had even ordered a charge against the Russians and scattered the cavalry to the divisions' front, but they had merely reformed and their artillery continually blocked the route of march of the two divisions.

Casualties were very heavy; the National Guardsmen had lost over a third of their number, the line of dead and dying marking their line of march and their stands in square. Starting with only 4,300 men in the ranks, the two divisions were dwindling rapidly and the Russian artillery fire was firing rapidly and accurately, causing more casualties by the minute.

As more Russians gathered like vultures over dying prey, there were eventually over 20,000 Muscovite cavalry surrounding the two divisions, charging and being repulsed in turn. Russian Guard cavalry had joined the mêlée and the gigantic horsemen roared through the smoke to smash against the National Guardsmen's squares only to take yet another repulse. The French were in six mutually supporting squares, but one was finally decimated by Russian artillery fire and collapsed. The survivors attempted to reform into tight knots to resist the next charge, but were overrun. They refused quarter and were killed where they stood.

Sniffing success, the Russian horsemen closed in for the kill. One French square, commanded by General Delort, was shot to pieces and Delort ordered them to lay down their arms to save the survivors' lives. Still, the remaining belligerent survivors refused to quit, merely closing ranks and 'marched the more proudly'.

One Russian officer carrying a flag of truce was shot down by the defiant French survivors. The fighting was savage, the blood-encrusted survivors, lips blackened by biting off the end of countless cartridges, still refused to quit. Pacthod, however, wounded – his broken right arm was 'hanging useless and bleeding – and wishing to save the lives of his survivors, moved out of his square to talk to the next Russian officer bearing a flag of truce. The Russian, pleading for Pacthod to surrender was told by a grim, unyielding Pacthod that 'I will not discuss terms under the fire of your batteries. Cease your fire and I will stop mine.'

One square, being ruined by Russian artillery fire and the last to hold out, was overrun by Russian cavalry. The survivors stayed in tight groups of still defiant men and finally with a shout headed for the nearby marshes and five hundred of them managed to escape. The remaining survivors were surrendered by Pacthod to the praise of the Tsar and the Russian commanders. The swords of the French commanders were returned immediately, the Russians honouring more than able opponents. The running fight of the two divisions had been nothing short of epic. Pacthod's surrendered remnants numbered about 1,500, most of them wounded. Around 500 had escaped. More than 2,000 were killed or wounded in the sixteen-mile fight. General Delort stated that 'Every one did more than honour demanded, but I cannot find words to describe the behaviour of the National Guards. The words "brave" and "heroic" are inadequate to give an idea of their conduct.'[5]

CHAPTER 13

RED MICHAEL

The battles of Quatre Bras and Ligny, 1815

People who think of retreating before a battle has been fought ought to have stayed home. NEY

Tell the grenadiers that any man who brings me a prisoner will be shot. ROGUET

Look what their light cavalry have done to us! Imagine what their cuirassiers will do. WILLIAM OF PRUSSIA

Order, counter order, disorder. FRENCH MILITARY PROVERB

17:00 16 June 1815, Gemioncourt Farm, Belgium
The sound of firing to their front was a growing crescendo as Guiton's brigade of Kellermann's cavalry corps trotted towards the crossroads of Quatre Bras. As the battlefield exploded into view, Kellermann spotted Red Michael talking with his aide, Colonel Heymes, and came forward to report. Guiton halted the cuirassier brigade and deployed it in two lines, one regiment behind the other.

After a brief, heated exchange with the short-tempered marshal, Ney ordering Kellermann to 'crush them, ride them down!', Kellermann furiously galloped back to his luckless troopers, reining in his horse so violently that it slid on its hind legs along the slick ground trying to respond to his rider's wishes. Leaving his sabre in its scabbard Kellermann bellowed '*En avant!*' to the startled brigade. Regimental trumpeters stumbled with their trumpets, bringing them to their mouths to sound the charge, dutifully echoed by the company trumpeters all along the line. With a thunderous '*Vive l'Empereur!*' the brigade drew sabres and sunk spur, charging from the halt.

The pounding of 4,000 hooves literally shook the ground as the wave of massive armoured horsemen crested the low-lying hills which rose immediately in front of the Anglo-Dutch position. The leading ranks of the armoured juggernaut held their sabres point towards the enemy, each succeeding rank held them above their heads. Led by experienced, veteran officers and trumpeters mounted on easily recognised white or grey horses, the grim troopers followed their commanders into the waiting inferno.

Spotting two regiments in open order, Kellermann led his troopers in a whooping, hell-for-leather charge out of nowhere that trampled the surprised infantry before they could form square. Both the 33rd and 69th Regiments of Foot were overrun, the 69th being thoroughly cut to pieces losing a colour. The 33rd bolted for the rear, receiving a battery volley from nearby French artillery company for good measure.

Not stopping to reorganise, the cuirassiers overran an English artillery battery, sobering the gunners who tried to fight back using rammers and handspikes. Heedless of the increased volume and accuracy of the enemy's gunfire, Kellermann's two regiments swept on, crunching through a Brunswick square, scattering the black-coated Germans like tenpins.

The now hatless Kellermann led the brigade on to the threshold of the crossroads, momentarily clearing the field, but left unsupported by the witless Ney, his cuirassiers were now being shot down by accurate British musketry in increasing numbers. Rallying his exhausted troopers, Kellermann and Guiton led them back towards the French positions. Kellermann's horse was shot out from under him, pinning him to the ground. Freeing himself from his dead mount, he was scooped up by two troopers as they galloped past. Clinging to one stirrup from each man, the little general was carried between the two cuirassiers back to their line of departure.

———— ✳ ————

The Emperor had returned with the violets in the spring just as they had said he would. Jean de l'Epée had picked up the abandoned throne from the hapless Bourbons in a bloodless coup aided both by the army and a restless, unhappy populace. His eagles again 'flew from steeple to steeple'.

The Bourbons had fled to Belgium and with them those that had betrayed the Emperor the previous year, such as the 'ingrate' Marmont. The reformed and immensely expensive Maison du Roi had done nothing to defend Louis XVIII. They could not match Napoleon's veterans in a street brawl, a stand-up fight or in loyalty to their sovereign.

Napoleon offered the allies, now engaged in dividing up the spoils from their victory in 1814, peace, but they instead declared him a wolf's head, an international outlaw, and both sides again prepared for war. Once again armies marched and counter-marched across Europe to settle their differences.

Many of the Emperor's old comrades and commanders reported for duty.

Davout, who had refused to take service under the Bourbons was made Minister of War and to him fell the task of getting the French army ready for campaign. Suchet, Soult, Rapp, Savary and others duly reported for duty and were given commands and positions of trust as in the old days.

Davout's monumental task was to get the French army ready to take the field against the allies.[1] This was accomplished without resorting to the hated conscription, but there were weakness in this new army, christened the Armée du Nord. Berthier was not available as chief of staff, having gone into Germany after escorting Louis XVIII ('Louis the Unavoidable') to Belgium and safety. Unfortunately for Napoleon and the Armée du Nord, Berthier fell from a window and was killed on 1 June.

What Napoleon finally decided on was to name Soult as chief of staff and major general of Nord. The staff assembled, though having some of the stalwarts of earlier years such as Bailly de Monthion, was not as strong or as skilled as Berthier's staffs had been, even in the lean years of 1813–14. Soult's choices for his personal aides-de-camp were poor and overall the function of staff and organisation were among the main reasons for French failure in Belgium.

New corps organisation had to be created, and their commanders were carefully chosen, many of them being much better soldiers than the marshals they had replaced. Grouchy was deservedly promoted to marshal and given command of the Cavalry Reserve; Mortier was assigned with the Guard as usual. The Guard itself was carefully rebuilt and its commanders selected. Curial, one of the Guard's own commanders, was found to be unsuitable, but Friant and Morand, as well as Pelet and Pere Roguet were back to command. Guyot and Lefebvre-Desnoettes commanded the heavy and light cavalry, respectively; harness, horses, guns and ancillary equipment scrounged and requisitioned to get the Guard artillery up to strength and ready for active service.

Secondary armies were formed to protect and defend the French frontiers until Napoleon could defeat the Anglo-Dutch and Prussian armies in Belgium and march to their aid. Knowing the struggle could be a long one and planning for it, the Emperor planned the campaign thoroughly and hand-picked the independent commanders with special care.

Remembering the less-than-stellar performance of his army commanders in 1813 and 1814, he chose experienced, competent officers to command on the eastern and southern marches. Rapp would defend in the east in Alsace and Lorraine where he was well known and popular. Suchet, the one marshal to come out of Spain with his reputation not only intact but enhanced, would defend against Austrian incursion from Piedmont. Lamarque was sent into the Vendée where a Royalist revolt had again broken out and Decaen would watch the Spanish frontier.[2]

Napoleon, clearly grasping the strategic situation, ordered the Armée du Nord to concentrate on the Belgian frontier behind the protection of the northern fortresses. The army was composed of five corps d'armée, all under experienced generals of division. Quietly and efficiently, overcoming staff foul-ups, troops and units mustered and marched to their assembly areas, some of the larger formations finishing their organisation on the road. The Guard, as usual, stayed in and around Paris until the last minute to confuse allied intelligence.

Nord was tightly concentrated and prepared to strike across the border while the allied armies were still in their cantonment areas. Within Nord, however, were certain weaknesses. Many regiments and brigades were under strength. While composed of veterans, the troops and higher level commanders had not worked together before and many of the senior generals were mistrusted because they had willingly served the Bourbons after the First Abdication. The troops and regimental officers were ready to go forward unquestioningly into the fire, but many of the senior officers were just plain worn out.

One unfortunate incident that did not help matters as the campaign opened was the defection to the allies of General Bourmont, who commanded one of Gérard's divisions. Blücher had no time for traitors of any ilk and bluntly told the shocked Royalist that 'the son of a female dog was always the son of a female dog'.

Gérard, who among others had vouched for Bourmont's fidelity, was shocked and humbled. He was told by Napoleon that 'It was just as I told you, General; what is blue is blue, and what is white is always white.' It should be noted that Davout was against Bourmont's appointment and had suspected the deserter's sentiments accurately.

Wellington's Anglo-Dutch army did not approach the quality of the expert force which had won in Spain and southern France. Many of the Peninsular regiments, 'Wellington's Invincibles', were away in other theatres, such as North America, and had far to come and would not make it home for the campaign. There were too many new, inexperienced troops in the English, Scottish and Irish regiments in Belgium and there were never enough expert light infantry, such as the famous 95th Rifles, to go around. His artillery was excellent and his cavalry was well-mounted. The Duke attempted to get some of his old Portuguese outfits, his famous 'fighting cocks,' to deploy to Belgium for active service, but that proved to be impossible. His Hanoverian contingent was untried, except for the excellent King's German Legion; the Brunswickers were of uneven quality. Many in the Dutch and Belgian units had lately been in the service of France and their loyalty was debatable. All in all it was an 'odd-lot' collection.

Blücher's Army of the Lower Rhine was fleshed out with many untrained and untried Landwehr. Prussian artillery was largely ineffective; the supply services non-existent. Prussia's ruthless attitude and demeanour in provinces gained from the Congress of Vienna had aroused much resentment which was reflected in the attitude in the sullen and sometimes unwilling recruits obtained from the newly 'liberated' areas. The mutiny of the Saxon contingent before the campaign began was a good example of the problems encountered by the Prussians in assimilating their new provinces.[3]

Facing these two armies and their experienced commanders, the Emperor was still highly confident of victory. On 15 June he loosed his offensive across the Belgian border between Wellington and Blücher. Catching both armies and their commanders by surprise, Napoleon supposedly caused Wellington to remark, 'He has humbugged me, by God.'

Thrusting Nord like a rapier into the Charleroi region of southern Belgium, Napoleon effectively forced the Armée du Nord between his two most dangerous opponents. The allied advanced units were thoroughly defeated by the fast moving French spearheads, Zieten's corps being mauled in the process. Napoleon had gained the strategic advantage of interior lines by which he could, properly applying mass and economy of force, defeat each army separately, but he had to hurry.

The vital Charleroi bridge was captured intact by a determined rush of the sailors and engineers of the Imperial Guard, being employed after Vandamme was late moving out. Pajol galloped the bridge after it was cleared, the offensive being now able to continue. Hustling the corps forward, despite Soult's staff mishaps and Vandamme's tardiness, Napoleon was prepared to engage the allies separately. He was confident that his veterans were more than a match for the allies.

The Emperor divided his army into two wings, Ney taking the left and Napoleon the right. Ney was a curious case. Some competent historians believe he was suffering from 'battle fatigue' after the rigours of the Russian campaign. Besides his yeoman work at both Borodino and the Berezina, he was the last Frenchman to come out of Russia. His fumblings as an independent commander in 1813 deprived Napoleon of a decisive victory on at least two occasions. Additionally, his lead in the marshals' mutiny in 1814 was the catalyst that brought about Napoleon's abdication. However, whatever his mental state in 1815, he was still a driving, inspiring troop leader and was revered and followed by the rank-and-file.

Born in the Saar in 1769, Ney was another of the Grande Armée's 'Germans' and entered the Royal Army in 1788 in a hussar regiment. In 1792 he was promoted to sergeant major and was a colonel by 1794. Ney was an excellent drillmaster, but many times a lax disciplinarian off the battlefield. A driving, aggressive fighter, he led from the front, sometimes as a corps and army commander losing control of the action as a whole. By 1799 he was a general of division. His entire service up to 1800 was with the Rhine armies. He greatly distinguished himself at Hohenlinden in 1800 and, with Grouchy and Richepanse, was largely responsible for Moreau's decisive victory there over the Austrians. A competent tactician when he kept his wits about him, he was never a strategist. He was probably at his best as a corps commander. He was a failure as an independent commander in 1813, botching one of the Emperor's best planned battles at Bautzen.

Ney's real talent lay in rearguard operations. He was a superb leader of men as he showed repeatedly. A curious mixture of personality traits, Ney was hot-tempered and foul-mouthed, he had a devoted wife to whom he was faithful and he played the flute. An expert 'general of execution,' he could lead a corps into the assault like 'a captain of grenadiers' and bungle a simple manoeuvre when he became unsure of himself. Sent to Spain with Masséna in 1811 he was relieved for insubordination. Napoleon soon employed him again through 1814. The troops called him the 'Red Lion' and 'Red Michael'. He was arrested by the Bourbons after Waterloo and was tried for treason and shot. His wife was made to pay for the firing squad. His trial was something less than fair.

Initially, Napoleon was loath to employ him. He also was not too appreciative of the 'iron cage' remark after landing in Gulf Juan. He finally sent word to Davout in Paris that if Ney wanted to participate in the campaign he needed to get to the northern frontier quickly. Reaching Nord on 15 June with a single aide-de-camp and a small staff, he assumed command over the corps of Reille and d'Erlon as well as Kellermann's cavalry corps.

Ney pushed for Quatre Bras with Reille's corps leading the offensive. Only 8,000 men and sixteen guns under the youthful, cheerful Prince of Orange were in position to defend the crossroads. With at least 20,000 veterans available, all French, and as many en route, Ney could have overwhelmed the token force that had been sent to stop him. However, both he and Reille had fought against Wellington in Spain, were aware of his tactical skill and wary of a trap. Lefebvre-Desnoettes and his Guard light cavalry had flushed the Belgo-Dutch outposts from nearby Frasnes in a hot little fight, the action being prompted by

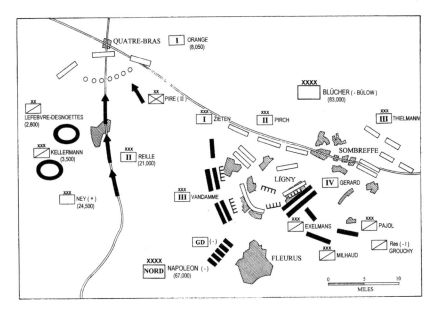

The Battle of Quatre Bras
Ney was too cautious in his initial movement to contact at the crossroads, and fed in his troops piecemeal, when a coordinated attack would have overwhelmed the relatively small force of Dutch–Belgians initially at the crossroads. What resulted was a see-saw engagement with the allies feeding in troops as they arrived, and the French fighting furiously under Ney's confusing generalship. The battle ended in a draw with the French back at their line of departure.

incoming potshots from the town and Bachelu's division of Reille's corps coming under attack. This small prelude to the main engagement opened the action, the troops in Frasnes taking to their heels back to their main positions, their stragglers being scooped up as prisoners. While this was going on, five Nassau battalions quietly occupied the crossroads.

Quatre Bras itself was a small, poor hamlet of three to four worn-down peasant hovels. At the juncture of the Charleroi and Nivelles roads, it became an objective of strategic importance in the campaign, if only briefly. The roads ran roughly north-south and east-west, providing good lateral communications between the two allied armies as well as an excellent axis of advance for the French. It is safe to assume that the troops of both armies arriving in the vicinity virtually swamped the inhabitants.

South-west of the crossroads lies the wood of Bossu, thick and impassable to formed bodies of troops, but skirmishers in open order could traverse it without too much trouble. To the south were the Gemioncourt Farm and the village of Piraumont. The south-east of the road junction were the two small villages of Grand and Petit Pierrepoint. The ground was covered with grown wheat and the rolling terrain was perfect for Wellington's favourite tactic of a reverse-slope defence. The terrain was also suitable for cavalry action and for artillery to manoeuvre.

The allied armies greatly feared a French surprise attack on the morning of 16 June. Napoleon wanted to defeat the Prussians first and then deal with Wellington. The allied dispositions confirmed this decision was sound. Blücher was much more concentrated than the Anglo-Dutch. Further, the Prussians were further south towards the French frontier than their allies.[4]

Ney received his orders to occupy Quatre Bras by 11:00 on 15 June. Soult lacked the knack of being able to read Napoleon's atrocious handwriting or of putting Napoleon's intentions into a simple, cogent operations order. Upon receipt of the order, Ney lackadaisically moved out with Reille and d'Erlon in a long, strung-out column, supported only by Lefebvre-Desnoettes and his Guard cavalry. Kellermann and his cavalry corps was still far to the rear.

The few Dutch-Belgians in and around Quatre Bras, with no cavalry and only two companies of artillery, must have viewed the seemingly overwhelming French advance with great trepidation. They were deployed through the wheat fields and woods to give an impression of greater numbers, they knew they could not hold out against a determined offensive for any length of time. The flood of Reille's corps debouched before them from march column into line of battle, the normally disorganised appearance of a French unit on the march completely changing into a disciplined, battle-ready force at the orders of their commanders. The outnumbered Dutch-Belgians could only count their rounds of ammunition and wait, the sweat of fear and anticipation soaking through their uniforms. When would their support arrive?

However, the gods of war had not ceased to smile on the allies. Two Dutch-Belgian generals, Perponcher and Rebecque, one a division commander and the other the Prince of Orange's chief of staff, knew what to do and reacted promptly. Couriers flew north from the crossroads urgently seeking anyone who could come to their support. The two Dutch-Belgians settled down to fight a delaying action until that support could arrive.

Wellington was fortunate in having these two officers in position facing the French. They knew their business and their decision to hold might have changed the course of the campaign. They deployed the available infantry division, most of the available units being deployed between the two Pierrepoints and the Gemioncourt farm. Light infantry was pushed forward to screen the positions and others hustled to occupy Piraumont.

Ney attacked tardily at 14:00 with the leading elements of Reille's II Corps. Swiftly advancing on the axis of the Charleroi road, and effectively supported by Pire's light cavalry division, Reille buffeted the Belgo-Dutch units ahead of him, warily watching for an English surprise. Ney outnumbered Orange at this point by three to one and should have made short work of Orange's single division. Wary of a trap, his cautious advance was going to cost the French dearly by the end of the day.

Bachelu's division, leading Reille's attack, rushed Piraumont and cleared the enemy light infantry from the hamlet in a nasty little bayonet fight. Continuing the attack, Bachelu attempted to outflank the Belgo-Dutch battalions in and around the Gemioncourt Farm. Under heavy pressure, these units attempted an orderly withdrawal into the wood of Bossu but were jumped by Pire's ranging light cavalry and cut to pieces. Attempting to rescue the decimated infantry, Merlen's recently arrived cavalry brigade clumsily collided with the French chasseurs and lancers and were thoroughly mauled and were driven off the field in something of a panic.

Around 15:00 Picton's English division came panting on to the battlefield (Wellington also reached the battlefield around 15:00 after his meeting with Blücher). Picton had wisely chosen to ensure his troops were fed before marching to Quatre Bras; consequently, they arrived later than planned. Behind them, the Duke of Brunswick's black-coated contingent was following Picton onto the battlefield. Picton aggressively counter-attacked the victorious French, knocking Bachelu's division back on their heels and for a moment gaining the allies some breathing space.

Wellington had reached the battlefield shortly before Picton's arrival and witnessed the counter-attack by the 92nd Foot, a highland regiment. The highlanders were initially roughly handled by Bachelu's hard-fighting veterans and the newly arrived infantry division of General Foy, an old horse artilleryman who had faced Wellington in Spain. Driving the British savagely back, they nearly took out the Duke himself, forcing him to take shelter with the Scotsmen. Determined close-quarter fighting by Picton finally checked both Bachelu and Foy.

Pire was involved in this mêlée and some of Picton's units were roughly handled. Pire also routed a militia battalion and captured eight guns.

The action was becoming desperate as each division of the II Corps was committed as they came up, Ney giving little thought to a coordinated attack. This could have been the result of his normal 'practice' of forgetting about the units not being under his direct supervision. Another factor could have been a reported thumping hangover both he and the members of his staff may have had after a drinking bout the night before. Neither possibility was of help to the tired French infantry desperately attempting to destroy the allied troops in and around the crossroads.

For whatever reason, Ney was losing control of the action. Though still able to control the field, he seemed unable to concentrate the mass needed either to defeat the allies outright or hurt them enough to drive them from the field. The advantages gained by the Emperor's strategic move the day before were being wasted.

Ney attempted an envelopment of the allied left flank with two of Reille's divisions. Simultaneously on the French left, Prince Jérôme manoeuvred his newly arrived division through the wood of Bossu, successfully clearing it of both the enemy and the growing number of stragglers taking shelter in the forest. Swarms of French voltigeurs scrambled through the underbrush fighting a catch-as-catch-can action which finally overwhelmed the enemy defenders. Punching into the open ground beyond the wood, Jérôme's victorious infantry pounced on the newly arrived Brunswickers.

Stubbornly holding their ground, Brunswick's Germans refused to withdraw before the hated French. A vicious firefight developed, both sides littering the field with dead and dying. Finally, the Brunswickers were on the verge of being overrun as enterprising French infantrymen in open order lapped around their flanks. Launching himself into their midst leading his cavalry against the Ière Légère, the Duke attempted to rally his sagging line, but took a round through the stomach. Seeing their commander fall, the dispirited and defeated Brunswickers broke up and fled, chased by Jérôme's infantry. The unfortunate 'Black Duke' had followed his father in being killed by the French, continuing what had become a rather grim family tradition.[5]

Reille's three infantry divisions now shouldered forward and the two Pierrepoints, which were south of the wood of Bossu, were in French hands by 15:30. Advancing in skirmisher swarms, the French infantry literally smothered the allied units, shooting their lines to pieces. The British light infantry engaged the French voltigeurs and chasseurs in a game of skirmisher cat-and-mouse, but superior numbers were beginning to tell. Backing up these tirailleurs en grandes bandes, French artillery began to dominate the field, breaking up allied attacks and wrecking several allied units, sometimes with point-blank canister fire.

However, all was not lost for the allies. More reinforcements were reaching the crossroads. All Wellington had to do was hold. The available French units had been more than enough to overwhelm the allies early on, but the continued arrival of allied reinforcements and Ney's inexpert direction of the battle, were giving the allies time to hold and reorganise.

Kempt's English brigade, as well as more Nassau battalions, now arrived and slammed into Jérôme's division driving him back into the wood. Seeing this, the quick-witted Foy swung his division on its axis outflanked Kempt and taking his brigade in enfilade. The ubiquitous Pire again pounced on a target of opportunity, but keeping a cool head in a crisis, Kempt rapped out an order and his brigade formed square by battalion against Pire's light horse and repulsed the attack, driving off Pire with loss. For the time being, the patched allied line held.

However, Kempt's brigade was defeated by Bachelu's artillery and the 108ᵉ Ligne and were charged by the Iᵉʳ and 6ᵉ Chasseurs (Pire) but were able to form square again as they fell back under the unrelenting pressure of the French light cavalry and supporting artillery.

The British 42nd Foot, the famous Black Watch, now advanced against the French in line. The ever-vigilant Pire swung his lancers into line and caught the highlanders from behind before they could form square. A desperate struggle in the wheat ensued, lance against bayoneted musket, the regimental commander of the 42nd falling mortally wounded and the enraged highlanders shooting cavalrymen from the saddle in revenge. The French attack was grimly pressed and the unfortunate highlanders were decimated. The swarming French cavalry broke up every attempt of the 42nd's survivors to form square, but the Scots toughly formed themselves into tight, indigestible knots around their officers and colours. The 42nd's losses were so heavy that they had to be formed with another regiment which had also suffered heavy losses for a single composite battalion for the battle two days hence.

The remainder of Pire's division, two regiments of chasseurs à cheval, launched themselves against the 28th and 44th Foot. British commands of 'Ready, present!' were matched by desperate shouts of 'Vive l'Empereur' from the French. Caught in line, the 44th were methodically slaughtered, their colours being taken and re-taken, but the 28th, to Picton's cry of '28th, Remember Alexandria!' coolly faced their second rank to the rear and fought off the French horsemen. Pire penetrated the Namur wood and ruined a Hanoverian battalion in the process..

The 15:15 message from Imperial Headquarters now arrived, informing Ney that 'the fate of France is in your hands'. Goaded by the Imperial spur, he immediately redoubled his efforts, but the reinforcements he was expecting, d'Erlon's I Corps, did not materialise. Ney was under the impression that d'Erlon's corps belonged to him and did not understand that d'Erlon had been ordered to Ligny to support the Emperor's main effort there.

D'Erlon's corps was hotfooting it for Quatre Bras when it was intercepted and diverted by one of Napoleon's hard-riding aides-de-camp, possibly General La Bédoyère. Knowing the Emperor's intentions and not needing to see any message from Soult, he immediately informed d'Erlon that he must march to

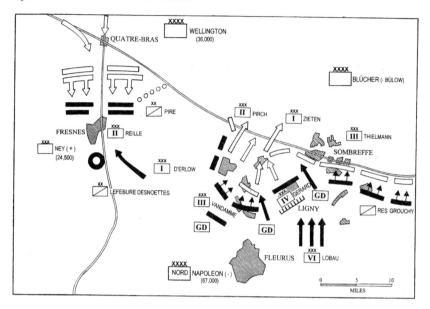

The Battle of Ligny: the Decisive French Attack

The failure of d'Erlon to support the French left and envelop the Prussians ruined Napoleon's initial plan. However, the decisive attack by the Imperial Guard, supported by Gerard's IV ruined Blücher's centre and drove the Prussians from the field. The artillery concentration and the attacking units are shown.

Ligny and strike the Prussian right flank with his entire corps. Immediately responding, d'Erlon changed direction and moved across country towards the smoke and roar of the struggle at Ligny.

When Ney discovered that d'Erlon was marching away from Quatre Bras he sent an aide in hot pursuit to bring d'Erlon back. Ney believed that if d'Erlon was not available he could not defeat Wellington. Probably, he was unaware of Napoleon's intention and the instructions d'Erlon had received from one of Napoleon's ADCs.

Rapidly approaching the Ligny battlefield, d'Erlon was caught by Ney's ADC. For whatever reason, which has never been satisfactorily explained, d'Erlon dropped off Durutte's division and Jacquinot's cavalry brigade to support them, without informing either Napoleon or Soult, and turned around heading back to Quatre Bras without firing a shot. The I Corps troops did not even have to clean their muskets that night.

Back at the crossroads, the seesaw battle continued. Ney could not quite win, but Wellington's position was rapidly falling apart. Jérôme again attacked the exhausted allied survivors but again was held off by desperate fighting. Around 17:00 Kellermann rode in with his leading brigade, commanded by Guiton. Ney immediately, and without support, ordered Kellermann to attack the allied centre, being berated by Ney for not having his entire command to hand. Kellermann, amazed at both the anger and the order, asked for clarification and was told to ride down the enemy and crush them.

The intrepid Kellermann placed himself at the head of the lone brigade and ordered a charge from the halt. Kellermann turned to his troopers and bellowed 'Charge at full gallop! Forward march!' In his report of the action afterwards, Kellermann remarked that 'I used great haste so as not to allow my men time to shrink, or to perceive the whole extent of the danger in front of them.'

The brigade, consisting of the 8^e and 11^e Cuirassiers, crested the hill mass in front of the allied position like a steel tipped wave and crashed into whatever lay in their path. Two English regiments were caught in line by the steel juggernaut, one, the 69th Foot, losing their King's colour to the cuirassiers. The other, the 33rd Foot was hit and scattered by the massed heavy cavalrymen. An English artillery company was also caught, the gunners being mown down by the giant cavalrymen and the traces for the gun teams being cut before the victorious cuirassiers thundered on. Brunswick infantry in square were overrun, the square broken, and the brigade, winded and now taking fire from massed infantry, finally reached the crossroads.

Ney failed to exploit this advantage and the brigade had to fight its way out of what was becoming a deathtrap. Leading his men out, Kellermann's horse was shot out from under him, dismounting the general and leaving him open to death or capture. Two of his troopers scooped him up between them, taking him back to the French lines holding on to their stirrup leathers.

Ney's failure to support Kellermann's cracking of the allied centre was a missed opportunity that cost him the battle. At 18:15 Cooke's English division arrived, composed of three British Guards regiments. This gave Wellington a three-to-two numerical superiority of which the Iron Duke immediately took advantage. Stiffly counter-attacking all along the line, the reinforced Anglo-Dutch slowly but steadily pushed back the hard-fighting French to their line of departure. The French light cavalry once again ranged the battlefield, mauling the Guards battalions and at one point sending them scurrying for cover in the woods, but Ney could not coordinate a concentrated French effort and again an advantage melted away. The drawn battle ended by 20:30, though 'bickering' continued until about 21:00.

On the same day to the south-east near the village of Ligny, Napoleon came to grips with the main Prussian army under Blücher. Napoleon's aim, as always, was the destruction of his enemy on the battlefield. Poor staff work by Soult and Ney's errors would cripple Napoleon's initial plan. Ney for his part probably only partially understood what Napoleon wanted him to accomplish.

In any event, the battle of Ligny was one of Napoleon's best-fought battles. There, Blücher massed over 80,000 Prussians against 67,000 French. Napoleon took the initiative, attacking a superior army in a strong defensive position among solidly built villages, and not only turned the Prussians out of their chosen positions, but inflicted casualties on the Prussians of three to one.

Blücher's position was deceptively strong, the Prussians occupying a tangle of walled enclosures and small villages, each of them a ready-made strong-point. Ligne brook was small, but deep and impassable to both artillery and cavalry without a bridge or a usable ford. There were weaknesses in the old Prussian's dispositions, however. His right was in the air giving Napoleon an open opportunity to flank and trap Blücher's units in that sector. Further, the Prussian dispositions among the villages gave their front an irregular trace, which gave the French, especially their artillery, myriad opportunities for enfilade fire which were taken advantage of and which the French artillerymen employed with all their usual professional skill.[6]

Moreover, Bülow's IV Corps was not involved in the fight. He was arguably the best of the Prussian corps commanders and his presence, and numbers, might have actually tipped the scales in favour of the Prussians.

Further Prussian weaknesses were the lack of a central army artillery reserve, the artillery, despite well-thought out reforms of that arm after 1807, still being the poor relation to the infantry and cavalry.[7] Last, Blücher had decided to fight whether or not Wellington came to support him. The old hussar, the famous 'Marshal Forward', was a fighter of the first order, though with no claim to being a strategist and a rather poor tactician. He was at his best in a desperate tactical brawl, which Ligny had all the makings of before the first shot was fired in anger.

The battle started in mid-afternoon and Napoleon wrote to Ney around 14:00 that he was about to attack Blücher and that he, Ney, should immediately attack and 'drive away' any allied force to his front. He then should wheel to the right and envelop Blücher's right flank. It was a planned battle of annihilation, similar to Napoleon's plan at Bautzen in 1813. Ney would fail to accomplish this mission again in Belgium.[8]

By 14:30 Napoleon had Vandamme's III Corps, Gérard's IV Corps, the Imperial Guard (less Lefebvre-Desnoettes' Guard Light Cavalry division which was supporting Ney) and Grouchy's Cavalry Reserve with Pajol's, Milhaud's and Exelman's cavalry corps. Lobau's VI Corps was within supporting distance. Girard's division of Reille's II Corps was attached to Vandamme.

Napoleon opened his attack at approximately 14:30 with Vandamme going against Blücher's left flank and Gérard attacking the Prussian centre. Both had excellent artillery support. Grouchy was on the French right with one of Gérard's division to hold the Prussian left flank in place. Vandamme was the main effort with Gérard's mission to take and hold Ligny.

At 15:15 Lobau was ordered forward and orders were sent to Ney ordering him to advance against Blücher's right rear immediately. In vicious fighting, Vandamme cleared the St Amand salient, the fighting favouring the French, being more experienced in this type of combat in built-up areas than the Prussian infantry.

However, the stubborn Prussians had finally stopped both his and Gérard's advance in no-quarter fighting. Blücher unwittingly kept sending battalions into the massed fire of the French artillery that had the Prussian corps of Pirch (II Corps) and Zieten (I Corps) in an unrelenting cross-fire. The French artillerymen hammered the hapless Prussians mercilessly. Prussian units kept advancing and were chewed up one after the other. Prussian units were becoming intermixed and confusion was becoming greater as the Prussian commanders lost control of the action.

Seeing the battle 'ripen' to his advantage, Napoleon massed the Imperial Guard infantry for the decisive assault against the Prussians. That coupled with the enveloping manoeuvre that had to be on the way from Ney would trap at least half of the hapless Prussian army between Ney and Gérard, with the Guard attacking between them to overrun at least two Prussian corps.

As has already been related, Ney fumbled his mission and d'Erlon's I Corps marched and countermarched all day. Its approach to the Ligny battlefield actually startled Vandamme's corps, causing some confusion as to who the advancing troops actually were – allied or French. This confusion caused Vandamme's effort to falter and he actually lost ground to the Prussians. This confusion also caused a major Prussian counter-attack.

The resurgent Prussians surged forward and Zieten's troops recovered two of the three villages in the St Amand complex and were fighting in the third village when the Imperial Guard appeared. At the same time, Thielmann's cavalry attacked but this was contained expertly by Grouchy. Having been given a breather by the Guard's appearance, Vandamme's weary infantry again attacked and recovered most of the lost ground.

By 18:30 Napoleon confirmed that the errant column off his left flank was d'Erlon. Realising his initial plan was ruined, he massed the Guard against the Prussian centre and loosed them against the Prussians around 20:00. Gérard again attacked, his troops moving between the Guard's assaulting columns and the Prussian centre was shattered at first impact. French artillery, as it had on other fields such as Friedland and Lützen, paved the way for the French assault.

Zieten's cavalry, led by Blücher riding into the maelstrom like a lieutenant of hussars, charged the mass of infantry. The Guard infantry formed square and ruined the charge. Blücher's horse was killed under him and he was ridden under by Milhaud's cuirassiers. He was saved by his devoted aide-de-camp, Nostitz, and the French cavalrymen had no idea they had nearly captured the Prussian commander. Blücher's loss to the Prussians would have been an irretrievable loss to the allied cause.

One Prussian Uhlan regiment, the 6th, commanded by Lützow, the famous partisan commander from 1813, attacked a French infantry regiment in square, thinking they were merely National Guard troops because of their motley appearance. Unfortunately for the unlucky Lützow, they happened to be the 4e Grenadiers à Pied of the Imperial Guard. The solid Guardsmen coolly presented arms and shot the Uhlans to pieces with disciplined, regular volleys. Lützow was unhorsed, wounded and captured, and over eighty of his troopers were shot down. Appearances can be deceiving.

A Royalist émigré who was present at Ligny and saw the fighting stated that the French were 'either a legion of heroes or of devils' and were not the inexperienced, worn out troops of the campaign in France of the year before.

The Prussian 1st (Koningen) Dragoons, 2nd Kurmark Landwehr Cavalry and the Brandenburg Uhlans, also charged the Imperial Guard and were broken on their squares or were repulsed by Milhaud's cuirassiers and the Dragoons of the Imperial Guard.

The Prussians were defeated all along the line and at least two of the three corps engaged had been mauled. While it was not the victory Napoleon wanted, it was a good start to the campaign. French casualties had been approximately 11,500. The Prussians, on the other hand, had suffered 34,000 casualties, which included about 12,000 who deserted during their retreat from yet another lost field. The French rested on the battlefield and regimental bands were heard playing 'La Victoire á Nous'.[9] The next day the main French army under Napoleon would advance and face Wellington's Anglo-Dutch army near a little hamlet named Mont St Jean. And the Prussians, with Blücher hors de combat temporarily and his chief of staff, Gneisenau, withdrew to Wavre and not eastward.[10] Their subsequent movement would be to Wavre and eventually to the soon-to-be epic battlefield near Mont St Jean to seal a dear-bought allied victory.

General Gaspard Gourgaud gave a fitting comment on the performance of the French troops in the campaign in Belgium in 1814:

Never did the French troops so well display their superiority over all the troops in Europe, as during the short campaign, in which they were so constantly inferior in numbers. It may be truly said, that if, in these great disasters, the French army lost all, it at least preserved its honor.[11]

The victory at Ligny is overshadowed by the battle of Waterloo two days later. However, four French generals performed excellently at Ligny and clearly demonstrated that French military talent had not degenerated by the end of the Empire.

Hyppolyte-Marie-Guillaume Pire (1778–1850) emigrated in 1791 and had service in the Régiment de Rohan, an émigré unit, in 1794. With the Armée de la Vendée in 1796, he volunteered for the newly raised a in 1800 at the outset of the Marengo campaign. Appointed a maréchal des logis, he was a captain by 1805 and thereafter rose rapidly.

Promoted to chef d'escadron in 1806 he was appointed one of Berthier's aides-de-camp in 1807 and was appointed as the colonel of the 7e Chasseurs à Cheval that year. He went into Spain with the Emperor's second invasion, again as one of Berthier's 'hellions' and was promoted to general of brigade in 1809. He served with the Armée d'Allemagne assigned to Montbrun's division in Davout's III Corps. He served in Russia, Saxony in 1813 and in the campaign of France in 1814. He was promoted to general of division in 1813.

Rallying to Napoleon in 1815, he was given command of a light cavalry division which performed superbly at Quatre Bras, ranging the battlefield and running roughshod over allied infantry units.

Jean-Baptise Girard (1775–1815) began his military service with the Volont-aires au Bataillon de Réquisition du District de Bayols in September 1793. The next year he was in Italy and was promoted to sous-lieutenant in 1796. In January 1799 he was made a chef de bataillon and a chef de brigade the next year. In 1800 he served in the Marengo campaign as chief of staff to Monnier.

In 1805 he was assigned to the Cavalry Reserve as a staff officer and was promoted to general of brigade in November 1806 with Suchet's division in the V Corps. He served in Spain from 1808–11 and was in Russia assigned to Victor's IX Corps. He remained with Eugène in the newly christened Army of the Elbe in early 1813 and was in the siege of Magdeburg from 1813–14.

He rallied to Napoleon in 1815 and was assigned as a division commander, stoutly fighting at Ligny, but was unfortunately mortally wounded. His hard-used division remained behind as the rest of the army moved out to lick its wounds and could have been employed to wreck Gneisenau's amateurish pursuit on the evening of Waterloo. It is an interesting 'what if' regarding this division if Girard was still commanding it that day.

Dominique Joseph René Vandamme (1770–1830) was a Fleming with red hair and a violent temper. One of the best of the Grande Armée's fighting commanders, it was said that only Davout could control him – and even he had trouble doing it. However, for all of the colourful history left by Vandamme, a good part of it is probably, and unfortunately, apocryphal.

He enlisted in 1788, apparently deserted in 1790 and re-enlisted in 1791. Initially an instructor with the volunteers, he rose rapidly, becoming a general of brigade in 1793 and a general of division by 1799. His service during the Wars of the Revolution was with the Rhine armies. When assigned to the Grande Armée after 1805, when he was one of the two division commanders who made the decisive attack at Austerlitz on the Pratzen, it was usually in secondary areas and in command of foreign troops. He reduced the Prussian Silesian fortresses in 1806–7 and commanded the Württemberg troops in 1809. He rowed with Jérôme in 1812 and was unjustly relieved because of it.

In 1813 he commanded the I Corps and, not being supported by St Cyr after Dresden, got himself trapped by the allies during the pursuit and was defeated and captured at Kulm. After returning to France the next year he was turned away by the Bourbons and enthusiastically joined Napoleon in 1815 and was given command of the III Corps.

Napoleon reportedly said of him, 'If I had two of you, the only solution would be to have one hang the other' and that Vandamme was perfect to lead an assault upon hell itself, as he had no fear of God nor the devil. Napoleon also told Davout to take good care of him in 1813 as good fighting men were growing scarce.

The last general officer that had been an integral part of the command and control system of the Grande Armée is not very well known. François Gédéon Bailly de Monthion (1776–1850) had been Berthier's understudy and chief subordinate in the Grand Quartier Général Impérial for years and was an officer of proven skill and ability.

He was commissions a sous-lieutenant in the 74e Ligne in 1793, being promoted to lieutenant in 1795. That same year he was promoted again to captain adjoint and was assigned to the Armée de Sambre-et-Meuse from 1796–7. He was aide-de-camp to General Turreau in 1797 and from 1797–9 he served consecutively with the Armées de Mayence, Helvetie and Danube. He served with distinction at the defence of Kehl. He was with the Armée d'Italie in 1800, but was transferred to Berthier's staff in 1800 and was promoted to chef d'escadron in the 9e Chasseurs à Cheval. With the Grande Armée on the staff in the campaigns of 1805, 1806 and 1807 he served with skill and devotion and proved himself to be an excellent staff officer.

In served with Murat in Spain in 1808 as a senior staff officer and was promoted general of brigade that year. He was back with Berthier and the Armé d'Allemagne in 1809, serving as Berthier's primary assistant chief of staff. He served in Russia in the same capacity and was Eugène's chief of staff at the end of the retreat after Berthier became ill. He was again Berthier's assistant in 1813–14, taking over from Berthier and running the staff more than competently if Berthier was not present or if he was ill. He served Soult as the primary assistant chief of staff with the Armée du Nord in 1815, but the two did not get on and the army's efficiency suffered for it.

Napoleon would have made a better decision if he had made Bailly de Monthion a marshal in 1815 and had made him Major General to replace Berthier. No one officer knew the job better than de Monthion and if he was not Berthier's equal as a chief of staff, he had been trained by Berthier and would have served Napoleon as well as Berthier had done.

CHAPTER 14

GLORY COSTS TOO MUCH

Eugène never caused me the least chagrin. NAPOLEON

If I had two marshals like Suchet, I not only would have conquered Spain, but would have kept it. NAPOLEON

Part I Eugène de Beauharnais

09:00, 4 January 1813, Posen, The Grand Duchy of Warsaw
The grey-haired, stocky officer stood at the window of the miserable building now serving as the office of the Major General and Chief of Staff of the Grande Armée, or actually what was left of it; if the starving, ragged and frost-bitten survivors trying to rally at the end of the great retreat could be called 'Grande'. He stood with his arms behind his back, noticing the white-uniformed troops of the regiment of black men from Naples in formation in the snow, thinking how incongruous it looked. Grizzled veterans from the Old Guard were conducting an inspection for guard mount, slowly and methodically going up and down the ranks, checking weapons and ammunition.

The army was in a mess. Ammunition was low, losses crippling, so many key subordinates dead or dying, frost-bitten stragglers wandering in every day to contribute more or less to the army's hollow combat strength. Eble and Lariboissière had just died; the Emperor had left for Paris a month ago, promising to bring back reinforcements. Murat had just deserted and the command of these gallant remnants had devolved onto Prince Eugène, the Emperor's stepson.

To Eugène's credit, he had hesitated to take command, but someone had to, someone all would obey. The marshals were quarrelling again; no one would take orders from anyone else. Only Davout was demonstrating any sense at all.

If they did not straighten things out, the Russians would be on the Elbe in a week. There were already rumours of Cossacks in their rear and there was not enough cavalry left to find out. Their losses in horses in Russia had been incredibly heavy; the cavalry was crippled and much of it was Murat's fault.

Eugène was due in about fifteen minutes. He had finally consented to assume command late last night. Now they had much work to do and Napoleon had to confirm Eugène in command as soon as possible to stop this senseless bickering among the marshals and senior generals. There was still time to draft some necessary orders before Eugène's arrival, although there were few of the chief of staff's gallant 'hellions' left to deliver them. Too many friends and comrades had been left behind dead or captured inside Russia. With a heavy sigh and a shrug of his shoulders, the officer at the window turned and resumed his seat at his desk, took out his pen and paper and started to write. Marshal Berthier, major general and chief of staff of the Grande Armée was once again at work, waiting for the first commander he had served other than Napoleon since 1796.[1]

There are two general officers who generally do not receive the historical recognition that is their due. Both served loyally and ably throughout the period 1800–14 and one served further in 1815.

The first, Eugène de Beauharnais (1781–1823) was the son of Josephine by her first husband, Alexandre de Beauharnais, who had been a general of the Republic and had been executed during the Terror. Eugène reportedly had first met Napoleon when he had approached him on his own to ask that the sword of his father be returned to him. Napoleon was impressed by Eugène at that first meeting and, after he married Josephine, he legally adopted both Eugène and his sister Hortense.

Eugène has been described as a 'long, lean cavalryman' and joined the Armée d'Italie in 1797 after Rivoli and made the campaigns in Egypt and Syria as one of Napoleon's aides-de-camp.

On his return to France with Napoleon, he was given a commission in what would become the Chasseurs à Cheval of the Guard and participated in the battle of Marengo. Napoleon constantly coached and taught the young Eugène and made him his viceroy in the newly christened Kingdom of Italy. Deemed too young and inexperienced to command the Armée d'Italie in the 1805 campaign (that billet going to the experienced Masséna), he devoted himself to his post and subjects and became a competent administrator and de facto head of state for his new kingdom.

When Austria attacked the French Empire, without the benefit of a declaration of war in 1809, Napoleon was forced to give the command of the

Armée d'Italie to Eugène. An inexperienced and very young general, Eugène had teething problems and his first effort against the Austrians on 16 April 1809 was a definite defeat. Eugène was willing to learn from both defeat and the advice of his generals, and the rest of the campaign was a record of success. Eugène repeatedly outmanoeuvred and outfought his Austrian opponents throughout the rest of the campaign.

Eugène's generalship improved and matured throughout the campaign. Napoleon's correspondence to him during this period is 'a virtual field manual' on how to command an army in the field, but if the innate talent to command was not inherent in Eugène's character, the outright success of the Armée d'Italie would have certainly been diminished. On 8 May, Eugène and his army made an assault crossing of the Piave River and defeated the Austrians under the Archduke John decisively. This victory opened the way for a pursuit of the defeated Austrians into southern Austria and an eventual juncture with the Armée d'Allemagne in time for the battle of Wagram.

Eugène is undoubtedly the most underrated and ignored general officer of the period in any army. Beginning as an inexperienced army commander, he developed into a capable general and independent commander who could figuratively make bricks without straw and succeed where other older and more inexperienced officers might fail. Innovative, loyal, intelligent and skilful, his operations in Russia proved him to be a commander that was careful of the lives of his men, the very devil in boots to inefficient administrative officers and a deadly opponent on the battlefield. His performance in 1813–14 showed signs of genius, especially his defence of northern Italy in 1814. He has never been given his due by historians.

Given command as an inexperienced officer of the Armé d'Italie for the campaign of 1809, Eugène matured into an experienced, skilled commander who was careful of the lives of his men, learned from his mistakes and could be trusted to command on his own successfully. Eugene's performance in Russia, especially during the retreat when he rescued Ney's corps which had become trapped behind Russian lines and given up for lost, was exemplary. His performance at Maloyaroslavets before the retreat began is also noteworthy, commanding on the field and defeating Kutusov.

Eugène constantly improved throughout his career. Described as a 'long, lean cavalryman' he was an officer in the Chasseurs à Cheval of the Guard at Marengo, later commanding the regiment. Appointed as Napoleon's Viceroy in Italy, he ruled firmly but fairly and tolerated no corruption either in government or in the Armée d'Italie.

Napoleon had to employ him as the commander of the Armée d'Italie in 1809, most of the Grande Armée then being employed, with its fighting commanders, in Spain. At first hesitant and being defeated by the Archduke John at Sacile, Eugène learned form his mistakes and skilfully manoeuvred and fought his army until they made a junction with the Armée d'Allemagne in Austria, fighting together at Wagram.[2]

Commanding the IV Corps of the Grande Armée in Russia, Eugène proved to be an outstanding corps commander, his Italians doing some of the finest fighting of the campaign. Eugène's performance at Maloyaroslavets and during the retreat were exemplary. When Ney's corps was cut off from the main army during the retreat and thought to be lost, it was Eugène that found him and brought him in with his survivors. His actions upon assuming command of the remnants of the Grande Armée after Murat's desertion at the end of the retreat, at Berthier's urging and without waiting for Napoleon's concurrence or direction, undoubtedly saved the Grande Armée cadres and survivors.

Eugène built up an effective army to face the Prussians and Russians while Napoleon was organising a new Grande Armée to come east. Eugène's Army of the Elbe expertly traded space for time and numbered nearly 60,000 effectives when Napoleon took the field in April 1813. He was then sent to Italy.

Eugène held northern Italy in 1814 in a brilliant campaign that defeated all comers, rebuffing Murat's and the allies' offers of a crown in Italy if he turned on Napoleon. After the first abdication, he retired to Bavaria with his wife and remained there during the Hundred Days – some sources maintain that he did not want to go back to France and others that he was in semi-arrest. Whatever the case, it is doubtful that his father-in-law, the King of Bavaria, would have allowed him to return to serve Napoleon again.

There were two generals who were key subordinates under Eugène in 1809. Both are generally ignored by historians as they usually served in secondary theatres, as in Italy in 1809. Both are outstanding officers and deserve their due.

Paul Grenier (1768–1827) was a private in the Régiment de Nassau-Infanterie (later the 96ᵉ Ligne) in 1784, rising to corporal in 1788, sergeant in 1789, fourrier in 1790 and sergeant-major in 1791. He was an adjutant sous-officier by 1792 and won his epaulets that year as well as promotion to captain. He served at Valmy, Jemappes, Hondschoote and Wattignies.

Promoted to adjutant general chef de brigade in 1793 with the Armée de la Moselle, made chef de brigade the next year, winning his general's stars the same year serving with Championnet and at Fleurus. With the Armée de Sambre et Meuse from 1794–97, he was promoted to general of division the same year, gaining command of the 10ᵉ Division of that army. Transferred to command of the 2ᵉ Division of Sambre et Meuse the next year, he was later transferred to the Armée d'Angleterre under Hoche (1798).

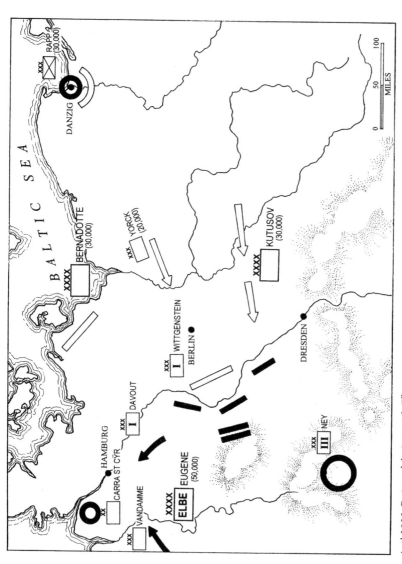

Strategic Situation, April 1813: Eugène and the Army of the Elbe

Eugène, urged by Berthier, took command of the wreck of the Grande Armée after Murat's desertion in January 1813. His subsequent operations from January to April 1813, when he linked up with Napoleon marching east from France, mark him as one of the most able generals of the period. His mission was to hold the Empire's eastern marches and to build up an effective army. Continually bassled by Napoleonic correspondence from Paris, Eugène carefully and methodically built up an army of almost 60,000 troops from frozen veterans, sullen allies, and newly arrived conscripts. He also kept his own counsel when necessary, and although he gave up more territory than Napoleon wished, he kept the allies, who significantly outnumbered him, at bay until Napoleon's arrival in April.

Again transferred, this time to the Armée d'Italie in 1798, he was successful against the Russians at Bassignano in May of 1799. Briefly serving again with Championnet in the Armée des Grandes Alpes, he was soon back with Italie. In 1800 he served with the Armée du Rhin and replaced St Cyr as a corps commander in June of that year. He defeated the Austrian general Kray that summer and fought at Hohenlinden in December.

Generally during the Empire his service was with the Armée d'Italie as a corps commander and his is one of the reasons Eugène was so successful in 1809. The next year Grenier was made the Inspector General of Infantry for the Armée d'Italie and also served as chief of staff to Murat in Naples, which had to be an interesting assignment. Serving with Augereau in 1812, he was back with Eugène in 1813–14 as a corps commander. In 1815 he served in the defence of Paris.

Grenier is one of the unsung heroes of the Grande Armée. Usually serving in secondary theatres, his value and merit generally went unrecognised and he was probably associated with Moreau because of his service in Germany in 1800. Loyal, steadfast and very competent, he served Eugène faithfully in good times and bad and he deserves much more recognition than he generally gets.

Jean-Baptiste Broussier (1766–1814) is another general officer that seldom gets his due. He served with distinction in 1809 under Eugène and started his career in 1791 as a captain in the 3rd Bataillon Volontaires de la Meuse. Promoted to chef de bataillon in 1794 he served with the Armée de Sambre et Meuse from 1794 to 1796 in the 43e ligne. In the Armée d'Italie in 1797 he was promoted to chef de brigade à la suite by Napoleon in March of that year.

The next year he was on Duhesme's staff with the Armée du Rome and was promoted provisional general de brigade by Championnet in 1799. Broussier served with distinction under both of these commanders and was in Loison's division in the Marengo campaign, fighting at Fort Bard during the Alps crossing.

After some staff assignments under Murat and in the Armée d'Italie, he was promoted to general of division on 1 February 1805 and was made chief of staff of the Armée du Nord in November of that year. He commanded a division under Lefebvre in 1806 and went back to command a division in the Armée d'Italie that summer. He stayed with Italie through 1809, defeating Gyulai at Callendorf on 24 June. He also served at Graz and Wagram.

He was under Eugène again for the invasion of Russia, serving throughout the campaign and in 1813 he was the commander of the 3rd Division of the Corps of Observation of Mayence (Mainz). Late in the year he became the commandant of Strasbourg and Kehl. He died the next year.[3]

One of the best soldiers and cavalrymen of the period was Pierre Montbrun (1770–1812). He was very likely the most skilful of Napoleon's cavalry corps commanders. He enlisted as a private in the Ier Chasseurs à Cheval, and by hard work and competence, fought his way up to Colonel and regimental commander of that regiment. He enlisted in 1789 in the Chasseurs d'Alsace, which became the Ier Chasseurs à Cheval, won a battlefield commission and was a captain by 1797.

A chef d'escadron in 1799, he was promoted to chef de brigade in 1800 and given command of the 8e Dragons. From 1803–5 he commanded his old outfit, the Ier Chasseurs à Cheval in Davout's command, which eventually became the famous III Corps. Davout ensured he was promoted to general of brigade in 1805. In 1806 he was with the Armée du Naples, first in Reynier's division and then with the Division Espagne. He commanded the cavalry in the V Corps in 1806, but was transferred to command the Württemberg cavalry under Vandamme in Silesia. Later that year he commanded the cavalry of Jérôme's IX Corps but was back with the V Corps under Masséna this time in 1807. He commanded Victor's cavalry in Spain (I Corps) and commanded the Guard cavalry detachment that rode to the support of the Polish Light Horse at Somosierra.

In 1809 he was with the Armée d'Allemagne and commanded Davout's corps cavalry division in the campaign against the Austrians that year, winning distinction in the fighting around Ratisbon, proving himself an excellent senior commander who could think for himself and command both infantry and cavalry. Sent to Eugène's Armée d'Italie, he fought excellently at Raab, but was back with Davout for Wagram. He was in Spain and Portugal in 1810–12 and went into Russian commanding the II Cavalry Corps. He was killed in action at Borodino that September.

He was aggressive, intelligent, an excellent tactician and leader of men.

Part II Marshal Suchet

08:30 17 April 1810, near the village of Pina, Aragon, Spain
Lieutenant Berthod of the 10^e Escadron of the *Gendarmerie* of Spain was having the wound to his right leg dressed after a sharp little action against one of the local guerilla bands. The lieutenant grimaced as the wound was cleansed with alcohol, courtesy of a bottle of wine liberated by one of his troopers, and after the dressing was applied tightly to the wound, he stood up to ensure he could walk and mount his horse. Satisfied, he limped over to his mount and hung his sword belt from the saddle and recovered his regulation bicorne. Then he went to talk to his maréchal des logis.

The gendarmes had won, defeating a larger guerilla band, and they were cleaning up the area, collecting captured weapons and making sure that the dead guerillas actually were dead. The wounded brigands the gendarmes had captured were bound securely before departing for Pina. The gendarmes had lost one dead and four wounded, including their lieutenant. The thirty-eight gendarmes, however, had killed ten of the enemy and wounded at least fifty, most of which had either escaped or were in hiding until the gendarmes moved on. The gendarmes had also lost four horses killed in the action out of fourteen present. That was really a shame, as good horses were harder to replace than troopers, even highly regarded gendarmes. Spain was a hard place to campaign.

After speaking to his maréchal des logis, the lieutenant mounted his horse, who was thankfully unhurt, to await the assembly of his detachment. Most of the detachment was made up of *gendarmes à pied*, so they had no mounts to worry about. The troopers who had lost their horses were doubly unhappy – they would have to walk back to Pina in the column and help to guard the prisoners, as well as find new mounts upon returning. The maréchal des logis, a grizzled veteran of many years' service, barked his command to the detachment to assemble, the troops formed up with the prisoners in the middle of the little column and behind the lieutenant and the mounted gendarmes, the little column began its slow trek back to Pina, flank, front and rearguards out. This was still Spain, and they knew they were being watched.[4]

The Iberian peninsula proved to be the graveyard of military reputations for a number of Napoleon's marshals. Soult lost more battles than he won, though he successfully pacified his area of responsibility. Victor, Marmont, Augereau, Moncey, Ney and Jourdan proved themselves incapable of dealing with the situations they had to confront, both Victor and Marmont being defeated by Wellington. Masséna, quite possibly the most talented of the marshalate, was not only a failure in the Peninsula, but it proved to be his last active command.

Louis-Gabriel Suchet was the only one of Napoleon's generals to be made a marshal because of success in Spain. He also was granted a Spanish title by his Emperor and not only was he successful militarily in Spain, but he also excelled as an administrator and successfully pacified Aragon. He later did the same for Catalonia and Valencia, never with an army that numbered more than 50,000 men. Suchet realised that the goodwill of the Spanish people was paramount in his campaigns in eastern Spain. The Spaniards were left to rule themselves, managing their own budget, levying their own taxes and policing their own people. Suchet abolished old, corrupt or inefficient institutions, such as trade restrictions, and the provinces prospered.

Eastern Spain 1809–14: Suchet's Operations
Suchet's operations from 1809 to 1814 were based in Aragon and Catalonia, and spread southwards. Tarragona and
Valencia were two of the prizes that Suchet's Army of Aragon captured, as well as defeating two British expeditions from
Sicily. Suchet was almost uniformly successful in his operations, as well as generally pacifying his base of operations in
Aragon and Catalonia, but in 1813–14 had to conform to the general French situation in Spain and was forced to
evacuate Valencia in 1813. He was the only French general to win his baton in the Peninsula.

Suchet was the son of a silk merchant in Lyons, reportedly somewhat wealthy, but that did not stop young Suchet from volunteering to defend *La Patrie* in 1793. By 1796 he was serving in the Armée d'Italie as a lieutenant colonel and he was promoted to colonel by Napoleon because of his proficiency and competence. In 1799 he was a general of division and had experience, and an excellent reputation, both as a commander and a staff officer.

In 1800 he was still with the Armée d'Italie, and when the Austrian avalanche came down on him and Masséna before the Marengo campaign began, Suchet became de facto commander of the 'other half' of the Armée d'Italie that was not bottled up in Genoa with Masséna. Suchet performed brilliantly on the Var as an independent army commander, defeating the Austrian Elsnitz and starting his own offensive eastward after the Armée de la Réserve crossed the Alps.

Suchet commanded a division in V Corps in 1805–7 and was posted as commander of the neglected III Corps in Spain in 1809. His first battle in command ended being a lost cause, as his neglected troops ran away from outnumbered Spanish at Alcaniz on 23 May 1809. Setting his jaw and rolling up his sleeves, Suchet set to work revitalising his new army, which by now had been renamed the Army of Aragon. Restoring discipline and ensuring his troops were regularly paid, clothed and properly equipped, Suchet conquered and pacified Aragon. The next three years saw Suchet conquer two more provinces, more than adequately endowed with fortresses, and captured approximately 77,000 prisoners and 1,400 guns.

After his defeat at Alcaniz, Suchet had to face the Spanish under Blake again or risk losing hard-won Saragossa. Defeating Blake's initial attack and then counter-attacking, Suchet won a hard-fought action which, while not decisive, went a long way into injecting confidence back into his small army. Three days later Suchet attacked and routed Blake at Belchite, saving Saragossa and restoring the situation in Aragon.

1810 was a very active year for Suchet in eastern Spain. He took Lerida and Mequinenza, and Harispe won a neat little victory over the Spaniards Ibarrola and O'Donnell, inflicting 3,500 casualties for a loss of only 120. The 13th Cuirassiers distinguished themselves in this action, hitting the Spanish flank and overrunning the Spanish troops who tried to make a stand, sabring those who ran for it.

At the end of the year Tortosa was besieged, the city surrendering in early January. Tarragona was the next target, but it was a stubborn nut to crack. However, by methodically launching skilful assaults at the city's defences, it was taken by Suchet in June 1811, with losses of 4,000 French to the Spanish losses of over 22,000. This victory gave Suchet his promotion to marshal.

Suchet and the Army of Aragon now moved to take Valencia. Beginning his advance against Valencia in September 1811. He defeated his Spanish opponent, Blake, at the battle of Saguntum in October and drove him into Valencia, eventually taking not only the city, but Blake's army with it in January 1812.

The years 1811–12 marked a change in Spain, especially in eastern Spain. Napoleon had begun to siphon off many units from his armies in Spain to support the invasion of Russia. Suchet, while still successful, was having trouble maintaining his gains, but remained victorious. Two British amphibious expeditions from Sicily were forced to re-embark because of Suchet's energetic campaigning. Harispe won another spectacular victory over O'Donnell at Castalla in July, completely routing the Spanish with losses of over 3,000. French losses were under 200.

However, at the end of 1813 Suchet's army had been reduced to just 17,000 and he had to execute a methodical withdrawal back to France. Some garrisons were left with orders to hold out as long as possible. Some, such as Robert's garrison at Tortosa, held until the shooting stopped, but by then the French, and Suchet, had retired back into France.

Jean-Isidore Harispe (1768–1855) was undoubtedly Suchet's best division commander in Spain, first serving as his chief of staff when Suchet took over the III Corps and then being given command of an infantry division. This much-wounded and skilled officer began his military career as the captain commandant of a Free Company in March 1793. The next year he was a chef de bataillon commandant of the 2e Bataillon Chasseurs Basques and was soon promoted to adjutant general chef de bataillon.

He was nominated a provisional chef de brigade on the battlefield in 1794 and was constantly employed in various billets. He was with the Armée de Reserve and the Armée de Grisons in 1800, transferring to the Armée d'Italie the next year.

He was the commander of the 16e Légère in 1802 and was assigned to Augereau's corps from 1802–5. He was a brigade commander in Desjardin's division in 1805 and 1806 and was wounded at Jena. In 1807 he was promoted to general of brigade in the IV Corps, also serving in the I Corps and the Corps de Reserve under Lannes. He was a brigade commander in Verdier's division and was wounded again at Friedland.

He went into Spain in 1808 and served there until the French withdrew. He was wounded at Alcanitz in 1809 and faithfully served and distinguished himself under Suchet and Soult. In 1815 he rallied to the Emperor and was given a division on the Spanish frontier under Clausel. Suchet thought very highly of Harispe, who was quite possibly the best division commander in Suchet's command. Suchet also thought very highly of General Habert, another of his subordinates.

Heinrich von Brandt, the ubiquitous Polish officer in the Vistula Legion who made such interesting character sketches has this to say about Suchet:

> Two days later our commander-in-chief (Suchet) paid us an unexpected visit. He reviewed us, thoroughly examined the arms and equipment of the men and congratulated us on our good turn out. He gave Solnicki ('a soldier who deserved his respect') a warm handshake and this compliment was probably due to our report on the Monzon affair. Our previous commanders had never bothered to pay us such visits, but this one had an excellent effect on the men.[5]

When von Brandt was wounded and had distinguished himself, he found out after regaining consciousness in the hospital that Suchet had come by to see him and award him his much-deserved Legion of Honour. Suchet was not only a good soldier and commander, he looked after his men and took special care of his wounded.

After conducting a minor operation and returning to his unit, von Brandt tells an interesting story of how he was taught to write an after-action report, the lesson being taught to him by his company commander:

> On the next morning Solnicki, the former commandant of Monzon, called me into his room and I found him rather agitated. 'I have received,' he told me, 'the order to write a full report on yesterday's battle. Would you sit down there and set the ball rolling. Here is a pen, ink, and paper.' I sat down, and regurgitated a brief resume of what had happened, adding the number of dead and wounded, some fifteen men. I read all this off to the captain and he pointed out that I had missed a couple of essential details. He then dictated some additions and corrections, which had the effect of turning this minor skirmish into a colourful struggle of heroic proportions, and accorded full credit to its fortunate outcome to himself. 'That, my friend, is how you write a report.'[6]

Note this hilarious characterisation of General Habert, who – to use words ascribed to another general of another army, undoubtedly Habert's intellectual equal – was 'stout of heart and arm, if thick of head':

> Laval, always remembered with respect in the French Army, was a tiny little man whose puny appearance contrasted markedly with his great reputation. The soldiers called him 'the miller' on account of the grey overcoat he was always seen in. He seemed somehow to be overshadowed by the general of our brigade, Habert, a giant of a man with a huge mane of jet black hair and athletic build

but with no particular merit other than exceptional bravery. A typical example of this was an occasion when we were digging-in in a street leading to a crossroads which was still in the enemy's hands. We had thrown up a barricade in order to provide cover and so we could cross from one side of the street to the other without too much danger. The barricade was not very high and it was necessary to duck when passing along behind it so as to avoid the fire of the Spanish. Tall men, like Habert, really had to bend right over. Just as he was in the course of varying out this particular manoeuvre one of the soldiers, lying flat on his belly by the barricade, made the frivolous remark, 'So, generals get scared too, do they?' Habert, furious, spun around, seized the insolent offender by the arms, carried him out into the middle of the street and drew himself up to his full height. Suddenly a volley was fired at the strange pair and the soldier dropped dead, hit by five or six bullets. Incredibly, the general got away with nothing more than a bruise on his arm. He gave the soldier's corpse a good kick, called him a f———— conscript and continued on his rounds. I must add that this act of brutal courage did not offend the comrades of the deceased and they agreed that the general was in the right, saying, 'He did the right thing. It was a shocking thing to say to a general.[7]

Von Brandt also tells of the heart-felt grief that Habert displayed for heavy losses to his own men. Habert was undoubtedly a man of complex character and that there was more to him than met the eye.

Prince Eugène and Marshal Suchet are two of Napoleon's shining stars in the pantheon of French commanders of the period. They are also two of the most neglected. Studying their campaigns offers much insight into the operations conducted in secondary theatres away from Napoleon the Grande Armée. Napoleon trusted them both and neither ever let the Emperor down. They were the equal, if not the superior of the allied commanders they faced and are due the credit they won on the battlefields of the First Empire.

CHAPTER 15

THE ART OF COMMAND

An assessment

The man in the ranks is not a model of wisdom in every respect, but he is a mighty shrewd judge of his own commanding officer; no lying bulletin can throw dust in his eyes, no advertising swashbuckler can pass as a hero. The court-martial which sits round a bivouac fire may be very informal, but it has an 'instinct for reality'. I pin my faith to the judgement of the Grognards of the Old Guard. They spoke of him as l'Homme. UNKNOWN

Who hath not served cannot command. JOHN FLORIO

I object to saying things twice. PLAUTUS

I am a man under authority, having soldiers under me; and I say to this man, Go, and he goeth; and to another, Come, and he cometh. MATTHEW, VIII.9

07:30 2 April 1814, On the Drawbridge of the Fortress of Vincennes, outside Paris
The veteran cavalryman with the wooden leg, nicknamed *Jambe de Bois*, stood at the gate of the old fortress watching the Russian emissary from General Barclay de Tolly prance triumphantly across the wooden drawbridge. The cavalryman, who was Governor of Vincennes, commanding the fortress in the name of the Emperor, was a former Old Guardsman and had lost his leg at Wagram in 1809. He was tough, competent and as hard and unyielding as the fortress he commanded. Vincennes was the main arsenal for Paris and it was stocked to the top with weapons and ammunition which the victorious allies, as represented by this cocky Russian officer, desperately wanted.

The evening before, the crusty commander of this fortress had led 250 men on a raid, taking up abandoned weapons and equipment left behind in Paris by the departing troops of Marmont and Mortier, who had lost the battle for French capital. The allies had expected, by the terms of the armistice with the two marshals, to enjoy the fruits of their victory in France's capital, but a good portion of the expected meal had been recaptured by the wily old cavalryman and taken back into the fortress. The Russians were not pleased. The perfectly uniformed and accoutred Russian, who was obviously a carpet knight and not a soldier, was here to demand the surrender of the fortress of Vincennes. The Governor, accompanied by his staff, looked upon him with nothing but contempt.

As the Russian reached the gate, the two exchanged salutes and the Russian immediately demanded that Jambe de Bois surrender Vincennes. The Governor replied, 'I will only surrender this fortress on the orders of His Majesty, the Emperor.' The Russian was perplexed, as the French inside the fortress were hopelessly outnumbered and could not hope to hold the arsenal against a determined attack supported by artillery. The Russian explained to the Governor that the allies had completely surrounded the fortress and that they would starve him out.

Jambe de Bois, supported by the looks of disdain towards the Russian on the faces of his staff, replied, 'Try it.'

The Russian officer, caught completely off guard by the Frenchman's stubborn reply, threatened to have the fortress attacked and destroyed, 'We'll blow you up.'

Unruffled, the Governor stated simply and matter-of-factly: 'Go ahead, and we'll all go up in the air together, and if we should pass one another in mid-air, I won't promise not to give you a scratch.'

The Russian, taken aback with the statement of intent from the Governor, threatened the Frenchman and again demanded that the fortress be surrendered in accordance with the terms of the armistice.

Jambe de Bois looked the Russian straight in the eye and spoke slowly and distinctly, 'The Austrians took one of my legs. Let them return it, or come take the other. In the meantime, I advise you to stay clear of my guns, if you do not wish to feel their effect.'

With that comment, General Pierre Dausmesnil, late of the Chasseurs à Cheval of the Imperial Guard and now Governor of Vincennes, turned on his one remaining heel and stumped back into the fortress, dutifully followed by his staff, leaving the Russian dandy in open-mouthed amazement at the gate.[1]

What is 'command' and how do you go about doing it? This is an age-old question and one that is continually asked and discussed at military academies, leadership conferences and seminars and, most importantly, by those who aspire to be commanders . . . Is command an 'art' or is it some esoteric quality that is innate in some and not in others? Can it be taught or is it instinct? Is it part of a man's character and is it to be sought out as something to be done? I hope that this volume has answered at least some of these questions and raised others – my main hope for this book is that it will stimulate more research and more writing on the subject.

The question has been asked for centuries and I do not believe there is any one answer to it. Command is a quality hard to define, just as leadership is, and it applies not only to generalship, but also at the lower levels, such as the platoon and company. The commander, whoever he is, has to put himself in front of his troops, one way or another, and using whatever leadership qualities or styles he has must impose his will on those subordinate to him. Easy on paper, it is not easy in execution. What makes one commander successful and another not? Is it a combination of qualities or having them all, if such a list exists?

This study has given examples of good commanders and some not so good. It has also, I hope, demonstrated that there are limits that even good commanders reach. Oudinot was an excellent division commander, an average corps commander and completely out of his depth as an independent army commander. He was also hampered by the fact that he took thirty-four wounds in twenty-three years. Lannes was killed before his full potential was reached, and he was one of the most talented of Napoleon's senior commanders. An ideal advance guard commander and an excellent tactician, he also showed himself skilled in siege operations. One of the things that Lannes did do was devote himself to the study of his profession, undoubtedly prompted by his lack of education when he first enlisted.

Other generals in this study are worthy of emulation, even today, and of further study. Davout never failed in any mission assigned to him by his Emperor. He was never defeated and was both an excellent tactician and strategist. An interesting 'what if' would have been if he had commanded on the Berlin front in 1813 instead of Oudinot. In many ways Davout was the most competent of the marshals and his steadfast honesty and incorruptibility were outstanding. His three division commanders from 1806–12 are also worthy of much study and they have generally been neglected. It was one of the most successful command teams in military history.

Eugène has to rank on the first echelon of French commanders of the period and he is also the most ignored. He is a prime example of Napoleon teaching at least some of his subordinates in both the art of war and how he expected them to wage it. Suchet is another outstanding independent commander who is also in the shadow of others. Unfortunately he never faced Wellington in the peninsula, which will beg questions as long as this period is studied.

What of the 'might-have-beens'? Desaix, the 'most balanced' of Napoleon's subordinates trained Davout, Savary and Rapp. He learned from both victory and defeat and was an outstanding leader, commander and general. His early death was a great blow to Napoleon and there is no doubting that Napoleon held him in high esteem, reorganising the Armée de Reserve on the march to give him a corps command. Desaix saved Napoleon's career. Kléber, Marceau, Championnet, Leclerc and other talented commanders in the French service also died before their time and too many have been forgotten.

Why did Reynier lose at Maida and Soult at Albuera? Both were more than competent and probably should have won. There is no satisfactory answer. Were they not served well by their subordinates? Or did they make too many mistakes in the field. Soult fought outnumbered at Albuera, but that was nothing new for a French army. Reynier was not an inspiring commander (neither was St Cyr) and that was a great disadvantage when commanding French troops.

Many, if not most, of Napoleon's generals came up from the ranks. They were given the opportunity by the great social upheaval of the French Revolution and the emigration of the greater majority of the French officer corps of the old Royal Army. Sixteen of the twenty-six marshals had enlisted service and rose from the ranks. What made them outstanding combat leaders and some of them excellent generals? Frederick N. Maude said it succinctly and gives insight into the mindset of the times and what these men were really like:

> Theirs was a case of the 'survival of the fittest' in a terrible hard school of selection . . . Only born leaders of men could have survived such an ordeal. They may have been, indeed they often were, illiterate, rapacious, jealous and vindictive, but they all possessed that power which defied all examinations to elicit – viz the power to get the last ounce of exertion and self-sacrifice out of the men under them, without recourse to legal formalities or the application of authorised force.[2]

John Elting gives a further viewpoint on the marshalate and what these men were made of. His assessment of many of the marshals is also an insight into their character and abilities:

> . . . hard men, toughened to wounds, cold winds, and hunger. Some, like Lefebvre, took their sons, grown tall enough, on their road to the muttering guns. Whatever their background, most were honourable, and the worst were not without some decencies. Massena might be a swindler, Augereau an adventurer, Soult sometimes dubious. But Davout, Bessières, and Serurier rode past riches to be had for only a little reaching; Mortier would wave aside costly gifts offered him in a conquered city.

War and the years wrought harshly with them. Lannes, Bessieres, and Poniatowski dead on the field of honor; Massena, Lefebvre, and Serurier aged and impotent; Ney grown bald and irresponsible; Soult fat, grumpy, and mistrusted.

Massena, Davout, and Suchet were the masters, capable of independent missions. So, to a lesser degree were St Cyr, Soult, and — for a while — Macdonald. Lannes, had he lived, might have ranked with their best. The rest were human projectiles who required their Emperor's aim and impulse.[3]

He comments further on the generals who never made marshal, either because of a lack of opportunity or recognition, or having been killed in action. Unfortunately, the contributions of these men, so critical to the early formation and character of the French armies of the period that became the Grande Armée, are generally overlooked:

Other men — so many of them dead, worn out, shunted aside or exiled — had shaped the French armies as much as those new marshals of 1804. They were the might-have-beens, the men who should have been marshals had they survived — high-hearted Desaix, whom Napoleon thought the best-balanced of his lieutenants, and gallant young Marceau. Whether the sharp-minded Hoche and resentful Kléber would have accepted a baton is an unanswered question . . .[4]

Napoleon himself, so well served by the officers mentioned in this volume, had myriad comments to pass on about being a commander. The following is most illuminating and succinct in its judgements and opinions:

The first qualification in a [commander] is a cool head — that is, a head which receives just impressions, and estimates things and objects at their real value. He must not allow himself to be elated by good news, or depressed by bad. The impressions he receives, either successively or simultaneously in the course of the day, should be so classed as to take up only the exact place in his mind which they deserve to occupy; since it is upon a just comparison and consideration of the weight due to different impressions that the power of reasoning and of right judgement depends. Some men are so physically and morally constituted as to see everything through a highly coloured medium. They raise a picture in the mind on every slight occasion and give to every trivial occurrence a dramatic interest. But whatever knowledge, or talent, or courage, or other good qualities such men may possess, nature has not formed them for the command of armies, or the direction of great military operations.

Command is always sought by the best of professional soldiers, and it can be a lonely job, but one for which there is no substitute. Old Marshal Boufflers wrote: 'The higher we rise, the more isolated we become; and all elevations are cold.' It is absolutely true, but command is also fulfilling and to paraphrase an old American military axiom, there is no substitute for it. Wellington stated that he liked to 'walk alone' and that undoubtedly referred to command. To abrogate that authority is often fatal. Admiral Lord Nelson pronounced that councils of war usually end in counselling retreat, which usually leads to defeat. That is undoubtedly why Napoleon seldom used them. Further, Napoleon, a commander upon whom authority sat easily, would undoubtedly have agreed.

Clausewitz knew the value of leadership, generalship (they are not the same thing) and the force of personal example:

> You have to have seen the steadfastness of one of the forces trained and led by Bonaparte . . . seen them under fierce and unrelenting fire – to get some sense of what can be accomplished by troops steeled by long experience in danger, in whom a proud record of victories has instilled the noble principle of placing the highest demands on themselves. As an idea alone it is unbelievable.

French General de Fezensac, promoted for skill and valour after Russia, was succinct on what good leadership could do to motivate subordinates to accomplish any task, at any time and against any odds:

> This habit of attempting anything, with the weakest of forces, this insistence that nothing was impossible, this unlimited confidence in success, which at first gave us one of our greatest advantages, was fatal to us in the end.[5]

As to the importance of good, solid commanders to the troops they lead, the army they are in and the country they serve, von Moltke the Elder stated that 'The military commander is the fate of the nation.' Napoleon's myriad sayings and maxims are most enlightening, perhaps one of the most illuminating being that 'An army of lions commanded by a deer will never be an army of lions.'

Last, to command and to be in charge, is at once gratifying and terrifying. Men's fates are in the commanders hands. Some decisions are matters of life and death; all decisions made by a commander at any level affect the soldiers under his command, in peace or war. The ultimate responsibilities of the commander are to the men he commands, the commander he serves and to the nation.

'First, one must see . . .'

Finally, this testimony to the devotion Napoleon inspired in the men of the Grand Armée perhaps sums up what leadership realy is:

I never took any other oath of allegiance but that of fidelity to Napoleon and his dynasty; that oath I have kept; I shall keep it. I never uttered but one political exclamation, and it, I hope, will exhale itself with my dying breath: VIVE L'EMPEREUR NAPOLEON!   ADELBERT J. DOISY DE VILLARGENNES

THIS TIME THERE WERE TOO MANY

Plançenoit, 1815

More dreadful-looking fellows than Napoleon's guard I had never seen. They had the look of thoroughbred, veteran, disciplined banditti. Depravity, recklessness, and bloodthirstiness were burned into their faces . . . Black mustachios, gigantic bearskins, and a ferocious expression were their characteristics. BENJAMIN HAYDON

As long as there are a few veterans, you can do what you want with the rest. DE SAXE

What soldiers! These are no longer the spiritless wrecks of Arcis-sur-Aube. They are either a legion of heroes or of devils. ANONYMOUS FRENCH EMIGRE

18:00 18 June 1815, Plançenoit, Belgium

The Armée du Nord had pounded the Anglo-Dutch army mercilessly all day long and a decision on the battlefield had yet to be reached. Repeatedly the French had come close to overwhelming Wellington's exhausted survivors, only to be frustrated by the innate toughness of the allied infantry who had grimly settled down to hold or die on the ridge Wellington had picked for them.[1]

Several infantry squares had been cut up or had collapsed during the French cavalry charges, some units being caught in line and overrun, and allied colours had been captured in the process.[2] The allied artillery fire had greatly slackened as guns had been dismounted by French counterbattery fire, and casualties among the gun crews had been heavy, victims either of artillery fire or the successive French cavalry charges.[3] Other allied battalions, English, Hanoverian, Brunswick or Nassau, still in square, were being blown to pieces by point-blank artillery fire, the aggressive French gunners having manhandled their pieces to within 100–250 yards of the allied line.[4]

Swarms of French skirmishers were dealing with the remaining allied skirmishers, either driving them in or engaging in close range fire fights less than eighty yards from the allied line.[5] Other French tirailleurs were opening a deadly fire on the main allied line, at times making the allied position untenable, the mutual support of skirmisher and artillery fire being a deadly combination.[6] If this tactic had been employed earlier, Mont St Jean might have been a French victory.[7]

However, Wellington's line still held and Napoleon needed a quick decision. The Prussians were knocking at the door of his right flank and the small, exhausted VI Corps under Lobau was encountering extreme difficulty keeping them off Napoleon's flank and line of communication. Duhesme's Young Guard division had been sent to hold the key village of Plançenoit to support Lobau, but they had been ejected by superior numbers of vengeance-minded Prussians.

Bitter, no-quarter fighting raged through the village, houses and streets being taken and retaken. Hand-to-hand fighting in and around the church and cemetery had caused that key location to change hands repeatedly. Finally, Duhesme had taken a mortal wound and most of the Young Guard were firmly ejected from the village. A tough, die-hard element still held the cemetery, forming the rock around which the Prussian flood ebbed and flowed, but the odds were becoming too long. Fourteen Prussian battalions were in and around the village and posed a definite threat to the French rear. Prussian artillery fire was landing near the Old Guard battalions covering Napoleon's headquarters.

The Emperor ordered Morand to send two Old Guard battalions against the Prussians and to retake Plançenoit 'with the bayonet'. General Pelet, in his shirtsleeves, took command of the task force. Putting himself at the head of the two battalions, he turned to the bearskin-topped mass and forbade them to load their muskets, telling them to put their faith in cold steel. The Guard drummers beat the *pas de charge* and Pelet led the two veteran battalions into the burning hell that was now Plançenoit.

Passing the dying Duhesme, who was being held upright in his saddle by two of his Young Guardsmen, the two battalions shrugged aside the fugitives who blocked their path. Led by a mace-swinging drum major, Stubert, the Grenadiers and Chasseurs drove into the centre of the wrecked village, passing the cheering Young Guard survivors in the church cemetery. Wading into the Prussians, the grim drum major braining a Prussian with every swing of his heavy, leaded mace, the Guardsmen carved a bloody swathe through the Prussians. The rallied Young Guard followed their 'elder' comrades into the assault.

At seven-to-one odds, the Old Guardsmen did not fire a shot. The Prussians were savagely bayoneted, clubbed and herded from the village. That mission accomplished, Pelet continued his attack after clearing the village of the enemy.

Prussian artillery fire from beyond the village finally stopped the two battalions, and they withdrew into the village after having their ranks dressed by Pelet. They retired in perfect order, and the Prussians did not pursue. 3,000 Prussian casualties marked the path of the Old Guard attack.

Joined by the surviving Young Guard in the village, they held their positions against Bülow's Prussians for the rest of the action as Nord gradually fell apart behind and around them. The Young Guard died in the village, but the intrepid Pelet rallied and led his two battalions in a break-out to the south, saving their eagle. Progressing south away from the Prussian pursuit, Pelet guided his command to the sound of the Guard drummers beating *La Grenadière* and *La Carabinière* through the fading light. The pursuing Prussians, more interested in the easy pickings of running fugitives, left them and other formed units alone, bypassing them and went of in search of easier prey.

APPENDIX

THE LAST RESERVE

The Imperial Guard, 1804–15

At Tilsit, in a review for the the sovereigns, Tsar Alexander, while viewing the Old Guard pass in review, asked Marshal Ney where were the men who had given the Guardsmen such terrible scars. Ney's reply was blunt and succinct: 'Sire, they are all dead.'

Theirs was a case of the 'survival of the fittest' in a terribly hard school of selection . . . Only born leaders of men could have survived such an ordeal. They may have been, indeed they often were, illiterate, rapacious, jealous, and vindictive, but they all possessed that power which defied all examinations to elicit – vis. the power to get the last ounce of exertion and self-sacrifice out of the men under them, without recourse to legal formalities, or the application of authorised force.

FREDERICK N. MAUDE

10:00 30 October 1813, near Hanau, Franconia

The retreat from Leipzig had been a horse-killing nightmare. The artillery train drivers slept in the saddle as their weary mounts trudged down the rutted roads, following the gun team or caisson in front of them. The mounts of the horse artillerymen plodded along, foot artillerymen wearily walked, but the men, horses and guns of the Imperial Guard artillery stuck together. It was march or die, and everyone from their commander, General Drouot, to the newest conscript knew it. The veterans put their heads down and their shoulders into it, veteran cavalrymen and horse artillerymen periodically dismounted and led their horses, to save them in case of emergency

Down the road from Hanau mounted couriers drove their lathered mounts to spread the alarm. The turncoat Bavarians, with the help of some stray Austrians and Cossacks, were blocking the way home and the weary, dispirited and depleted corps of MacDonald and Marmont, numbering barely 7,000 survivors, were heavily outnumbered.

The Bavarians under Wrede were attempting to stop the retreating units of the Grande Armée from crossing the Rhine and getting home and that definitely would not do.

Orders came as shouted commands up and down the column. The artillery of the Guard, including forty-eight of the Emperor's 'pretty girls', his 12-pounders, were immediately ordered forward. Drouot shouted some quick instructions to his subordinates and pounded up the road with his aides-de-camp to reconnoitre battery positions for his artillerymen and their deadly guns. Company commanders hastily conferred with their lieutenants and NCOs, and these latter trotted up and down their company columns, shaking and cuffing awake the exhausted train drivers as well as their cannoneers. The column came awake, shouldered their packs and muskets and humped forward, the train drivers urging their dead-tired horses forward one more time. It was an emergency and everyone knew it.

Down the road they came, trace chains rattling against caisson and gun carriage, the Guard foot artillery running to catch up, bearskins bobbing along the column in the autumn bleakness. Drouot's hard-riding aides directed the companies into their selected positions, and battery commanders and first sergeants bellowed out commands, as company drummers beat *la Diane*, the long roll and train trumpeters playing their calls to direct the gun teams into the appropriate manoeuvre, veteran horses knowing the calls and not needing urging from their drivers.

The deadly 12-pounders swung into position, trails were dropped by cannoneers and the companies laid their pieces to their capitaines' commands. The situation was desperate, the exhausted line infantry had been driven back in desperate fighting to a distant tree line. At the urgent command, *'Feu!'* the Guard companies opened a deadly fire against the enemy infantry, causing considerable loss and denting their offensive.

The Old Guard infantry was ordered forward, the Chasseurs advancing in open order as skirmishers, literally hissing their disgust at their late allies, the Grenadiers deploying in line, attacking the allies in an irresistible flood – a bayonet-tipped, bearskin-topped line of huge veterans, who had the look of 'disciplined *banditti*'.

Allied cavalry massed and charged the Guard artillery companies. Trails swung round, canister loaded, and again the bronze mouths belched fire, smoke and death, mowing down the allied horsemen in ranks. Their charge carried the survivors among the artillerymen, who grabbed muskets, rammer staffs and handspikes, knocking shocked cavalrymen out of their saddles as they defended their guns. Almost immediately, the French Guard cavalry was among them, driving the allies back or sabring them where they stood. The artillery companies were saved and they continued their pounding of Wrede's improvised army.

In the Grande Armée's rear came the Guard's artillery park, escorted by the respected and feared elite gendarmerie of the Guard, led and commanded by the deeply respected General Radet, the Grande Armée's Provost and another of the Empire's 'iron men'. On reaching the battlefield, and staying behind the battle line, Radet had circled the artillery trains and park for all-round defence, the two battalions of Guard infantry accompanying him spread out inside this perimeter. A roaming horde of Cossacks, sighting this seemingly easy, and quite tempting, target, came out of the woods at the dead run, their horses straining at bit and bridle. As quick-witted as he was tough, Radet manned the available guns with his infantrymen, greeting the Cossacks with point-blank canister that dropped scores of Cossacks and horses. Surprised and overwhelmed, they broke and fled. The hard-riding, tough gendarmes rode out in pursuit, gathering prisoners and hopelessly scattering the shattered remnants.

The Imperial Guard was the Grande Armée's, and Napoleon's, ultimate reserve. The mere sight of the Guard's bearskins could send enemy commanders into mental convulsions and also make the Guard a priority target on the battlefield. Its presence was an insurance policy for the hard-used line units and it gave the Emperor a handy reserve of very reliable troops composed of infantry, cavalry and artillery. It was the Grande Armée's insurance policy.

The Guard's origin is an interesting combination of the military and political. Half of its ancestry came from the *Garde du Corps Legislatif* and the *Garde du Directoire* both of which were formed as guard units for the Revolutionary governments. The other ancestor was Napoleon's Guides, first formed in Italy as a mounted guide unit and commanded by Captain Bessières and later increased in strength for Egypt and made up of infantry, cavalry and artillery. Some of the Guides came back to France when Napoleon did, the rest remaining to help strengthen Kléber's hand.

From these units the *Garde des Consuls* was formed. It was far from the disciplined veterans that would eventually evolve into the Imperial Guard. Its first action was Marengo, where the cavalry performed excellently and the infantry and artillery was committed on the French right to help slow down the general Austrian advance – they suffered heavy casualties and fought well, withdrawing with the rest of the French right flank and later participating in the French counter-attack precipitated by Desaix's arrival with Boudet's division.

The Guard, which Napoleon wanted to be both a well-uniformed and disciplined show horse outfit as well as a reliable combat organisation had teething problems. Its first commander, Lannes, spent too much on uniforms, went badly into debt and had to step down. No-nonsense and practical Bessières took over the Guard's internal administration and accounts and the rough spots were eventually overcome.

A tough infantry commander was also brought in for the Grenadiers who needed a strong hand and a man they could respect. Dorsenne was just what the Guard needed and he was so strict that even the toughest grenadier in the regiment was said to tremble before him when being inspected. Dorsenne came from the line, was an experienced officer of many wounds and gave the Guard infantry exactly what was needed. He earned the respect and devotion of the regiment and was both revered and feared by them. Elzear Blaze swore that the man had no nerves under fire and ignored incoming artillery rounds with his back to them in the hell that was Essling in 1809 when the Guard infantry had to stand and take it with no appreciable reply from the outgunned French artillery. He was wounded at Essling and later died in July 1812 from a trepanning operation on his skull, the result of that old wound.

Jean-Roche Coignet's admission to the Guard came from his service in Italy in 1800 where he was noticed by Berthier and brought to Napoleon's attention.

> General Berthier came galloping up, and said to me, 'What are you doing there?' 'General, you see what I have done. This gun is mine. I took it all by myself.' 'Do you want something to eat?'
>
> 'Yes, general.' (He talked through his nose.) Then he turned to his groom and said, 'Give him some bread.' And taking out a little green memorandum book, he asked my my name.
>
> 'Jean-Roche Coignet.'
> 'Your demi-brigade?'
> 'Ninety-sixth.'
> 'Your battalion?'
> 'The first.'
> 'Your company?'
> 'First.'
> 'Your captain?'
> 'Merle.'
>
> 'Tell your captain to bring you to see the First Consul at ten o'clock. Leave your gun and go and find him.'
>
> Then he galloped off, and I, delighted, went as fast as my legs would take me to rejoin my company, which had turned into a road to the right.[1]

That evening the captain took me by the arm, presented me to the colonel, and told him what I had done during the day. He answered, 'Why, captain, I knew nothing about this!' Then he shook me by the hand, and said, 'I must make a note of it.' 'General Berthier wishes to present him to the Consul at ten o'clock this evening,' said my captain; 'I am going to take him.' Ah! I am glad of it, grenadier.

We went to see General Berthier, and my captain said to him, 'Here is my grenadier who captured the gun, and since then he has saved my life and that of my first sergeant. He killed three Hungarian grenadiers.' 'I will present him to the Consul.' Then General Berthier and my captain went to see the Consul, and after talking a while with him they called me in. The Consul came up to me, and took me by the ear. I thought he was going to scold me, but, on the contrary, he was very kind; and still holding me by the ear, he said, 'How long have you been in the service?' 'This is my first battle.' 'Ah, indeed! It is a good beginning. Berthier, put him down for a musket of honour. You are too young to be in my Guard; for that, one must have made four campaigns. Berthier, make a note of him at once, and put it on the file. You may go now,' said he to me, 'but you shall one day be one of my guards.'[2]

Coignet was below the height requirement for Grenadiers, even though he had been one in the line, and Davout had a direct solution for that problem:

... we started off at once to go to the house of General Davout, colonel-general of the foot grenadiers. He received us pleasantly, and said, 'You bring me a sapper who has a fine beard.' 'I want to keep him in my company,' said my captain to him; 'he has a musket of honour. But he is very small.'

He made me stand beside him, and said, 'You are not tall enough for a grenadier, 'But I would like to keep the place, general.' 'We must cheat the measure. When he passes under the measure make him put some packs of cards in his stockings. You see,' he said, 'he's too short by an inch or more. Never mind, you will see that with two packs of cards under each foot, he will pass all right; you must go with him.' 'Certainly, general.' 'If he be accepted he will be the smallest of my grenadiers.' 'But he is to be decorated.' 'Ah! That makes a difference, do your best to have him accepted.'[3]

Coignet's description of the Guard's uniform is both accurate and admiring:

Nothing could be handsomer than that uniform. When we were on dress parade we wore a blue coat with white lapels sloped low down on the breast, a white dimity waistcoat, gaiters of the same, short breeches, silver buckles on the shoes and breeches, a double cravat, white underneath and black on the outside, with a narrow edge of white showing at the top. In undress, we wore a blue coat, white dimity waistcoat, nankeen breeches, and seamless white cotton stockings. In addition to all this we wore our hair brushed out in front like pigeon's wings, and powdered, and a queue six inches long, cut off at the end like a brush and tied with a black worsted ribbon, with ends exactly two inches long. Add to this the bearskin cap and its long plume, and you have the summer uniform of the Imperial Guard. But one thing of which I can give no real idea is the extreme neatness which was required of us. When we left barracks the orderlies inspected us, and if there was a speck of dust on or shoes or a bit of powder on the collar of out coats we were sent back. We were splendid to look at, but abominably uncomfortable.[4]

Coignet's admiration for his new commander Dorsenne echoed the sentiments of the entire regiment:

But a colonel, named Dorsenne, came to us from Egypt, covered with wounds; he was just the sort of soldier needed to discipline and drill an efficient guard. In a year's time we might have served as a model for the whole army. He was so severe that he made the most unruly soldier tremble; he reformed all abuses. He might have been held up as an example for all our generals, both for courage and bearing. A finer looking soldier was not to be seen on the battlefield.[5]

As initially organised by First Consul Bonaparte the Consular Guard consisted of a regiment of Grenadiers à Pied, a regiment of Grenadiers à Cheval, a company of light infantry (chasseurs à pied) and a company of guides à cheval (chasseurs à cheval), with a company each of artillery and artillery train (the artillery company was half horse and half foot artillery). It was a small Guard with a strength of only 2,089 all ranks and would blossom under the Empire to over 112,000 in 1814.

After Marengo the Guard was hammered into the form and organisation that it would keep throughout the Empire. Its internal organisation and discipline was 'perfected' and the Guard's commanders were handpicked by Napoleon. Upon Napoleon's assumption of the title Emperor, the Consular Guard became the Imperial Guard. Candidates for the Guard had to have ten years' service and an impeccable service record. Those that did not keep up to that standard were sent back to the line. Guardsmen held one rank higher per grade than the line (one wag remarking that even the Guard's donkeys had the rank of mules) and Napoleon himself reviewed every promotion of every man, the uniforms the

Guard regiments would wear, as well as the assignments the personnel were given. Coignet described in detail an inspection by Napoleon:

We were informed that the First Consul was to inspect our barracks, and that we must be on the lookout for him. But he took us by surprise and found us in our beds; he was accompanied by his favourite general, Lannes . . . The Consul went through all the rooms and finally came to my bedside. My comrade, who was six feet four inches tall, stretched himself out on seeing the Consul beside our bed; his feet stuck out of the bedstead more than a foot. The Consul thought that there were two grenadiers in a line, and came to the head of our bed to assure himself of the fact, and passed his hand along the body of my comrade, to be sure he was not mistaken . . . [Napoleon stated] 'these bedsteads are too short for my grenadiers. Do you see, Lannes? all the beds of my guard must be changed. Make a note of it, and have new bedsteads made for the whole guard; these will do for the garrison' . . . The Consul delivered a severe lecture to all our officers, and looked into everything; he had a piece of bread brought to him. 'That is not the right kind,' said he. 'I pay for white bread, I wish to have it every day. Do you understand, Lannes? Send your orderly officer, and order the quartermaster to come to me.' To us he said:

'I will review you on Sunday; I want to see you. There are malcontents among you. I will hear your complaints.' Then they returned to the Tuileries. In the order that he sent for the Sunday review, Colonel Dorsenne recommended that nothing should be neglected in the uniforms of the men. The whole store of clothing was turned upside down; all the old uniforms were renovated, and he inspected us at ten o'clock. He was so stern that he made the officers tremble. At eleven o'clock we set out for the Tuileries; at noon the Consul came down to review us mounted on a white horse, which, it was said, Louis XVI had ridden. This horse was of great beauty, with a tremendous mane and tail; he marched through the ranks with the step of a man; he was a magnificent-looking horse.

The Consul made us open ranks; he walked slowly and received many petitions; he took them himself and then handed them to General Lannes. He stopped wherever he saw a soldier present arms, and spoke to him. He was pleased with our appearance and ordered us to march past. We found some casks of wine at the barracks, and a quart of it was distributed to each man. The petitions were almost all granted, and the contentment was general.[6]

In 1804 there were now a regiment each of Grenadiers à Pied and Chasseurs à Pied, as well as the Grenadiers à Cheval and the Chasseurs à Cheval, which were Napoleon's personnel escort and conducted themselves as such. Grenadiers, both foot and mounted, were big men, five feet six inches (French) and the Grenadiers à Cheval were a black horse regiment, (as would be the Artillerie à Cheval and the Gendarmerie d'Elite). There were two companies each of artillery and train troops. In 1806 the horse artillery would become a regiment of six companies supported by a battalion of train d'artillerie.

In 1801 a company of veterans was added to the Guard, as was a squadron of Mamelukes, which had come back from Egypt with the army. They were organised by Rapp, one of Napoleon's aides-de-camp, and served gallantly at Austerlitz and on other bloody fields. They were attached to the Chasseurs à Cheval and lasted in various strengths throughout the Empire.

A squadron of gendarmes was taken into the Guard in 1802, evolving into the 'feared and respected' Gendarmerie d'Elite, who were issued a bearskin with a visor, the same type that would be adopted by the newly formed regiment of Artillerie à Pied in 1810. Drouot was assigned that task and took his new regiment into action at Wagram in 1809 where it distinguished itself. After the campaign, the shako originally issued to Drouot's companies was replaced by a bearskin, along with the organisation of a band and a sapper detachment.

The navy furnished picked sailors to form what eventually became the Sailors (*Marins*) of the Guard, a generally hard-working and hard-luck outfit that was lost at Baylén in 1808. Many of the seamen were kept in prison hulks and became expert escape-artists, enough of them getting away to reconstitute a company for further service.

In 1804 Napoleon introduced Velites into the Guard, thus making the Guard not only a combat organisation, but a military school as well. The infantry regiments were the first to get the new charges, the artillery and cavalry regiments received theirs the next year. The reward for three years' satisfactory service as a Velite was a commission as a sous-lieutenant in the line. Less satisfactory candidates were either sent to a line regiment as a fourrier, to the Guard as an enlisted man, or to one of the military schools. The practice was curtailed after 1807, but the Guard cavalry kept them until 1811. They were taken on campaign and employed in combat. All in all, it was a pretty demanding method of getting a military education, though undoubtedly an interesting one.

In 1806 the Guard was enlarged, a practice that was maintained until the end of the Empire in 1815. The *Dragons de la Garde Impériale* or Guard Dragoons were organised, Friedland being their first campaign. Their sponsor was reputedly the Empress Josephine, hence their unofficial title of the 'Empress's Dragoons'. The Guard infantry was 'reinforced' by two regiments, the fusiliers/grenadiers and the fusiliers/chasseurs. Both became distinguished units, the fusiliers/grenadiers later being given the privilege of wearing their hair in a queue as the senior regiments did. These were the regiments that distinguished themselves at Essling in 1809, being led by Mouton and Rapp against Rosenberg's corps in the town, retaking it from the Austrians and ejecting them from the village.

The year 1807 saw the formation of the famous Regiment of Polish Light Horse, the Chevau-Légers Polonais who would be re-armed with lances in 1809 and renamed the Ier Chevau-Légers Lanciers de la Garde Impériale. They had a very rough start as soldiers, but were reined in by Lasalle and other patient instructors and distinguished themselves in their first action at Somosierra in Spain. That action brought them Guard status and they became a famous regiment. One squadron accompanied Napoleon to Elba in 1814 and fought at Waterloo in 1815.

More infantry was formed as Guard units in 1809 and after. The first were two regiments each of tirailleurs/grenadiers and tirailleurs/chasseurs. These were small regiments, only two battalions of four companies each and their commanding officers were majors. Two regiments each of conscripts-grenadiers and conscripts-chasseurs were also formed. The pick of the conscripts went into these new regiments and their purpose was to fight. As the seemingly endless wars ground on, more regiments were added to augment the Guard infantry, eventually there being nineteen each of tirailleurs and voltigeurs. In 1811 the Flanquers-Chasseurs were formed from the sons of gamekeepers and employees of the forestry ministry. It was an elite unit, though after Russia and heavy losses conscripts were drafted into the regiment to reconstitute it. It was uniformed in green, as was the regiment of Flanquers-Grenadiers raised in 1813, though the latter was made up of conscripts.

Besides the Poles, other foreign units that were taken into the Guard included two units from Holland after it was annexed to France which became the 3e (Dutch) Grenadiers à Pied and the 2e Chevau-Légers Lanciers, the famous Red Lancers. The Velites of Florence and Velites of Turin were taken into the Guard in 1809 and 1810, respectively, and Murat's half-organised Lancers of Berg had quasi-Guard status and performed excellently in Spain, distinguishing themselves against the British cavalry at Villadrigo. However, as with other German units in 1813 it had to be disarmed in November of that year, although one squadron stayed loyal and was part of the garrison of Mayence (Mainz) under Morand.

In 1812 after much squabbling, Napoleon finally established the hierarchy of the Imperial Guard into Old, Middle and Young. The Old Guard consisted of the Ier Grenadiers à Pied, Ier Chasseurs à Pied (as well as the noncommissioned officers of the 2e Grenadiers à Pied and the 2e Chasseurs à Pied), the Grenadiers à Cheval, Chasseurs à Cheval, Mamelukes, Ier Lanciers, Elite Gendarmes, as well as the two artillery regiments (horse and foot), engineers, veterans and the non-commissioned officers of the Young Guard artillery.

The Middle Guard consisted of the two fusilier regiments, the Dutch Grenadiers, the enlisted men of the 2^e Grenadiers and 2^e Chasseurs, the 2^e (Dutch) Lancers, all the artillery train battalions, the two Italian Velite units, the Dutch veterans unit and the ouvriers. The Young Guard were all of the other infantry regiments, the enlisted men of the Young Guard artillery companies, and the Regiment of the National Guard of the Imperial Guard.

In 1811 the Battalion of Instruction, also known as the Battalion of Fontainebleu, was organised, which merely formalised what the Guard had been doing since the induction of Velites into the Guard. There were three battalions of instruction and their function was to train fusiliers as sergeants and picked Young Guardsmen as corporals. Those that successfully completed the course were sent to the line as cadre, which gave back to the line what had originally been taken out.

The Guard was rebuilt twice: once after Russia and again in 1815. Four big regiments of mounted Gardes d'Honneur, uniformed and equipped as light cavalry, were formed, but their 'seasoning' went slowly and they were not committed to action until after Leipzig, performing well at Hanau in 1813 and one of the regiments distinguishing itself at Reims in 1814. Napoleon also organised three light cavalry regiments of *éclaireurs* (scouts) that were committed far too early before completing their organisation, but performed well for all that. They were each attached to a senior Guard cavalry regiment.

For 1815 four regiments each of Grenadiers à Pied and Chasseurs à Pied were organised and the two fusilier regiments were not reorganised. All of the grenadiers and chasseurs were designated Old Guard and there were no Middle Guard units, only Old and Young Guard. The Young Guard was supposed to have six regiments each of tirailleurs and voltigeurs. Because of organisation difficulties, only three regiments of each went into Belgium. They formed a division under Duhesme and fought gallantly in the defence of Plançenoit. There was also a 2e Regiment de Chasseurs à Cheval organised but it did not join the army until after Waterloo.

The general officers of the Imperial Guard were a varied and colourful lot in an army of colourful characters. Generals were sometimes rotated between the Guard and the line and some of the more distinguished are described here.

François Roguet (1770–1846) began his military career as a private in the Infantry Regiment Guyenne in 1789. He service during the Revolutionary Wars was mainly in Italy. A captain in 1793, he was a chef de bataillon in 1786 and a chef de brigade by 1800. In 1803 he was promoted to general of brigade.

Assigned to the VI Corps (Ney's) in 1805 and was with the Grande Armée from 1805–7. He was wounded and taken prisoner at Guttstadt in 1807.

Roguet went into Spain in 1808 but went to Austria with the Imperial Guard in 1809. He was made colonel of the 2e Grenadiers à Pied on 5 April 1809. At the conclusion of the Wagram campaign he went back to Spain where he served until again pulled out, this time for the Russian campaign.

He was promoted to general of division in 1811 and commanded the 2nd Young Guard division under Mortier in Russia. He was again a Guard commander in Germany in 1813 and commanded the 6th Young Guard Division in Belgium in 1814. Roguet rallied to Napoleon in 1815 and commanded Guard troops in the Waterloo campaign. He was famous for his command in Belgium against the Prussians: 'Any grenadier who brings me a prisoner will be shot.'

A driving, relentless commander, he took good care of the troops in his charge, being nicknamed by them 'Père' (Father) Roguet.

Pierre Berthezène (1775–1847) volunteered with the 5e Bataillon de l'Herault in September 1793. Almost immediately, he was promoted to sergeant major. He served with the Armée d'Italie from 1794–1801 and, chosen by acclamation for his epaullettes, he was promoted to lieutenant in November 1795. He had a succession of junior staff assignments, including aide-de-camp to General Compans from 1795–1800, and was promoted to chef de bataillon in 1800.

He was major of the 65e Ligne in 1806 and colonel of the 10e Légère in 1807, serving with the Grande Armée in 1807 and the Armée d'Allemagne in 1809. He was appointed as adjutant general of the Imperial Guard in December 1811 and commanded a brigade of Young Guard troops under Delaborde in 1812. He served at the Berezina and again commanded a Young Guard brigade in 1813 under Dumoustier and was promoted to general of division in August of that year.

Given command of a division under St Cyr, he was taken prisoner when St Cyr was forced to capitulate later that year. He rallied to Napoleon in 1815 and commanded a division in Vandamme's III Corps in Belgium.

Jean-Marie-Pierre-François Lepaige Comte Dorsenne (1773–1812) was a volunteer in the bataillon de Pas-de-Calais in 1791. By 1792 he was a captain and served with the Armée du Nord until 1794. With the Armée de Sambre et Meuse until 1796, he went to Italy with Bernadotte's division where he served in the 61e Demi-brigade.

Dorsenne was promoted to chef de bataillon by Napoleon in 1797 and went to Egypt with Desaix in 1798, serving there until repatriated in 1801. He was promoted to chef de brigade of the 61^e Ligne in 1802 and was hand-picked by

Napoleon to straighten out the Grenadiers of the Guard. Immaculate in appearance and bearing, Dorsenne was exactly what the Grumblers needed. It was said that the most veteran grenadier would tremble if Dorsenne stepped in front of him. Firmly but fairly, the handsome colonel straightened out the Guard infantry, making them a model for the army.

Promoted general of brigade and colonel in the Imperial Guard in 1805, Dorsenne was with the Grande Armée from 1805–7. It was he that led the bayonet attack on the Russian infantry column that penetrated to Napoleon's command post at Eylau. In Spain in 1808, he was with the Armée d'Allemagne in 1809, commanding the Guard infantry at Essling, setting the example in front of them as they were pounded by Austrian artillery. Calmly ordering his men to close ranks as men fell, he was wounded in the head, but stayed at his post. Blaze in his memoirs states that he believed that Dorsenne had no nerves at all, being able to turn his back to an artillery bombardment while commanding his troops and not looking behind him for incoming rounds.

Promoted to general of division in 1809 he was sent back to Spain and stayed there to 1811 and died in Paris in July 1812. Coignet also mentions Dorsenne in his memoirs and greatly admired the man. He did not care for Madame Dorsenne, however.

Philibert Guillaume Duhesme (1766–1815) commanded the National Guard in his home canton in 1789. In 1791 he was a captain in the 2e Bataillon de Volontaires de Saône-et-Loire, with the Armée du Nord from 1792–4 and became a noted commander of light infantry, later writing a book on the subject. Promoted to Lieutenant Colonel in the 4e Bataillon France de Hainault in 1792 and to general of brigade in 1794, he was the commanding general of the 5e Division of the Armée de Sambre et Meuse in December 1794 and was of the 10e Division of the Armée du Rhin et Moselle the next year, being assigned to the 6e Division of the same army in April 1796.

The next month he was given the 7e Division and was with the Armée du Rhin to 1798 serving with both St Cyr and Desaix. From there he served consecutively in the Armées d'Italie, Romain and Naples. He was a corps commander in the Armée du Reserve in 1800 and commanded a division under Masséna in 1805 in Italy.

He served in Italy from 1805–7 and was sent into Spain in 1808. He served in Saxony in 1813 and in the campaign in France in 1814. In 1815 he rallied to Napoleon and was given command of the Young Guard division that went into Belgium with the Armée du Nord. He fought well at Waterloo and was mortally wounded in the fight for Plançenoit on the French right flank.

Louis Lepic (1765–1827) had an interesting early career being in, consecutively, the Lescure Dragoons, Chasseurs des Trois Eveches and the 2e Chasseurs à Cheval from 1781–91. He was promoted to brigadier in 1787. He was assigned to the Garde Constitutionelle du Roi in February 1792 and was a maréchal des logis in the Dragons de la Republique in September of that year. Thereafter he rose rapidly, being promoted to captain in October of 1792 and shortly thereafter to lieutenant colonel.

In March 1793 he was appointed a chef d'escadron in the 15e Chasseurs à Cheval and served with the Armée d'Italie from 1796–1801. He was promoted to chef de brigade in the 15e Chasseurs in 1799. He fought at Marengo in 1800 and thereafter served again in the Armée d'Italie in 1805 until transferred to the Grande Armée, being appointed as Colonel Major of the Grenadiers à Cheval of the Imperial Guard in December 1805. With the Grande Armée from 1805–7, taking part in the great French cavalry charge at Eylau in February 1807, leading the Grenadiers à Cheval in a wild chevauchee which found him and some of his troopers trapped behind the reformed Russian lines. Summoned to surrender, he and his troopers cut their way out and reached the French lines.

Lepic served in Spain in 1808 and was with the Armée d'Allemagne in 1809. Back to Spain and Portugal from 1810–11, Lepic made the Russian campaign and was promoted to general of division in 1812. Nominated colonel of the 2e Régiment des Gardes d'Honneur, he led them through the 1813 campaign in Saxony. Declared unfit for service, he commanded the 21st military district in late 1813–14. He rallied to Napoleon in 1815 and was on the Imperial staff that year.

Jean-Jacques-Germain Pelet-Clouzeau (1777–1858) started his military career as an engineer, volunteering in 1800. In 1805 he came to the attention of Masséna, who was then the commander of the Armée d'Italie. Pelet served with Masséna from then until Masséna's eventual relief after failing in Portugal and Spain in 1810.

Pelet matured as a soldier under Masséna's watchful and professional eye, learning how to command and lead troops. Trusted, intelligent and loyal, Pelet eventually became Masséna's senior aide-de-camp and served ably in Italy, Poland, Germany and Portugal, where he became friends with Eble.

In the campaign of 1809 at the battle of Eckmühl, Pelet distinguished himself commanding a light infantry unit as well as temporarily commanding a Baden cavalry detachment before Ratisbon. His exploits during the campaign were mentioned in the Bulletins, but he was not mentioned personally, as his name was unknown; he was referred to merely as the 'reconnaissance officer'.

After Masséna's disgrace, Pelet was assigned to the Grand Quartier-General Impériale for the invasion of Russia. He had requested command of an infantry regiment, but was refused. However, he was finally granted his wish and assumed command of the 48ᵉ Ligne on 11 October 1812. Surviving the retreat, he was promoted to general of brigade and commanded a Young Guard brigade in Saxony in 1813.

Fighting throughout 1813 and 1814, Pelet rallied to the Emperor after the latter's return from Elba in 1815. Given command of the 2ᵉ Régiment des Chasseurs à Pied of the Old Guard, Pelet earned undying fame with his attack and defence of Plançenoit on the French right flank at Waterloo.

Etienne Radet (1762–1825) began his interesting career as a private in the Sarre Infantry Regiment in 1780, rising to corporal in 1781 and sergeant in 1782. By 1787 Radet had transferred to the Marchaussée, the forerunner of the Gendarmerie as a corporal. In 1789 he was a sous-lieutenant in the National Guard, being promoted to full lieutenant the same year. He made captain in 1790 and major the next year. He was appointed adjutant major of the 2ᵉ Bataillon Volontaires de la Meuse and promoted to chef de brigade in 1794.

In 1798 he was transferred to the Gendarmerie as a chef de legion to re-organise Avignon's gendarmes. Promoted to general of brigade in the Gendarmerie in 1800 he was assigned the mission by the First Consul of re-organising the entire Gendarmerie. He was also later responsible for organising the Neapolitan Gendarmerie as well as the Gendarmerie of Hamburg.

Radet was also instrumental in kidnapping the Pope and was appointed the Grande Prévôt of the Grande Armée in 1813 in Saxony. He played a prominent part in the victory at Hanau as the Grande Armée was leaving Germany. In April 1815 after Napoleon's return he was assigned as Inspector General of Gendarmerie and was the Grand Prévôt of the Armée du Nord in Belgium. His comments on the general indiscipline of the troops on the march north are noteworthy. He was wounded at Waterloo and proscribed by the Bourbons upon their return.

Antoine Drouot (1774–1847) was 'a simple, honest, awkward gunner'. Born on France's eastern marches, he graduated from the Metz artillery school in 1793. Drouot was a foot artilleryman and his initial combat service was with the Armée du Nord and the Rhine armies and he was promoted captain in 1796. Further service saw him on both the Rhine and in Naples, serving at the Trebbia under Macdonald. He was on Eble's staff in 1800–1 and fought at Hohenlinden in 1800.

He commanded the 14ᵉ Compagnie of the 1ᵉʳ Régiment d'Artillerie from 1803–4, was promoted to chef de bataillon in 1805. He had the interesting distinction of having been aboard ship and fought at Trafalgar that year. After his return he was made the inspector for the manufacture of arms at Mauberge along with serving on the general staff of the Grande Armée in 1805.

He was promoted to major in the 3ᵉ Régiment d'Artillerie à Pied in 1807 and was named inspector at Charleville that year. In Spain the next year, he was chosen by Napoleon to organise and command the new foot artillery regiment of the Imperial Guard, which he led in the Wagram campaign. Wounded at Wagram, he took part in Lauriston's large battery that supported Macdonald's attack. Returning home after the campaign with his regiment, he completed their organisation, including procuring a band, sappers and the famous visored bearskin to replace the shakos they wore in Germany on campaign. After Wagram he was promoted to colonel and was made a Baron of the Empire.

Drouot went into Russia and served throughout 1812 and 1813. At Lützen in early 1813, he expertly commanded and led the large battery that attacked the allied centre and destroyed it with point-blank canister fire, paving the way for the decisive assault of the Guard that won the day. At the battle of Hanau, after Leipzig, he commanded the large Guard artillery battery that dominated the field, fighting hand-to-hand alongside his beloved gunners when almost overrun by allied cavalry until the Grenadiers à Cheval counter-attacked and routed the enemy horsemen.

He fought stoutly through 1814, accompanied his Emperor to Elba and rallied to Napoleon in 1815. He served loyally and ably with the Armée du Nord in Belgium and, on Napoleon's second abdication, was refused permission to accompany him to St Helena. Deeply intelligent (dubbed the 'Sage of the Grande Armée' by the gunners that revered him) and religious, he read his Bible every day. He refused to take a pension from the Bourbons until well after Napoleon's death.

Jean-Baptiste Bessières (1766–1813) was the last man in the army to wear his hair powdered, in wings and a queue. He was always impeccably uniformed, a stern disciplinarian and was usually employed by Napoleon in the Guard's interior administration. Honest, loyal and 'something of a man apart' he was also an expert cavalrymen who took excellent care of both men and horses.

Starting his military career in the King's Garde Constitutionelle, he was probably 'on the wrong side' in the Tuileries massacre, but survived to find his way south of Paris and enlist in a cavalry regiment. Elected a sous-lieutenant in 1793, he served on the Spanish frontier being promoted to captain in his regiment by 1795. The next year saw him in Italy where he came to Napoleon's attention and was given command of Napoleon' s Guides. He had found his niche.

An outstanding combat leader, he made all of the major campaigns of the Grande Armée. He usually commanded the cavalry of the Imperial Guard, but he was given other assignments on campaign to give him experience. He matured professionally as he grew older. Ineffective as a cavalry corps commander in

1806, by 1808 he routed a larger Spanish force at the battle of Rio Seco.

In 1809 with Murat absent, Bessières commanded the Cavalry Reserve and did it so expertly that many considered him a better commander than Murat. He was better trained than Murat, knew how to look after his men and horses and not waste them on campaign. Just as brave and gallant as Murat, he was undoubtedly more intelligent and a better soldier.

Bessières made the Russian campaign and was back in the saddle for 1813. He was killed by an artillery round near Rippach before the campaign had really got started.

One last general officer of the Guard is neither famous nor well-known. An artilleryman who played the flute in his leisure time and left an excellent memoir, his name is Jean-François Boulart (1776–1842), commonly called 'Bon'.

In 1793 he was a student at the artillery school at Chalons and was commissioned into the 2ᵉ Artillerie à Pied that year. In quick succession, he served with the Armée du Rhin from 1793–7, the Armée du Rome in 1798 and the Armée d'Italie in 1799, fighting at Novi that year. He was with Suchet on the Var in 1800 and was promoted to captain in 1801.

1803 found him with the 5ᵉ Artillerie à Pied, but he transferred to the more dashing and glamourous 5ᵉ Artillerie à Cheval, which must have cost him quite a bundle on new uniforms. He rose steadily from then on was chef de bataillon in 1806, chef d'escadron that same year, transferred to Guard horse artillery in 1807 and a major in the Guard foot artillery regiment after Wagram. Boulart was appointed to command the artillery in Curial's Guard division in 1812. He ended as a general in command of Rapp's corps artillery in 1815.

Boulart served at Jena, Ostrolenka, Friedland, Spain, Essling, Wagram, Smolensk, Borodino, the Berezina, Leipzig, Hanau, La Rothière and Montereau. His memoirs are full of anecdotes from a professional soldier with a sense of humour. He did his duty, no more no less, and was proud of his guns and men and of being an artilleryman.

Napoleon wanted a large and impressive Guard for a number of reasons, the most important of which being a highly trained and reliable force of all arms under his personal command to be committed when and where necessary. It was no mere Palace Guard. No single officer was ever entrusted with the command of the Imperial Guard. Napoleon saved that honour for himself.

While the Old Guard infantry regiments were not usually engaged in combat, the Guard cavalry and artillery were employed freely starting with the battle of Austerlitz in 1805. The Young and Middle Guard infantry regiments were regularly committed to action, especially after 1809. One outstanding exception to that rule was at Borodino in 1812 when, though urged by subordinates to commit the Guard to finish off Kutusov, Napoleon refused, believing that his 'last reserve' must be kept intact. It was probably a grave error in judgement on Napoleon's part.

It is worth noting that the greater majority of the Guard infantry were not Old Guard, but belonged to the Young and Middle Guard, with the exception of the Waterloo campaign. The Old Guard battalions that made the final assault at Waterloo belonged to the junior regiments that were newly raised. They attacked, outnumbered and not en masse, and were defeated by overwhelming numbers of allied troops. The senior regiments formed square and stopped the allied pursuit long enough for much of Nord to get away. Pelet's two Old Guard battalions in Plançenoit broke out and made their way to safety, saving their eagle. An Old Guard foot artillery company ran out of ammunition and went through the motions of loading and firing which bluffed the allied cavalry into a momentary halt. Finally, the Guard cavalry formed Nord's rear guard, forming in line of battle with the Guard Lancer regiment on the right and the Grenadiers à Cheval on the left of the line. British cavalry coming off Wellington's ridge rode for the lancers, until the French and Poles 'presented' lances at the halt. The British horse veered from them to their right and instead attacked the Grenadiers à Cheval, who met them with a volley from their muskets, dropped them, drew swords and charged. When the Grenadiers à Cheval left the battlefield, it was in perfect order, the last of the Armée du Nord to depart, still lordly in manner, with their bearskins visible for all to see.

British artist Benjamin Haydon described the Old Guard infantry when he saw them at Fontainebleu in 1814:

> More dreadful looking fellows than Napoleon's Guard I had never seen. They had the look of thoroughbred, veteran, disciplined *banditti*. Depravity, reckless-ness, and bloodthirstiness were burned into their faces . . . Black moustache, gigantic bearskins, and a ferocious expression were their characteristics.[7]

At the beginning of the 1815, Captain Mauduit described the Ier Régiment des Grenadiers à Pied as follows:

> The average height of the grenadiers was five feet, six inches [French] . . . The average age of the grenadiers was 35 years old . . . The average [length of] service . . . was 15 years and as many campaigns . . . Long-tested by marches, fatigues, deprivations, bivouacs . . . the grenadier of the Guard was lean and thin. Obesity was unknown in our ranks . . . A particular mark of the affectation of the grenadier of the Guard was his earring. It was his first expense upon arrival into

the Corps . . . A comrade of his pierced his ear and introduced a lead wire until the day when his budget permitted him a ring of gold . . . The uniform of the grenadier for the march or . . . combat was the blue greatcoat . . . blue pants black gaiters and the fur bonnet . . . Each grenadier had his water bottle hung from his cross-while belting and convenient to his right hand . . . If a regiment of grenadiers of the Old Guard was magnificent on the Champ de Mars, on the field of battle it was sublime! There, each grenadier became a hero that neither cannonballs, not shells nor canister, nor musket balls made flinch.[8]

Finally, a word from the poet Chateaubriand, bringing to the descriptions of the Guard something that only a poet could do:

> In order to spare the king [Louis XVIII] the sight of foreign troops, it was a regiment of the Old Guard who lined the route. I do not believe that human faces ever wore so threatening and terrible an expression. Those battle-scarred grenadiers, the conquerors of Europe, who had seen so much, who smelled of fire and powder; those same men, robbed of their Captain, were forced to salute an old king, disabled by time not war, watched as they were by an army of foreigners in Napoleon's occupied capital. Some, moving the skin of their foreheads, brought their great bearskins down over their eyes as if to avoid seeing anything; others turned down the corners of their mouths in angry contempt; others again showed their teeth through their mustachios, like tigers. When they presented arms it was a furious movement and the sound made one tremble. Never have men been put to so great a test and suffered such agonising torment. If they had been called upon to exact vengeance, it would have been necessary to exterminate every one of them or they would have devoured the earth.[9]

The Imperial Guard's appearance on the battlefield was enough to send opposing commanders into mental convulsions. The steadfastness of the Old Guard at Essling under an incessant cannonade was enough to persuade the Austrians from a final attack on the French line. Dorsenne at Eylau in 1807 destroyed a column of Russian grenadiers with the bayonet only after the Russians had penetrated the French position. Dorsenne's Old Guard infantry stood and took punishment from the Austrian artillery by closing and keeping ranks after their comrades had been hit and went down. They not only maintained their position but steadied wavering troops from nearby line units. Old Guard infantry shocked Wrede by their unexpected appearance at Hanau in 1813. The subsequent attack by the Old Guard ruined whatever chance Wrede had of stopping the Grande Armée leaving Germany.

NOTES

Notes to Introduction

1 Coignet, *The Notebooks of Captain Coignet: Soldier of the Empire 1799–1816*, pp. 101–3

2 The guillotine.

3 Napoleon had battle honours placed on the colours of the Armée d'Italie in 1796–97 to boost morale.

4 It is interesting to speculate whether these officers would have supported Napoleon's *coup d'état* in November 1799.

5 Augereau had deserted from different European armies, one of which was the Prussian Army, hence the nickname. When observing the 'march past' of the haul of Prussian prisoners at Jena in 1806, he noticed that his old company had been captured and that the company commander and 1st Sergeant were still the same after twenty years. He was more than gracious to them.

6 Marie-Louises were the too-young conscripts of 1814, named after their young Empress. Some careless authors list the conscripts of 1813–14 as 'Marie-Louises', but the term actually applies to those of 1814 only.

7 Elting, *Swords Around A Throne*, p. 12.

8 Davout's name was originally spelled d'Avout; Desaix's was Des Aix.

9 An excellent reference for that campaign is *The Blue Nile* by Alan Morehead.

10 There is a very good modern biography of Lannes by Margaret Chrisawn, *The Emperor's Friend*. One delightful story concerns Lannes's return to his native village after being promoted to general officer rank. One old woman in the village, who was sometimes on the receiving end of Lannes's mischievous adventures when he was little, told him he was still 'a little twerp.'

11 As cited in Elting, p. 55.

12 As cited in Elting, p. 64.

13 Britten Austin, *The Great Retreat*, p. 257.

14 A conversation with John Elting in 1995.

15 Elting, p. 703. The original reference is in the *Bulletin de la Sabretache*, VI, p. 395. This incident took place during Carnot's expert defence of Antwerp in 1814. The sentry's

shot was accompanied by Carnot's sarcastic refusal and he addressed Bernadotte as 'a prince, born a Frenchman, who knows so much about the standards of honourable conduct.'

16 Lachouque and Brown, *The Anatomy of Glory*, p. 479. General 'Père' Roguet was the officer who would disband the Ier Grenadiers à Pied of the Imperial Guard, the 'old of the old' on 11 September 1815 'without a murmur'.

17 Elting, p. 141.

18 Esposito and Elting, *A Military History and Atlas of the Napoleonic Wars*, Biographical Sketches. In an era when the quip and wise retort are common place, this comment has to take first place.

19 Some sources state that when hit Montbrun exclaimed 'nice shot' but that is undoubtedly apocryphal.

20 For von Funck's candid appraisals of the French generals and marshals, some quite surprising, see his memoir, *In the Wake of Napoleon*.

21 Elting, pp. 153–4.

Note to Prologue

1   The best reference for the Poles action at Somosierra is *Les Polonais à Somo-Sierra en Espagne en 1808* by Colonel Andrzej Niegolewski, who was the only officer of the squadron to make it to the top of the pass with the squadron. It is much more accurate than either Thiers's account or de Segur's fable.

Notes to Chapter 1

1   Esposito and Elting, *A Military History and Atlas of the Napoleonic Wars*, Map 60.

2   Marshal de Broglie was the first general to organise his troops into divisions in combat. These were the forerunners of what would develop into the divisions and the corps of the Napoleonic armies.

3   General Jean-Baptiste de Gribeauval was responsible for developing the most complete artillery system in Europe before 1800. His system, and the artillery doctrine that accompanied it, carried the French artillery through the Napoleonic period. For a full explanation of Gribeauval's developments and reforms see the article 'The Cannon's Breath' by the author. There are two excellent biographies of Gribeauval in French, by Lt Col. Hennebert and Pierre Nardin.

4   Guibert's *Essai de Tactique* was a modern volume that stressed mobility and the offensive, as well as an army of citizen soldiers. He contradicted his *Essai* in his second treatise, *Defense du système de guerre moderne*, in which he stated that 'The vapours of modern philosophy heated my head and clouded my judgement'.

5   Pierre Bourcet, who started the French staff college at Grenoble in 1764 as well as founding the French general staff, and who was the foremost staff officer of his day and an expert in mountain warfare, wrote *Principes de la guerre de Montagnes*. He was the forerunner of Louis-Alexandre Berthier, the first of the great chiefs of staff of history.

6   Mesnil-Durand wrote *Fragments de Tactique, ou six mémoires* (three more *mémoires* were added later). He opposed much of what Guibert had written and opposed the abolition of the chasseur (light infantry) companies that had been instituted by de Broglie.

7   After Gribeauval, the du Teil brothers, Jean and Jean-Pierre (sometimes referred to as Jean and Joseph) were the most influential of the French artillerymen. They codified French artillery doctrine in the very useful and influential *De l'Usage de l'Artillerie Nouvelle dans la Guerre de Campagne*. It was the only doctrinal publication of the period above the usual *règlements*.

8   For an excellent coverage of the French military reformers of the period 1763–89 see Quimby, *The Background of Napoleonic Warfare*.

9   Davout was one of the few, if not the only, French senior officer who wore eye-glasses in combat. He had a special pair made that tied at the back of his head.

10 Columns. Generally speaking, when the term 'column' is used during the period, it means an infantry battalion in column which would either be one or two companies in width. Two companies were termed a 'division.'

11 Troops in line. The regulation French line was three-deep during the period. In 1813 Napoleon changed this to two-deep. Many times French infantry commanders would not form the regulation three-deep line, preferring to form their units in a heavy skirmish line backed up by a second line of battalion columns which would 'feed' the first line as ammunition was expended. This was used by the French at Jena and in other actions during the period. See Griffith's and Lochet's excellent articles in *Empires, Eagles, and Lions*.

12 Pirch had been a Prussian officer and his 'influence' was either a speed bump or a few steps backward in the reform process. Trying to make Frenchmen into Prussians just did not work.

13 Quimby, *The Background of Napoleonic Warfare*, p. 233.

14 Ibid, p. 234.

15 Ibid, pp. 234–6.

16 Ibid, pp. 245–6.

17 Ibid, pp. 236–43.

18 Rochambeau was de Broglie's son-in-law and would later command the excellent expeditionary force that was sent to North America in 1780. He would share in the allied victory at Yorktown, Virginia in October 1781. One of his staff officers was the young Alexandre Berthier. Rochambeau's artillery train was composed of Gribeauval's new pieces.

19 Quimby, p. 243.

20 Ibid, pp. 242–3.

21 Luckner served with the allied army under Prince Ferdinand of Brunswick during the Seven Years War. He was Frederick the Great's brother-in-law.

22 Ibid, pp. 245–7.

23 Joly de Maizeroy is the author of *Théorie de la Guerre* and was a proponent of warfare

of manoeuvre and generally supported de Broglie, and, obliquely, Mesnil-Durand.

24 Quimby, p. 270.

25 The use of light troops and skirmishers was as old as the ancient Greeks and Romans. However, the new French tactical system was the first to employ light infantry in open or skirmish order in conjunction with formed units on the battlefield, the two working together offensively to forge a new weapon. See Duffy, *The Military Experience in the Age of Reason*, p. 279.

26 Luvaas, *Napoleon and the Art of War*, p. 51.

27 Rothenberg, *Napoleon's Great Adversary: The Archduke Charles and the Austrian Army 1792–1814*, p. 33.

28 Ibid., pp. 145–6. See also *The British Light Infantry Arm* by Gates, pp. 21, 27, and 29.

29 Because Gribeauval's far-reaching reforms greatly affected education of both artillery officers and NCOs, the French artillery had once again gained the reputation as the best in Europe by 1789.

30 Elting, *Swords Around A Throne*, pp. 532–6. See also Quimby, pp. 300–44.

31 Gates, pp. 33–4.

32 Elting, p. 535.

33 Lynn, *The Bayonets of the Republic*, pp. 219, 227, 230 and 231.

34 Gates, p. 21.

35 Elting, p. 533.

36 Ibid., p. 535.

37 Ibid., pp. 207–8. Masséna was bluntly reminded of this by his subordinates when he overlooked this tradition. He corrected his error.

38 Luvaas, p. 44.

39 Ibid., p. 6.

40 Elting, p. 531.

41 Ibid., 531.

42 The voltigeurs, because of the overall efficiency and general combativeness, became known as *der kleinen manner* (the little men).

43 There can be much confusion in the use of the term 'column' especially regarding the French. There were heavier formations towards the end of the Empire, but the usual formation used was the handy battalion column, which could advance across terrain in a line of battalion columns quite rapidly and maintain their cohesion. MacDonald's formation for his division at Wagram, which was formed with Napoleon's approval, was a large hollow oblong with the rear open. When it hit the Austrian first line, it shattered it on impact. It was supported by Lauriston's 102-gun artillery battery.

44 Lachouque and Browne, *The Anatomy of Glory*, p. x. (Latest edition, Greenhill 1997).

45 For a detailed comparison of the field artillery systems of the period see my *Artillery of the Napoleonic Wars 1792–1815*.

46 Gribeauval's new system was thoroughly tested, the result being that it was far superior to the older, obsolete French Vallière System of 1732. However, because of

the politics of the French court, and a long, bitter dispute between Vallière's son and Gribeauval, it was not until the mid-1770s that Gribeauval's system was put into complete production and adopted.

47 Kiley, p. 57.

48 Ibid, p. 68.

49 Louis de Tousard, *The American Artillerist's Companion*, p. 45.

50 For a good discussion of the different belligerents' horse artillery, see Kiley, pp. 112–21.

51 Lynn, p. 283.

52 Detaille, *L'Armée Française*, p. 112.

53 Berthier is usually characterised as nothing but a 'chief clerk'. In fact, he was the pre-eminent chief of staff of his day and instituted many staff procedures that are still in use today. He did have influence on Scharnhorst and the development of the Prussian General Staff. Thiebault said of him in 1796: 'Quite apart from his specialist training as a topographical engineer, he had knowledge and experience of staff work and furthermore a remarkable grasp of everything to do with war. He had also, above all else, the gift of writing a complete order and transmitting it with the utmost speed and clarity . . . No one could have better suited General Bonaparte, who wanted a man capable of relieving him of all detailed work, to understand him instantly and to foresee what he would need.' General Custine also thought highly of Berthier: 'I can speak of him with more knowledge than anyone else, for it was I who formed him in America . . . I know of no one who has more skill or a better eye for reconnoitring a locality, who accomplishes this more correctly, and to whom all details are more familiar. I shall perhaps find someone who can replace Berthier, but I have not yet discovered him . . .' The Duc de Lauzan stated that Berthier 'has all the necessary qualifications for making an excellent chief of staff'. Napoleon, with whom Berthier served for eighteen years stated in 1796 that 'General Berthier, chief of staff, has spent his days fighting at my side and his nights at his desk: it would be impossible to combine more activity, good will, courage, and knowledge . . .' and that Berthier had 'talents, activity, character . . . everything in his favour'. At Lodi in 1796, Napoleon described 'the intrepid Berthier, who was on that day a cannoneer, cavalier, and grenadier'. Ferdinand von Funck, the Saxon liaison officer at Napoleon's headquarters stated in 1807 that 'Berthier . . . in spite of a rough exterior . . . was not an unkindly man and, although hard and irascible, was amendable to reasonable representations. His often cross-grained manner was, as a rule, a consequence of the pressure of work, under which he all but succumbed. All the problems connected with the needs of the army and of their transport in war were thrown on him as Minister for War and Chief of the General Staff, The armies were scattered from Bayonne to the bug, from Calabria to the Helder, and as far as Stralsund; they were shifting their position incessantly, had to be supplied and directed, and the whole of it passed through [Berthier's] hands. However ably his office staff supported him, he always was and remained the clearing house through which all business was

transacted.' 'It was Napoleon who inaugurated every plan, improvised the means for carrying it out, and by imbuing all with his own zeal made everything possible. It was General Berthier who, the plan of the chief once conceived, identified himself thoroughly with it, divided and subdivided the work to be done, assigning to each one the particular task by which he was to cooperate with every other member of the army, smoothing over difficulties, providing for every contingency. His anxious solicitude, which kept him ever on the alert, his undaunted cooperation, were never relaxed until success was achieved . . .' 'Berthier was also the most indefatigable person I knew, and when I one day congratulated Count Daru on his wonderful power of sustaining fatigue and doing without sleep, he said to me, 'The Prince of Neufchatel is even stronger than I am; I never spent more than nine days and nights without going to bed, but Berthier has been in the saddle for thirteen days and nights at a stretch . . .' Berthier's contemporaries consistently placed him at the crux of the successes of the Grande Armée, as did Napoleon.

54 Elting, p. 82.

55 Ibid., p. 84.

56 See Elting's excellent paper 'Jomini, Disciple of Napoleon?' for an accurate overview of Jomini's character and competence level. A short version is in his *The Superstrategists*, pp. 148–61.

57 Thiebault, *An Explanation of the Duties of the Several Etats-Major in the French Army*, pp. 22–4.

58 Ibid., pp. 19–21.

59 Ibid., pp. 12–15.

60 Ibid., p. 15.

61 Von Brandt, *In the Legions of Napoleon*, p. 186.

Notes to Chapter 2

1 Lanza, *The Source Book for the Marengo Campaign*, p. 72.

2 Ibid., p. 72.

3 A corps d'armée was the smallest force of all arms in the French Army from the Marengo campaign onward. Napoleon and other French commanders were toying with this organisation from at least 1796, as the division of all arms, was proving to have deficiencies. The establishment of the corps gave the corps commander his own staff and left the divisions with their own staffs and commanders. In effect, the corps was a headquarters with corps troops assigned (artillery, engineers, administrative staff, etc.) and it was assigned a number of divisions, from two to five, with which it would operate. Divisions, though usually permanently assigned to the corps, could be detached to another corps headquarters if necessary, and other divisions attached from other units. If necessary, provisional corps could be 'stood up' for special situations. This was done in the Marengo campaign when Desaix arrived from Egypt; in 1805 when an VIII Corps was formed and assigned to Mortier; in 1807 for Lannes, and again for Lannes in the first half of the campaign

of 1809 as he had just arrived from Spain. It was a highly flexible organisation which gave the French an immense administrative, tactical and combat advantage over their enemies.

4 Lanza, pp. 79–80.

5 Ibid., p. 80–1.

6 Luvaas, *Napoleon on the Art of War*, p. 88.

7 Sargent, *The Campaign of Marengo*, p. 24.

8 Coignet, *The Notebooks of Captain Coignet*, p. 76.

9 Ibid., p. 76.

10 Petit, *Marengo*, p. 25. The thirty-minute fight of the Consular Guard infantry is an interesting microcosm of the battle of Marengo. Some accounts have the entire Guard infantry going into action, 800 strong, losing a third of their number, and withdrawing with the rest of the French army. Austrian accounts from 1823 have the Guard infantry being destroyed by Austrian cavalry commanded by Frimont. Neither account is accurate. While there were undoubtedly about 800 Guard infantrymen on the field, the action for which they are famous was probably fought by only 500–600 Guardsmen, and their losses were probably about fifty per cent of the unit engaged. The rest, either in formation as Petit states, or in groups withdrawing as best they could, disengaged and made it back to friendly lines. Their colour was saved by Lieutenant Aune. The unit was in the French counter-attack, so the Austrian secondary claim that they had been destroyed is inaccurate. That they were involved in the counter-attack was stated by Generals Monnier, Dupont, and Berthier, and was noted in the *Journal of the Army of the Reserve* by Major Broussier. During the fight, they either formed square as noted in the *Bulletin of the Army of the Reserve*, or they fought in line, and they very well could have been hit in the rear by Frimont, as the Austrian account states. They are not mentioned at all in General Melas's account of the battle. Coignet notes in his account that a battalion of the 43^e Ligne was hit in the rear by Austrian dragoons and destroyed. That happening twice in the same action in the same way is much too coincidental. Probably there were at least 200 survivors from the Guard's thirty-minute delaying action and they very well have been reinforced with the other 300 Guard infantry that were on the field, which would account for the total of 800. What those other 300 Guardsmen were doing is unknown, but they may have been those that were taking ammunition up to the firing line that Coignet talks about. The commander of the Guard infantry in their thirty-minute fight was Soules and the other battalion commander was Tortel. They may have been placed under the command of Stabenrath, an officer on Berthier's staff and who is mentioned being employed in that capacity in one of the French after action reports. Finally, from the awards list for the Consular Guard at Marengo, it is clearly indicated that the Guard infantry distinguished themselves, in this their first fight as a unit. Napoleon was not in the habit of granting awards for valour for a unit that was destroyed, and his remark after the action that a unit of 500 could fight its way out of a difficult situation may have been referring to the Guard infantry.

11 Coignet, p. 77.
12 Sargent, p. 225.
13 Elting, *Swords Around A Throne*, pp. 601–2.
14 Chandler, *On the Napoleonic Wars*, p. 87.

Notes to Chapter 3

1 Esposito and Elting, *A Military History and Atlas of the Napoleonic Wars*, Map 46.
2 Elting, *Swords Around A Throne*, p. 60.
3 Esposito and Elting, Map 50. Ferdinand deserting his army while it was in danger of being encircled is, to a soldier, contemptible. Equally contemptible, many of the senior Austrian commanders, Schwarzenberg included, went with him. Mack to his credit, refused, and stayed with his men. He was also left holding the proverbial bag and was court-martialled and imprisoned for Ulm while Ferdinand was neither punished nor censored. Schwarzenberg did get Mack reinstated in 1819. Ferdinand accomplished nothing constructive for the rest of the campaign.
4 Stutterheim, Major General, *A Detailed Account of the Battle of Austerlitz*, pp. 145–6.

Notes to Chapter 4

1 Reynier had recommended evacuating Egypt because of his belief it was not worth the effort. Napoleon wasn't pleased.
2 Once the Ière Leger had been defeated, the battle was virtually over. This principle part of the action apparently lasted for only about fifteen minutes.
3 Oman, *Studies in the Napoleonic Wars*, p. 54.
4 Esposito and Elting, *A Military History and Atlas of the Napoleonic Wars*, Biographical Sketches.
5 Elting, *Swords Around A Throne*, p. 160.
6 Chandler, *On the Napoleonic Wars*, pp. 138–9.
7 Ibid., pp. 142–3. There was some misinformation applied to Maida by Charles Oman, basically stating that the French had attacked in column, instead as has been shown, in line. Oman later corrected his error, but his initial oversimplification of 'column versus line' has to a large degree, stuck. That is unfortunate, but the evidence that the French attacked in line at Maida is conclusive. Reynier stated in a letter to Joseph Bonaparte in July 1806 that the 1st leger had attacked in line, and a French officer present at Maida later wrote that the order to form and attack in line came from Reynier himself.

Notes to Chapter 5

1 For example, the Duke of Baden was made a Grand Duke, and the Electors of Württemberg and Bavaria were made kings.
2 This was Sergeant Guindey. He was later taken into the Imperial Guard and assigned to the Grenadiers à Cheval and was awarded a commission. He was killed in action at Hanau in 1813.

3 Esposito and Elting, *A Military History and Atlas of the Napoleonic Wars*, Map 63.
4 Vialannes was tardy arriving on the battlefield because of 'personal business' on his part. He was not Davout's cavalry commander in the next campaign.
5 In theory, the commander-in-chief of the Prussian Army was the king. If the king was a good soldier and knew his business, as in Frederick the Great's case, all should go well. With Frederick William, however, what resulted was even more confusion after Brunswick was shot.
6 Funcke, *In the Wake of Napoleon*, pp. 101–2.
7 Von Brandt, *In the Legions of Napoleon*, pp. 39–40.
8 Von Brandt, p. 201.
9 White, *The Enlightened Soldier*, p. 128.
10 Ibid., p. 154.
11 Ibid., p. 154–5.
12 Craig, *The Politics of the Prussian Army*, p. 22.
13 Ibid., p. 23.
14 Ibid., p. 24.
15 Duffy, *The Army of Frederick the Great*, pp. 309–16. The Prussian officers themselves referred to the recruits as 'riff raff.'
16 Craig, p. 24.
17 Ibid., p. 25.
18 White, pp. 56, 64.
19 Paret, *Yorck and the Era of Prussian Reform*, pp. 96, 104 and 112.
20 Paret, *Clausewitz and the State*, p. 125.
21 Grawert's misadventures, as well as those of General Ruchel at Jena's ending can be found in Maude, *The Jena Campaign 1806*, pp. 147–77 and Petre's *Napoleon's Conquest of Prussia*, pp. 121–64 with comments on strategy and tactics at pp. 165–80. The Prussian view of Jena and Auerstadt is in Jany's *Geschichte der Preussischen Armee*, Volume III, pp. 561–93.
22 Petre, p. 130.
23 Elting, *Swords Around A Throne*, p. 517.
24 White, pp. 59, 66, 70 and 77.
25 Ibid., p. 58.
26 Ibid., p. 59
27 Ibid., p. 76–8.
28 Ibid., p. 77.
29 Ibid., p. 73.
30 Ibid., p. 62.
31 Ibid., p. 62.
32 Ibid., p. 78.
33 Ibid., p. 62.
34 Paret, *Yorck and the Era of Prussian Reform*, p. 145.
35 Ibid., p. 126.

36 Of all the reforms the French either started or completed before the shooting started in 1792, it was their organisation and functioning of their staff system which was the most important. Berthier built on the provisional staff instruction that was prepared for the staff corps in the 1780s (and probably for which he was one of the officers that prepared it), making the first unofficial staff manual when he was with the Armée d'Italie in 1795. From that came Thiebault's two excellent staff manuals, and the French were organising their staffs at army and division level into staff sections with specific duties for each section, and each section being under an assistant chief of staff before Napoleon took command of the Armée d'Italie in 1796. Compared with this, the general staffs of the other major belligerents were behind. The Austrians did not organise into staff sections until 1800–1 and as late as 1809 still did not have staffs at the division level. They organised into corps d'armée on the French pattern that year, but the corps staffs were overworked, having the administrative burden from their subordinate divisions thrown back on them. The Prussian general staff was not efficiently organised until after 1807, at the urging and under the leadership of Scharnhorst and Gneisenau. By 1815, the Prussian General Staff was still in the embryonic stage. The Russian staff organisation was at best chaotic. Russian commanders, especially Suvorov, prized Austrian staff officers, but the Russians did not have as efficient a staff organisation as any of the other major belligerents. The British, especially Wellington, had a general staff that was tailored to the mission at hand. Wellington's staff was efficient and trusted, but it was organised by Wellington himself, and he did not allow his subordinates much latitude in their operations. For the French staff organisation and functioning, see Elting's *Swords Around A Throne*, Colonel Vachée's *Napoleon at Work*, Watson's biography of Berthier, Thiebault's two staff manuals, and Martin van Creveld's *Command in War*. For an overall view of the staff development of the staffs of the major belligerents, see Brigadier General Hittle's *The Military Staff*, which must be used with care. For the Austrians see Rothenberg's *Napoleon's Great Adversary*, as well as his *The Army of Francis Joseph*. Wellington's staff is excellently described and analysed in Ward's *Wellington's Headquarters*. The Prussian staff problems and organisation are adequately described in Gorlitz's *The German General Staff* and Craig's *The Politics of the Prussian Army*.

Notes to Chapter 6

1 Kiley, *Artillery of the Napoleonic Wars 1792–1815*, p. 187. For an excellent view of Russian tactics of all branches, see *Tactics of the Russian Army of the Napoleonic Wars* by Alexander and Yurii Zhmodikov.
2 Esposito and Elting, *A Military History and Atlas of the Napoleonic Wars*, Map 73.
3 Russian artillery officers of the period were particularly unskilled. See Wilson, The *Campaigns in Poland 1806 and 1807*, p. 22. The Russians were enthusiastic about their artillery employment. Their divisions, for example, would have as many guns attached as a French corps, etc. Their artillery fire would be effective by the sheer

weight of the bombardment as at Eylau.

4 Petre, *Napoleon's Campaign in Poland*, p. 183.

5 After being ordered to advance by Napoleon, Murat merely rode to the head of his divisions and turned his horse toward the enemy and led off. The division followed. It was an incredible, low-key example of personal leadership.

6 The Russian cavalry charges at Eylau lacked dash and sometimes momentum. Charles Parquin, of the 20ᵉ Chasseurs à Cheval mentions that they met a Russian cavalry advance at the halt, fired their carbines in a volley and then charged, defeating the Russian cavalry which had advanced on them at the walk. The 20ᵉ Chasseurs were on the Grande Armée's left flank.

7 Ryan, *Napoleon's Elite Cavalry*, plate 37. Lepic was one of the Grande Armée's characters, in an army of characters. The Russian summons to surrender came from a Russian dragoon officer: 'Surrender, General! Your courage has carried you too far-you are in our lines.' Lepic's reply was typical: 'Look at those mugs and tell me if they want to surrender!' motioning to the Grenadiers à Cheval who were with him. Then he bellowed 'Grenadiers, follow me!' When Napoleon saw him after his return to the French lines, Napoleon said to him 'I thought you had been made a prisoner, General, and I was deeply pained!' Lepic's retort to Napoleon's obvious concern was 'Sire, you will never hear but of my death.'

Notes to Chapter 7

1 Lannes at been shot in the neck at the siege of Acre in the Holy Land during the Egyptian campaign. The wound left him with a permanent 'tilt' to his neck.

2 Murat was still at Heilsberg, and Grouchy was the senior cavalry division commander.

3 Esposito and Elting, *A Military History and the Napoleonic Wars*, Map 79.

4 The decisive part of Senarmont's unprecedented action is here where he decided to go against the Russian centre on his own. Senarmont changed artillery from a supporting arm on the battlefield to an arm that was the equal of the infantry and cavalry. It could not only manoeuvre and provide 'close and continuous fire support', but clearly demonstrated that it could hold ground. The infantry, for the duration of this artillery action, was now the supporting arm and Senarmont's quick-witted behaviour changed the French main effort from the right flank to the centre.

5 See the section on Senarmont in *Grand Artilleurs* by Girod de l'Ain. Senarmont's after-action report is most helpful, as is the I Corps after action report. Senarmont's letter of 15 June to his brother clearly states that he walked the ground after the action and estimated 4,000 Russians dead on the field. See Kiley, *Artillery of the Napoleonic Wars*, p. 200.

6 Esposito and Elting, Map 81.

7 Petre, *Napoleon's Campaign in Poland*, p. 324. Yermelov in his memoirs refers to Senarmont's large battery as 'that . . . ghastly battery. See *The Czar's General* by Yermelov, p. 100. One of the footnotes on the same page of that volume states that Senarmont 'virtually wiped out entire regiments'.

8 The excellent historian, Margaret Chrisawn, whose biography of Lannes has set a new standard for biographies of the marshals.

9 Esposito and Elting, *Biographical Sketches*.

10 Von Brandt, *In the Legions of Napoleon*, p. 54.

11 Von Brandt, p. 65.

Notes to Chapter 8

1 Davout, with his foresight in establishing an intelligence network in the soon-to-be theatre of operations in 1808–9 had ample warning of the impending Austrian offensive. He also employed his light cavalry boldly, sending them on deep reconnaissance in Austrian territory. Davout had a knack of training cavalrymen. Montbrun rose from buck private to colonel and commander of the 1er Chasseurs à Cheval under Davout, and Jacquinot, Pire and other outstanding cavalrymen at one time or another had served under Davout's command. Davout was a demanding commander and a hard man but he stood up for his officers, even if they failed, if they had acted under the orders he had given them. He also remembered, unlike some of his peers, competence displayed by his subordinates, and was conscientious about rewarding them for a job well done. He was an ideal commander, and was not above apologising for an injustice. See *Napoleon's Finest* by Scott Bowden, p. 99. Davout fully deserved the unofficial title bestowed on him by his troops: 'The First'.

2 Charles had instituted many reforms between 1805 and 1809. One thing he could not do, however, was make up for the innate inefficiency of his corps commanders and senior generals, as well as the slowness of the Austrian army on campaign. The Austrians had an outstanding chance of success in this campaign, but lost it by not moving fast enough and taking advantage of the initially slow French concentration.

3 French operations around Ratisbon, which ended in the complete defeat of the Austrian offensive deserve to be called masterly. Napoleon later considered them the best manoeuvres of his career. In actuality, the Austrians were lucky to escape with an army that was still intact. Francis' refusal to seek peace after the repeated defeats at Ratisbon, Landshut and Eckmuhl was foolish, and led to Wagram and another humiliating peace.

4 Rapp's comment in his memoirs on the counterattack into Essling was 'I was charged to take the two remaining Young Guard battalions to the support of the others . . . Our five battalions attack and shatter [the enemy] with the bayonet . . . we are the masters of the village.'

5 Napoleon's comment to Rapp after the action, again according to Rapp's memoirs, was 'If you ever did well in not executing my orders you have done so today.' Apparently, Napoleon appreciated initiative and his commanders thinking for themselves.

6 Josef Smola was not only the outstanding Austrian artilleryman of the period, but was one of the best in any army. His concentration of almost 200 guns at Essling is the largest concentration of the period. However, it was merely a supporting action,

not an attack as Senarmont's was at Friedland or Drouot's was at Lützen. It did overpower the French artillery, literally blowing them off the field, and part of Lannes's II Corps at least attempted to leave the field. The Old Guard, however, stood and took it, which prohibited any Austrian infantry attack.

7   Coignet, *The Notebooks of Captain Coignet*, pp. 176–9.
8   Blaze, *Life in Napoleon's Army*, p. 103–4.
9   Sargent, *The Campaign of Marengo*, p. 224.

Notes to Chapter 9
1   British siege operations in the Peninsula were poorly run. There were not enough specialised engineer troops in Spain to support sustained siege operations, and many British sieges were either failures or they culminated in costly assaults by British infantry. That they finally succeeded in reducing the fortresses besieged is a tribute to the gallantry of the British soldier.
2   The actual number of colours taken at Albuera is usually disputed. Remnants of some are in the Invalides today, but at least one colour was retaken on the battlefield. Some of the artillery battery that was overrun was also recovered. The same arguments linger about Waterloo. For example, British accounts insist that no infantry squares were broken during the French cavalry attacks. However, Brigadier Pilloy, a French cuirassier who actually charged the British squares, is emphatic in his letters that he rode over and through British infantry in square. What probably happened is that British squares were reduced by casualties and collapsed, but the survivors toughly re-formed in knots of infantrymen to remain 'safe' against the French cavalry. One British eyewitness stated that the 27th Foot, the Inniskillings, were 'literally dead in square' on the ridge. Further, apparently five allied colours were taken by French cavalry at Waterloo. They were recovered after the battle in a farm house, so the loss was not permanent. It should also be noted that the losses in some British regiments were so heavy that their colours were sent to the rear to prevent their loss.

Notes to Chapter 10
1   St Cyr later admiringly remarked of the Swiss under his command that they were 'stronger than nature.'
2   Napoleon believed that after taking Moscow and defeating the main Russian army under Kutusov that Alexander would at least negotiate with him. Alexander had vowed not to treat with Napoleon as long as the French remained on Russian soil and refused to talk to Napoleon. This was at least partly because of a fear of his own nobles. Alexander did not want to end up like his father.
3   What is usually ignored when dealing with the Russian campaign is the extent of the Russian losses which exceeded 250,000. Russian irregular and militia losses are unknown. Total Russian and French losses for the campaign were probably about even.

4 The Cossacks were undisciplined, did not care for artillery or massed infantry fire and were judged by Antoine de Brack as being the best light cavalry in the world. They also took honours as the best looters of the period.

5 A total of six artillery companies were reformed from the arsenal at Orsha.

6 This was one time that Napoleon should have listened. The possession of the pontoon train at the Berezina would have saved many lives. It should be noted that pontoniers were artillerymen, not engineers. Eble himself was an artillery officer. The commander of the I^e Bataillon des Pontonniers at the Berezina was Major Chapuis. His immediate superior was Colonel Chapelle. Both of them reported to Eble.

7 At the Studenka ford, the Berezina would have been 100 metres wide with a depth of 2–2.3 metres. The pontoniers, engineers and sailors would have had to construct twenty-four spans per bridge between 4.25 and 4.5 metres long and there would have been twenty-three trestles per bridge. Even though trestle bridges were the specialty of the engineers, pontoniers also had the knowledge, skill and ability to construct and emplace them.

8 Britten Austin, *The Great Retreat*, p. 220.

9 Dombrowski was a character. At a formal function he once tripped in front of the assembled personages to his great embarrassment. In this case at the Berezina, he did the best he could in a very bad situation.

10 Britten Austin, p. 223. Vaudancourt was very critical of Bronikowski's performance and the loss of Borisov and its bridge.

11 Oudinot's correspondence with Berthier for the period is more than interesting:

The enemies been pushed back from one position to the next as far as Borisov, where our light cavalry, supported by a regiment of cuirassiers, made an extremely brilliant charge. Upon which he withdrew in disorder into the town, which we'd have entered together with him if he had not set fire to a bridge which lies at its entrance.

There are two more passages: one at Stadkov, a mile upstream, and the other at Oukholoda, two miles downstream from Borisov. The aim of the movements noticed yesterday evening on the enemy's two flanks was to occupy these crossing points, which are all guarded. During the night it has not been possible to carry out any reconnaissances exact enough to be sure which is the most favourable point for throwing a bridge.'

Also included was Corbineau's report and that he had sent Corbineau to seize the ford at Studenka. He further stated that he would throw the bridge during the night and that he faced about 20,000 Russians and that he would do all he could to deceive the Russians as to the actual crossing site.

Monseigneur. Your Serene Highness will see from the report of General Aubry who at this moment has just got back from Studenka at the moment I've received your latest dispatch, that the passage is far from being assured. The enemy doesn't seem to be at all being put off the scent and it is certain it's Setingel's troops, coming from Beresino, who are facing that ford. A peasant who yesterday served as guide to a column of about 6,000 Russians, and who escaped from their hands, has told us that column has today made a movement in the opposite direction. But despite the obstacles presented to crossing at Studenka I think we should manage to overcome them provided I am promptly supported, for, within a few hours, I shall find myself between two hostile army corps. The river at that point is deeper than it was three days ago.'

Monseigneur. Unless ordered to the contrary, I shall attack the enemy at Borisov tomorrow. Yet I must draw Your Excellency's attention to the fact that, even if I should manage to drive him out of the town, it's probable he'll burn the bridge, whose re-establishment would be absolutely impractical. This will be confirmed to you . . . by all who know the Berezina's swampy banks and Borisov's formidable position.

12 Britten Austin, p. 232.

13 Ibid., p. 231. Rochechouart referred to the Borisov bridge as the 'interminable . . . accursed bridge.'

14 Elting, *Swords Around A Throne*, p. 229.

15 Britten Austin, p. 229.

16 Esposito and Elting, *A Military History and Atlas of the Napoleonic Wars*, Map 124.

17 Two of them are reproduced in the plate section.

18 Gourgaud, *Napoleon and the Grande Armée in Russia*, p. 247.

19 Yet, when Davout's troops crossed the bridges, they did so in perfect order to 'fife and drum'.

20 Kutusov had never defeated Napoleon and was undoubtedly tired of coming in second. His failure to support Wittgenstein and Tshitshagov at the Berezina clearly point to a reluctance to face Napoleon again. His warning to Tshitshagov supports this.

21 Caulaincourt, *With Napoleon in Russia*, p. 244.

22 Britten Austin, p. 255.

23 Ibid., p. 254.

24 Caulaincourt, p. 236.

25 Britten Austin, p. 260.

26 Ibid., p. 260.

27 Ibid., p. 256.

28 Ibid., p. 261.

29 Ibid., p. 257.

30 Ibid., p. 263.

31 Ibid., p. 261.

32 Ibid., p. 263.

33 Ibid., p. 266.

34 Victor had faced and been defeated by Wellington in the Peninsula. It appears that he learned from his mistakes. His rear-slope defence at the Berezina against Wittgenstein looks like it was copied from Wellington. The Russians sometimes

penetrated his defences, but were always ejected by expertly launched counter-attacks. Most of Victor's troops were Germans and Poles with less than a year's service.

35 Lachouque and Brown, *The Anatomy of Glory*, pp. 263 and 265. Anywhere Napoleon bivouacked was called the 'palace,' be it in the open, in a barn, or an actual palace.

36 Elting, p. 377. The Swiss stand was truly magnificent. Though repeatedly assaulted, they did not give up a foot of ground. Their division commander, General Merle, was noted by Napoleon as being worth 'four marshals'.

37 Britten Austin, p. 248.

38 Ibid., p. 289.

39 Ibid., p. 289.

40 Ibid., p. 290.

41 Ibid., p. 290.

42 Ibid., p. 291.

43 Elting, p. 377.

44 Britten Austin, p. 293.

45 Ibid., p. 293.

46 Lachouque and Brown, p. 264.

47 Elting, p. 263. Apparently only four or five guns were lost in the ford during the crossing. The remainder, over 200, were got away.

48 Kiley, *Artillery of the Napoleonic Wars 1792–1815*, p. 232.

49 Esposito and Elting, Map 125.

Notes to Chapter 11

1 There are two sources that are valuable for this series of incidents. First, there is *Metternich The Autobiography 1773–1815*, pp. 179–93, and *Napoleon Bonaparte: An Intimate Biography* by Vincent Cronin, pp. 339–43. The Austrian alliance with the allies in 1813 was a done deal before Metternich met with Napoleon to act as a 'mediator'.

2 Esposito and Elting, *A Military History and Atlas of the Napoleonic Wars*, Map 134.

3 There are indicators throughout the period that Alexander was a coward. He was certainly no soldier. Throughout the 1813–14 campaigns the allied sovereigns accompanied the allied army on campaign, which undoubtedly thrilled the allied commander-in-chief, Schwarzenberg. Alexander did not have the moral courage in this instance to face Napoleon on the battlefield, even though the allies outnumbered the French by two to one.

4 Moreau had been a successful Republican general. He was uncooperative with Napoleon during the Marengo campaign, and was later implicated in a Royalist plot against the First Consul which forced him into exile. Showing up to 'advise' the allies in 1813 did demonstrate his true colours. Both the allies and French were not surprised that he was hit by French artillery and mortally wounded at Dresden. Some undoubtedly thought it was divine retribution and deserved. There is a most interesting story of Moreau and his dog when he was hit at Dresden. It is in Charles Parquin's memoirs.

Notes to Chapter 12

1 Having to face the Imperial Guard would be enough to send shivers up the spine of the most resolute commander. Wrede had seen them on more than one occasion, as he had been a long time comrade of the French, from at least 1805. Napoleon's comment was 'Poor Wrede. I could make him a count. I couldn't make him a general.'

2 Mortier was not the best of the marshals, but he was reliable, loyal, a skilled tactician and an excellent combat leader. His performance in 1814 delaying the allies from the French frontier was exemplary, especially when compared to Marmont's and Victor's 'droopy-plumed' performance.

4 Blücher was quite a character. His nickname, 'Marshal Vorwarts' (Marshal Forward), fitted him exactly. He was not the sharpest knife in the allied drawer, but he was the most aggressive and pugnacious, even though he was nearly in his dotage by 1813–14. He hated Napoleon, the French Revolution and the French, wanted revenge for 1806, was undaunted by defeat and had an excellent chief of staff in Gneisenau. Blücher was one of the main reasons the allies won in 1813–14.

5 See *La Sabretache*, Volume 9, 1901, the Rapport du General Delort, p. 312, for the after-action report for La Fère-Champenoise.

Notes to Chapter 13

1 One of the overlooked accomplishments of the Hundred Days was the reconstitution of the French Army for active service on campaign. The army had been neglected and badly treated by the Bourbons. Units had been intermixed, the Young Guard disbanded, the Old Guard banished from Paris, and many officers were retired or placed on half-pay, their places taken by Royalists who either had little or not military experience or they had served with the allies against France. The man responsible for preparing the army for war was Marshal Davout.

2 One of the more intriguing aspects of the Hundred Days is that the independent commanders Napoleon picked were either successful in their assigned missions, or performed impossible tasks with competence, and some with brilliance. Colonel Bugeaud, who was the commander of the 14^e Ligne on the Piedmontese frontier, heard of Napoleon's second abdication and received his regiment's eagle on the same day. The war was ostensibly over, but the Austrians were still advancing. Bugeaud addressed his troops, stating 'Soldiers of the 14th here is your eagle. If the Emperor is not longer our sovereign, France endures. Forward!' Bugeaud led his 1,400 against 8,000 of the enemy and routed them.

3 The Saxons who had been forcibly impressed into the Prussian service by the Congress of Vienna had mutinied before Napoleon's return from Elba. Apparently they went after Blücher, crashing through his headquarters front door, shouting 'Long Live Napoleon!' while he unhesitatingly exited through the rear. Other Germans, such as those in the Rhineland were not too happy with their new Prussian overlords either, not being used to being ruled so harshly.

4 The Anglo-Dutch army was dispersed in 'peacetime' cantonments, while the

Prussians were emplaced somewhat ready to deploy. They were also watching the French frontier and could react to a French offensive much quicker than Wellington's army could.

5   This duke was the son of the Duke of Brunswick who was mortally wounded at Auerstadt in 1806.

6   Wellington's alleged comment that the Prussians would be damnably mauled by fighting at Ligny turned out to be quite accurate.

7   The Prussian artillery arm was the worst of the main belligerents in the Napoleonic period. It performed poorly in 1806 and though it gradually grew more proficient from 1813 on, and its organisation and command and control had greatly improved, it still had problems. The Prussians had no artillery school until 1791, and did not have a complete artillery system, the System of 1812, until 1816. But they had learned. For more information, see Kiley, *Artillery of the Napoleonic Wars*.

8   In both instances, Napoleon planned battles of annihilation. Why he relied on Ney both times is a mystery. Davout, Suchet, Soult, or a plethora of other French commanders would have executed the planned envelopments with much more skill and drive. For Jomini's problems, see Elting's *The Superstrategists*.

9   'The Victory is Ours.'

10 This was the strategic situation of the campaign. The joker in the pack, however, was Grouchy. In one of the myriad 'ifs' of this campaign, the Prussians could have been prevented from joining Wellington on the 18th, at least in the strength that they did, if Grouchy's pursuit had been more aggressively handled.

11 Gourgaud, *The Campaign of 1815*, p. 132.

Notes to Chapter 14

1   Napoleon and Berthier, although the professional relationship between them is too often underplayed, had one of the most successful command relationships in military history. It is much more significant than the similar relationship between Blücher and Gneisenau, and Berthier was definitely Gneisenau's superior as a chief of staff. After the crossing of the Berezina, Napoleon departed for Paris, as he was urged to do by his principal subordinates. Murat was left in command, but soon deserted and went back to Naples. No marshal would take orders from another, and Berthier convinced Eugène to take command. Eugène was reluctant, but took Berthier's sage advice, and showed himself to be an excellent strategist. However, what is usually overlooked is Berthier's decisive part in this sequence of events. He was truly a remarkable man and soldier.

2   Napoleon's correspondence with Eugène during this period is basically a 'field manual' on how to conduct Napoleon's method of waging war. Eugène paid attention, and after his first errors and defeats, his generalship matured and his performance was excellent and successful. The best study in English on Eugène's campaign in Italy and Austria in 1809 is Epstein's *Prince Eugène at War: 1809*.

3   During the campaign, one of Broussier's regiments, the 84e Ligne under Colonel

Gambin, were caught alone in Graz by an Austrian army under General Gyulai. With 1,200 men under arms, Gambin stood off over 10,000 Austrians in the St Leonard Cemetery in Graz, until relieved by the 92^e Ligne under Colonel Nagle. The 84^e's stand against Gyulai lasted at least fourteen hours. Austrian losses could have been as high as 1,200 killed and 800 wounded, with an additional 500 taken prisoner. They also lost two standards. French losses could have been as high as 400 killed and wounded from the 84e Ligne. The 84e Ligne was granted a unit award in the form of a plaque which was born on their eagle, with the motto *Un Contre Dix* (One Against Ten). This was only one of two unit awards of this type given during the period in the Grande Armée. The other was for the 128e Ligne for the action at Rosnay in 1814, *Un Contre Huit* (One Against Eight). For an excellent rendition of the Graz action, see John Walsh's excellent article 'The French Zulu'.

4 Martin, Captain, *La Gendarmerie Française en Espagne et en Portugal,* p. 339.

5 Von Brandt, *In the Legions of Napoleon,* p. 75.

6 Ibid., p. 71.

7 Ibid., p. 65–6. Von Brandt also recalled that he thought General Andoche Junot was 'not right in the head,' an interesting observation in that Junot later went insane and committed suicide in Illyria.

Notes to Chapter 15

1 Ryan, *Napoleon's Shield and Guardian,* pp. 257–60.

2 As quoted in Esposito and Elting, *A Military History and Atlas of the Napoleonic Wars,* Biographical Sketches.

3 Elting, *Swords Around A Throne,* pp. 154–5.

4 Ibid., p. 157.

5 *Roots of Strategy,* Book 3, p. 242.

6 Doisy de Villargennes, *Reminiscences of Army Life under Napoleon Bonaparte,* p. iv.

Notes to Epilogue

1 See both Siborne, *History of the Waterloo Campaign,* pp. 310–40 and Ropes, *The Campaign of Waterloo A Military History,* p. 310.

2 For allied squares being broken during the French cavalry charges, see Houssaye, *Napoleon and the Campaign of 1815,* p. 212: 'Several [squares] were shaken and partially broken, if not crushed and scattered altogether' and p. 424, where he cites General Delort as stating that 'several squares were broken.' Brigadier Pilloy, a trooper in the 9th Cuirassiers, maintained that he charged three times against an English square, finally riding 'over and through it'. His narrative is paraphrased in Elting's *Swords Around A Throne* on p. 658. The full account from his letters is contained in *Carnets de la Sabretache,* volume 14, 1906, pp. 505 and 558. Regarding colours taken from the Anglo–Allied army, sources claim between four and six (see Elting p. 658). Captain Klein de Kleinenberg of the Chasseurs à Cheval of the Imperial Guard is credited with capturing one, as are the 9th and 10th Cuirassiers. The figure could be as low as

three, but four is probably the most likely number.

3 Siborne, pp. 327, 331–2; Ropes, p. 310.

4 Houssaye, p. 216; Siborne, p. 332; Ropes, p. 310.

5 Houssaye, p. 216.

6 Chesney, *Waterloo Lectures*, p. 216; Houssaye, p. 216; Ropes, p. 310; Siborne, p. 314, 331–2, 335.

7 Ropes, page 310.

8 See 'Jean-Jacques Pelet: Warrior of the Sword and Pen' by Donald D. Horward in *The Journal of Military History*, Volume 53, Number 1, dated January 1989.

Notes to Appendix

1 Coignet, *The Notebooks of Captain Coignet*, p. 68.

2 Ibid., p. 70.

3 Ibid., p. 95.

4 Ibid., p. 104.

5 Ibid., pp. 98–9

6 Ibid, pp. 99–100. This clearly demonstrates Napoleon's care of his troops and their welfare. It also demonstrates that he could be a 'ten-eyed devil' during an inspection.

7 Elting, *Swords Around A Throne*, p. 183.

8 Bowden, *Armies at Waterloo*, pp. 56–7.

9 Baldick, *The Memoirs of Chateaubriand*, p. 266.

BIBLIOGRAPHY

A significant source for the period is the *Carnet de la Sabretache*, and here are listed the main articles used for this study.

Premier Volume, 1893 'Le Journal de Marche du Colonel Lataye, 1805', p. 139.

'La Garde Consulaire', p. 233.

Volume 2, 1894 'Composition et organisation de l'équipage de guerre de l'Empereur Napoleon en 1812, p. 5.

'Les Generaux des Cuirassiers et leur Armure', p. 96.

'L'Armée expeditionnaire d'Angleterre', pp. 120, 167, 236.

'Le Ier régiment des chevau-legers lanciers polonaise de la Garde sur les campagnes de 1813 et 1814,' p. 275.

'Une conversation de Bernadotte en 1814,' p. 290.

'Mémoire presente a l'Empereur Napoleon Ier sur l'organisation du service d'etat-major, 1805,' p. 499.

Volume 3, Paris 1895 'Le 7e Corps a Eylau', p. 3.

'Leon Aune, Deuxième Grenadier de France, p. 156.

'Les marins de la flotilla et les ouvriers militaries de la marine pendant la campagne de 1809 en Autriche,' pp. 145, 206, 274, 385.

Volume 4, 1896 'Bataille d'Eylau,' p. 81.

Volume 5, 1897 'Un pèlerinage du bord de la Beresina', p. 200.

'Bataille de Friedland (Journal d'operations du Ier corps de la Grande Armée', p. 325.

Volume 6, 1898 'Les chevau-legers polonais de la Garde dans la campagne de 1813–1814,' pp. 177, 220, 301, 472.

'Le récit de Langeron sur la Bataille de Paris (30 March 1814),' p. 193.

'Notes de voyage du general Desaix,' pp. 577, 701, 801.

Volume 7, 1899 'Notes de voyage du general Desaix, 1797,' p. 2.

Le general Lasalle à Varsovie (aout–septembre 1807)', p. 14.

'Les debuts de l'Armée du Rhin (1799),' p. 288.

'Le general Moreau à l'armée du Rhin (novembre 1799–février 1800)', p. 588.

Volume 8, 1900 'Documents relatifs à la tenue provenant des archives du Général Baron de Stabenrath, p. 41.

'La campagne de 1809 en Italie – Journal historique du 52ᵉ régiment de ligne (10 avril–12 juillet), p. 449.

'Le général d'Hautpoul à Austerlitz, p. 632.

'Le général Delaborde, p. 713.

Volume 9, Paris, 1901 'Un Episode de la retraite de Russie – lettre d'un officier d'artillerie', p. 279.

'Rapport du General Delort au Ministre de la Guerre sur le combat de Fere-Champenoise, p. 312

'La cavalerie de la Garde à Waterloo, p. 360.

'Journal d'un mois de campagne à la Grande Armée, p. 449.

'Campagne et captivité de Russie (1812–1813), pp. 620, 686.

'Au sujet de deux ouvrages manuscripts du Général Bardin, p. 707.

Volume 10, 1902 'Episode de la Bataille de Dresde, p. 32.

'Portrait de Baron Lejeune, en tenue de colonel aide de camp du maréchal Berthier, 1809, p. 515.

'Le Général Comte Pacthod, p. 547.

Volume 11, Number 1, 1903 'Armes d'honneur decernées à la Garde consulaire après Marengo, p. 57.

Volume 11, Number 2 La garde à Paris, p. I.

Volume 12, 1904 'Souvenirs du 14ᵉ legère (1805–1812), p. 106.

'Le général Dautancourt et la gendarmerie d'élite pendant les Cent-Jours', pp. 129, 216.

'Guindey', p. 228.

Volume 14, 1906 'Les Généraux du grand-duche de Varsovie de 1812 à 1814', p. 415.

'Le combat de Krasnoe et la retraite de Ney sur le Dnieper', pp. 519, 626, 683.

'Le centenaire d'Iena et d'Auerstadt', p. 577.

'Notes et documents provenant des archives du général baron Ameil', p. 711.

Volume 15, Paris 1907 'Le Centenaire de Friedland', p. 321.

'Notes et documents provenant des archives du général baron Ameil,' pp. 18, 65, 129, 193, 189, 441, 489, 569.

'Souvenirs du général baron Teste, pp. 65, 113, 162, 250.

'Soldats d'Eylau, p. 89.

'Soldats d'Heilsberg et de Friedland, p. 354.

'Lettres du Brigadier Pilloy, pp. 505, 558.

Deuxième Serie, Volume 7, Paris 1908 'Le passage du grand Saint-Bernard', p. 413.

'La campagne de 1809 en Italie-Journal historique du 52e regiment de ligne.' p. 449.

Deuxième Serie, Volume 8, 1909, 'Le centenaire d'Essling et de Wagram', pp. 3321, 515.

'Les assiégeants de Saragosse, page 107.

'Une glorieuse relique de 1809 – La plaque à devise de l'aigle du 84ᵉ de ligne, p. 528.

Deuxième Serie, Volume 10, 1911 'Lettre de Berthier annoncant à Josephine la victoire de Marengo,' p. 336.
'Souvenirs du général baron Teste,' pp. 593, 657, 737.
Deuxième Serie, Volume 11, 1912, 'Souvenirs du général baron Teste,' pp. 17, 97, 161, 225, 289, 371.
'Le général de division Comte Compans,' p. 241.
Troisième Serie, Volume 1, 1913, 'Une letter de Masséna en 1800,' p. 40.
'Lettre du maréchal Davout, prince d'Eckmühl, relative au général comte Friant,' p. 497.
Troisième Serie, Volume 9, 1926, 'Le 3e regiment de grenadiers a pied (1810–1813),' p. 214.
'Les companies d'élite de la Cavalerie (1801–1815),' p. 358.
'Les gendarmes d'ordonnance (1806–1807),' p. 540.

Adkin, Mark, *The Waterloo Companion*, Aurum, London and Stackpole PA, 2001.
Alexander, Don W., *Rod of Iron: French Counterinsurgency Policy in Aragon during the Peninsular War*, Scholarly Resources Inc., Wilmington DE, 1985.
Anon., *German Military Dictionary*, War Department, Washington, 1944.
Aubrey, Octave, *Napoleon Soldier and Emperor*, J. B. Lippincott Company, New York, 1938.
— *Les Pages Immortelles de Napoleon*, Editions Correa, Paris, 1941.
Aurelius, Marcus, *The Emperor's Handbook*, Scribner, New York, 2002.
Baldick, Richard, *The Memoirs of Chateaubriand*, Alfred Knopf, New York, 1961.
Barrère, Albert, *A Dictionary of English and French Military Terms*, Hachette, London, 1942.
Barres, Jean-Baptiste, *Memoirs of a Napoleonic Officer*, The Dial Press, New York, 1925.
Becke, A. F., *The Battle of Waterloo*, Greenhill, London, 1995.
Belloc, Hilaire, *Napoleon's Campaign of 1812 and the Retreat from Moscow*, Harper and Brothers Publishers, New York, 1926.
Bertraud, Jean-Paul, *The Army of the French Revolution*, Princeton University Press, Princeton NJ, 1988.
Bezotocnii, V. M., A. A. Vasilii, A. M. Gorshman, O. K. Parkaev and A. A. Smirnoff, *The Russian Army, 1812–1814*, Moscow, 1999.
Bourgogne, Sergeant *Memoirs of Sergeant Bourgogne*, Peter Davies, London, 1926.
Brack, Antoine de, *Light Cavalry Outpost Duties*, Demisolde Press, San Diego, 2000.
Brandt, Heinrich von, trans. and ed. by Jonathan North, *In the Legions of Napoleon: The Memoirs of a Polish Officer in Spain and Russia 1808–1813*, Greenhill, London, 1999.
Brett-James, Antony, *1812: Eyewitness Accounts of Napoleon's Defeat in Russia*, Macmillan, London, 1967.
Britten Austin, Paul, *1812 The March on Moscow*, Greenhill, London, 1993.
— *1812 Napoleon in Moscow*, Greenhill, London, 1995.
— *1812 The Great Retreat*, Greenhill, London, 1996.
— *1815 The Return of Napoleon*, Greenhill, London, 2002.
Brown, Anne, and Howard C. Rice Jr, trans. and eds, two volumes, *The American*

Campaigns of Rochambeau's Army, Princeton University Press, Princeton NJ and Brown University Press, Providence RI, 1972, (c. 1890).

Boulart, Bon, *Mémoires Militaires du General Bon Boulart sur les Guerres de La Republique et de L'Empire*, La Librarie Illustrée, Paris, nd.

Bowden, Scott, *Armies at Waterloo*, Empire Games Press, Arlington TX, 1983.

— and Charles Tarbox, *Armies on the Danube, 1809*, The Emperor's Press, Chicago, 1989.

— *Napoleon and Austerlitz, The Glory Years 1805–1807, Volume I*, The Emperor's Press, Chicago, 1997.

— *Napoleon's Grande Armée of 1813*, The Emperor's Press, Chicago, 1990.

— *Napoleon's Finest: Marshal Davout and His 3rd Corps, Combat Journal of Operations, 1805–1807*, Military History Press, Madison WI, 2006.

Bucholz, Arden, *Hans Delbrück & the German Military Establishment*, University of Iowa Press, Iowa, 1985.

Busch, Otto, *Military System and Social Life in Old Regime Prussia, 1713–1807: The Beginnings of the Social Militarization of Prusso-German Society*, Humanities Press, Inc., Boston 1997.

Camon, H., *Quand et Comment Napoleon à conqu, son Systeme de Bataille*, Paris. 1935.

Camon, H., *Napoleon's System of War*, trans. and annot. by George F. Nafziger, The Nafziger Collection, West Chester OH, 2002.

Caulaincourt, A. L. A. de, *With Napoleon in Russia*, William Morrow, New York, 1935.

Chandler, David, *On the Napoleonic Wars*, Greenhill, London, 1994.

— ed., *Napoleon's Marshals*, Greenhill, London, and Macmillan, New York, 1987.

— *The Military Maxims of Napoleon*, Macmillan, New York, 1988.

— *The Art of War in the Age of Marlborough*, Sarpedon, New York, 1994.

Chardigny, Louis, *Les Maréchaux de Napoleon*, Tallandier, Paris, 1977.

Charrie, Pierre, *Drapeaux et étendards de la Revolution et de l'Empire*, Copernic, Paris, 1982.

Chesney, Charles *Waterloo Lectures*, Greenhill, London, 1997.

Chlapowski, Desirée, *Memoirs of a Polish Lancer*, Emperor's Press, Chicago, 1992.

Chrisawn, Margaret S., *The Emperor's Friend: Marshal Jean Lannes*, Greenwood Press, London, 2001.

Clausewitz, Carl von, *The Campaign of 1812 in Russia*, Greenhill, London, 1982.

Coignet, Jean-Roche, *The Notebooks of Captain Coignet*, Greenhill, London, 1989.

Connelly, Owen, *Napoleon's Satellite Kingdoms*, Free Press, New York, 1965.

— *The French Revolution and Napoleonic Era*, Holt, Reinhardt, and Winston, New York, 1991.

Corvisier, Andre, ed., *A Dictionary of Military History and the Art of War*, Blackwell Press, Cambridge MA, 1994.

— *Armies and Societies in Europe 1494-1789*, Indiana University Press, Bloomington IN, 1979.

Craig, Gordon A., *The Politics of the Prussian Army 1640-1945*, Oxford University Press, Oxford, 1955.

Creveld, Martin van, *Command in War*, Harvard University Press, Cambridge MA, 1985.

Cronin, Vincent, *Napoleon Bonaparte: An Intimate Biography*, William Morrow, New York, 1972.

Damamme, Jean-Claude, *Les Soldats de la Grande Armée*, Perrin, Paris, 1998.

Davidov, Denis, trans. and ed. by Gregory Troubetzkoy, *In the Service of the Tsar Against Napoleon*, Greenhill, London, 1999.

Davout, Louis N., *Operations du 3e Corps, 1806–1807, Rapport du Maréchal Davout, Duc d'Auerstadt*, Paris, 1896.

Dempsey, Guy, *Napoleon's Mercenaries: Foreign Units in the French Army Under the Consulate and Empire, 1799–1814*, Greenhill, London, 2002.

Denoeu, François, *Military French*, D. C. Heath, Boston MA, 1943.

Detaille, Eduard, trans. by Maureen Carlson Reinartsen, *L'Armée Française An Illustrated History of the French Army, 1790–1885*, Waxtel & Hasenhauer, New York 1992.

Doisy de Villargennes, J. Adelbert, *Reminiscences of Army Life under Napoleon Bonaparte*, Robert Clarke and Co., Cincinnati OH, 1884.

Douglas, Howard, Major General Sir, *An Essay on the Principles and Construction of Military Bridges and the Passage of Rivers in Military Operations*, Thomas and William Boone, London, 1832.

Duffy, Christopher, *The Military Experience in the Age of Reason*, Atheneum, New York, 1988.

— *The Army of Frederick the Great*, rev. ed., The Emperor's Press, Chicago, 1996.

— *Austerlitz 1805*, Cassell and Co., London, 1977.

Du Teil, Jean, *The New Usa of Artillery in Field Wars: Necessary Knowledge*, The Nafziger Collection, West Chester OH, 2003.

Elting, John R. *Swords Around A Throne: Napoleon's Grande Armée*, The Free Press, New York, and Weidenfeld, London, 1988.

— *The Superstrategists*, Scribner's, New York, 1985.

— trans., *Military Life Under Napoleon: The Memoirs of Captain Elzear Blaze*, The Emperor's Press, Chicago, 1995.

— Cragg, Dan, and Deal, Ernest, *A Dictionary of Soldier Talk*, Charles Scribner's Sons, New York, 1984.

— *Notes for Instructors, Department of Military Art and Engineering*, West Point, New York, 'Napoleon's Campaign in Russia,' 1964.

Epstein, Robert M., *Prince Eugène at War*, Empire Games Press, Arlington TX, 1984.

Esdaile, Charles, *The Peninsular War, A New History*, Penguin Books, London, 2003.

— *Fighting Napoleon: Guerillas, Bandits and Adventurers in Spain 1808-1814*, Yale University Press, New Haven CT, 2004.

Esposito, Vincent J. and John R. Elting, *A Military History and Atlas of the Napoleonic Wars*, Greenhill, London, 1999.

Eystsurlid, Lee, W. *The Formative Influences, Theories, and Campaigns of the Archduke Carl of Austria*, Greenwood Press, London, 2000.

Faber du Faur, Jonathan North trans. and ed., *With Napoleon in Russia*, Greenhill, London, 2000.

Fain, Baron, *Napoleon: How He Did It, The Memoirs of Baron Fain First Secretary of the Emperor's Cabinet*, Proctor Jones Publishing Company, San Francisco, 1998.

— *Memoirs of the Invasion of France, 1814*, London, 1834.

Fallou, L., *La Garde Impériale (1804–1815)*, Krefeld, Paris, 1975.

Fezensac, Raymond de, trans. by A Knollys, *A Journal of the Russian Campaign*, Ken Trotman Ltd, Cambridge, 1988.

Fletcher, Ian, ed, *Voices from the Peninsula: Eyewitness Accounts by Soldiers of Wellington's Army 1808-1814*, Greenhill, London, 2001.

Forrest, Alan, *Soldiers of the French Revolution*, Duke University Press, London, 1990.

— *Napoleon's Men: The Soldiers of the Revolution and Empire*, Hambledon and London, London and New York, 2002.

— *Conscripts and Deserters: The Army and French Society during the Revolution and Empire*, Oxford University Press, New York, 1989.

Fraser, Edward, *The War Drama of the Eagles*, Murray, London, and E. P. Dutton, New York, 1912.

Funck, Ferdinand von, trans. and ed. by Oakley Williams, *In the Wake of Napoleon*, John Lane, London, 1931.

Gallaher, John G., *The Iron Marshal: A Biography of Louis N. Davout*, Feffer & Simons, Inc., London, 1976. Reprinted by Greenhill, London, 2000.

Gates, David, *The Spanish Ulcer A History of the Peninsular War*, W. W. Norton, New York, 1986.

Gates, David, *The British Light Infantry Arm c. 1790–1815*, Batsford, London, 1987.

Gill, Jack, *With Eagles to Glory*, Greenhill, London, 1992.

Girod de l'Ain, Maurice, *Grands Artilleurs: Drouot, Senarmont, Eble*, Berger-Levrault, Paris, 1895.

Glover, Gareth, *Letters from the Battle of Waterloo: Unpublished Correspondence by Allied Officers from the Siborne Papers*, Greenhill, London, 2004.

Gorlitz, Walter *The German General Staff: Its History and Structure, 1657–1945*, Hollis Carter, London, 1953.

Gourgaud, Gaspard, *Napoleon and the Grand Army in Russia*, Anthony Finley, Philadelphia, 1825.

Graves, Donald E., ed., trans. by Jonathan Williams, *De Scheel's Treatise on Artillery*, Museum Restoration Service, Alexandra Bay NY, 1984.

Griffith, Paddy, *The Art of War of Revolutionary France*, Greenhill, London, 1998.

Griffith, Paddy 'Bressonet's '*Etudes Tactiques sur la Campagne de 1807*' in *Empires, Eagles, and Lions* vol. II, no. 2, September/October 1993.

Haythornewaite, Philip, *The Armies of Wellington*, Arms and Armour Press, London, 1994.

— *Who Was Who in the Napoleonic Wars*, Arms and Armour Press, London, 1998.

— *Wellington's Army The Uniforms of the British Soldier, 1812-1815*, Greenhill, London, 2002.

Headley, J. T., *The Imperial Guard of Napoleon: from Marengo to Waterloo*, Charles Scribner, New York, 1851.

Heinl, Robert D. Jr, *Dictionary of Military and Naval Quotations*, United States Naval Institute, Annapolis MD, 1966.

Hennebert, E. *Gribeauval: Lieutenant-General des Armées du Roy, Premier Inspector General du Corps Royal d'Artillerie (1715–1789)*, Paris, 1896.

Herold, J. Christopher, ed. and trans., *The Mind of Napoleon: A Selection of his Written and Spoken Words*, Columbia University Press, New York, 1955.

Hertenberger, H. and F. Wiltschek, *Erzherzog Karl der Sieger von Aspern*, Styria, Graz, 1983.

Hittle, J. D., *The Military Staff*, Stackpole, Harrisburg, 1961.

Hochedlinger, Michael, *Austria's Wars of Emergence 1683–1797*, Longman, New York, 2003.

Hoen, M. von, and Alois Veltze, *Krieg 1809, II Band, Italien*, L. W. Seidel & Sohn, Vienna, 1908.

—, Hugo Kerchnawe and Alois Veltze, *Krieg 1809*, vol. IV, Appendices.

Holtman, Robert B., *Napoleonic Propaganda*, Greenwood Press, New York, 1969.

Hopton, Richard, *The Battle of Maida 1806: Fifteen Minutes of Glory*, Leo Cooper, Barnsley, 2002.

Howard, Douglas, *An Essay on the Principles and Construction of Military Bridges and the Passage of Rivers in Military Operations*, Thomas and William Boone, London, 1832

Howard, John Eldred, *Letters and Documents of Napoleon: Volume I The Rise to Power*, The Cresset Press, London, 1961.

Horward, Donald D., Editor, *Napoleonic Military History, A Bibliography*, Greenhill, London, 1986.

Horward, Donald D., 'Jean-Jacques Pelet: Warrior of the Sword and Pen', *The Journal of Military History*, vol. 53, no. I, January 1989.

Hourtoulle, F. G., *Le General Comte Charles Lasalle 1775–1809*, Copernic, Paris, 1979.

— *L'Epopee Napoleonienne*, Histoire et Collections, Paris, nd.

— trans. by A. Mackay, *Soldiers and Uniforms of the Napoleonic Wars*, Histoire et Collections, Paris, c. 2004.

— trans. by A. Mackay, *The Empire at its Zenith*, Histoire et Collections, Paris, c. 2003.

— trans. by A. Mackay, *Borodino, the Moskva: The Battle for the Redoubts*, Histoire et Collections, Paris, 2000.

— trans. by A. Mackay, *Jena, Auerstadt: The Triumph of the Eagle*, Histoire et Collections, Paris, 1998.

— trans. by A. Mackay, *Wagram: The Apogee of the Empire*, Histoire et Collections, Paris, 2002.

— trans. by A. Mackay, *1814: The Campaign for France: The Wounded Eagle*, Histoire et Collections, Paris, 2005.

Houssaye, Henry, *Iena et la Campagne de 1806*, Paris, 1912.

— *1815: La Premiere Restauration; Le Retour de l'Isle d'Elbe; Les Cent Jours*, Flammarion, Paris, 1939.

— *Napoleon and the Campaign of France, 1814*, Worley Publications, Felling, 1994.

— *Napoleon and the Campaign of 1815: Waterloo*, Uckfield, Naval and Military Press, 2004.

Howard, Michael, ed., *The Theory and Practice of War*, Indiana University Press, Bloomington IN, 1975.

— *Clausewitz*, Oxford University Press, Oxford, 1983.

Hudleston, F. J., *Warriors in Undress*, Little, Brown, and Company, Boston, 1926.

Jany, C., *Die Preussische Armee von 1763 bis 1807*, vols III and IV, Biblio Verlag, Osnabruck, 1967.

Johnson, David, *The French Cavalry 1792–1815*, Belmont Publishing, London, 1989.

— *Napoleon's Cavalry and its Leaders*, Holmes and Meier, New York, 1978.

Journal Militaire, Année 1809, Paris 1809.

Kiley, Kevin F., *Artillery of the Napoleonic Wars 1792–1815*, Greenhill, London, 2004.

Kiley, Kevin F., 'The Cannon's Breath: Jean-Baptiste Vaquette de Gribeauval and the Development of the French Artillery Arm 1763–1789' *First Empire Magazine* no. 81, March/April 2005, pp. 12–18.

Labaume, Eugene, *A History of the Invasion of Russia by Napoleon Bonaparte*, John W. Parker, London, 1844.

Lachouque, Henry, and Anne Brown, *The Anatomy of Glory*, Greenhill, London, 1997.

— *Waterloo*, Arms and Armour Press, London, 1972.

—, Jean Tranie and J-C Carmigniani, *Napoleon's War in Spain, The French Peninsular Campaigns, 1807–1814*, Arms and Armour Press, London, 1982.

Lanza, Conrad, *Source Book of the Marengo Campaign in 1800*, The General Staff School, Fort Leavenworth, Kansas, 1922.

Lawford, James, *Napoleon's Last Campaigns 1813–1815*, Roxby Press, 1977.

Le Diberder, Georges, *Les Armées Francaises à L'Epoque Revolutionnaire 1789–1804*, Collections du Musée de L'Armée, Paris, 1989.

Ledru, A., *Montbrun 1809*, Paris 1913.

Lefebvre de Behaine, C., *La Campagne de France, Napoleon et les Allies sur le Rhin*, Perrin et Cie, Paris, 1913.

Leggiere, Michael, *Napoleon and Berlin*, University of Oklahoma Press, Norman Oklahoma, 2002.

Lejeune, Louis-François, *Mémoires du Général Lejeune: : 1792-1813*, Editions du Grenadier, Paris, 2001.

Lemaire, Jean-François, *Les Blesses dans Les Armées Napoleoniennes*, Lettrage, Paris, 1999.

Linck, Tony, *Napoleon's Generals The Waterloo Campaign*, The Emperor's Press, Chicago, 1993.

Lochet, Jean 'War Against Prussia, 1806: Comparison of French and Prussian Tactics During the Campaign of 1806–1807' *Empires, Eagles, and Lions* vol. II, no. 2, September/October 1993.

Longford, Elizabeth, *Wellington Years of the Sword*, Harper and Row, New York, 1969.

Luvaas, Jay, *Napoleon on the Art of War*, The Free Press, New York, 1999.

Lynn, John A., *The Bayonets of the Republic, Motivation and Tactics in the Army of Revolutionary*

France, 1791–1794, Westview Press, Boulder CO, 1996.

Mackesy, Piers, *War in the Mediterranean 1803–1810*, Longmans, Green, and Company, New York, 1957.

Madelin, Louis, *Les Cent-Jours Waterloo*, Librarie Hachette, Paris, 1954.

Marbot, Marcellin, *The Memoirs of Baron de Marbot*, two vols, Longmans, Green, and Co., London and New York, 1892. Reprinted Greenhill, London, 1988.

Markham, J. David, *Imperial Glory*, Greenhill, London.

Marmont, Auguste, *Memoires du Maréchal Marmont Duc de Raguse de 1792–1841*, vols 2, 5, & 7, Paris 1857.

Martin, Emmanuel, *La Gendarmerie Française en Espagne et en Portugal (Campaagnes de 1807 à 1814)*, C. Terana, Paris, 1998.

Maude, F. N., *The Jena Campaign*, Greenhill, London, 1998.

Meneval, C. F. de, *Memoirs of Napoleon Bonaparte*, vols I and II, PF Collier, New York, 1910.

Mercer, Cavalie, *A Journal of the Waterloo Campaign*, Greenhill, London, 1988.

Metternich, Clemens von, *Metternich the Autobiography, 1773–1815*, Ravenhall Books, Welwyn Garden City, 2004.

Meunier, Hugues-Alexandre-Joseph, *A Treatise upon the Regulations of the French Infantry*, George Nafziger, West Chester OH, 2000.

Mikaberidze, Alexander, *The Russian Officer Corps in the Revolutionary and Napoleonic Wars*, Savas Beattie, El Dorado Hills CA, 2005.

Morvan, Jean, *Le Soldat Imperial*, two vols, Teissedre, Paris, 1999.

Muffling, Carl von, *The Memoirs of Baron von Muffling*, Greenhill, London, 1997.

Muir, Rory, *Tactics and the Experience of Battle in the Age of Napoleon*, Yale University Press, Newhaven, 1998.

Muller, W., *Relation of the Operations and Battles of the Austrian and French Armies in the Year 1809*, London, T. Goddard Military Library, 1810.

Nafziger, George, *Imperial Bayonets*, Greenhill, London 1996.

Nardin, Pierre, *Gribeauval Lieutenant General des Armées du Roi (1715–1789)*, Fondation pour les études de defense nationale, Paris, nd.

Niegolewski, Andre, *Les Polonais A Somo-Sierra: En Espagne en 1808*, Librarie des Deux Empires, Paris, 2001.

Noel, Jean-Nicolas-Auguste, ed., trans. and introd. by Rosemary Brindle, *With Napoleon's Guns, The Military Memoirs of an Officer of the First Empire*, Greenhill, London, 2005.

Oman, Carola, *Napoleon's Viceroy: Eugène de Beauharnais*, Hodder and Stoughton, London, and Funk and Wagnalls, New York, 1966.

Oman, Charles, *A History of the Peninsular War*, vol. IV, Greenhill, London, 1996.

— *Wellington's Army*, Edward Arnold, London, 1913. Reprinted Greenhill, London, 1986.

— *Studies in the Napoleonic Wars: The Bulletins of Napoleon's Grande Armée, 1805–1814*, Greenhill, London, 1989.

Paret, Peter, *Yorck and the Era of Prussian Reform*, Princeton University Press, Princeton

NJ, 1966.

— *Clausewitz and the State: The Man, His Theories, and his Times*, Princeton University Press, Princeton NJ, 1985.

Parker, Harold T., *Three Napoleonic Battles*, Duke University Press, Durham NC, 1983.

Pelet, Jean Jacques and Donald D. Horward, eds, *The French Campaign in Portugal 1810-1811*, University of Minnesota Press, Minneapolis MN, 1973.

Petit, Joseph, *Marengo, or the Campaign of Italy by the Army of Reserve, Under the Command of the Chief Consul Bonaparte*, Philadelphia, 1801.

Petre, F. Lorraine, *Napoleon and the Archduke Charles*, Greenhill, London, 1991.

— *Napoleon's Last Campaign in Germany – 1813*, Greenhill, London, 1992.

— *Napoleon's Campaign in Poland, 1806 – 1807*, Greenhill, London, 1989.

— *Napoleon's Conquest of Prussia*, Greenhill, London, 1993.

— *Napoleon at Bay 1814*, Greenhill, London, 1994.

Phipps, Ramsay, *The Armies of the First French Republic*, 4 volumes, Oxford University Press, London, 1926–1939.

Pigeard, Alain, *Dictionnaire de la Grade Armée*, Tallandier, Paris, 2002.

Quimby, Robert, *The Background of Napoleonic Warfare*, Columbia University Press, New York, 1957.

Rauchensteiner, Manfried, *Die Schlacht von Aspern am 21. und 22. Mai 1809*, Heeresgeschichtlichen Museum, Vienna, nd.

Regnault, Jean, *Les Aigles Impériale et le Drapeau Tricolore 1804–1815*, J. Peyronnet, Paris, 1967.

Richardson, Robert, *Larrey: Surgeon to Napoleon's Imperial Guard*, Quiller Press, London, 2000.

Ropes, John Codman, *The Campaign of Waterloo, A Military History*, Charles Scribner's Sons New York, 1893.

— *The First Napoleon*, Houghton Mifflin, Boston, 1885.

Ross, Steven T., *From Flintlock to Rifle, Infantry Tactics, 1740–1866*, Frank Cass & Co. Ltd, London, 1996.

Rothenberg, Gunther, *Napoleon's Great Adversary, Archduke Charles and the Austrian Army 1792–1814*, Batsford, London, 1995.

— *The Emperor's Last Victory*, Weidenfeld and Nicholson, London, 2004.

— *The Army of Francis Joseph*, Purdue University Press, Ashland OH, 1976.

— *The Military Border in Croatia: A Study of an Imperial Institution*, University of Chicago Press, Chicago, 1966.

— Kiraly, Bela K., and Peter F. Sugar, *East Central European Society and War in the Pre-Revolutionary Eighteenth Century*, Columbia University Press, New York, 1982.

Rudorff, Raymond, *War to the Death: The Sieges of Saragossa 1808–1809*, Purnell, London, 1974.

Ryan, Edward, *Napoleon's Elite Cavalry*, Greenhill, London, 2001.

— *Napoleon's Shield and Guardian: The Unconquerable General Daumesnil*, Greenhill, London, 2003.

St Hilaire, Emile Marco de, *Histoire de la Garde Impériale*, Victor Lecou, Paris, nd.

Sargent, Herbert H., *The Campaign of Marengo*, A. C. McClurg, Chicago, 1897.

Schneid, Frederick C., *Napoleon's Conquest of Europe: The War of the Third Coalition*, Praeger, London, 2005.

Scott, Samuel F., *From Yorktown to Valmy The Transformation of the French Army in an Age of Revolution*, University Press of Colorado, 1998.

—— The *Response of the Royal Army to the French Revolution: The Role and Development of the Line Army 1787–1793*, Clarendon Press, Oxford, Bouolder CO, 1978.

Segur, Philippe-Paul de, *Napoleon's Campaign in Russia*, Time-Life Books, Chicago, 1985.

Shanahan, William O., *Prussian Military Reforms 1786–1813*, AMS Press, New York, 1966.

Sherwig, John M., *Guineas and Gunpowder: British Foreign Aid in the Wars with France, 1793–1815*, Harvard University Press, Harvard Massachusetts, 1969.

Siborne, W., *History of the Waterloo Campaign*, Greenhill, London, 1995.

Simms, Brendan, *The Struggle for Mastery of Germany, 1779–1850*, St. Martin's Press, New York, 1998.

—— *The Impact of Napoleon: Prussian High Politics, Foreign Policy, and the Crisis of the Executive, 1797–1806*, Cambridge University Press, Cambridge, 1997.

Six, Georges, *Dictionnaire Biographique des Généraux & Amiraux Français de la Revolution et de L'Empire (1792–1814)*, Paris, Bordas, 1947.

Smith, Digby, *Napoleon's Regiments*, Greenhill, London, 2000.

—— *Armies of 1812, The Grande Armée and the Armies of Austria, Prussia, Russia, and Turkey*, Spellmount, Staplehurst, 2002.

Stussi-Lauterburg, J. *Beresina 1812*, GMS, Zurich, 1986.

Stutterheim, Major-General, Pine Coffin, trans., *A Detailed Account of the Battle of Austerlitz*, London, T. Goddard, 1807.

Tarle, Eugene, *Napoleon's Invasion of Russia*, Octagon Books, New York, 1984.

Thiebault, Paul, *An Explanation of the Duties of the Several Etats-Majors in the French Army*, London, 1801.

Thiry, Jean, *Marengo*, Editions Berger-Levrault, Paris, 1949.

Thomason, John W., Jr, Editor and Illustrator, *Adventures of General Marbot*, Charles Scribner's Sons, New York, 1935.

Tousard, Louis de, *American Artillerist's Companion*, C and C Conrad and Company, Philadelphia 1809. Reprinted by Greenwood Press, New York, 1969.

Tulard, Jean, *Dictionnaire Napoleon*, Fayard, Paris, 1987.

—— *Napoleon, ou le mythe du sauveur*, Fayard, Paris, 1987.

Tranie, J. and Carmigniani, J. C., *La Patrie en Danger 1792–1793, Les Campagnes de la Revolution*, tome I, Charles Lavauzelle, Paris, 1987.

—— *Napoleon et l'Autriche-La Campagne de 1809*, Copernic, Paris, 1979.

Tsouras, Peter G., ed, *The Greenhill Dictionary of Military Quotations*, Greenhill, London, 2000.

Vachée, Col., trans. by Frederick Lees, *Napoleon at Work*, PDI Publishing, 1995.

Vallotton, G., *Les Suisses a la Berezina, a la Baconniere*, nd.

Vignalles, de, *Précis Historique des operations militaires de l'Armée dItalie en 1813 et 1814 par le Chef de l'Etat-Major-general de cette Armée*, Paris, 1817.

Walsh, John, 'The French Zulu,' *Miniature Wargames Magazine*, no. 278, June 2006.

Ward, S. P. G., *Wellington's Headquarters A Study of the Administrative Problems in the Peninsula 1809–1814*, Oxford University Press, Oxford, 1957.

Wartenberg, Count Yorck von, *Napoleon as a General*, Kegan Paul, London, 1902.

Watson, S. J., *By Command of the Emperor: A Life of Marshal Berthier*, Ken Trotman Ltd, Cambridge, 1988.

Wenge, August, *Die Schlacht von Aspern*, Berlin, 1900.

Whitcomb, Edward, A., *Napoleon's Diplomatic Service*, Duke University Press, Durham NC, 1979.

White, Charles, *The Enlightened Soldier: Scharnhorst and the Militarische Gesellschaft in Berlin, 1801–1805*, Praeger, New York, 1989.

Wilson, Sir Robert, *The Campaigns in Poland in 1806 and 1807*, Worley Publications, Felling, 2000.

Willcox, Cornelis de Witt, *French English Military Technical Dictionary*, Harper, New York, 1917.

Willing, Paul, *Napoleon et ses Soldats, Tome 1 L'Apogée de la Gloire (1804–1809)*, Collections Historiques du Musée de l'Armée, Paris,

— *Napoleon et ses Soldats Tome 2 de Wagram à Waterloo (1809–1815)*, Collections Historiques du Musée de L'Armée, Paris, 1987.

Yermelov, Alexy, ed. by Alexander Mikaberidze, *The Czar's General: The Memoirs of a Russian General in the Napoleonic Wars*, Ravenhall, London, 2005.

Yonge, Charlotte M., *Memoirs of Colonel Bugeaud*, Worley Publications, Felling, 1998.

Zhmodikov, *Tactics of the Russian Army in the Napoleonic Wars*, two vols, The Nafziger Collection, West Chester OH, 2003.

INDEX